Making the World Global

Making the World Global

U.S. Universities and the Production
of the Global Imaginary

ISAAC A. KAMOLA

DUKE UNIVERSITY PRESS
Durham and London
2019

Designed by Matthew Tauch
Typeset in Minion Pro and TheSans C4s
by Copperline Book Services

Library of Congress Cataloging-in-Publication Data Names:
Kamola, Isaac A., author.
Title: Making the world global : U.S. universities and the
production of the global imaginary / Isaac A. Kamola.
Description: Durham : Duke University Press, 2019. | Includes
bibliographical references and index.
Identifiers: LCCN 2018047266 (print)
LCCN 2019005716 (ebook)
ISBN 9781478005612 (ebook)
ISBN 9781478004172 (hardcover)
ISBN 9781478004738 (pbk.)
Subjects: LCSH: Education, Higher—United States—Finance. |
Universities and colleges—United States—Finance. |
Educational fund raising—United States. | Education and
globalization.
Classification: LCC LB2342 (ebook) | LCC LB2342 .K34 2019
(print) | DDC 378.1/060973—dc23
LC record available at https://lccn.loc.gov/2018047266

Cover art: World map with countries scaled to
represent the percentage of foreign students studying in
the United States, by country of origin. Source:
www.ghemawat.com.

To Serena, Harvey, and Callia.

You are my world.

Presumably, if one is a factory worker, it is on the factory floor that one's politicization, one's consciousness, comes out in day-to-day struggle. And if I am an academic, and so long as I remain an academic, I must attempt to make the most important political input during those very many hours that I spend contributing to teaching or researching or whatever other aspects of academic life may come into play.

—WALTER RODNEY, *Walter Rodney Speaks* (1990)

Contents

ix   PREFACE

xvii   ACKNOWLEDGMENTS

1   Introduction: Globalization and the World

PART I. REPRODUCING THE NATIONAL IMAGINARY

29   1. "Creative Imagination" Is Needed: W. W. Rostow and the Rise of Modernization as a National Imaginary

62   2. "The World's Largest . . . Development Institution": Robert McNamara and the National Development Imaginary

PART II. MARKETING THE GLOBAL IMAGINARY

83   3. "Marketing Can Be Magic": Theodore Levitt and Globalization as a Market Imaginary

118   4. "Realities of the Global Economy": A. W. Clausen and the Banker's Global Imaginary

PART III. REPRODUCING THE GLOBAL UNIVERSITY

141   5. "Stakeholders and Co-investors . . . Have 'Reform' on Their Mind":
Kenneth Prewitt and the Defunding of Area Studies

168   6. "An Opportunity to Transform the University and, Frankly,
the World": John Sexton and the Global Networked University

189   Conclusion: Reworlding the Global

195   NOTES
231   REFERENCES
269   INDEX

Preface

On June 23, 2016, the United Kingdom voted to end its membership in the European Union. This vote, called Brexit, became one primal scream in a growing economic and ethnonationalist rejection of the geopolitical project President George H. W. Bush once termed the New World Order. This global order, based upon a post–Cold War vision of greater cultural integration, free trade, expanded institutions of global governance, and the fluid movements of peoples, commodities, and money, had, until very recently, been assumed by many to be the self-evident and unquestioned trajectory of our shared human future. While many scholars bristled at the particular phraseology of the "end of history" (Fukuyama 1989, 1992) or the arrival of a "flat" world (Friedman 2005), since the last decade of the twentieth century it had become hard to imagine the world as anything other than global. However, in the wake of Brexit and the election of Donald Trump, Pankaj Ghemawat—NYU professor of global business management—summed up what many were already thinking. In a piece published in the *Harvard Business Review*, Ghemawat wrote that people "are scrambling to adjust to a world few imagined possible just a year ago," namely that the "myth of a borderless world has come crashing down" (2017, 112). While Ghemawat goes on to demonstrate the empirical robustness of globalization, he nonetheless acknowledges the unexpected fragility of the global imaginary.

I wrote and conceptualized much of this book at a time in which the global imaginary seemed much more stable than it does today. While a graduate student at the University of Minnesota during the 2000s, I was immersed in heady discussions about globalization, global governance, and whether the war on terror constituted a rejection—or an expression—of this emerging global reality. While everyone seemed to be talking about globalization, I found myself puzzled by the fact that globalization remained an agonizingly ambiguous and incoherent concept. Everyone seemed eager to declare the world global, yet reluctant (or unable) to convincingly explain what globalization actually meant.

My dissertation was an attempt to think through this paradox.[1] I argued that efforts to develop a more coherent understanding of globalization ignored the fact that the concept of globalization depended upon deep contradictions and incoherencies. While academic debates about globalization focused on establishing the specific definitions, causalities, time lines, and qualities of globalization, I argued that these discussions depend upon a prior commitment to imagining the world as indisputably global. Take for example the 2010 KOF Index of Globalization, which ranks countries in terms of their levels of globalization.[2] In this account, Belgium and Austria rank first and second. Interestingly, the Cayman Islands rank 187 out of 208 despite housing a significant portion of the world's offshore banking accounts. Afghanistan and Iraq are similarly ranked very low on the globalization index (183rd and 193rd, respectively) despite being focal points in a global war on terror and the sites of massive multinational military interventions. What makes trade, foreign direct investment, portfolio investment, telephone traffic, tourism, internet usage, and the per capita number of McDonald's and Ikea stores KOF indicators of globalization but not, for example, the number of offshore accounts or foreign troops per capita? What does (and does not) count as global, in other words, is simply assumed to be self-evident such that the scholarly concept of globalization becomes an exercise in studying those things already imagined as global (Kamola 2013). The concept of globalization requires already imagining the world as global, and then applying the term "globalization" to reference this imagined object.

The durability of the global imaginary, despite the conceptual shakiness of globalization, explains how the term "globalization" reached such prominence during the 1990s and early 2000s. As a result, over a short period of time, a diverse ecosystem of concepts attempting to understand the world as a single sociopolitical space became quickly replaced by the "epistemic monoculture" of globalization (Santos, Nunes, and Meneses 2008). For example, during the 1970s many scholars within the disciplinary field of International Relations deployed the term "world politics" to theorize and popularize a rethinking of international politics in contrast to the realists' exclusive focus on politics between nation-states and to including accounts of transnational, domestic, and subnational actors (for example, see Bull 1977). The same year Hedley Bull published *The Anarchical Society*, Robert Keohane and Joseph Nye published *Power and Interdependence*. In their introduction, Keohane and Nye (1977, 3) wrote that "we live in an era of interdependence" which, while "poorly understood," is visible in the "widespread feeling that the very nature of world politics is changing" and that "multinational corporations, transnational social movements, and international organizations" are shaping the world into a single unit. By the 1990s and early 2000s, however, debates about world politics and complex interdependence became subsumed by the language of globalization. In their introduction to the 2001 revised version of *Power and Interdependence*, for example, Keohane and Nye wrote that their concept of interdependence was simply a precursor to, and a prophetic statement of, globalization. While interdependence was the buzzword of the 1970s, globalization was that of the 1990s (Keohane and Nye 2001, 228). Globalization simply means more interdependence.

I found the epistemic monoculture of globalization particularly troubling because critiques of globalization often simply turned into demands for a different form of globalization, such as "alter-globalization," "global civil society" (Kaldor 2000, 2003), "grassroots globalization" (Appadurai 2000, 2001), "justice globalism" (Steger 2008), or "globalization from below" (Kellner 2002). Globalization, in other words, has become both the horizon upon which to understand contemporary social life as well as its alternative. Conceptualizing political alternatives using the language of globalization is particularly concerning given that the language of globalization has been largely shaped by Western intellectual traditions, "northern epistemologies" (Santos 2007a), and to the exclusion of "southern theory" (Connell 2007a, 2007b).

Whether Brexit, Trump, and the popular reemergence of the ethnonationalist right are historical blips or the beginning of a scary new chapter of human history remains to be seen. This troubling conjuncture, however, does make shockingly visible the fact that the global imaginary has never simply unfolded toward some predetermined, inevitable, and linear future. *Making the World Global* argues that the global imaginary is something produced, over time, and within particular material conditions. As these material conditions change, so too do our shared political, social, and cultural imaginaries. This book examines how relationships between universities, the American state, philanthropic organizations, and international financial organizations created the conditions within which it became common for faculty, students, administrators, parents, policymakers, business leaders, and funders of higher education to imagine the world as global. Specifically, this book documents how the state-sponsored Cold War university—which imagined the world as an international system composed of discrete nation-states, with the U.S. at its center—was gradually replaced by more marketized forms of academic knowledge production and, in the process, created the conditions within which globalization became a particular object of knowledge.

Making this argument entails examining academic knowledge about globalization from the point of view of reproduction. This includes examining how, over the past decades, the world of American higher education was remade into a certain site for the reproduction of knowledge about the world as global. Those transformations within the American academy, of course, exist in relation to the restructuring of higher education in Africa as well. Placing these worlds within a contrapuntal relationship helps to demonstrate the structured and material hierarchies and asymmetries that continue to organize not only the production of academic knowledge but also what it means to say the world is global.

The Real Labor of Knowledge

This argument stems from the premise that academic knowledge—the books and articles we read and write, classes we take and teach, the conferences we attend, and curricula we develop—are all products of human labor. Like T-shirts, sugarcane, and automobiles, academic knowledge is similarly produced by specific people working within particular material conditions. These material institutions, social relationships, collective practices, and shared meanings constitute the worlds of academic knowledge production.

This theoretical commitment to understanding academic knowledge in terms of social reproduction was something I first learned through practice. As a graduate student during the first decade of the twenty-first century, I came to see my own practices of study, as well as my teaching and professional training, as occurring in relation to political and economic transformations taking place at the University of Minnesota. During this period, the administration was actively engaged in strategic positioning aimed at making the university more competitive, exclusive, and in line with its so-called peer institutions. This involved prioritizing strategic initiatives, often at the expense of students, clerical and service staff, and graduate employees. It included closing General College, the primary point of access for first-generation, minority, and lower-income students. Rather than boldly stating an unwavering commitment to valuing employees and prioritizing an inclusive student population, the administration instead adopted cookie-cutter institutional policies aimed at transforming the university into "one of the top three public research universities in the world" (University of Minnesota 2007, 3), all repackaged within its corporate "Driven to Discover" rebranding effort.[3]

Within this context, a vocal and organized group of staff, students, graduate workers, and some faculty mounted considerable political opposition to these changes.[4] We protested the seemingly inevitable neoliberal transformation of our institution, working tirelessly to highlight, politicize, and theorize the university as a political space. We identified how our institution was becoming less concerned with critical, intellectual life and more obsessed with developing alternative revenue streams, climbing the rankings, and establishing corporate relationships. We critiqued these changes as betraying the democratic potential of higher education, as the commercialization of education and intellectual life, and a forfeiture of the democratic mission of public education. We walked the picket lines, organized a graduate employee union, occupied administrative buildings, went on a hunger strike, published articles, and hosted scholar-activist conferences. In doing so, we came to see the University of Minnesota not merely as a space we passed through en route to a degree and a (rapidly vanishing) tenure-track job, but rather as a complicated political institution, one with long and problematic histories built on exclusion, marginalization, and dispossession. We also saw, however, the University of Minnesota as an institution that, despite its many hierarchies, injustices, and pathologies, also contained democratic possibility and opportunity. We learned that political and economic contestations could open alternative possible futures.

Within this political and theoretical cacophony, I still attended my classes, took my comprehensive exams, and arrived at a dissertation topic. Facing funding constraints and departmental pressures to reduce time to degree, I abandoned my plan to complete field research on the relationship between collapsing coffee prices and genocide in Rwanda, and instead turned to the flashy concept of globalization. This subject could be studied from anywhere and did not require extensive field research or language skills. I was informed that one month in South Africa would be more than sufficient in terms of fieldwork. Instead of hurdles, I found that the University of Minnesota, like most American universities, was undergoing a number of reforms and curricular changes—in line with its strategic planning—aimed at establishing itself as a global university, which included placing considerable institutional support behind faculty and students doing work on globalization. My dissertation research, for example, was funded by the Office of International Programs (OIP), which, originally established in the 1960s to connect the school's strengths in agricultural research with the broader Cold War development agenda, now served as the catchall office for administrating scholarships, student research abroad, overseeing "system-wide international policies and initiatives," and developing "scholarly initiatives of faculty, colleges, and graduate students."[5] Administrators saw OIP as making it possible to "leverage outside grants for faculty to continue international research" (Katzenstein 2009).

Only in retrospect did the obvious become evident: that the dissertation I ultimately wrote could not be disaggregated from the material conditions within which I was writing it. Later, when applying for academic jobs in the years immediately following the 2008 financial crisis, it continued to be abundantly clear that writing about some things (and not others) was directly affecting access to funding, professional opportunities, and full-time employment. However, while these very practical, financial, and strategic relationships profoundly shape what one writes, they often remain unspoken. I came to see the systemic failure to acknowledge the material relationships making academic practices possible as enabling a vision of the academy as a zero point: that detached vantage from which one can falsely claim to look out, describe, and understand a world existing out there (Mignolo 2011, xvii). If we reject the notion of the university as a zero point, and understand colleges and universities as instead worldly institutions, then we must also take seriously the fact that institutions of higher education are always particular, provincial, and embedded sites of political and economic struggle. However, even in such acknowledgment, there remains a deep desire to imagine universities as universal. After all, it is only from such a lofty vantage that one can write, think, study, and teach about the world as an abstraction, knowable from a point of transcendence. It becomes possible to talk about politics, democracy, or class as concepts and ideas, rather than—as we learned on the picket lines—very real, complex, and unsolvable conflicts, with very real consequences, that ultimately cannot be resolved by a well-argued piece of prose or around the seminar table. Imagining the university as a zero point, in other words, makes it possible to fool ourselves that, as students and scholars, we inhabit an immaculate perch that invests our academic practices as either engaged in an apolitical quest for truth or as the fountain of critical political engagement playing out at the level of ideas.

However, the hard lesson I learned through practice was that universities and colleges do not exist as detached from some real world, but rather are themselves always structured and structuring, produced and reproduced, and profoundly intertwined with the world or, more accurately, within a plurality of worlds. The university is a real world, just like the sweatshop, the plantation, and the shop floor. However, unlike T-shirts, sugarcane, and automobiles, the primary things being reproduced within the worlds of higher education—in addition to disciplined and indebted students, educated citizens, and skilled workers—are knowledge, expertise, and imaginaries. Drawing from this insight, this book does not seek to better conceptualize what globalization actually means, where it comes from, how it works, or whom it affects, but rather to understand why the world came to be imagined as global within the world of American higher education. Therefore, rather than returning to academic debates for insights into how to better conceptualize globalization, *Making the World Global* instead asks, What was the massive expansion of global-speak a symptom of?

Acknowledgments

The production of knowledge is always a social and collective project. As such, this book is indebted to the labor and shared intellect of so many people, including a large number of good, gracious, and brilliant friends. It is only their love, friendship, and intelligence that brought this project to light.

From those formative graduate student days in Minnesota, I am particularly indebted to Asli Çalkivik, Kartik Raj, Michael Nordquist, Wendy Clement, Garnet Kindervater, Jonathan Havercroft, Mike Kramer, David Leon, Çiğdem Çidam, Jonneke Koomen, Eric Richtmyer, Caley Horan, and Henriët Hendriks, as well as members of Bud Duvall's dissertation writing group. My understanding of politics is richer because of the sisters and brothers of AFSCME Local 3800, especially Jess Sundin, Steff Yorek, Phyllis Walker, Gladys McKenzie, Brad Sigal, and J. Burger; and the greater strike support community, including Nick and Kate Woomer-Deters, Andrew Hamilton, Ty Moore, Rosemary Fister, Marion Traub-Werner, Richa Nagar, Lily and Sofi Shank, Nate Laurence, and so many others. Thanks also to the many comrades of the GradTRAC-UE Local 1105 union drive—we came so close—as well as the co-organizers of the "Re-thinking the University" and "Re-working the University" conferences, including Amy Pason, Matt Stoddard, John Conley, Morgan Adamson, Lucia Pawlowski, Steven Koskela, Elizabeth Johnson, and Noah Ebner. Thanks and solidarity to Susan Kang, who brought me to my first labor rally. Eli Meyerhoff was—and continues to be—at the heart of this entire enterprise, as co-organizer, coauthor, reader of countless drafts, friend, and fellow dreamer.

In addition to the many faculty who worked so hard to train our often unruly cohort of students, the department of political science during the first decade of the twenty-first century would not have been possible without the late-night custodian Steve (thanks for the key . . .), Wayne Howell, Judith Mitchell, Alexis Cuttance, Beth Ethier, Bob Hamburg, Steve Hanson, and Mark Ollenburger. And, of course, life in Minneapolis would not have been the same without Tony at the Red Dragon, Jason at the Uptown, Pat at the Wienery, and all the folks at the Hard Times Café.

Many thanks to those faculty who not only played an important role in my intellectual development but also advised, mentored, and looked out for me at key junctures: Bud Duvall, Manfred Steger, David Blaney, Lisa Disch, Tarak Barkawi, Premesh Lalu, Antonio Vazquez-Arroyo, August Nimtz, Teri Caraway, Timothy Kaufman-Osborn, and Paul Apostolidis.

Being on the job market during the years immediately following the 2008 financial crisis meant that, like so many scholars braving this new world of higher education, I spent several years in academic vagabondage. Dartmouth College's Department of Government showed, especially Bill Wohlforth, considerable hospitality to an unemployed spouse. I owe a huge debt of gratitude to Jill Morawski, who, as director of Wesleyan University's Center for the Humanities, took a chance on me during a particularly vulnerable time. I will always be grateful to Jill as well as Joseph Fitzpatrick, Matt Garrett, Margo Weiss, and Nima Bassiri for that critical year as an Andrew W. Mellon postdoctoral fellow. The following two years at Johns Hopkins were all the richer, intellectually and personally, because of Alex Livingston, Merike Andre-Barrett, Drew Walker, Kevin Darrow, Lauren Wilcox, Siba Grovogui, Lori Leonard, Bill Connolly, Jane Bennett, Anatoli and Jacqui Ignatov, Casey McNeil, Tim Vasko, and the colleagues at the Friday Africa seminar. Sam Chambers and Rebecca Brown shared unparalleled hospitality, advice, support, professional guidance, and commiseration. The American Council of Learned Societies' New Faculty Fellows program funded these two years in the great city of Baltimore. This fellowship program was designed to help newly minted PhDs weather the post–financial crisis academic environment— a program just as needed today as a decade ago. I am incredibly grateful to the ACLS for this opportunity.

At Trinity College, Ben Carbonetti, Sonia Cardenas, Stefanie Chambers, Mary Dudas, Diana Evans, Andy Flibbert, Thomas Lefebvre, Reo Matsuzaki, Lida Maxwell, Kevin McMahon, Tony Messina, Anna Terwiel, and Abby Fisher Williamson have proven the most supportive and impressive departmental colleagues. Our department administrator, Mary Beth White, is beyond amazing in every way. The Trinity chapter of the American Association of University Professors—you know who you are—also continues to give me great strength and optimism. Colleagues Jennifer Regan-Lefebvre and Reo Matsuzaki provided outstanding feedback on earlier drafts of this project as part of a Trinity Institute for Interdisciplinary Studies (TIIS)–funded Junior Faculty Research Fellowship. A TIIS Manuscript Fellowship brought together Andy Flibbert, Garth Myers, Vijay Prashad, Allen Stack, and Himadeep Muppidi for a pivotal rethinking of the project. Lior Azariya provided exceptional research assistance for chapter 6.

Vijay, in particular, made a number of transformative comments on various drafts, including the memorable: "Stop calling these your empirical chapters . . . they are your only chapters." The book is mercifully shorter, and more focused, thanks to his input.

A hearty thanks also goes out to the archivists and staff at the Baker Library at Harvard Business School, including Rachel Wise, Melissa Murphy, and Tim Mahoney; Myles Crowley and the staff at MIT's Institute Archives and Special Collections, as well as Elisabeth Kaplan and the staff of the University of Minnesota archive. Mike Kramer provided great comradery and accommodation while in Cambridge for research. Nancy Smith and Amanda Bollacker were exceptionally helpful in procuring the images for the book.

Draft chapters were presented at the Western Political Science Association (2013 and 2014), International Studies Association (2016), and at the American Political Science Association (2016) meetings. Many thanks to the audiences and discussants, particularly Samantha Majic. The virtual writing group of Anatoli, Eli, and Chris Buck provided essential feedback on early drafts of this manuscript. Amentahru Wahlrab and Jonathan Havercroft provided careful readings of later drafts. And Robert Vitalis's many readings of the whole manuscript and meticulous attention throughout have been helpful beyond measure.

I would like to thank Elizabeth Ault at Duke University Press for her steadfast support and clear guidance, as well as Jason Weidemann at University of Minnesota Press and three anonymous reviewers for their exceptional feedback in the last stages of the project. Kristy Johnson, Liz Smith, and Karen Fisher provided careful copyediting that was beyond heroic.

My final and biggest thanks, however, goes to Serena Laws. Thanks for your continual support and steadfast friendship. I love you dearly.

Introduction

Globalization and the World

All academics have participated in gatherings . . . where budget constraints, political decisions, promotion opportunities, off-the-cuff ideas, and institutional strategies are coated with the gloss of intellectual necessity and scientific progress. Yet academics write disciplinary history as if such meetings never take place or have any epistemic effect. The denizens of the cave seem indeed quite reluctant to talk about their natural habit, and they much prefer to have others believe that they inhabit a region of pristine ideas and celestial doctrines.

— NICOLAS GUILHOT, "One Discipline, Many Histories" (2011)

In the immediate aftermath of the terrorist attacks of September 11, 2001, the American intelligence community—which had experienced years of downsizing and retirements—began actively reassessing its "workforce planning" and developing more vigorous strategies for expanding its "human capital" (Negroponte 2006; Nemfakos et al. 2013). American colleges and universities became important partners in developing the "scholars and scholarship" necessary to populate the "national security, military, and intelligence agencies" with those deemed capable of executing the global war on terrorism (Martin 2005, 27). For example, in 2008 Secretary of Defense Robert Gates announced, in a speech before the Association of American Universities, the creation of the $60 million Minerva Consortium designed to encourage social scientists to engage in research deemed essential for national security (Gonzalez 2014, 93). Similarly, anthropologists were recruited into the Human Terrain System and deployed alongside soldiers in Iraq and Afghanistan to provide information about "local customs, kinship structures, and social conflicts" (Glenn 2007, 1). The National Academies collaborated with the Office of University Programs at the Department of Homeland Security to develop strategies for better integrating colleges and universities into homeland defense (National Research Council 2005). Security agencies, including the Central Intelligence Agency (CIA), actively recruited on campus—including covering the tuition for students possessing "critical skills" and who agreed to serve in the agency after graduation (Giroux 2008, 69–71; see also Golden 2017a, 2017b). New and well-financed academic and professional programs, centers, and institutes on counterterrorism and homeland security began popping up at a wide range of institutions.[1] College and university campuses also became the domestic front in this global war on terrorism, as scholars with dissenting views were harassed and fired, academic freedom curtailed, and foreign students surveilled (Nelson 2004, 359; Carvalho and Downing 2010).

The recruitment of colleges and universities into this "military-industrial-academic complex" (Giroux 2007) is not unique to the post-9/11 world. In fact, these recent collaborations are explicitly modeled on efforts developed during the Cold War (Martin 2005, 27; National Research Council 2005, 9–13; see also chapter 1).[2] Major differences remain, however. During the Cold War, scholars collaborating with the security apparatus were employed to actively reproduce a vision of the world as a strategic space occupied by discrete nation-states, operating within an international system of states, and with the United States at its center. However, by the early twenty-first century, the social sciences were producing large volumes of scholarship dedicated to studying globalization, globality, globalism, global governance, global capitalism, global supply chains, global communications, global trade, global cities, global security, global policy, and global justice. Scholars and students in 2001 were actively engaged in the practice of imagining the world as a vast, interconnected global space. It was within this horizon that President Bush declared before a joint session of Congress, "Our war on terror begins with al Qaeda . . . [but] will not end until every terrorist group of global research has been found, stopped and defeated" (Bush 2001). By December 2001, the war on terror had been officially named the Global War on Terrorism, or GWOT for short. In 2005 efforts surfaced to rename the conflict the Global Struggle against Violent Extremism" (G-SAVE) (Gardner 2010, 304). While considerable debate existed within the Bush administration about what constituted a war on terrorism, no one doubted that this was a global war. The assumption that terrorist attacks necessitated a global response did not arrive spontaneously. Rather, by 2001, it had already become common—if not perfectly banal—to claim that the world existed as a single, global space.

This was particularly true within the world of higher education. In fact, the previous year, Justin Rosenberg observed that "we live today in a veritable 'age of globalisation studies,' in which one academic discipline after another is gaily expanding its remit into the 'global' sphere and relocating its own subject matter in a geographically extended, worldwide perspective" (2000, 11). The "age of globalization studies" Rosenberg describes was clearly evidenced in the massive proliferation of academic writing on globalization during the 1990s and early 2000s as well as the rush to create global studies departments and programs; the expansion of book series, edited volumes, readers, journals, conferences, and professional associations dedicated to the topic; and the rewriting of class titles, textbooks, syllabi, and job postings to include a focus on global issues and globalization.[3] This shift in academic focus went hand in hand with institutional efforts to globalize colleges and universities, including expanded opportunities for students to engage in global experiences abroad, developing interdisciplinary programming with a global focus, and creating global partnerships with universities around the world. By 2003, nearly 50 percent of American colleges had mission statements emphasizing teaching students to "thrive in a future characterized by global interdependence" (Hovland 2006, 11).[4] Today, global studies programming exists at more than three hundred American colleges and universities, some with multimillion-dollar facilities and more than a thousand undergraduate and graduate student majors (Steger and Wahlrab 2017, 14–15).

Despite the considerable embrace of globalization studies all around him, Rosenberg remained skeptical. In his seminal 2005 essay "Globalization Theory: A Post Mortem," Rosenberg argued that the academic obsession with globalization was little more than a faddish response to short-term political and economic trends. Globalization theory, he argued, emerged from a specific and fleeting historical moment defined by the "collapse of the Soviet Union," the "rapid restructuring of the international system," and the "crisis of Keynesianism and Bretton Woods" (Rosenberg 2005, 64). These events, he argued, unleashed a wave of "speculative and transnational capital" that washed over the former communist countries like an engorged river crashing upon a "flood-plain." This "conjunction" resulted in the "frenzied expansions, integrations, realignments and transformations that gave the period its overwhelming theme of spatial change" (64). By the mid-2000s, Rosenberg argued, the specific historical conditions that gave rise to globalization theory had largely subsided, opening a "new conjuncture" in which the concept of globalization "no longer provide[d] an ideologically plausible guide" (63). Considering these developments, the "*concept* of 'globalization'" had to undergo a "historical post mortem" that involved "an *empirical* reassessment of the 1990s" to explain why "'globalization' became the craze that it did" (5; emphasis in original).

Rosenberg's analysis of globalization is compelling, reminding his readers that concepts are always born within certain political and economic moments. In doing so, he warns against projecting the specific present into an inevitable future. However, Rosenberg's analysis misses two crucial points. First, the rise of global studies was not just an academic response to changes taking place (out there) in the world but, closer at hand, an intellectual adaptation to changes taking place within the world of higher education itself. The end of the Cold War not only remade political and economic relationships between the United States, Soviet Union, and the Bretton Woods institutions, but profoundly altered the relationships of academic knowledge production as well.

Second, while Rosenberg accurately acknowledges that the heated academic debates over globalization have largely subsided from their peak in the 1990s and early 2000s, his argument fails to appreciate the thing actually produced during this period: namely, the global imaginary. While Rosenberg focuses on the limitations of the concept of globalization, the 1990s and early 2000s were, even more importantly, a time when it became ubiquitous, and seemingly self-evident, to imagine the world as global. While academics debated whether globalization was new or old, good or bad, strengthening or weakening the state, singular or plural, spatial or temporal, modern or postmodern, these debates all assumed that the concept of globalization more or less accurately represented the world as it was: global. Even as globalization emerged as a hotly contested concept within the academy, and the social sciences in particular, the claim "the world is global" became self-evident and common sense (Kamola 2013).

Making the World Global, therefore, argues that rather than examining the particularities of the post–Cold War conjuncture as the origin of the concept of globalization (as Rosenberg suggests), we instead focus our attention on the question of reproduction. Rather than concept formation, this book examines knowledge production. In doing so, it becomes possible to ask a different question: How did the world of American higher education become a particular location within which it became widely possible to imagine the world as global? Answering this question requires establishing a different theoretical terrain. To do so, I first examine the difference between globalization as a concept (a term that claims to represent a unique phenomenon) and the global imaginary.[5] I then examine what it means to study the global imaginary as produced and reproduced within the worlds of higher education.

Imagining the World

Writing about the world as global requires imagining an object of study that cannot actually be seen. No individual can stand outside the social whole and represent a single world from some point outside itself. This is because knowledge about the world is always produced within a world. As such, knowledge about the world, as global or otherwise, reproduces the social relationships that make such knowledge possible. The practice of photographing—or imaging—the earth from outer space provides a useful analogy for thinking about knowledge as always reproduced within a world.

For most of human history, images of earth were speculative and limited to artistic representations, given that "earthbound humans" could only experience a "tiny part of the planetary surface" and therefore relied upon "their imagination" to "grasp the whole of the earth" (Cosgrove 2001, ix). The first photographic images containing the planet's curvature were taken in 1935, from manned aerial balloons floating nearly fourteen miles above the earth's surface (Poole 2008, 56–58). During the early years of the space race, the first photos of earth were taken by manned space expeditions within earth's orbit, and therefore presented earth front and center. Starting with Explorer VI in 1959, unmanned spacecraft were able to take black-and-white images of earth from outer space. However, prior to digital photography, these satellites captured photographs on film, developed the film onboard, converted the images into digital information, and relayed the data back to earth, where the pictures were reassembled into grainy, colorless printouts (Poole 2008, 72–73). This changed when the crew of Apollo 8 took the first color image of earth from outside earth's orbit.

The iconic *Earthrise* photo was shot with a 70 mm handheld Hasselblad

FIG. I.1 Bill Anders, *Earthrise*, December 24, 1968.

camera by Apollo 8 astronauts, on December 24, 1968, as their craft circum-
navigated the moon looking for possible future landing locations (Maher
2004, 526).[6] Forty years later, astronaut Lovell recalled that "Bill [Anders]
had the camera with colour film and a telephoto lens. That is what makes
the picture. Earth is about the size of a thumbnail when seen with the naked
eye from the Moon. The telephoto lens makes it seem bigger and gives the
picture that special quality" (McKie 2008).[7]

Upon returning to earth, the *Earthrise* photo was cropped and disseminated by NASA, with the first widely replicated color print appearing on the
cover of *Life* magazine's January 10, 1969, edition, under the issue title "The
Incredible Year '68: Special Issue." This image, however, was significantly
modified from the original. The lunar surface was cropped out completely,
and the earth rotated 120 degrees counterclockwise. The obscured section of

LIFE
'68
The Incredible Year
SPECIAL
ISSUE
The earth as seen
from Apollo 8 in space,
showing the outlines of
North and South America
JANUARY 10 · 1969 · 40¢

FIG. I.2 Cover of *Life* magazine, January 10, 1969. Image courtesy of Getty Images, the LIFE Premium Collection.

the planet—directly above the lunar surface in the original—was tucked under the magazine's banner.[8] In other words, the specificity of the shot, made possible during a lunar fly-by, is erased, and the earth comes to stand in for itself. The context that made the image possible is replaced, leaving only the object earth situated against the black background of space. The modified photograph offers an image of earth as a single, self-evident thing, simply observable as it really is, from a point outside itself.

While it might be tempting to read the *Earthrise* photo as simply a more accurate and objective depiction of earth as a physical space, this photograph always represented "an Earth perspective" (Poole 2008, 29).[9] Since its inception, this image has been given meanings based on its worldly contexts. For example, coming at the end of a year that saw students occupy universities from Paris to Mexico City, black power fists raised on the Olympic podium, the assassination of Martin Luther King Jr. and Robert Kennedy, race riots in major American cities, the Tet Offensive, eroding support for the war in Vietnam, as well as Soviet tanks rolling into Czechoslovakia, *Earthrise* helped construct a certain vision of a world that did not actually exist: a "visual confirmation of American democracy's redemptive world-historical mission . . . [ushering in] the universal brotherhood of a common humanity" (Cosgrove 2001, 260). The edited image on the cover of *Life* became an inspiration among antiwar and environmental activists who appropriated the image to conjure an imagined human community without war or ecological devastation (Weir 2007, 106; Poole 2008, 152). To this day, *Earthrise*, along with the subsequent 1972 *Blue Marble* photograph taken by Apollo 17, remain the two most reproduced images of earth. These images are ubiquitous within advertising, publications, and marketing material, and populate the "symbols of 'global' educational, humanitarian, and ecological issues" (Cosgrove 2001, 257).

While *Earthrise* appears to simply capture the world as it is, the very possibility of this image cannot be disaggregated from Cold War politics. After the Soviet Union launched Sputnik in 1957, the Kennedy administration responded with a commitment to send a man to the moon by the end of the decade. Former Nazi rocket engineers tasked with designing intercontinental ballistic missiles developed the Saturn V rockets that propelled the Apollo missions. The 1968 Apollo 8 launch was initially scheduled to test the lunar landing vehicle within the earth's orbit. However, foreign intelligence sources learned that the Soviet Union was planning a lunar flyby the following year. If successful, this would give Russia another first in the space race (in addition to first satellite, first living animal, first man and woman in space, and first space walk, among others). The already scheduled Apollo 8 mission was therefore hastily reassigned as a lunar flyby. As a result, it not only became the first manned craft outside earth's orbit but also lacked the landing module mounted on the front of the craft—the presence of which would have blocked the *Earthrise* photo (Poole 2008, 19). The photo was also made possible by the fact that, starting with the Gemini 9 flight in 1966, all manned space expeditions were required to have a media strategy that included capturing photographs and TV footage for public consumption (Poole 2008, 71).[10]

The practice of photographing earth from outer space is not entirely different from imagining the world as global, as practiced within academic print culture.[11] Unable to exit the earth's orbit, colleges and universities are always and already worldly institutions, grounded in long histories and inscribed within vast economic, social, political, and cultural structures and practices. Despite being located within vast overdetermined social relationships, those students, scholars, and administrators inhabiting the world of higher education often imagine universities as extraworldly spaces from which to orbit—and gaze down upon—the world below. In claiming to simply reflect upon the world, seeing it as it actually is, the university often fades from the foreground, cropped out of the imaginary. In this process, colleges and universities increasingly are perceived as ivory towers located above and outside the world. In reality, however, there is no outside from which to view the world as a single thing, global or otherwise. A university is not a capsule floating outside the world's orbit. As such, academic knowledge is never merely a snapshot of the world outside itself.

Making the World Global is an effort to better understand how the world came to be imagined as global from within the world of American higher education. It is a multidecade and multisited story focusing on individual thinkers, the institutions they inhabit, and the imaginaries rendered possible within—and outside of—the American academy. The book starts by examining the reproduction of a national imaginary within American higher education during the Cold War. During this period, considerable effort went into remaking American higher education, and the social sciences particularly, into a space for imagining the world as a system of discrete nation-states. As the colleges and universities changed during the 1980s and 1990s, so too did the knowledge produced within them. An emphasis on area studies and national development gave way to regimes of knowledge production that favored imagining different worlds as all parts of a same global whole.

Treating higher education as engaged in the practice of world making offers a substantially different analytic than that found in most studies of higher education. The scholarship on higher education often relies upon an "impact model" (Hart 2002, 12) in which the global forces of globalization, marketization, and corporatization come crashing down upon local academic institutions. Two things—the university and globalization—collide and institutions of higher education adapt to this new reality. Such accounts, based on the assumption of linear causality, have little space for understanding the ways in which colleges and universities are actually active participants in the production, and reproduction, of the world.

The World of American Higher Education

What does it mean to study the academy not as an Archimedean point outside the world—as a transcendent tower from which to gaze at a world existing down below—but rather as itself part of the world? What does it mean, in other words, to study the academy as a site of world making? To answer this question, let me first briefly sketch the broad contours of the academic literature on higher education to mark my significant departure.

This book is an intervention into the growing and important literature documenting the corporatization, commercialization, commodification, privatization, and neoliberalization of higher education (Soley 1995; Slaughter and Leslie 1997; Aronowitz 2000; Bok 2003; Kirp 2003; Slaughter and Rhoades 2004; Washburn 2005; Newfield 2008, 2016; Bousquet 2008; Tuchman 2009; Ginsberg 2013; Giroux 2014; Fabricant and Brier 2016). Much of this literature focuses on the crisis of education taking place within American institutions. For example, studies examine how market forces within higher education increase indebtedness, exacerbate social inequality, and undermine academic freedom (Williams 2006; Adamson 2009a; Mullen 2010; Nelson 2010; Mettler 2014). Other studies explore possible political responses to such marketization, including unionization and the cultivation of the academic commons (Martin 1998; Johnson, Kavanagh, and Mattson 2003; Harvie 2004; Berry 2005; Shukaitis and Graeber 2007; Krause et al. 2008b; Edufactory Collective 2009; Kamola and Meyerhoff 2009). Some of the best studies document the effects market logics have had on particular disciplines, and most notability the humanities, where austerity and market rationality have been experienced for many decades (Ohmann 1976, 2003; Guillory 1993; Bérubé and Nelson 1995; Readings 1996; Nelson 1997; Newfield 2003; Donoghue 2008; Nussbaum 2010). There is also a growing effort to demonstrate that this crisis is not new, but an extension of the fact that higher education is deeply entwined with a long history of slavery, colonization, imperialism, and other forms of racialized oppression (Dugdale, Fueser, and Alves 2011; Ferguson 2012; Wilder 2013; Harney and Moten 2013; Pietsch 2013; Chatterjee and Maira 2014; Pietsch 2016; Stein and Andreotti 2016). There is a growing amount of literature examining how market and neoliberal logics have had catastrophic effects on national education systems around the world (Chou, Kamola, and Pietsch 2016b; Mittelman 2018), including in Canada (Côté and Allahar 2007), the U.K. (Holmwood 2011; Pritchard 2011; McGettigan 2013), Latin America (Rhoads and Torres 2006), and Africa (Diouf and Mamdani 1994; Zeleza and Olukoshi 2004; Afoláyan 2007; Mamdani 2007). This largely critical body of work exists parallel to a mushrooming practitioner-led literature that examines the relative costs and benefits that accompany the "globalization of higher education" (Odin and Manicas 2004; Suárez-Orozco and Qin-Hilliard 2004; Altbach 2007; Weber and Duderstadt 2008; Altbach, Reisberg, and Rumbley 2009; Bassett and Maldonado-Maldonado 2009; Wildavsky 2010).

Making the World Global intervenes in these important conversations in three specific ways. First, it breaks down the common narrative of American higher education as "a linear movement of progressive expansion, democratization, and inclusion interrupted" by the marketization of higher education (Stein and Andreotti 2016, 5). Most critical studies of American higher education—especially those organized around the narrative of crisis—imagine the post–World War II period as a golden age of American higher education. The democratization and expansion of higher education during this period, the argument goes, became foreclosed upon as the institutions faced wave after wave of commercialization starting in the 1980s.[12] This narrative, however, does injustice to the fact that American higher education has always been closely tied to practices of coloniality, enclosure, and dispossession (Kamola and Meyerhoff 2009; Wilder 2013). Therefore, rather than using the terms of ascent and decline, or democracy and crisis, this book examines American higher education as a contested world or multiple worlds. In doing so, one can trace the massive expansion of American higher education during the Cold War as explicitly tied to American imperialism, including efforts to defeat popular anticolonial movements. Parallel to its alliance with the military apparatus, however, the world of American higher education also includes considerable contestation and rebellion. The militarized university exists alongside, simultaneous to, and overdetermined by the utopic demands of students, faculty, and campus workers seeking to imagine a world otherwise. In this way, the institutions we inhabit today can be thought of as the amalgamation of nonlinear histories that include slavery and land dispossession, American colonial and imperial expansion, and shifting practices of capitalist accumulation, as well as powerful political, social, and cultural demands for a more just and inclusive world. The university, in other words, is not one thing; it is many, as it contains multitudes. Consequently, the knowledge produced within the academy is not only shaped by these histories but embodies their deep and living contradictions.

Second, while most literature on higher education focuses on the effects of commercialization on students, faculty, staff, disciplines, democracy, and society as a whole, this book looks at how these changing social and economic relations also shape the production and reproduction of academic—and specifically social scientific—knowledge. In doing so, it becomes possible to understand the world of American higher education not simply as the victim of political and economic changes coming from outside, but rather a location within which the world is continually produced and reproduced at the level of the imaginary. This book examines how the transformation of the world of higher education not only affects the academy and the disciplinary practices we engage in, but also the very concepts, terms, and imaginaries that become widespread across many worlds.

And, finally, this study differs from much of the academic literature on higher education in having a much more expansive understanding of what constitutes the world of American higher education. Much of the literature focuses primarily on colleges and universities, and sometimes government policies. However, scholars who narrowly focus on the university often miss the ways in which nonacademic institutions profoundly shape—and are shaped by—the world of higher education. As chapters 2 and 4 on the World Bank as well as chapter 5 on the Social Science Research Council (SSRC) demonstrate, academic ideas often circulate outside the academy, become adopted and incorporated into policy, and then travel back into the world of higher education. In other words, *Making the World Global* demonstrates how the world of American higher education might be perceived in ways profoundly connected with other sites of social production and reproduction.

Even with this expansive understanding of higher education as a contested and material world, I should note that focusing on American institutions does provide a limitation. On the one hand, the American academy is unlike any other university system. It is a vast, heterogeneous mix of public state institutions (including large flagship research institutions, state colleges, technical schools, and community colleges) as well as private research and professional universities, religious colleges, small liberal arts schools, and for-profit institutions. American higher education is not actually a system at all but rather a "historically specific by-product of the incorporation, adaption, and bastardisation of other university models" (Chou, Kamola, and Pietsch 2016a, 4–5). This heterogeneity is exacerbated by the fact that these vastly heterodox institutions engage in a wide range of activities, which may include providing undergraduate, graduate, and professional instruction; facilitating academic research; delivering sporting, cultural, and extracurricular activities; developing housing and retail properties; engaging in urban revitalization; providing continuing education, military training, and extension services; patenting technology and incubating corporate entities; and so on. Clark Kerr (2001), former President of the University of California, famously preferred to talk of a multiversity rather than a university. While this uniquely American model does not exist elsewhere in the world, it is widely appropriated, also in the "spirit of strategic adaptation, emulation, and incorporation" (Chou, Kamola, and Pietsch 2016a, 5). Therefore, the lessons learned examining American higher education might be particular to this world, or they might speak to broader universal—or multiversal—tendencies.

I should also note that focusing on American higher education is not an endorsement of the claim that universities, in the United States and elsewhere, possess a monopoly on the production of knowledge. Today the production of knowledge is widely dispersed, taking place in numerous locations: everything from the mass media, social media, and blogging platforms to prestigious think tanks, philanthropic foundations, corporations, nonprofit organizations, and data-gathering international institutions. For example, as chapters 2 and 4 demonstrate, the worlds of higher education—in the United States and across Africa—are profoundly affected by knowledge produced within the World Bank. Similarly, in recent decades, think tanks have greatly expanded their influence over policy and public discussion, often through producing and disseminating the specialized, expert knowledge once considered the sole domain of higher education institutions (Rich 2004;

McGann and Sabatini 2011). That being said, the university is still unique in this changing terrain of knowledge production. In addition to providing advanced credentialing, universities also cultivate much of the ideas, personnel, and legitimacy that flows across these dispersed networks of knowledge production.

To study how changes in the world of American higher education shape the practice of imagining the world as global, this book focuses on a small handful of elite institutions, some academic (Massachusetts Institute of Technology, Harvard Business School, and New York University), others philanthropic (SSRC) and financial (World Bank). All these institutions are located in a handful of East Coast cities: Cambridge, New York, and Washington, DC. Similarly, the central figures around which I have arranged this narrative are all white men (W. W. Rostow, Robert McNamara, Theodore Levitt, A. W. Clausen, Kenneth Prewitt, and John Sexton). This choice of institutions and leading characters is intended to illustrate—and awkwardly draw attention to—the very real hierarchical organization that continues to shape the world of higher education more generally. The American academy is, after all, still very much organized according to gendered and racial hierarchies. According to the American Association of University Professors, for example, men are still more likely to secure tenure and tenure-track positions, with women constituting just 34.6 percent of full-time faculty in 2009 (down from 38.4 percent in 1976). Women only make up a minority of full professors (28 percent), but a majority of academics on contingent contracts. Within college administration, only 23 percent of university or college presidents are women (Curtis 2011). In terms of racial inequity, 84 percent of tenure and tenure-track professors are white (and 60 percent white males) and only 3 and 4 percent, respectively, are black and Hispanic; among university presidents, the vast majority—89 percent—are white (Hamer and Lang 2015, 906).

If American higher education is a world organized over many decades to facilitate the mass reproduction of a global imaginary, and if hierarchy and exclusion profoundly structure this world, what does this tell us about how we have come to imagine the world as global?

Worlding the Global within American Higher Education

Walter Mignolo rightly argues that "delinking from coloniality" includes recognizing that the "American and the European Academy are not hubs of the decolonial" (2011, xxvii). Why then write a book about how six white males inhabiting elite East Coast academic, philanthropic, and financial institutions reimagined the world? I argue that there is critical work to be done in destabilizing and denaturalizing the imaginaries produced within these institutions. While not necessarily a work of decolonial theory, I hope *Making the World Global* can be read as an ally—or better yet, an accomplice—to the project of decolonizing the university.

Over the past few decades, and in relation to a dramatic expansion of higher education across the Global South, there is a growing demand that scholars around the world actively engage non-Western, and often nonacademic, sources of knowledge.[13] Raewyn Connell (2007a, 2007b), for example, calls for a greater attention to "southern theory"; Canagarajah (2002, 5–6) critiques the academic research article as reducing the Third World to "raw data" that requires "theorization/interpretation by the West to pass into the accepted stock of knowledge"; Portuguese scholar Boaventura de Sousa Santos argues that "another globalization" (2007b, xvii) is possible but requires moving "beyond northern epistemologies" (2007a) and confronting "the massive epistemicide upon which Western modernity built its monumental imperial knowledge" (Santos 2007c, 29; see also Santos 2014). Jean and John Comaroff argue that taking Africa as one's "point of departure" makes it possible to observe the multiple ways in which the European and American worlds are evolving toward Africa (Comaroff and Comaroff 2011, 7). I share an enthusiasm for this critical, political, and epistemic project (for example, Kamola 2014a, 2017; el-Malik and Kamola 2017). Why then write a book focusing on the production of knowledge within American universities? Or, more accurately, why focus on those institutions most complicit in concocting, disseminating, normalizing, and reinforcing "theory from the north"? I do so for three reasons.

First, personally and practically, American higher education is the world within which I live and work. American institutions of higher education are where I learned much of what I know, where I've spent the majority of my life, and what provides the food on my table and a roof over my family's head. In this way, I am compelled by Walter Mignolo's call to recognize and affirm one's locality and embodied practices as the sources of all knowledge claims.

Mignolo argues that a decolonial politics rejects "the *hubris of the zero point*," disavowing knowledge claims (including critical ones) that assume "a disembodied subject beyond location" (2011, xvii, xxiv, emphasis in original). Following Mignolo's mantra that "I am where I do and think" (2011, xvi; see also Mignolo 2000), my engagement with the world of American higher education stems primarily from the fact that I come from this particular world. In fact, everything from how my waking day is spent to what I think (and how) is shaped by the world of American higher education. I sincerely hope that doing my "homework" (Gusterson 2017)—that is, examining the networks of power, influence, and intellectual reproduction that shape the world in which I live—makes it possible to see American higher education not as a locationless platform from which to know the world, but rather as a complex and particular site in which worlds are produced and reproduced, including at the level of the imaginary. Academic knowledge, even if we might desire to claim otherwise, is produced within certain institutions and under specific conditions. Acknowledging this requires, for me, being attentive to the ways in which American higher education has a long history closely entwined with coloniality, imperialism, and finance capital.

Second, as American universities are being emulated and exported around the world, a small handful—the Harvards, MITs, and New York Universities—stand in as the prototypes of the American academy. However, these elite institutions constitute only a small handful of the more than 4,700 postsecondary institutions in the United States.[14] This book seeks to understand how a handful of schools came to be imagined as the totality of American higher education. In asking this question, it becomes evident that the institutions that now constitute the export face of American higher education are themselves coproduced within their shifting entwinements with the American military apparatus and vast amounts of private, and philanthropic, funding.

And, finally, studying the world of American higher education makes it possible to see the global not as a fact but rather as a place-in-the-world. On this point I am deeply influenced by James Ferguson's masterful book *Global Shadows*, which starts with the argument that the tendency to imagine Africa almost exclusively in terms of "crisis," as a "failure," and a "problem" to be solved, has caused scholars to abstain from writing about Africa as a whole, preferring instead "detailed ethnographic knowledge of local communities" (Ferguson 2006, 2–3). He argues that, rather than shying away from writing about Africa, scholars should instead think of Africa as a category "through which a 'world' is structured" (5). Africa is, in other words, a way of understanding the world produced through the various, heterogeneous, contested, and deeply political practices that surface when one tries to perform the impossible—that is, imagine a diverse, multifaceted, and heterogeneous continent as a coherent whole. *Making the World Global* extends Ferguson's argument to think of the global as also a place-in-the-world. After all, the global, like Africa, is a "historically and socially constructed" category, created in ways that are "in some sense arbitrary" (5). Like Africa, the global is a meaningful and very real term. Businesspeople, politicians, and citizens make decisions about production, governance, migration, warfare, regulation, trade, investment, immigration policy, and military intervention based on how they imagine the world as global. And like Africa, the global is an imaginary constructed and circulated through asymmetrical economic and political relations. However, unlike the category Africa—which Ferguson points out structures a world that is geographically confined and defined in terms of "lacks, failures, problems, and crises" (8)—the global structures a world imagined as transparent, self-evident, geographically boundless, and brimming with (real or potential) abundance and opportunity. Ferguson correctly contends that "we can no longer avoid talking about 'Africa' if we want to understand the wider order of the 'world'" (7). I would add that we also cannot understand the "world" without also understanding "the global" as a particular constructed imaginary.

To study the global as an imaginary, one made possible through the worldly practices of knowledge production, each of the following chapters examines different knowledge producers and the material locations where such production takes place. The book does not claim that these locations and individuals are the originators of such imaginaries. There is no ground zero in the production of the global imaginary. Rather, the production and reproduction of a global imaginary within American higher education emerged over a long period of time, often in asynchronous and haphazard ways. For example, in interviews with some founding thinkers of globalization, Steger and James (2015) find no single answer to the question of when and why their interviewees embraced the language of globalization. For George Modelski, the insight came out of his work on macro-world organization. Arjun Appadurai came across the term "globalization" in the popular press after the fall of the Berlin Wall, around the same time he was invited by Mike Featherstone to contribute to what became the groundbreaking *Theory, Culture and Society* special issue "Global Culture." Growing up speaking French,

Saskia Sassen was first inspired by the French term *globale* but began using the word "globalization" "because it seemed to be an emerging term in the academy. If you wanted to be efficient in a short conversation, or on a panel, or over lunch, or over drinks, 'globalization' was the term you used" (James and Steger 2014b, 462). The following chapters, therefore, should not be read as a linear story, but rather as preliminary sketches covering a handful of vignettes within a vast, complex, and overdetermined set of social relations.

The chapters, however, might also be read contrapuntally—not only with each other, but also with the institutional worlds that the reader inhabits. Edward Said argues that texts cannot be treated as independent of the "certain legal, political, economic, and social constraints" that shape their "production and distribution" (1983, 32). To read a text as coming from a world, Said suggests a contrapuntal method—one that begins by identifying that which is absent or obfuscated within a text and, in bringing it to the fore, juxtaposes these retrieved absences against the original, surface-level reading.[15] Said takes the concept of the contrapuntal from music; the contrapuntal occurs when "various themes play off one another, with only a provisional privilege given to any particular one" (1993, 51). The existence of different themes allows for one to see both the structure of the music and the variation: "in the resulting polyphony there is concert and order, an organized interplay that derives from the themes, not from a rigorous melodic or formal principle outside the work" (Said 1993, 51). The contrapuntal method, therefore, allows one to highlight the particularities as well as the structural ordering of one's object of study. A contrapuntal method does not simply argue for plural and relativistic reading—it does not simply "valorise plurality"—but is instead "a plea for 'worlding' the texts, institutions and practices, for historicizing them, for interrogating their sociality and materiality, for paying attention to the hierarchies and the power-knowledge nexus embedded in them" (Chowdhry 2007, 105).

In reading each chapter against one another, and the book against the reader's own institutional practices, we might begin to see the particularities (as well as the reoccurring structures)—the themes and variations—that organize the worlds of higher education. By understanding academic knowledge as produced and reproduced within such worlds, we are not only better positioned to understanding what we mean when we say the world is global but, more importantly, able to see globalization not as an external force but rather an imagined relation reproduced within our daily activity. Doing so creates an opportunity not only to imagine the world otherwise but also to imagine, design, and create the kinds of relations, institutions, and practices that might make new imaginaries possible.

Chapter Outline

This book is divided into three sections. The first section examines the production of social scientific knowledge during the decades following World War II. During this period, the Cold War university worked closely with philanthropic organizations, the federal government, and financial institutions to imagine a world divided into nation-states, organized into an international system, and with the United States at its center. Chapter 1 focuses on how the federal government and philanthropic organizations profoundly transformed American colleges and universities into exceptionally well-funded strategic reserves of knowledge used to manage the rise of American empire. Faced with Soviet competition and decolonization across the Third World, the new fields of area studies, international studies, and International Relations received unprecedented funding. As exemplified in the work of W. W. Rostow, a veteran of the Office of Strategic Services during World War II and faculty at MIT's Center for International Studies (CENIS), the national imaginary became the foundation of modernization theory. The chapter demonstrates how, throughout Rostow's writings, the world became imagined as composed of discrete nation-states, each with its own trajectory toward Western-style democratic and capitalist modernization. This national imaginary circulated widely within the academy, the federal government, and development agencies, and shaped not only how the world was imagined but also America's strategic posture toward the rest of the world.

Chapter 2 examines how a Rostowian national imaginary moved into the World Bank in the late 1960s, and the effect this had on shaping higher education policies across the Third World. Trained at Harvard Business School and serving as an Air Force statistician during World War II, Robert McNamara became influenced by modernization theory while in the Johnson administration. During his tenure as president of the World Bank, McNamara not only greatly expanded the institution's lending capacity but also transformed the World Bank into one of the largest producers of economic knowledge. Reproducing a national development imaginary, McNamara profoundly shaped World Bank policy toward newly independent African countries, including in the realm of education. Seeing education—including higher education—as central to national development, the McNamara Bank made funding African universities a priority. One unintended consequence was the creation of African universities as vibrant centers of anticolonial intellectual thought aimed at imagining the world otherwise.

The second section examines early efforts to reimagine the world as global within business schools and the World Bank. Chapter 3 situates Theodore Levitt's 1983 *Harvard Business Review* article "The Globalization of Markets"—widely credited with popularizing the term "globalization"—within his general approach to marketing. Levitt argued that marketing professionals should not simply ask customers what they want but cultivate a "marketing imagination"—namely, the ability to imagine what the customer wants, even before he or she articulates these desires. Understood in this way, Levitt's article on globalization can be read less as an argument about whether the world is global than as a marketing manifesto encouraging companies to imagine the world as if it were global. The chapter examines how Levitt's global imaginary spread rapidly throughout the business world such that companies began to adapt their marketing strategies. In a very short period, globalization became a powerful heuristic through which business leaders and professional marketers reimagined foreign markets as already prone to, and desirous of, American products.

Chapter 4 returns to the World Bank, examining how the national development imaginary gave way to reimagining the world as a single financial market. McNamara's successor—former Bank of America president A. W. Clausen (1981–86)—arrived at the World Bank with a banker's global imaginary, which shaped all aspects of the institution's response to the Third World debt crisis. The proliferation of structural adjustment, and an emphasis on calculating rate of return, brought about dramatic changes to the world of higher education. Rather than seeing higher education as an essential component of national development, the Clausen Bank envisioned higher education as a market relationship, a private good—"human capital"— quantifiable as the difference in wages between those with and without education. This reimagining of the value of higher education justified a radical defunding of higher education across Africa and, consequently, the further solidification of the United States as an unrivaled center of academic knowledge production.

The final section examines how ideas about globalization, first produced within the business schools and cultivated within the worlds of business, finance, and development, returned to American universities as the very logic by which higher education is marketed, funded, and administered. Chapter 5, for example, examines how American social sciences adopted the language of globalization during the 1990s within the context of increasing economic pressures on post–Cold War higher education. As the federal government and philanthropic foundations pulled back funding, many colleges and universities began pursuing investments from private donors to offset these considerable losses. Chapter 5 focuses specifically on the debates within the SSRC during the mid-1990s. Publicly, SSRC president Kenneth Prewitt explained the council's shift away from area-based grant funding as driven by the fact that the world was now global, and therefore the institution must change to reflect changing times. However, internal discussions make it clear that the SSRC was facing considerable financial difficulty and saw this reprioritization as a way to please their stakeholders and coinvestors. This chapter contextualizes the rise of global studies as itself a symptom of a changing political economy of higher education.

Chapter 6 examines the rise of study abroad, the practice of recruiting foreign students, and the creation of branch campuses as various strategies for globalizing American universities and colleges. Often talked about as inevitable responses to the fact of globalization, this chapter argues that these practices should instead be read as institutional adaptations to the economic pressures facing the world of higher education. The chapter focuses on the effort by New York University, under President John Sexton, to transform itself into a global network university, through the creation of branch campuses in Abu Dhabi and Shanghai. This chapter identifies an edu-theological global imaginary guiding Sexton's thinking about higher education. Sexton portrays research universities, and NYU particularly, as "ecumenical gifts" to the world, facilitating a new age of cosmopolitan interconnection. This global imaginary, however, renders invisible the very real exploitations that made the building of NYU's global branch campus in Abu Dhabi possible. The chapter argues that the rhetoric around global higher education often fails to reveal the financial incentives at work in shaping how universities imagine, value, fund, and intellectually engage their global commitments.

Making the World Global concludes by arguing that if knowledge about the world is shaped by the material conditions under which such knowledge is produced, then knowing the world differently involves not only developing new concepts, theories, and terminologies but also—and even more fundamentally—creating new conditions of academic knowledge production. The conclusion calls for developing a broader cartography and ecology of academic knowledge production, from which it might be possible to produce new ways of knowing the world—ways of imagining the world that resist the assumption that the world is already, self-evidently global.

Notes toward an Investigation (Optional)

While it might be tempting to read *Making the World Global* as an empirical or historical story, I consider it a work of theory, constructed through close—and symptomatic—readings of texts produced within particular conjunctures.[16] While I hope the contours become evident as the book unfolds, I am aware that the broader theoretical argument might remain entangled within a thicket of names, institutions, and events. For those interested in taking the scenic route, a saunter among the trees, please feel free to skip this section. However, for those interested in a more clearly blazed trail through the forest, and who don't mind the mixed metaphor, this section offers a quick look under the hood at the book's theoretical underpinnings.

In answering the question "What is global-speak a symptom of?" the common answer would probably be something like this: growing academic attention to globalization during the 1990s occurred because the world was becoming increasingly global. This answer, however, assumes that what is (and is not) global remains largely self-evident. This assumed self-evident quality of the global rests upon the image of the world as a finite spherical space being drawn ever closer together. In other words, the claim that the world is global depends upon the spatial metaphor of the world as a globe.

This book instead argues that globalization should be studied from the point of view of reproduction. I draw this distinction, between a spatial metaphor and a point of view of reproduction, from Althusser's (2001a) essay "Ideology and Ideological State Apparatus (Notes towards an Investigation)." This essay, written in France months after the university occupations of May 1968, examines—among other things—the changing social function "the School" plays in shaping how people imagine the world around them. The essay rejects the economistic Marxist descriptions of ideology, in which economic production (the base) determines all aspects of the superstructure. This essay instead lays out a framework for studying sociopolitical relations as complexly overdetermined. To this end, Althusser critiques the base-superstructure model—in which capitalist production is directly and caus-ally responsible for reproducing all aspects of social life (the family, religion, the state, etc.)—not because he finds this analysis incorrect, but because it depends upon a limited "spatial metaphor: the metaphor of a topography" (Althusser 2001a, 90). The base-superstructure metaphor assumes, in other words, that a building's foundation determines the shape of all subsequent floors. While Althusser states that this spatial metaphor reveals many im-portant things about the structure of capitalism (such as the fact that "the base . . . in the last instance determines the whole edifice"), it simultaneously limits how the world can be known as a social whole.[17] Althusser argues in-stead for "go[ing] beyond" the descriptive metaphor of topography in favor of adopting "*the point of view of reproduction*" (91–92, emphasis in original). To do this, he proposes examining how different registers and apparatuses overdetermine each other to reproduce a social whole. Rather than a linear understanding of causality (i.e., base determines superstructure), Althusser argues that the social whole is instead a constantly shifting assemblage of semiautonomous social registers immanent to each other. Different appa-ratuses and registers, what we might call worlds, constantly overdetermine each other in ways that are organized by the relations of production but not solely determined by them. A certain college or university, for example, is an institution that shapes the kinds of practices possible within it. It is not, however, simply one thing but rather an overdetermined set of relationships between disciplines, departments, students (and families), faculty, admin-istration, alumni, donors, workforces, architecture, curricular decisions, branding, endowments, professional organizations, and geographical loca-tion, all shaped by—but not reducible to—broader trends within the political economy of higher education, and the world economy more generally. Over-determined structure, in other words, is immanent, contested, contradictory, and lived.

Therefore, examining globalization from the point of view of reproduc-tion requires treating globalization or globalism not as simply an ideology reflecting specific class interests (for example, Rupert 2000; Steger 2002) but rather as "*the imaginary relationship of individuals to their real conditions of existence*" (Althusser 2001a, 109, emphasis in original). Produced within the world of higher education, globalization represents an imaginary relation-ship reproduced by individuals as they collectively ascribe meaning to their social world (the entirety of which cannot be seen, and therefore must be imagined). Because the social whole cannot be objectively seen from some outside vantage point, subjects must imagine themselves in relation to their real conditions. Althusser illustrates this act of reproduction using the Pascalian example of a person attending church who kneels, prays, makes the sign of the cross, and confesses. It is not some preexisting faith in God, or a false opiate fabricated by the ruling class, that motivates these very real activities but rather the practices themselves, as organized by the apparatus of the Church, which produce belief in an imagined God (Althusser 2001a, 114).

Applying this argument to globalization, one can understand the global imaginary as having "*a material existence*" since it always "exists in an apparatus, and its practice, or practices" (Althusser 2001a, 112, emphasis in original). In other words, within the apparatus of the university, individuals engage in the material practices that reproduce an imagined relationship to the world as global. Like faith in God, understanding the world as global does not originate from some transcendent truth learned from standing outside the world, but rather from the repeated practices taking place within the apparatus of the university. This book attempts to demonstrate how changes within the world of higher education created the conditions within which it became possible to imagine one's relationship to the world as global. Rather than kneeling, bowing, and praying, for academics and students our daily activities include attending classes, meetings, and talks, applying for grants, writing papers, teaching, studying, and all the other practices that constitute the world of higher education. It is through these changing practices that we reproduce a global world at the level of the imaginary.

I realize that many readers might be skeptical of using the controversial Althusser, and his long out-of-fashion version of structural Marxism, as a guide for understanding the reproduction of national and global imaginaries within American higher education. I hope that the rest of the book, taken as a whole, demonstrates how this approach—and the productive tensions implied within it—might facilitate efforts to understand, contextualize, reimagine, and remake the institutions of higher education within which we live and work. For those who remain skeptical, I have two points of clarification. First, my reading of Althusser is far from conventional. I contend that by "reading Althusser as Althusser reads Marx," it becomes possible to see the limitations within Althusser's own theoretical apparatus as shaped by the conjuncture within which he wrote. If one takes Althusser's essay, originally written within the contested post–May 1968 French university, and rereads it today within the contemporary American neoliberal university, it becomes possible to identify a different Althusser than the one so widely critiqued during the 1970s and 1980s (for example, Thompson 1995; Rancière 2011). This Althusser is flexible enough to appreciate the multiple, competing, contingent, singular, and contested worlds that exist as overdetermined relationality. In doing so, he presents a theoretical approach that, on the one hand, insists upon the centrality of capitalist accumulation while, on the other hand, avoids the economistic readings of Marx that remain very much prevalent among Marxist scholars as well as their critics. This new Althusser offers a decentered, diffused, immanent, and infinitely contradictory understanding of capitalism. This vision of overdetermined complexity, I argue, destabilizes any claims that the production of knowledge takes place at some point outside the world.

Whether his focus is Lenin (Althusser 2001b), Marx (Althusser and Balibar 1999), Machiavelli (Althusser 1999), Rousseau (Althusser 2007), Montesquieu (Althusser 2007), or even himself (Althusser 2003, 226), Althusser commonly employs the method of reading a theorist within the conjuncture in which they wrote. Doing so makes it possible to identify the limits, absences, and possibilities made possible by that conjuncture. *Making the World Global* models this method, organizing each chapter around reading the work of one individual, and using this rereading to map the conjunctures that make such knowledge possible.

Second, Althusser's analysis pushes back against the notion that political change comes from academics engaged in radical spontaneity originating from elsewhere. Arjun Appadurai, for example, also called for a politics of reimagining globalization. He rightfully claims that *"the imagination as a social process"* is "central to all forms of agency" and therefore "the key component of the new global order" (Appadurai 1996, 31). To explain this process, he articulates the contemporary imagined worlds as shaped by five "global cultural flows"—ethnoscapes, mediascapes, technoscapes, financescapes, and ideoscapes (Appadurai 1996, 33–43). Making the world differently therefore requires imagining it differently. To this end, Appadurai calls on academics to reimagine globalization in ways that avoid disciplinary constraints and area studies limitations while reinvigorating an analysis of locality. However, this urgent call assumes that political change takes place when individual academics choose to adopt new imaginaries (Appadurai 2000, 3; see also Appadurai 2001). While Appadurai focuses on the academy as one important location for imagining globalization differently and calls upon academics to craft their contributions in ways that might assist grassroots activism, he nonetheless assumes that poverty and political struggle exists outside the academy. Conceptualized as privileged and nonmarginal, academics in Appadurai's account occupy an elite position from which to assist a politics existing elsewhere. Appadurai's call to imagine globalization differently, however, ignores the fact that the anxiety of falling wages, workplace speed-up, and job precarity is rampant not only outside the university but within it as well. The existing political economy of higher education, with its increasingly competitive job market, debt, precarity, and greater pressure to publish or perish, often punishes those who might otherwise wish to apply their skills to globalization from below. Except for an established academic elite, the choice to develop new global imaginaries outside disciplinary publishing is a difficult choice, with very real consequences. This book, therefore, exists at this tension: a desire for a radical and spontaneous new global imaginary and a caution that what appears individual and agentic is also already structured. This tension is not merely a conceptual academic debate about structure versus agency, but rather an unanswerable political question.

As Justin Rosenberg observes in his classic essay "Globalization Theory: A Post Mortem," one of Althusser's biggest failures—in addition to his "overcomplicated, even tortured" language—was an inability to demonstrate how to engage in a "historical method of conjunctural analysis" (Rosenberg 2005, 32). *Making the World Global* is an effort to take up this challenge and—from within the limits of the neoliberal American academy—use Althusser's insights to rethink why, and how, the world became imagined as global. Because the practices that made this book possible are simultaneously particular and structural, both my own and widely shared, I see the test of this book as whether readers can identify their own institutions and conjunctures reflected here. In doing so, we might begin to collectively see those broader dynamic structural relations—if not specific institutional contexts—responsible for reproducing knowledge about our world. And, in doing so, we might begin to intentionally construct counterinstitutions within which it might be possible to imagine the world otherwise.

I Reproducing the National Imaginary

1 "Creative Imagination" Is Needed

W. W. Rostow and the Rise of Modernization
as a National Imaginary

One thought ever in the fore—
That in the Divine Ship, the World, breasting Time and Space,
All peoples of the globe together sail, sail the same voyage,
Are bound to the same destination
—WALT WHITMAN, "One Thought Ever at the Fore"

In 1953, the Center for International Studies (CENIS) at Massachusetts Institute of Technology (MIT) submitted a proposal to the Ford Foundation requesting funding for what would become the new center's highly influential Economic and Political Development Program. Drawing on faculty expertise, the proposal laid out an ambitious research agenda focused on understanding comparative economic and political development across India, Italy, and Indonesia. The proposal argued that research on economic and political development had important strategic implications for the United States, observing that today "development of the underdeveloped countries is a decisive factor in world politics," especially given that "Asia and Africa have become primary arenas in the Soviet-American conflict" (CENIS 1953, 1). While world affairs are only "partially shaped by Great Power strategy," the actual contours, the proposal argued, involve "internal political and economic evolution" experienced in political and economic life (1). As such, development informs the "course of the larger power struggle and may, in the long run, determine its outcome" (1). The United States, therefore, has considerable interest in assisting "emergent nations," helping them "achieve economic growth" and forge "democratic institutions" (1). The center justified its funding request on the basis that closer study of economic and political development would "help define the kinds of policy and action" that would "aid and hasten" changes "in the desired direction" (1).

The following year, CENIS submitted a follow-up request, documenting preliminary findings about India, Italy, and Indonesia, overviewing the twenty-two research projects under way, listing the new faculty and specialists hired, and touting the collaborative relationships established between CENIS and the Indian and Indonesian governments (CENIS 1954, vi). The proposal acknowledged that such research "is large in both scope and conception" and requires "substantial financing" (CENIS 1954, vi). In 1958, the center presented another proposal to the Ford Foundation, arguing that in its short six-year history, the center had "assembled a well qualified resident staff of economists, political scientists, sociologists, historians, and others" engaged in "research programs relevant to four important areas of national policy: economic and political development, international communication, U.S.-Soviet Bloc relations, and American society in its world setting" (CENIS 1958, 1). The report concluded, however, that the center remained heavily dependent upon "short-term grants from the major foundations" and "U.S. government contracts," and needed long-term financial support of $2.24 million to hire core faculty in the behavioral social sciences and to fund ongoing research projects, fellowships, and academic scholarship (CENIS 1958, 1, 3, 29). Sustained funding was warranted because CENIS was a unique institution, one in which social scientists worked to expand human knowledge within an interdisciplinary setting—allowing individual scholars to harness their own "imagination, synthetic power, [and] insights" in ways that broke through the existing "common sense" (CENIS 1958, 7).[1] After many months of proposal reviews and clarifications, the Ford Foundation granted the center a long-term funding grant of $850,000 (approximately $7.3 million in 2018) (Office of Public Relations 1959, 1). Between 1952 and 1961, the Ford Foundation would provide $2 million to support the "three I's study" (Blackmer 2002, 67). By 1969, the center had annual expenditures of nearly $1 million ($6.8 million in 2018), with funding coming from government departments and philanthropic foundations (primarily Ford) in roughly equal portions, and research covering a wide range of topics on issues of economic and political development.[2]

The Center for International Studies at MIT was just one site within a rapidly changing world of American higher education. Prior to World War II, American colleges and universities received funding almost exclusively from student tuition, wealthy benefactors, and state governments. However, by the mid-1960s, the federal government—and the security apparatus in particular—had become the primary funder of higher education, creating nothing less than a "common-law marriage" between the federal government and leading universities (Kerr 2001, 37). This arrangement meant that universities no longer existed for the "training of 'gentlemen'" but instead preoccupied themselves fulfilling "national needs" (Kerr 2001, 36). This new relationship profoundly affected the production of academic knowledge within American higher education.

First of all, government and philanthropic funders transformed the social sciences into a standing reserve of expertise capable of being tapped in times of national need. This chapter demonstrates how, within the Cold War American university, the social sciences became a *standing reserve* of expert knowledge on issues concerning economic and security interests. Within the social sciences, this included producing academic knowledge and scholarly experts capable of knowing the contemporary non-Western world and international state system by enframing the world as a series of discrete national societies.[3] As the collaboration between social scientists, philanthropic organizations, and the security apparatus increased during the Cold War, many scholars found themselves working within new, well-resourced fields of area studies, international studies, and International Relations, often with the expectation that such training would be made available as needed for national security purposes.[4]

Second, this massive reorganization of the university—including the social sciences—meant that these new disciplines and well-funded centers, programs, journals, and professional organizations provided the material apparatuses within which it became possible to reimagine the world as composed of discrete national units, organized within an international system, and with the United States located at its center. At the unit level, the newly created area studies produced knowledge about the world as a series of national containers, each possessing a distinguishable national society, culture, and economy, and moving along a path toward modernization and maturation. At the systems level, the fields of International Relations and international studies reimagined the world as an international terrain within which these discrete national units operated. The assumed audience for both the unit- and systems-level analyses now included American foreign policy officials interested in harnessing such knowledge to expand American influence abroad, combat the Soviet Union, and tamp down on anticolonial insurgencies.

Within this milieu, modernization theory became one of the dominant new social scientific paradigms. As shown in this chapter, modernization theory provided a template for imagining the non-Western world as dividable into self-contained units that could be shepherded toward industrialization and democratization under the watchful eye of the United States. This imagined world stood in sharp contrast to the social scientific scholarship of the previous decades. Prior to World War II, the American academy was much smaller, whiter, more elite, and generally focused on American and European culture, history, society, politics, and economics. For example, during the first half of the twentieth century, the discipline of political science concerned itself primarily with understanding, advocating, and advancing American liberal democracy (Farr and Seidelman 1993, 107–12). In general, and with important exceptions (Vitalis 2015), American social scientists at major research universities prior to World War II demonstrated little interest in the contemporary non-Western world. However, the creation and transformation of area studies, International Relations, and international studies within the Cold War university created the possibility to produce knowledge about the entire world as a system of discrete nation-states, all traveling in the same direction. This imagined trajectory of modernization, not coincidentally, was the same end desired by American foreign policy experts.

This chapter examines how expanded government and philanthropic funding during the Cold War transformed the American social sciences into a site for the reproduction of modernization as a distinct national imaginary. The first section provides an overview of how the federal government and philanthropic organizations fundamentally reorganized the social sciences during the decades after World War II, including the shaping of area studies, International Relations, and international studies. This chapter then looks specifically at CENIS, and the work of W. W. Rostow particularly, as one example of how modernization as a national imaginary became widely produced and transmitted across these academic and policy circles.

Following World War II, the European imperial world order was severely challenged, including the colonial imaginaries accompanying it. Within this context, American universities—and area studies, international studies, and International Relations in particular—offered whole new fields of scholarship capable of reimagining the world, and America's new position, in ways useful to American policy makers, opinion makers, business leaders, and security experts. It was this vision of a world divided into discrete national economies and societies, and organized within an international political order, that, by the 1980s and 1990s, scholars of globalization would come to challenge.

War Mobilization and American Higher Education

The United States has never had a federal university system due to a strong cultural and political commitment to states' rights.[5] American higher education consists of a heterogeneous constellation of institutions: centuries-old elite private colleges and universities including Ivy League institutions, small liberal arts colleges, and historically black colleges and universities; massive land-grant institutions funded and governed by state governments; vocationally oriented state and community colleges; private research universities; and even for-profit institutions.[6] Historically, the federal government abstained from investing in higher education directly, choosing instead to leave university education to the discretion of states and private institutions.[7] In fact, prior to World War II, direct federal funding to higher education was limited to a small handful of vocational and extension programs, the occasional wartime mobilization, and special programs developed during the Great Depression (Axt 1952, chapter 4). During and after World War II, however, massive federal funding—in the form of tuition payments and agency grants—dramatically expanded the size and operating capacity of American colleges and universities. As a result, between 1945 and 1975, the number of undergraduates in American universities increased 500 percent; graduate student enrollments skyrocketed 900 percent; and more academics were hired during the 1960s than during the previous 325-year history of American higher education combined (Menand 2010, 64–65).

Prior to World War II, efforts to employ academics to conduct government research involved contracting out specific studies, effectively hiring institutions to complete discrete research tasks. As head of the National Defense Research Council during World War II, Vannevar Bush invented the policy of distributing grants to individual researchers (rather than institutions), but still offering universities "generous overhead rate[s]" that would more than cover institutional expenses and therefore garner university support for faculty participating in wartime research (Lowen 1997, 50).[8] As a result, many academic institutions became dependent upon federally funded research to subsidize all aspects of their operating budgets. By 1960, the federal government was funding higher education to a tune of $1 billion a year, with nearly 80 percent going to twenty elite universities. At Stanford, Berkeley, Caltech, MIT, and Harvard, for example, federal funding accounted for half of the research budgets, and between 15 and 80 percent of the overall operating budgets (Lowen 1997, 147–48).

This was part of a mass military mobilization of American higher education. During the war, the Office of Scientific Research and Development organized scientists, university physicists, chemists, and engineers to develop the scientific inventions widely credited with winning the war, including the atomic bomb, radar, and rocket propulsion, as well as life-saving medical breakthroughs such as penicillin and blood transfusion technology (Bush 1945; Cole 2009, 86–89). Coordinated by the Office of War Information, psychologists served in military units conducting psychological warfare (Needell 1998, 5). The Office of Statistical Control drew upon statisticians— including the young Harvard Business School professor Robert McNamara (see chapter 2)—to apply advanced statistical and computation techniques to logistical questions.[9] The Office of Strategic Services (OSS)—the precursor of the Central Intelligence Agency—recruited social scientists to provide interdisciplinary area-specific knowledge (Soley 1995, 77; Cumings 2002, 268). To this end, the OSS's Research and Analysis (R&A) branch "employed prominent historians, economists, sociologists, diplomats and other experts" organized into geographical units, with different groups focusing on Europe and Africa, the Far East, USSR, and Latin America (Liptak 2009, 17). By the end of the war, the R&A division had produced "3 million 3×5 cards, 300,000 captioned photographs, 300,000 classified intelligence documents, one million maps, 350,000 foreign serial publications, 50,000 books, thousands of biographical files and 3,000 research studies" (Liptak 2009, 17, 19).[10] Ivy League institutions became the primary recruiting grounds for the OSS (Winks 1987), leaving Arthur Schlesinger Jr. to note that, by 1942, the R&A branch had "raided" almost the entire faculty of the Harvard history department (Schlesinger 1992, 62; see also Smith 1972; Roosevelt 1976a, 1976b; Winks 1987; Chalou 1992). Many of the scholars who passed through the OSS and the Office of War Information created lasting professional connections that would propel them to the top of their academic fields after the war.[11]

In addition to mobilizing university faculty for the war effort, the U.S. military also sent enlisted men to 227 university and college campuses for language training as part of the Army Specialized Training Program. This program brought together faculty from foreign languages, culture, history, and other subjects to provide the basic language training and cultural familiarity required to "make communication between occupier and occupied easier" (Bendix 2003, 39; see also Hall 1947, 1; Fenton 2008, 264). These training programs proved so popular among university faculty that many programs remained in place even after the army stopped funding them in 1945. In many instances, these cross-disciplinary collaborations became the nucleus of campus area-studies programs.

At war's end, the "knowledge machine" mobilized to combat the Axis powers was never "dismantled," but rather "became the key adjunct to the permanent military economy of the Cold War" (Aronowitz 2000, 38).[12] In 1945, Vannevar Bush published the FDR-commissioned seminal report *Science: The Endless Frontier*, arguing that the federal government should make sustained financial contributions to universities in the name of national defense and economic growth. Making science analogous to settler colonialism, Bush argued, "Science offers a largely unexplored hinterland for the pioneer who has the tools for his task. The rewards of such exploration both for the Nation and the individual are great. Scientific progress is one essential key to our security as a nation, to our better health, to more jobs, to a higher standard of living, and to our cultural progress" (1945, 2; see also Lewontin 1997, 12–18; Cole 2009, 86, 106).[13] Bush recommended that the federal government create a national foundation that would "develop and promote a national policy for scientific research" (1945, 34), a policy that would come to fruition in 1950 with the formation of the National Science Foundation (NSF).[14] The NSF effectively channeled federal resources to university researchers, thereby incentivizing certain research agendas and providing resources for the massive expansion of higher education. The success of the NSF led to the expansion and creation of additional government funding agencies, including the Atomic Energy Commission, the Office of Naval Research, the National Aeronautics and Space Administration (NASA), and the National Institutes of Health (NIH), thus unleashing a tidal wave of federal funding into American higher education. While the government spent a meager $13 million on university research in 1940 (almost all on agricultural studies), a decade later fourteen federal agencies combined to fund academic research to the tune of $150 million (Axt 1952, 85–86). Within the social sciences, 96 percent of federal government funding came from the military (Washburn 2005, 43).

In addition to funding research, the federal government also paid for the mass expansion of American higher education through the 1944 Service-men's Readjustment Act—or GI Bill. The bill doubled college enrollment between 1938 and 1948 (from 1.3 to 2.6 million) with veterans making up half of total college enrollments in 1946 and 1947 (Axt 1952, 122, 126). Over a five-year span, the Veteran's Administration poured a billion tuition dollars into American colleges and universities (Axt 1952, 127).[15]

Producing the National Imaginary within the Cold War University

The great weakness in American scholarship is its provincialism.... Scholarship has an obligation to the nation and among other things it must be able to give correct answers about foreign places.
— ROBERT HALL, "Area Studies" (1947)

The massive expansion of federal and philanthropic investments in higher education during the Cold War shaped all aspects of academic knowledge production. Within the hard sciences, considerable money was now available to research technology that fueled the space and arms races, as well as for basic research in chemistry, physics, engineering, computer sciences, and other scientific fields, creating an increasingly interconnected "military-industrial-academic complex" (Leslie 1993). Within the humanities, scholars were enlisted to cultivate and promote a "national literature" (Readings 1996, 70), providing the nation with a "moral education," "national traditions," and "a unifying cultural identity" (Newfield 2003, 43).[16] Within the social sciences, the influx of governmental and philanthropic support institutionalized those new fields of scholarship deemed directly useful to the American security apparatus. The development and expansion of area studies, International Relations, and international studies worked together to reinforce "the same outcome: expanding American power" (Parmar 2011, 189).

Area Studies and the Reproduction of the National Imaginary

The creation of area studies within American higher education was a direct response to World War II. Prior to the 1940s, American policy makers had limited access to creditable knowledge about the contemporary non-Western world. The social science disciplines of economics, political science, and sociology—as practiced almost exclusively within American and European universities—were originally designed to study the markets, states, and civil societies of Western Europe and North America, treating the rest of the world as "somehow different" (Wallerstein 2004, 7). In fact, prior to 1940, American universities had graduated less than sixty PhDs on the "contemporary non-Western world" (Szanton 2004, 6).

During the 1930s, much of the knowledge about the non-Western world came from missionaries, foreign correspondents, members of the diplomatic services, amateur organizations for nonacademic enthusiasts (such as the American Oriental Society), and freelance travel writers (McCaughey 1980). Colonial administrators living overseas also contributed to this body of knowledge, writing as hobbyists on topics such as "archaeology, music, ancient literatures, and history" (Anderson 2016, 36). When studied within the academy, knowledge about the world outside Europe and North America was largely produced either in the discipline of anthropology, which studied "tribal" and "primitive" peoples, or in "Oriental studies," which examined ancient civilizations in "China, Japan, India, Persia, and the Arab-Islamic world" (Wallerstein 1997, 198). Furthermore, American social scientists studying the non-Western world often did so within the framework of European empire and colonial administration.[17]

There were, of course, important exceptions. For example, while historically white American research universities had few experts on contemporary Africa prior to World War II, scholars within historically black universities were actively writing about Africa in ways very different from the mainstream social sciences (Robinson 2004, 125–33; see also West and Martin 1997, 310–12; Vitalis 2015). For example, in 1946, W. E. B. Du Bois described his book *The World and Africa* as "a history of the world written from the African point of view," one that takes "the Negro as part of the world" (1965, viii). Leo Hansberry and Ralph Bunche taught classes on Africa at Howard University, and Du Bois taught a course on ancient Africa while at Atlanta University (Robinson 2004, 125–26, 128). During this period, African Americans created several journals and professional organizations dedicated to the joint study of Africa and African Americans, such as Carter G. Woodson's Association for the Study of Negro Life and History (West and Martin 1997, 310–12). Historically black colleges were also the first institutions to recruit African students, including Benjamin Nnamdi Azikiwe (the first president of independent Nigeria) and Kwame Nkrumah (the first president of Ghana), both of whom attended Lincoln University in the late 1920s and mid-1930s respectively (Robinson 2004, 127). Nkrumah went on to receive a master's degree in philosophy from the University of Pennsylvania and worked toward a PhD—which remained unfinished, possibly due to his committee objecting to his choice of writing on the philosophy of Western imperialism (Sherwood 1996, 61–65).[18] During World War II, Nkrumah worked with the Institute of Languages and Culture at University of Pennsylvania teaching African languages to students from the War Department (Sherwood 1996, 65–68). He also helped create the African Students Association, which brought together African students in the United States and Canada to advocate for African independence (Sherwood 1996, chapter 6). Those predominantly African and African American scholars seeking to study Africa outside the terms established by white American research universities often faced considerable material limitations. For example, African American scholars were limited to grant funding from only three private foundations (Rosenwald Foundation, General Education Fund, and Phelps-Stokes). And between 1936 and 1953, Ralph Bunche's Social Science Research Council (SSRC) grant remained the only example of a private foundation funding an African American to conduct field research in Africa (Robinson 2004, 132–33).[19]

During the decades following World War II, however, the study of the contemporary non-Western world became a well-funded priority within American higher education. Area studies became the designated location where much of this work took place. In the case of African studies however, the rapidly expanding scholarly interest and funding largely bypassed black scholars. As a result, this new field of scholarship treated Africa as a distinct and spatially bound area, imagined as existing outside "world-historical relationships with other continents, especially the Americas" (West and Martin 1997, 313). The material organization of African studies meant that "Africanists," trained within African studies programs and located within historically white universities, became the recognized experts on Africa, "jealously guarding its borders and interpreting the continent for the U.S. state and public" and, in so doing, reproducing Africa as limited to its territorial borders (West and Martin 1997, 313).

Area studies emerged as a concept during World War II as policy makers and military professionals became widely concerned that the existing academic disciplines failed to address the geostrategic needs of the United States (Wallerstein 2004, 9). Therefore, drawing on the interdisciplinary, area-focused research groups created by the OSS and other agencies during the war, the federal government—with considerable support from major philanthropic organizations—began institutionalizing area studies on university campuses. One of the first moves was the 1946 relocation of the oss's Soviet division to Columbia University, becoming the highly influential Russian Institute (Cumings 1998, 163). Over the following decades, the Pentagon, FBI, and CIA also funded area studies programs based on the premise that developing a working understanding of non-Western countries was a necessary tool for preventing countries from "falling into the hands of the communists" (Wallerstein 1997, 198).

This close tie among the social sciences, the security apparatus, and philanthropic organizations became an organizing principle of area studies as an intellectual project. In 1943, the SSRC Committee on World Regions published its first internal report calling for greater academic commitment to area studies, claiming that "the immediate need for social scientists who know the different regions of the world stands second only to the demand for military and naval officers familiar with the actual and potential combat zones" (quoted in Wallerstein 1997, 195). In December of the same year, Columbia University's Committee on Area Studies published a similar report calling for expanded graduate training in area studies.[20] These twin reports were followed up by the groundbreaking 1947 report *Area Studies: With Special Reference to Their Implications for Research in the Social Sciences* published by the SSRC's Exploratory Committee on World Area Research.[21] Written by Robert Hall, this report celebrated the role area studies played during World War II and chronicled the early successes of implementing area studies on college campuses.[22] It portrayed area studies as a scholarly endeavor necessary to advance social scientific knowledge while also providing the federal government with much-needed strategic policy analysis.

Since its inception, however, area studies remained conceptualized as a form of knowing the non-Western world through the lenses provided by the West. Hall's report, for example, modeled area studies on classics, which, he argued, offered a comprehensive understanding of the "Greek and Roman world" (1947, 12).[23] Just as John Stuart Mill credited knowledge of the Latin and Greek worlds as offering "differently colored glasses" from which to understand "other nations," Hall described area studies as similarly offering the insights needed to "live wisely in our new 'one world'" (14). Hall argued that recent developments in social scientific methodologies, new research practices, and greatly expanded transportation, as well as "financial support" that "far exceeds that of any preceding period," ensured that social scientists were now able to gather "precise knowledge of all other lands and all other peoples" (16). In this context, the collection of area-specific data opened the possibility of testing universal theories developed within the social sciences. Hall acknowledged that, up until now, "We have studied men isolated in the milieu of the North Atlantic, thinking that we have been studying man"; however, we cannot actually know the validity of these universal theories "until we know all other areas: We need the data of other areas to check our assumptions" (23–24).

Advancing social scientific knowledge by applying universal theories to data collected outside the North Atlantic was considered important because it provided the knowledge needed to manage a strategically contested world:

> Much of the research on foreign areas and cultures in the past has been done by men who had previously gained sound reputation from their publications on . . . Western Europe and the United States. The assumption has been that with this proved competence the scholar . . . could undertake similar study in, say, China or Khartoum. Those who have come to know well one foreign region or another have been able to recognize some very bad research done by otherwise highly competent men. As one converted academician who was called to Washington to head the research of a war agency put it, "I could draw on the best economic, political and other talent of the country. When a problem came up on country X, I would pass it to the best men available. The answers that came back were pure, indeed, in terms of accepted economic or political theory. They would doubtless have been workable answers to American and perhaps some European problems. But they were not the correct answers for country X." (Hall 1947, 24)

Hall advocated for area studies, therefore, by drawing a direct connection between advancing social scientific knowledge and training a standing reserve of expertise on China, Sudan, and countries X, Y, and Z to be tapped whenever a problem arose.

Philanthropic organizations responded positively to this SSRC report, quickly establishing a funding agenda that placed area studies at its center. The Carnegie Corporation was among the first funders of area studies, with its 1947 grant of $740,000 to Harvard's Russian Research Center (Cumings 1998, 163). The Rockefeller and Ford Foundations followed suit, creating a number of prominent area studies centers, including Far Eastern studies at Yale University, Far East and Russian studies at University of Washington, Soviet and East European studies at Columbia, Japanese studies at Michigan, and the New Nations Program at University of Chicago (Harootunian 2002, 156). African studies also received considerable attention during this period. The Ford Foundation spent $164 million between the early 1950s and 1974 on African studies alone, including the creation of centers at Columbia ($16.4 million), University of Chicago ($8.4 million), Yale ($6.3 million), and Johns Hopkins ($3 million), as well as Northwestern, Indiana, Boston University, UCLA, Harvard, Stanford, Michigan, and Wisconsin (Parmar 2012, 158). Between 1953 and 1966 the Ford Foundation spent $270 million on area and language studies programs at thirty-four universities (Cumings 1998, 163).[24] Foundations also funded academic networks, including workshops, conferences, professional associations, and journals. For example, the Carnegie Corporation helped found the African Studies Association (ASA) with a grant of $630,000, followed by subsequent funding from the Ford Foundation (Parmar 2012, 160–61). Less than two decades after the publication of Hall's report, there were more than 3,800 area specialists across 203 graduate programs in American higher education (Lambert 1973a, 17).

In addition to greatly expanded philanthropic support, the launch of Sputnik unleashed a deluge of federal funding for higher education (Clowse 1981). In 1958, Eisenhower passed the National Defense Education Act (NDEA), which not only increased the total amount of federal funding for higher education but also transformed civilian agencies into the "main spigots" of government largesse (Menand 2010, 67). Declaring that "the security of the Nation requires the fullest development of the mental resources and technical skills of its young men and women" (U.S. Congress 1958, Section 101), the NDEA provided expanded access to student loans, funds for modern languages instruction, National Defense Fellowships for graduate studies, and various programs to support the sciences, social sciences, and humanities, as well as a focus on improving high school instruction and teacher training. Title VI of the NDEA made $8 million available to create various language and area studies programs to train individuals "in such language[s as] are needed by the Federal Government or by business, industry, or education in the United States" (U.S. Congress 1958, Section 601; see also Hines 2001; Wiley 2001). These interdisciplinary area studies centers allowed students to learn modern languages alongside the "history, political science, linguistics, economics, sociology, geography, and anthropology" of their particular area of study (U.S. Congress 1958, Section 601). In addition to paying half the annual expenses of area studies centers, the NDEA helped cover the cost of "travel in the foreign areas, regions, or countries" as well as to bring foreign scholars to teach in area studies centers (U.S. Congress 1958, Section 601).

The result was a race to hire top scholars in area studies.[25] In the case of African studies, there emerged "nothing less than a scramble for trusted scholars" on Africa, "with research funds, promotion, and publication eagerly provided" (West and Martin 1997, 312). During the Cold War, African studies gained popularity and institutional support within the U.S. academy, with much of the funding driven by strategic concerns over the Soviet Union's involvement on the continent (Nader 1997, 130). African studies received considerable funding from the federal government, including NDEA grants and money from Title VI, U.S. Agency for International Development (USAID), and Fulbright, not to mention "the usual disciplinary funding through NSF, NEH, NEA, NIH," and indirectly through the Peace Corps (Guyer 1996, 13).

These intimate (and well-funded) working relationships between the federal government, philanthropic organizations, and the social sciences was further solidified with the creation of interdisciplinary working groups created to craft specific policy responses to anticolonial struggles in Latin America, Asia, the Middle East, and Africa. For example, the U.S. Army's Project Camelot assembled psychologists, anthropologists, and sociologists to develop a behavioral model of countries experiencing internal conflict, in the hopes that such models would be "predictive, and therefore useful, to military planners" (Herman 1998, 102). This research was justified on the ground that "relatively little is known . . . about the social processes" of non-Western countries, making it difficult to "deal effectively with problems of insurgency" in countries such as Argentina, Bolivia, Brazil, Colombia, Cuba, Dominican Republic, El Salvador, Guatemala, Mexico, Paraguay, Peru, Venezuela, Egypt, Iran, Turkey, Korea, Indonesia, Malaysia, Thailand, France, Greece, and Nigeria (official documents reprinted in Horowitz 1967, 48, 57).[26] Ending in political controversy, Project Camelot was slated to cost between $4 and $6 million and constituted a "veritable Manhattan Project for the behavioral sciences" (Herman 1998, 103).[27] The shuttering of Project Camelot, however, did not prevent a number of similar studies—including Project Simpatico (Columbia), Operation Task (Peru), and Project Agile (Vietnamese National Liberal Front)—from being funded by the Special Operations Research Organization and the Department of Defense (Herman 1998, 113). In 1967, under the moniker Project Themis, the Department of Defense poured $20 million into those social science departments and universities that agreed to foster greater connections between its social scientists, psychologists, and the military (Herman 1998, 114).[28]

The close working relationship between the federal government, philanthropic organizations, and American higher education resulted in a "vigorous expansion" of area studies, including rapid growth in the number of departments, centers, and programs as well as the journals, professional organizations, and grants supporting academic production (Solovey 2013, 1). As a result, in a few short decades, it became possible within American higher education to produce large amounts of academic knowledge about the contemporary non-Western world, much of which viewed the world "through the optic of the nation" and from the vantage of the American state specifically (Harootunian 2002, 160). Informed by functionalist and scientific approaches, Cold War area studies commonly downplayed historical and uneven power relations, focusing instead on how to redesign particular foreign nations to form "an orderly social system" (Harootunian 2002, 157). Most of the resources that went into the forming of area studies, however, stayed within "the *World* of U.S. Research Universities," comprising a few dozen prestigious private and public institutions (Robinson 2004, 119, emphasis in original). For example, despite decades of expertise gained from studying the continent, scholars at historically black colleges and universities were largely excluded from the expansion of African studies programs because the main architecture of the field—including Title VI centers, membership in the ASA, access to postdoctoral funding, and so on—remained almost exclusively in the hands of those at predominantly white research universities (Robinson 2004, 138–39).

The massive expansion of area studies during the decades after World War II provided the conditions within which it was possible to produce knowledge about contemporary non-Western countries and their internal dynamics. Considerable resources also went toward the expansion of the fields of International Relations and international studies, both of which were designed to provide policy makers with the tools for imagining these nations as operating within a system of states.

International Relations and the Reproduction of the National Imaginary

Prior to World War II, International Relations was formally codified within the American academy as an established subfield of political science with the formation of the American Political Science Association in 1904 (Guilhot 2011a, 8). However, for much of its early history, International Relations was little more than a hodgepodge of scholars working on topics as disparate as diplomatic history, moral theory, and international law. During these early years, International Relations and international studies were largely used interchangeably, and both fields primarily focused on maintaining international racial segregation and the purity of the white race, rather than studying something called the international state system (Vitalis 2002, 2015). During these decades, International Relations remained largely an "interdisciplinary field located on the margins of political science," without "methodological coherence," and operating as "a sort of commons . . . plowed by various disciplines ranging from economics to geography" (Guilhot 2008, 281). This gradually began to change as philanthropic funding reshaped the field of International Relations into a discipline capable of providing the American security apparatus the conceptual tools needed to imagine—and therefore manage—the world as an international state system.

In many ways, the discipline of International Relations has always been an outgrowth of philanthropic funding. Robert Vitalis argues that "it would be hard to imagine the advance of the discipline" of International Relations "in the United States and elsewhere in the interwar years" without the Rockefeller Foundation, which, by the mid-1930s, was financing its major institutions, including the Institute of Pacific Relations, Council of Foreign Relations, the Foreign Policy Association, the Royal Institute of International Affairs (London), and the International Studies Conference located in Geneva (Vitalis 2015, 85). The interest within the Rockefeller Foundation, as well as the Carnegie Corporation and Ford Foundation, owed much to a historically strong connection between these foundations and "the East Coast foreign policy Establishment," which was largely committed to defending "American-led global hegemony" and pushing back against isolationist tendencies within the academy, policy circles, and public opinion (Parmar 2012, 2). As early as 1935, the Rockefeller Foundation began providing generous funding to the Yale Institute of International Studies (YIIS) for academic training in International Relations. This institute would go on to cultivate a whole generation of realist theorists, often referred to as the Power School (Parmar 2012, 68–72). For example, William T. R. Fox—whose book coined the term "super power"—became assistant director of YIIS in 1944 and soon thereafter editor of the institute's new journal, *World Politics*. Within the Rockefeller-funded YIIS, "many of the founding myths of realism first took shape," as well as a political and intellectual commitment to use "the central issue of 'national security'" as the means to position the field of International Relations as relevant to policy makers (Vitalis 2015, 118–19). In the early 1950s, seven scholars affiliated with YIIS departed to form Princeton's Center for International Studies (also Rockefeller funded), while Fox left for Columbia's Institute for War and Peace Studies, and Max Millikan was tapped to head CENIS at MIT (Vitalis 2015, 119–20). A few years later, Kenneth Waltz—whose dissertation-turned-book *Man, the State, and War* is credited with solidifying the realist vision within International Relations—wrote that, without support from Columbia University's Institute of War and Peace Studies, and William T. R. Fox in particular, "it is difficult to see how there would be any book at all" (Waltz [1954] 2001, xv).[29]

Philanthropic foundations also funded the rise of realist approaches within the discipline. Early such examples include a series of 1948 meetings organized by the SSRC's newly formed Committee on International Relations. Convened by Frederick Dunn, these meetings aimed to establish International Relations as a distinct academic field.[30] Four years later, the Rockefeller Foundation, under the leadership of Dean Rusk, also took up the project of formalizing this still otherwise rudderless field.[31] Rusk sought to harness International Relations as a site for the training of "policy personnel for the State Department and other policy institutions" (Guilhot 2011, 10). In 1954, Rusk and Northwestern University professor Kenneth W. Thompson brought together Hans J. Morgenthau, Reinhold Niebuhr, Paul Nitze, William T. R. Fox, Walter Lippmann, Arnold Wolfers, Dorothy Fosdick, James Reston, and Don K. Price for a two-day conference aimed at formulating an overarching International Relations theory.[32] Thompson opened the Conference on Theory of International Politics with the observation that, while those studying international law received financial support from various professional organizations, "scholars in the field of international politics" do not enjoy such opportunities (quoted in Schmidt 2011, 88). While the workshop largely failed at its objective to establish a singular theory of International Relations, it nonetheless helped solidify the early core of a realist theoretical tradition within the subfield.

While area studies received the bulk of attention and funding between 1940 and 1960 (Vitalis 2015, 120), by the 1960s this newly organized security-focused, policy-relevant, realist International Relations had also attained institutional prominence. In addition to the institutes and working groups, Carnegie and Rockefeller funded the "material incentives—grants, jobs, fellowships" that institutionalized robust professional networks that enabled the spread of realist International Relations theory (Parmar 2012, 67).[33] The effects of these investments were clear. Even though the 1960s was a time of massive political mobilizations and decolonizing ferment across Africa, Asia, Latin America, and the Caribbean, the infrastructures created within the discipline of International Relations made it possible to imagine the world simply in terms of an anarchic international system. As a result, one is hard pressed to find a single International Relations scholar from this period who had anything to say about "arguably the single most significant transformation of the twentieth century" (Vitalis 2015, 120). In other words, philanthropic organizations and their well-funded academic institutes, centers, scholarly networks, and professional organizations so profoundly shaped the discipline of International Relations that there remained little space from which to imagine the world as anything other than an international system with the United States—and its interests—at the center.

This myopic disciplinary worldview was marketed using the self-narrative of the great debate, in which hard-nosed realism soundly defeated utopian and idealistic liberalism, thereby placing a dispassionate and scientific study of the international system at the heart of the discipline. It is now clear that a great debate between realism and liberalism did not actually take place (see, for example, Schmidt 1998; Wilson 1998; Thies 2002; Schmidt 2012), but was rather a pitch used to convince security elites about the usefulness of realist International Relations theory (Ashworth 2002). In this context, as the United States emerged as a superpower, policy makers had an increasingly large reserve of realist theories and trained academics to draw upon when shaping American foreign policy (Hoffmann 1977; Smith 1987; Cumings 1998, 170). This strategic reserve of academic knowledge and expertise proved highly useful among policy makers, not least because it made it possible to envision a more stable and peaceful world resulting from the prudent, rational, and measured deployment of American superpower.

International Studies and the Reproduction of the National Imaginary

Prior to the mid-1970s, American academics did not make a disciplinary distinction between International Relations and international studies (Vitalis 2002, 1). It was only later that the field of international studies would become distinct as a disciplinary space within which to preserve a more highly interdisciplinary intellectual tradition that existed prior to the realist dominance within the field of International Relations. Within the U.S., "chairs, programs, institutes, and associations" dedicated to international studies date back to the early or mid-1910s and historically focused on understanding "a world of increasing complexity and interdependence," while developing "practical strategies for administering territories and uplifting backward races" (Vitalis 2002, 2, 12). Often located in interdisciplinary centers and programs, international studies often draws in scholars from political science, International Relations, economics, sociology, geography, area studies, and other disciplines. During the decades after World War II, a number of highly influential international studies centers were created with a clear foreign policy focus. In addition to YIIS, these centers included Johns Hopkins University's School of Advanced International Studies (established 1943), CENIS (1952), the Foreign Policy Research Institute (1955), and Georgetown's Center for Strategic Studies (1962), which later changed its name to the Center for Strategic and International Studies to highlight its interdisciplinary approach to security questions.[34] In 1940, only two hundred scholars studied international studies, out of the total 150,000 academics located within the United States (McCaughey 1980, 14). Starting in the early 1950s, however, Rockefeller and Carnegie began spending millions of dollars establishing international studies centers on university campuses (Gendzier 1985, 111). As a result, between 1948 and 1970 the proportion of international studies degrees granted by the top twenty graduate programs doubled, with a large majority of graduates finding employment within the academy at rates matching, or exceeding, traditional disciplines (McCaughey 1980, 15).

The main professional organization representing the academic field of international studies—the International Studies Association (ISA)—emerged during the postwar years as the result of professional and intellectual discontent over the continued U.S.-centricity of the political science discipline. Scholars criticized the American Political Science Association for not paying significant attention to International Relations, as evidenced in the fact that annual meetings only allotted some two dozen panels to international politics (Vitalis 2015, 129–30, 219n3). Arnold Wolfers and Nicholas Spykman at YIIS initially discussed the idea of a standalone professional association for international studies. Others would make this a reality with the creation of the ISA in 1958. In the early days, ISA primarily brought together "West Coast professors and 'practitioners'" to address topics such as the effects of the nuclear context on the international system (Vitalis 2015, 130; see also Holsti 2014, 1–2) with the aim of advancing research that was of interest to "the U.S. governmental establishment" (Teune 1982, 2). The ISA started as an amateur operation, run single-handedly by Charles McClelland at San Francisco State, who launched the association's first journal with a grant from the New World Foundation and eventually hired its first professional staff in 1964 after receiving an annual grant of $15,000 from the Carnegie Endowment (Teune 1982, 2; Vitalis 2015, 130).

While international studies offers an interdisciplinary blend of International Relations and area studies, as seen in the discussion of CENIS, both imagined the world as a system of states, which could be profoundly reshaped by American foreign policy. The various institutional conditions created by federal funding and philanthropic organizations were an ideal environment for modernization theory to emerge as a guiding theory across the social sciences (Berger 2007). Like area studies, International Relations, and international studies, modernization theory imagined a world divided into different spatial units, with each nation evolving and modernizing in a linear fashion. Modernization theory worked across traditional disciplines as well as the new, or newly reordered, interdisciplinary spaces now springing up across the Cold War university. In this context, CENIS proved to be one of the major academic sites for the production, reproduction, and circulation of modernization theory.

Modernization theory's earliest architect, W. W. Rostow, clearly understood himself as creating a new imaginary. He acknowledged that his analysis offered "an act of creative imagination," giving U.S. policy makers simple and clear tools to understand the otherwise complicated causes and consequences of development taking place in the non-Western world (Rostow 1960, 166). He developed modernization theory by "compressing and making a kind of loose order of modern historical experience," such that one could gain "a degree of insight into matters which must of their nature be vicarious for us" (Rostow 1960, 166). For Rostow, distilling and abstracting the complex world into a story of modernization "give[s] us heart to go forward with confidence" knowing that, even during "moments of frustration and confusion," the "tricks of growth are not all that difficult" (1960, 166). Rather than becoming mired in the many obstacles and resistances to U.S. economic and political intervention—including a militant and rapidly decolonizing Third World—modernization theory made it possible for American (white and male) academics and policy makers to imagine these challenges as temporary obstacles to be overcome once non-Western countries followed the simple recipe of modernization. As Rostow described in an unpublished article intended for *Harper's* titled "The Agenda for 1957," "Practical men in authority do not usually believe that they use theories; but, consciously or unconsciously, they make their decisions in terms of *a picture of the world* around them which is, in effect, a simple, abstract, theoretical model" (1957a, 1, emphasis added). Rostow points out that the events of 1956—namely, student demonstrations in Budapest and the Suez Crisis—proved that policy makers "in Moscow, Washington, London and in the other capitals of the world" drew upon "images of the world which proved to be incorrect" (1957a, 1). As such, he argued, the goal for 1957 must be "readjusting American concepts and actions to the world as it revealed itself" (1957a, 1).

Modernization as a Picture of the World

Rostow's work on modernization theory was produced within a whole apparatus of knowledge production, most clearly institutionalized in CENIS.[35] The center grew out of a series of "brainstorming councils" organized by the Office of Naval Research between 1950 and 1951 aimed at harnessing the university to assist the formation of Cold War "strategy, tactics, and military hardware" (Needell 1998, 3; see also Gilman 2003, 156–60). The most well-known initiative emerging from these early meetings was Project Troy, which sought to develop psychological warfare tactics in response to the Soviet Union's jamming of the Voice of America. In exchange for $150,000 in State Department funding, MIT president James Killian assembled a group of academics from the fields of physics, electronics, psychology, anthropology, history, law, and economics, along with experts from government agencies and philanthropic organizations, to write a report addressing this Cold War setback (Needell 1998, 5–11). The final document not only examined the technical questions of how to transmit pro-American radio messages into the Soviet Union, but also—drawing upon the input of social scientists—which audiences to target, what questions to ask, what issues to emphasize, and how to craft the message (Needell 1998, 14–17).

Shortly after delivering the final report, Killian wrote to James Webb at the State Department about the possibility of continuing the collaboration in an institutionalized form—a "second phase of Project Troy" (Blackmer 2002, 17; see also Gilman 2003, 157–58). The State Department, claiming a lack of available funds, turned Killian down. However, Allen Dulles at the CIA was quick to offer funding (Blackmer 2002, 20). During the fall of 1951, CENIS embarked on its first project, the classified study of "Soviet Vulnerability" under the supervision of W. W. Rostow, just hired by MIT as an economic historian (Blackmer 2002, 21). In 1952, Killian reached out to MIT economist Max Millikan, who, wrapping up a stint at the CIA and Columbia University, agreed to join CENIS as its first director (Needell 1998, 23). Under his leadership, CENIS received generous funding from the CIA and Ford Foundation, and later Rockefeller and Carnegie Foundations (Gilman 2003, 158–59). Initially located in an east Cambridge warehouse, CENIS brought together "a wide variety of academic specialists" in order to "participate full- or part-time in classified research and discussions" within an academic setting (Needle 1998, 24). During the 1950s and 1960s, CENIS served as the institutional home for many prominent academics developing intellectual connections between area studies, international studies, and modernization theory, and was responsible for producing a vast literature on the relationship between modernization, development, and counterinsurgency (Gendzier 1998, 78–79; Gilman 2003, chapter 5). The cast of characters Millikan assembled was truly interdisciplinary and included scholars who studied the economics of foreign aid (Paul Rosenstein-Rodan), political psychology and the benefits of elite technocratic governance (Harold Lasswell), the links between the psychopathy of guerilla movements and the loss of traditional society (Lucian Pye), and the universal characteristics of modernization (Daniel Lerner), among others (Gilman 2003, 160–74). The young economic historian and former OSS operative W. W. Rostow was at the heart of this group.

Rostow had entered Yale University in 1932 at age fifteen, where he dedicated himself to the ambitious project of refuting Marx's conception of economic growth (Milne 2008, 25–26). He credits his "somewhat bizarre [undergraduate] education" at Yale as setting the stage for what would become his life's work. At Yale he was exposed to the "important philosophical notion" that "human perception works through arbitrary abstract concepts and therefore the reality of what we call facts is not without a certain ambiguity" (Rostow 1957b, 510). Taking this claim seriously, Rostow began to wonder: if all historical accounts are "shot through with implicit, arbitrary theory," why not make one's theory explicit (1957b, 510)? As a result, from a young age, he engaged the study of economic history driven not by disciplinary methodology, but rather by theoretical and political commitment: claiming that a "historian's method is as individual—as private—a matter as a novelist's style" (509). This led to a lifelong research agenda aimed at harnessing social scientific theories to explain "the interaction among the economic, political, social, and cultural sectors of whole societies," in other words, to "analyze whole societies in motion" (510). Rostow's ultimate aim in doing so was to refute "Marx's economic determinism," which "repelled" him (510).[36]

After Yale, Rostow attended Oxford as a Rhodes scholar (1936–38) and served as an SSRC fellow at Columbia (1939–40), before returning to New Haven to complete his PhD in economics (1940). During World War II, Rostow served in the OSS, first studying the economic strength of the Soviet Union to withstand German invasion (Gilman 2003, 161) and later in the London-based Enemy Objectives Unit, where he identified specific bombing targets that "would have the greatest, most prompt, and most long-lasting effects on the battlefield" (Rostow 1992, 49). In this capacity, he vigorously argued for bombing oil refineries and fuel stockpiles, vocally challenging the existing practice of targeting transportation and industrial infrastructures (Gilman 2003, 161; Rostow 2003, chapter 2). Rostow later credited his time at the OSS with instilling an "irreversible" calling for "public service" and for forging the "institutionalized links between intellectual life and national security" (1992, 56). He became increasingly convinced that academic knowledge could be deployed in the national fight against communism.

After the war, Rostow returned to his academic project of developing an anti-Marxist understanding of economic growth. His OSS experience, combined with an "unprecedented funding bonanza" within higher education, made him "a valuable commodity in Cold War America" (Milne 2008, 35). In 1946, Harvard University offered Rostow (age twenty-nine) a full professorship in economic history, which he declined in order to return to Oxford in a visiting position. He joined the United Nations Economic Commission for Europe in Geneva, in 1947, working on issues of European reconstruction, and spent a year at Cambridge University (Milne 2008, 36–37). Desiring to return to the United States, Rostow accepted a professorship in economic history at MIT—a position lobbied for by two friends from Yale who had also served in the OSS, Max Millikan and Charles Kindleberger (Milne 2008, 39–40). In 1951, a year after arriving at MIT, Rostow accepted a joint position at MIT's newly created CENIS.

It was within this context that Rostow produced some of the most important texts of modernization theory. Three intellectual commitments would form the core of his work: that nineteenth-century British industrialization served as a universal template for understanding economic change and modernization around the world; that modernization resulted primarily from changes taking place within a country; and, finally, that modernization resulted from broadly social, political, cultural, and not just economic transformations. Rostow's work imagined a world in which the United States could help direct countries down their natural paths toward Westernization simply by tinkering with their domestic composition. This national imaginary, produced in CENIS and in conversation with the security apparatus, was applied to a whole series of pressing policy questions concerning the U.S.'s position toward Russia and China, as well as the formerly colonized world. In doing so, Rostow reproduced an image of the world as composed of nation-states, naturally evolving together toward a common end, under the watchful eye of the United States. In this account, each nation matured into an advanced, industrialized, democratic, and capitalist country.

Rostow arrived in Cambridge, Massachusetts, with an impressive number of publications, most of which drew from economic theory, economic history, and troves of quantitative and statistical data to explain the domestic, political, and social factors that had given rise to nineteenth-century British industrialization.[37] His earliest work, for example, argued that the economic depression in Britain between 1873 and 1896 was triggered by shifts in domestic capital investment and national labor markets (Rostow 1938, 1939). Elsewhere he argued that "short-run economic fluctuations" between 1790 and 1850 resulted not only from smaller crop harvests but also from the "political and social events" that followed (Rostow 1941).[38] This work drew heavily from data collected in 1939, while he helped Columbia professor Arthur D. Gayer complete his study *The Growth and Fluctuation of the British Economy: 1790–1850* (Gayer, Rostow, and Schwartz 1953).[39] During World War II, Rostow authored articles examining British economic responses to the Napoleonic Wars—a case useful for thinking through "the postwar problems that we ourselves shall face" (1942a, 14)—and another examining the economic effects of price controls and rationing on wartime economies (Rostow 1942b).

During his first year at MIT, Rostow (1952b) published his most important book to date. Originating with a 1950–51 graduate seminar on economic history, *The Process of Economic Growth* laid out many of the core tenets of modernization theory. He clarified his long-held argument that economic analysis must include sociological, anthropological, psychological, and historical factors, all understood as changing over time. Still drawing primarily upon data from the British economy during the nineteenth century, Rostow argued that economic growth depended upon a whole host of "non-economic" factors, such as society's "propensity" to "apply science to economic ends," to "accept innovations," to desire "material advance," "consume," "have children," and successfully respond to "its environment" (1952b, 13–14).[40] Rostow would later describe this vision of national development as drawing less upon mathematical approaches to economics than upon a vision of the nation as a complex organism. Using the metaphor of the "biological science[s]," which understand national economic growth in terms of "the interplay between [the] human organism—man—and his physical environment," he focused on the "collective culture that man has developed" (Rostow 1954a, 1). He similarly argued that rather than drawing inspiration from "classical physics," economists should emulate biological studies of "comparative morphology" and, in doing so, study examples such as nineteenth-century British industrialization, which offer "the fully formed patterns we require for generalization" (Rostow 1956, 2).

While Rostow's theory of modernization was developed based on his study of nineteenth-century British industrialization, at CENIS his research agenda became less concerned with questions of British economic history and increasingly engaged Cold War policy debates. In the fall of 1951, Rostow and his CENIS colleagues engaged in a project examining "Soviet vulnerability," culminating in the publication of *The Dynamics of Soviet Society* in August 1952—a book that sought to develop a "conceptual frame" for examining change within Soviet society over time (Rostow 1952a, 3).[41] Rostow (1952a, xiii) introduced the book fully acknowledging that his training in British economic history of the nineteenth century made him a "layman" to the "complex and even treacherous field" of modern Russian studies. To address his limited area-specific knowledge, Rostow turned to his colleagues at CENIS as well as "many responsible authorities in and out of academic life," most notably Clyde Kluckhohn at a neighboring Cold War academic institution: Harvard's Russian Research Center (Rostow 1952a, xiii). The director of Harvard's Carnegie-funded center, however, was not himself a Russia expert, but rather an anthropologist specializing in Native American—and particularly Navaho—culture. Harvard sociologist Talcott Parsons acknowledged that more than a few "eyebrows were raised" over the fact that a non-Russian speaker, with no academic expertise in Russia, was made director of the Russian Research Center. However, Parsons credited Kluckhohn's abilities as a "general social scientist talented in administration," as well as his experience in the Office of War Information, as significant qualifications.[42]

The Dynamics of Soviet Society was circulated widely within the Eisenhower administration and became particularly influential as policy makers debated their response to Stalin's death (Rostow 2003, chapter 4). Based on this impact, the U.S. government commissioned CENIS to write a similar book on communist China the following year (Rostow 2003, 279). Unable to find a Chinese expert willing to write about communist China during the height of the McCarthy hearings, Millikan once again turned to Rostow. While Rostow expressed confidence he "had no left-wing past to hide from Senator McCarthy" (2003, 280), he once again voiced reluctance given his lack of area expertise. He changed his mind, however, when his wife, Elspeth, pointed out that he had "written extensively about the British nineteenth century without going there or mastering the dialect" (Rostow 2003, 280). The resulting book, *The Prospects for Communist China*, offers a long summary of China's political, economic, and social history, focusing on the rise of the Communist Party. Rostow expressed hope that the book would cultivate "a forward-looking American policy" and could "contribute marginally" to forming policy approaches not only with "guns and armed men, but also with capital and technique, with energy, and with a sense of human fellowship" (1954b, v, viii–ix).[43]

After developing a track record of providing strategically useful research on America's Cold War foes, Rostow and his colleagues at CENIS began turning their attention to understanding economic growth within so-called underdeveloped countries. Rostow's first major text on the topic, *A Proposal: Key to an Effective Foreign Policy* (cowritten with Millikan), was published in 1957. This book argued that the United States should greatly expand foreign aid as a tool for building political loyalties with the Third World. Like much of the work produced by Rostow, this book originated years earlier within a complex network of security, academic, and philanthropic interactions. In May 1954, Millikan and Rostow were invited to a two-day conference in Princeton organized by C. D. Jackson, a businessman, former psychological warfare staff member, and assistant to President Eisenhower. Many, including Jackson, felt that President Eisenhower's responses to the Chinese Revolution, China's invasion of Korea, and the French defeat at Dien Bien Phu were exceptionally tepid, underresourced, and overly reliant on nuclear deterrence and reinforcing European allies. Specifically, Eisenhower's policies were woefully oblivious to the inroads the Soviet Union and China were making in Asia, Africa, and elsewhere. Jackson sought out Rostow, Millikan, and other social scientists to help sketch out an alternative foreign policy agenda. This conference turned into a soirée of leading academics, businessmen, and politicians concerned with how the United States might simultaneously promote free trade and geopolitical stability (Gilman 2003, 175; Milne 2008, 52–54).

Jackson was so impressed with Millikan and Rostow's analysis that he encouraged them to submit a report justifying the refashioning of American foreign policy strategy around economic development aid. A draft report was circulated within academic and policy circles in 1954, among Congress members debating foreign aid expansion in 1956, and officially entered into the *Congressional Record* in 1957 (Gilman 2003, 176). Rostow even submitted the copy of the report to Eisenhower, including a prewritten speech that the president might use to announce the policy shift (Milne 2008, 53–54). After failing to gain traction within the administration, however, Millikan and Rostow revised the report for popular consumption as *A Proposal*, hoping to channel popular sentiment toward a redirected anticommunist strategy.

In this book, Millikan and Rostow argued that economic underdevelopment posed a major threat to the United States and should be responded to with a foreign policy that aggressively "promote[d] the evolution of a world in which threats to our security and, more broadly, to our way of life are less likely to arise" (1957, 3). They argued that the biggest threat came from the fact that "the bulk of the world's population" living outside "America and Western Europe"—namely, parts of the world that had historically been "politically inert"—had recently experienced "a great world revolution" such that they now shared "new aspirations for education, social improvement, and economic development" (Millikan and Rostow 1957, 4–5). Millikan and Rostow feared that "the Communist apparatus" was channeling these aspirations in ways threatening to American security:

> The dangers of instability inherent in the awakening of *formerly static peoples* would be present even in the absence of the Communist apparatus . . . but the danger is, of course, greatly intensified by the focus which both Communist thought and Communist organization give.
>
> The United States has not presented a consistent and persuasive alternative in terms of the democratic process. It is the unpleasant truth that the United States has come to be regarded increasingly in *the uncommitted areas of the world* as a power at best neurotic and at worst aggressive, preoccupied with military preparations and with a game of international power diplomacy which has no meaning for the newly awakened ordinary citizen. (1957, 6, emphasis added)

Drawing upon the assumptions of modernization theory, the report concludes that the U.S. government should respond by assisting in economic development as "one of the instruments" for blunting this international threat and, in doing so, "create an environment within which American society can thrive" (Millikan and Rostow 1957, 6).

During this period, Rostow became disillusioned with the Eisenhower administration's foreign policy and began forging a strong working relationship with Senator John F. Kennedy, including advising the senator on a bill expanding foreign aid to India (see Rostow 2003, 201–5; Milne 2008, 55–59). In 1958, Rostow took a leave from CENIS, returning to the U.K. on a Reflective Year Grant funded by the Carnegie Corporation. At the University of Cambridge, he turned his full attention to his long-held objective of proposing an anti-Marxist theory of national economic development (Milne 2008, 59–68). The result was the 1960 publication of his most influential text, *The Stages of Economic Growth: A Non-Communist Manifesto*, by Cambridge University Press. Building upon his early work, Rostow famously argued that economic development is an internal process whereby nations, beginning as agricultural, "traditional" societies, attain economic development by progressing through multidecade "stages" on their way to "maturity" (Rostow 1960). For Rostow, economic development requires centralizing political power within formal national institutions, industrializing the economy, producing goods for export, and adopting cultural practices that replace pre-Newtonian visions of a static world with a vision of dynamic human progress. According to Rostow, nations only fail to develop when domestic actors remain wedded to traditional practices, thereby preventing the kind of social, cultural, and political evolution that otherwise propels a people toward economic development. He argues that Communism has proven attractive to many because it also breaks down traditional society and helps launch countries toward modernity. However, while Communist societies are "capable of launching and sustaining the growth process," they also depend upon a "peculiarly inhumane form of political organization" (Rostow 1960, 164).

Compelled by *The Stages of Economic Growth*, and building on their existing friendship, John F. Kennedy tapped Rostow to serve as a foreign policy advisor during his 1960 presidential campaign. After the successful election, Kennedy brought Rostow into the administration as a deputy advisor on national security, working under McGeorge Bundy.[44] Rostow, however, eventually alienated many foreign policy advisors within the Kennedy administration with his desire to escalate the bombing of North Vietnam. After being exiled to the State Department, Rostow returned to the White House after Kennedy's assassination as Lyndon Johnson's national security advisor. It was during this time that the Rostow Thesis—the idea that the United States could win the war with expanded bombing of North Vietnam—became the administration's guiding principle (Milne 2008, 9–11).

Days after the Tet Offensive in 1968, Johnson met with his foreign policy team in the West Wing. After facing withering criticism over his proposal to exit Vietnam, outgoing secretary of defense Robert McNamara broke down in tears, yelling back at W. W. Rostow, his former mentor, "This goddamned bombing campaign, it's been worth nothing, it's done nothing, they've dropped more bombs than in all of Europe in all of World War II and it hasn't done a fucking thing" (Milne 2008, 3–5). A few weeks later, McNamara would step down as secretary of defense to become president of the World Bank (see chapter 2).

After Rostow left the Johnson administration, public criticism of his Vietnam strategy prevented him from returning to the elite East Coast universities that shaped his early career. He eventually accepted a position teaching economics at the Lyndon B. Johnson School of Public Affairs at the University of Texas. Interviewed later in life, Rostow would say that, when it came to "developing an effective American policy in underdeveloped areas," social scientists, working in the country's national interest, "have a role equivalent to that of the physical scientists in the arms race" (quoted in Gilman 2003, 160).

One should probably be cautious about accepting the claim that modernization theory, or any other social scientific approach for that matter, had a linear effect on shaping foreign policy during this tumultuous period. After all, the impact of ideas cannot be measured in the same way one observes a blast radius. As Bruce Kuklick (2006) points out, most Cold War intellectuals working in proximity to the American security apparatus failed to see their academic ideas incorporated into the fashioning of wartime strategy, with lofty academic ideas often serving merely as post hoc justifications for political calculations. In fact, within the Kennedy administration, Rostow's efforts to develop policy using the conclusions of *The States of Economic Growth* were widely ignored, and even outright mocked (Kuklick 2006, 1, 148–50). Rostow's lasting impact, however, comes less in policy outcomes than in producing modernization theory as a particular "conceptual framework" that makes it possible to reimagine American society as capable of "transform[ing] a world perceived as both materially and culturally deficient" (Latham 2000, 5). Whether or not his ideas shaped policy within the Eisenhower, Kennedy, or Johnson administrations, Rostow's modernization theory successfully reproduced a world imagined as a series of discrete national units, operating with their own internal dynamics, each being propelled down a common path toward Westernization. Within this vision, the United States plays an important role shepherding this development. By the 1950s and 1960s, it had become impossible to deny that the rapidly decolonizing world needed to be studied. Rostow offered a way of doing so that placed the U.S. at the center of this new order. However, this national imaginary, now omnipresent across the Cold War university, did not go uncontested.

Area Studies: Between Modernization and Decolonization

In many ways, Rostow's life and career resembled one dominant trajectory of the Cold War university. He inhabited a world of deeply intertwined academic, philanthropic, and government circles, in which the pursuit and production of academic knowledge was conducted in the name of the national interest. Within this context, the dominant theories of the day were designed not only to guide U.S. policies but also to make intervention around the world appear necessary and natural. With modernization as a national imaginary, it became possible to see the world as a collection of internally manageable national units, operating within an international system, both of which could be known by outside experts. However, this national imaginary—as reproduced in CENIS and Cold War universities more generally—contained considerable contradictions, making it difficult to fully harness area studies and international studies as standing reserves of geostrategic knowledge.

The massive increase in the numbers of students and faculty within American higher education after World War II resulted in greater diversity across this increasingly large university population. Between 1955 and 1965, for example, more students passed through American universities than during the previous three centuries. Included in this number were many African Americans, women, and members of other populations historically excluded from higher education (Rooks 2006, 13; see also Newfield 2008, 26–30). This greatly democratized student and faculty population demanded that universities and colleges create academic and disciplinary spaces that resembled the diversity now represented on campus. Well-funded area studies and international studies programs became some of the intellectual homes for these new populations of students and scholars, many of whom aligned themselves with civil rights, antiwar, and anticolonial movements. Area studies in particular enabled students and scholars to work with non-Western intellectuals and travel to decolonizing countries for research. Once in the field, many young scholars found it difficult to square their American academic, theoretical, and methodological training with the political struggles they were observing (and sometimes participating in). As a result, government-funded area studies programs unwittingly trained many young radical scholars, providing a fertile ground for the creation of a "bottom-up" method for studying the world's poor and marginalized (Wallerstein 1997). In one example, through a series of personal and professional connections, CENIS became the institutional home of Harold Isaacs—the Trotskyite journalist who had participated in the Chinese Revolution. While at CENIS, philanthropic organizations funded Isaacs's research on African decolonization and Jim Crow America (Vitalis 2015, chapter 8).

International and area studies therefore became well-funded and institutionally supported sites riddled with contradictions. Within Asian studies, for example, scholarly response to U.S. militarism in Indo-China sharpened into considerable backlash against modernization theory and the military-academic complex more generally.[45] Within the context of the 1968 Asian Studies Association annual conference, for example, more than three hundred scholars attended the graduate student–initiated Vietnam Caucus. The caucus provided not only an opportunity to "speak out *en masse* on the war" but also to debate the proper "relationship between 'Asian expertise' and the war," to express concern about "the financial structures that support and influence the profession," to question "the channeling of research to fill government needs," and to examine whether area experts could positively contribute "to public affairs" (Peck 1968, 2). What emerged from this meeting was a desire "to create a nation-wide inter-university student-faculty" organization (Peck 1968, 2), which came into existence as the Committee of Concerned Asian Scholars. This organization, and its journal the *Bulletin of Concerned Asian Scholars* (now published as *Critical Asian Studies*), helped to organize Asian studies scholars in ways that gave voice to a powerful critique of American imperialism.

These complex contradictions were also present within African studies. On the one hand, state and philanthropic actors imagined African studies in terms of what Martin Staniland called the "Washington formula," which sought to harness African studies "to the definition, defense, and deployment of U.S. interests and intentions in Africa" (quoted in Zeleza 1997b, 195; see also Staniland 1983).[46] However, many students and scholars within African studies also found themselves aligned with the civil rights, black consciousness, African anticolonial, Pan-Africanist, and antiapartheid movements. These tensions played out in the classroom and in scholarship, including contestations over the organization of knowledge production itself. For example, during the 1969 ASA meeting in Montreal, members of the Black Caucus "stormed the podium calling for the empowerment of black scholars within the ASA" (West and Martin 1997, 315). The scholar-protestors demanded greater political representation of black members within the association, greater attention to—and support for—Pan-Africanist research, and a "collective commitment to struggles for emancipation in Africa and the United States" (Zeleza 1997b). Two organizers of the Montreal protest, James Turner and Rukudzo Murapa, described their actions as responding to the fact that "black scholars have been continually consigned to a marginal position, and have been forced to languish in the underground of the academic world" because of "white racism" that continues to undermine "black scholarship by not providing adequate professional recognition and financial and institutional support" (quoted in Vitalis 2015, 137). Black scholars saw the ASA's working relationship with the Department of Defense and CIA as well as the association's failure to support African anticolonial struggles as exemplifying the ASA's "institutional racism" (West and Martin 1997, 315).

Students and faculty also protested universities themselves, targeting the transformation of academic campuses into extensions of the military apparatus. During the height of the Vietnam War, for example, MIT students and faculty protested recruiters from Dow Chemical (the makers of napalm), turned the student center into a sanctuary to protect an AWOL soldier facing imminent arrest, organized work stoppages, sit-ins, and teach-ins, disrupted a public presentation by former MIT faculty and NSA advisor W. W. Rostow, challenged MIT's president to justify research on first-strike missiles being conducted on campus, approved a student strike against troop escalations in Vietnam, and even occupied the president's office after smashing down the door with a battering ram.[47] At a laboratory work stoppage and teach-in at Kresge Hall on March 4, 1969, a group of science faculty circulated the "Beyond March 4" statement—which became the founding document of the Union of Concerned Scientists (UCS 2018). Along with the Instrumentation and Lincoln Laboratories, CENIS was a major target of protest.[48] In October 1969, 150 students occupied the center's offices (Bernhardt 1969).[49] On November 4, 1969, CENIS closed its doors, fearing protests during the November Action days (Staff 1969b), but this did not deter protesters from holding a mock trial for CENIS faculty accused of "serving U.S. Imperialism" while chanting, "We won't die for Pool and Pye" (Blackmer 2002, 217). In April 1972, eighty students staged a sit-in blocking the doors of the center (Giguere 1972). Students and faculty activists drew a clear connection between the military technology being developed in the scientific laboratories and the research projects under way at CENIS, highlighting the center's historical CIA connections as well as its Com-Com, International Communist, and Cambridge Projects.[50]

Across the social sciences—and most notably within the new, or newly reorganized, fields of area studies, international studies, and International Relations—a close relationship between academic production, the state security apparatus, and philanthropic funding profoundly reorganized the production of academic knowledge. As exemplified in Rostow's academic career, and most notably his work on the development and circulation of modernization theory, the Cold War university organized academic knowledge production to encourage scholars to produce knowledge about non-Western societies in ways useful for the security apparatus, and from the vantage of the American state. The Cold War university produced and reproduced the ability and desire to imagine the world as a system of nation-states that, through external nudging and prodding, might be compelled toward their natural development. While the national imaginary embedded within modernization theory would give way during the 1980s and 1990s as universities remade themselves into sites for the reproduction of the global imaginary, the new discourse of globalization would retain the core claim of modernization theory exemplified in Rostow's use of Walt Whitman's quotation (see epigraph): namely, that we are all fellow passengers, fundamentally headed toward the same destination.

2 "The World's Largest . . . Development Institution"

Robert McNamara and the National
Development Imaginary

> I have always regarded the World Bank as something more
> than a Bank, as a Development Agency.
> —ROBERT MCNAMARA, *"To the Board of Governors"*
> (September 1968)

In February 1968, Robert McNamara stepped down from his post as secretary of defense in the Johnson administration after coming to loggerheads with W. W. Rostow, Dean Rusk, and others over the country's Vietnam policy. Johnson facilitated a graceful departure for McNamara, nominating him to serve as president of the World Bank. Because the World Bank was a rather minor institution in world affairs at the time, many saw McNamara's move as a substantial demotion. However, over the course of thirteen years at the helm, McNamara transformed the organization into a major funder of economic development across the previously colonized world as well as a primary site for knowledge production about the world economy. The massive expansion of the World Bank's lending power, accompanied with its now vast knowledge production capabilities, made it possible to disseminate a national development imaginary across both the world of finance and the Third World. The policies that stemmed from this national development imaginary would play a role enabling a massive expansion of higher education across the Third World, and especially Africa.

McNamara formed his approach to economic development while at the Department of Defense, where he came to appreciate the ways in which "the security of this Republic" depended not only on a strong military but also on "developing stable patterns of economic and political growth both at home and in the developing nations throughout the world" (McNamara 1968, xi). He later acknowledged that although he arrived at the World Bank with no formal training in development economics, he was "not entirely a stranger" to issues of development because as secretary of defense he had come to understand "the connection between world poverty and unstable relations among nations" (McNamara 1973, 15). Like W. W. Rostow, McNamara imagined the world as divided into nation-states operating within an international system, and with the United States at its center. But McNamara also saw the World Bank as being uniquely well positioned to assist nations in achieving the domestic political, economic, and cultural changes necessary to achieve national economic development.

This chapter examines how ideas about national development created within the American Cold War university traveled into the World Bank and, with the financial backing of this institution, fundamentally reorganized the world of higher education. Two decades after World War II and intersecting with successful anticolonial struggles against European empire, the McNamara Bank became a focal point for both the reimagining and the remaking of the world into a system of independent national economies, operating within an international market, and with the U.S. at the center. Consistent with modernization theory, the McNamara Bank conceptualized itself as guiding countries toward national development by addressing a wide range of domestic issues, including health care, population growth, and education. Within this context, the World Bank envisioned itself cultivating a community of nations working together to achieve greater economic development and therefore geopolitical stability. In this way, modernization theory, as it traveled from American higher education into the World Bank, became one strategy for managing decolonization and incorporating newly independent countries into a world imagined as naturally and benevolently evolving into democratic and capitalist states.

One effect of this World Bank–funded national development strategy was the massive expansion of higher education across newly independent Africa, and the Third World more generally. The World Bank, guided by a national development imaginary, understood higher education as essential to developing the skilled workforce necessary for long-term economic growth. The expansion of African higher education that resulted from World Bank support, however, had the unintended consequence of creating the material conditions for the establishment of well-connected, and radical, centers of academic knowledge production. As a result, by the 1970s, there existed a vast heterodox ecosystem of academic knowledge production, much of it cultivated within Third World universities, which advanced radically different understandings of the causes of, and possible solutions to, the debt crisis. The Lagos Plan, for example, imagined economic mutual aid among African countries, while the Brandt Commission Report called for changing economic policies within northern countries to mitigate the challenges faced by countries in the South. These visions, however, would ultimately lose out during the 1980s to a reimagining of the world as a single global financial and knowledge economy (see chapter 4).

Before continuing, I should note that, while no longer common parlance today, I use the term "Third World" throughout this chapter for myriad reasons. First, during the period covered in this chapter (1960s through early 1980s) this term—along with "developing nations" and "lesser developed countries"—was still common parlance within the World Bank. In addition, during the 1970s and 1980s, the critiques of the term "Third World" as a geographically inaccurate, homogenizing, and denigrating term, and the rise of Global South as a discursive alternative, had not yet come into focus (see Esteva and Prakash 1998; Mohanty 2003; Berger 2004).[1] But, more importantly, as Vijay Prashad (2007) argues, the Third World was a political project still very much in contestation during this time. Though challenged in the face of the 1970s debt crisis, the project of anticolonial nationalism still offered viable political and economic imaginaries that proposed fundamentally different worlds than the ones ultimately crystalized in Reaganism, Thatcherism, and the World Bank's structural adjustment policies. There were still many widely imagined worlds, and possible interconnected futures, that could not yet be reduced to "global."

The McNamara Bank and National Development

When McNamara arrived at the World Bank in 1968, he brought with him a vision of national economic development very different from the infrastructure-oriented vision shared by his predecessors. Like Rostow, McNamara understood national development as entailing the remaking of a society from the inside, a process that required not only building infrastructure but also eradicating poverty and providing education, health care, population control, and a whole gamut of social opportunities. To execute this greatly expanded conception of national development, McNamara went about transforming both the research and funding capacities of the World Bank, turning the institution into a vast producer of economic knowledge with the capital to fund these greatly expanded policy areas. It was within this context that higher education took on new importance within the World Bank.

The International Bank for Reconstruction and Development (IBRD), or World Bank, was established in 1944 to provide large loans to help rebuild Europe after World War II.[2] During its first decades, the World Bank remained undercapitalized and on the brink of irrelevance, especially once the Marshall Plan displaced the immediate need for European countries to borrow to fund postwar reconstruction. A largely underfunded and rudderless institution, the World Bank operated more like a club in which a small staff debated the minutiae of a handful of loan packages (Finnemore 1997, 213). After initially making a few loans to European countries, the World Bank gradually began shifting its lending portfolio to include more loans to non-European countries, starting with Chile in 1947 (Kapur et al. 1997, 82).[3] Over time, the IBRD slowly shifted its focus from reconstruction to development. Initially inserted into the International Bank for Reconstruction and Development's name and charter as an afterthought, "development" was initially understood among the staff simply as a country's material productive capacity and the economic prospects it offered its citizens (Kapur et al. 1997, 95). As such, the World Bank's emphasis during the early years focused on facilitating the traditional banking practice of moving surplus capital to parts of the world with capital demands. Despite expanding into non-European countries, the World Bank still operated according to its chartered principles—channeling money from the private bond market into national, state-led, and capital-intensive projects that might not otherwise find funding in capital markets (such as electrical grids, power plants, dams, ports, or road systems). As with most commercial banks during this period, the World

Bank was relatively conservative, loaning money only to countries deemed creditworthy, with sufficient collateral, and often at levels significantly lower than the countries originally requested. As a result, the annual lending between 1949 and 1961 was a modest $428 million, far below the $15 billion annual budget originally imagined (Kapur et al. 1997, 90). Most of the loans went to countries with relatively high levels of per capita income, including Australia, Japan, Norway, Austria, Finland, France, and Italy (Kapur et al. 1997, 90, 93).

The 1959 Cuban Revolution, however, instilled a widespread fear among Western powers that extreme poverty in Asia, Latin America, and Africa created favorable conditions for communist insurgencies. The World Bank responded to this threat by establishing the International Development Association (IDA), which received contributions from wealthy countries (rather than private markets) and made this money available as highly subsidized loans to the world's poorest countries, specifically to those most vulnerable to communist insurrection. McNamara's predecessor, George Wood (1963–68), used the newly created IDA to recast the World Bank as a crusader against national poverty and expanded the institution's mandate to include people-centric projects such as agriculture, water, and education (Kapur et al. 1997, 14). The Kennedy administration described this policy as offering "cheap World Bank credits" for the purpose of "propping up sympathetic governments" (Mallaby 2006, 26). Within this context, McNamara would radically remake the World Bank by infusing this expanded and geostrategic vision of development with a zealous commitment to national modernization.

McNamara completed his undergraduate study at University of California–Berkeley in 1937. Because Berkeley was a land grant institution, students were required to participate in military training, and McNamara would later recount that his two years in the Army Reserve Officers' Training Corps (ROTC) had "a great impact on [his] life" (1995, 6). After graduation he earned his MBA from Harvard Business School in 1939 and, after a year at Price Waterhouse, returned to his alma mater as an assistant professor of accounting (Byrne 1993, 49). Throughout his career, McNamara would remain in close contact with the group of "academically inclined men" he met in Cambridge during this time, including David Bell, W. W. Rostow, McGeorge Bundy, Kenneth Galbraith, and Henry Kissinger (Jones 2007, 82).

Like Rostow and many others, McNamara was part of the mass mobilization of academics during World War II. Four months after the bombing of

Pearl Harbor, the Air Force recruited McNamara, and several of his Harvard Business School colleagues, to form the Office of Statistical Control. Housed at Harvard Business School, Statistical Control drew upon statistical analyses, game theory, and early advances in computing to develop operational and logistical strategies for the U.S. military (Byrne 1993, chapter 3). In 1943, McNamara traveled to England to work directly with the War Department and the U.S. Eighth Air Force division, eventually accepting an officer's commission (McNamara 1995, 9). At the end of World War II, Ford Motor Company hired McNamara and nine other "Whiz Kids" in the hopes that their data-driven approach would turn around the failing company. McNamara was so successful in this task that, in November 1960, he was offered the position of president of Ford Motor Company, the first non–family member to hold this post since 1906.[4] He was recruited nine months later by president-elect Kennedy to serve as secretary of defense.

While in Washington, McNamara worked closely with W. W. Rostow (Kraske et al. 1996, 168), whose book *The Stages of Economic Growth: A Non-Communist Manifesto* (1960) had gained a considerable following among American academics and policy makers. Rostow's vision of national development was shared across the American security apparatus, including USAID, the Council on Foreign Relations, the CIA, and the State and Defense Departments, which were beginning to express concern that large-scale infrastructure investments had not done enough to "win the hearts and minds of third world peasants" supporting revolutions in Vietnam and elsewhere (Goldman 2005, 69). In this setting McNamara embraced a vision of economic development as involving the internal remaking of societies as the cornerstone of combating poverty. After arriving at the World Bank, McNamara turned the institution's attention to funding programs that directly assisted the poorest populations, focusing specifically on addressing health provision, population growth, malnutrition, and low levels of education, while embracing a broader agenda of "society-wide interventions" (Goldman 2005, 69).

Toward this end Rostow and modernization theory influenced all aspects of the McNamara Bank. Whereas previous World Bank projects focused on large infrastructure projects that primarily benefited urban populations, McNamara concentrated on agricultural production in rural areas and on helping states provide "a certain level of welfare" to their populations (Finnemore 1997, 205). Hollis Chenery, McNamara's economic advisor (1970–72) and vice president for development policy (1972–78), was also heavily influenced by Rostow, and committed to the idea that the World Bank in particular could serve as the "locomotive of growth" necessary to push developing nations into the "take off" stage (Jones 2007, 97). For example, the 1974 report *Redistribution with Growth*—written by Chenery and members of the World Bank's Development Research Center, in collaboration with the Institute of Development Studies at University of Sussex, and supported by the Rockefeller Foundation—provided the intellectual framework whereby the McNamara Bank wove together its "traditional functions and activities" with "its new concerns with poverty alleviation" (Jones 2007, 99). For instance, Chenery argued that economic redistribution could be accomplished not by transferring wealth (such as through taxation) but by expanding services that disproportionately affected those sectors of the economy that benefit the poor most directly (Chenery et al. 1975). The role of the World Bank, therefore, was to guide nations in making decisions that could raise the living standards of the poorest populations. For McNamara, this involved combining "national resolve," "international cooperation," and "the resourcefulness of the entrepreneur," all in "partnership" with the World Bank (1981b, 20, 22).

To accomplish this vision of national development, however, McNamara required a more robust World Bank—one with greater capacity and expanded access to capital. As an experienced scientific manager of complex institutions, one of McNamara's first acts as president was to personally design and continually update elaborate data tables that provided him with "a complete and up-to-date picture" of institutional finances (Kraske et al. 1996, 172). He also reorganized the World Bank into a series of departments—Agriculture and Rural Development, Population, Health and Nutrition, and Education—tasked with researching and developing sector-wide policy recommendations (Jones 2007, 80). Rather than focusing on specific infrastructure investments, these new departments produced detailed research about the relative merits of investing in specific policy areas. McNamara further facilitated a rapid expansion in research and policy development by growing the World Bank's personnel from 1,600 to 5,700 and intentionally hiring staff from across the Third World, thus making the institution more representative of its primary clientele (Clark 1981, 169; Kraske et al. 1996, 179). While his predecessors governed the World Bank as a "culturally and intellectually homogenous club," McNamara encouraged "intensive debate and research" all "within a rapidly expanding and diversifying bureaucracy" (Jones 2007, 80). In this context, McNamara prioritized writing reports and data collection, and created numerous opportunities for collaborative research among bank staff, academics, and think-tank members (Finnemore 1997, 214). The World

Bank, now led by an academic, also saw itself as a producer of scientific and objective economic knowledge. Its now extensive bureaucracy, tasked with producing detailed knowledge about all aspects of economic development, modeled itself on the academy. In doing so, it shielded itself against critiques of operating according to political motivation, insisting upon a distinction between objective economic knowledge and political power (Downing 2012, 69). During McNamara's tenure, the World Bank emerged as a vast "knowledge-generating machinery" (Goldman 2005, 85).[5]

McNamara's expanded vision also required increasing the amount of capital at the World Bank's disposal. His first act as president was to call together top World Bank officials and urge them to compile a bold list of all the projects they wanted funded as "if there were no financial constraints," promising to find the money to make these programs possible (Clark 1981, 168).[6] Under McNamara, lending grew from $1 billion to $13 billion in 1981, with annual lending surpassing the total amount spent by the World Bank in the decades prior to his arrival (Kraske et al. 1996, 179).[7] McNamara also controversially expanded funding to the world's poorest countries by funneling surplus money borrowed by the IBRD into the IDA's coffers (Finnemore 1997, 213).

McNamara's commitment to national development through modernization, combined with an ability to provide the resources necessary to actualize this vision, made the World Bank quite popular among Third World leaders during the 1970s. McNamara regularly visited developing countries (fifty in his first term) and paid special attention to African countries and rural farmers (Clark 1981, 172). His wife, Margaret Craig McNamara, accompanied him on these trips and visited schools, hospitals, and clinics while he met with government officials and financial leaders (Clark 1981, 172). McNamara developed close working relationships with the leaders of newly independent African countries, including Jomo Kenyatta, Julius Nyerere, Kenneth Kaunda, and Léopold Sédar Senghor, and routinely sought their advice on issues of national development (Clark 1981, 172; Kraske et al. 1996, 170). Senghor referred to McNamara as a fellow poet, whose "intense efforts to help the Third World develop were to my mind those of an inspired man of action" (Senghor 1981, xiii).

McNamara routinely depicted the role of the World Bank as a partner working with countries to achieve the "development of the total national economy" (1973, 19). As McNamara described it, the World Bank would assist "countries to develop plans and to adopt wise and appropriate policies for development," while always keeping in mind that "it is their country, their economy, their culture, and their aspirations that we seek to assist" (1973, 22). It is not coincidental that these seemingly altruistic aims dovetailed nicely with American geostrategic objectives, with economic development in the Third World serving as a bulwark against the communist threat (Finnemore 1997, 211).

McNamara's image of the world as a series of national economies that, if properly tinkered with internally, could promote national development was quite clearly an imagined reality. As James Ferguson (1994) brilliantly illustrates in *The Anti-politics Machine*, during the 1970s the World Bank produced a development discourse that actively imagined economic development in exclusively national terms. Ferguson demonstrates how the World Bank imagined lesser developed countries (LDCs), such as Lesotho, as isolated, subsistence, and peasant-based national economies requiring greater integration into regional markets. This development discourse, however, conflicted with the academic discourse that understood Lesotho—a longtime exporter of both agricultural goods and labor to South Africa—as already well integrated into the regional economy.[8] This failure to capture the basic realities of Lesotho's economy, Ferguson argues, cannot simply be attributed to ignorance or the World Bank employing "second-rate academics" (1994, 27). Rather, the World Bank could only see itself as an institution capable of bringing development to Lesotho if it first imagined the country as a closed national economy in need of being acted upon by external institutions. The McNamara Bank, in other words, imagined countries as spatially isolated territories capable of being remade through the coordinated actions of national governments and the World Bank (Ferguson 1994, chapter 2).

The McNamara Bank encouraged many countries to borrow heavily to fund a whole host of social projects deemed necessary for the development of a modern national economy. One major recipient of World Bank attention and funding was education, including higher education.

Education as National Development

In 1961, the Rockefeller Foundation began its Education for Development program with the aim of "strengthening institutions of higher education in the LDC's with a view to making their teaching and research efforts more pertinent to national development" (Phillips 1976, v). By 1973, international organizations were spending $2.35 billion a year on education in developing countries, with a considerable amount going to higher education.[9] Among these institutions, the World Bank played a distinctly important role, not only in terms of providing funding but also in producing knowledge about the economic benefits of higher education.

McNamara was the first World Bank president to fully embrace education as essential to national development, placing it firmly at the center of the World Bank's antipoverty agenda.[10] During the early years of the McNamara presidency, considerable internal debate existed about what priority the World Bank should place on education, and whether to emphasize primary, secondary, tertiary, or adult education. Internal debates about the economic effects of education consumed considerable "intellectual energy" and manifested in the writing, circulation, and debating of countless reports and policy documents, including those by Harvard professor Edward Mason, World Bank director of education projects Duncan Ballantine, and the director of the World Bank's Office of Information, Harold Graves (Jones 2007, 81–88). In 1970, this internal debate culminated in *Lending in Education*, a document circulated among the executive directors, arguing that the World Bank should dramatically increase spending on education and, in doing so, avoid focusing exclusively on "short-run training of manpower" at the expense of projects that might have "long-term significance for economic development" (quoted in Jones 2007, 88). This shift in thinking set the precedent that the institution should make greater resources available for all levels of education, including the funding of teachers, technology, staffing, housing, and textbooks (Jones 2007, 89). In 1971, the World Bank published its first public report on education, which laid out the institution's view of education as important to national development. In addition to assessing the many issues facing the provision of education in developing countries—including growing political and social demand, population growth, limited teacher training, increasing cost, and insufficient government spending (World Bank 1971, 28)—the report also lays out an agenda for the World Bank to become "the largest financier of educational assistance" with the goal of quintupling the number of projects and total lending. The report unveiled a plan to increase the World Bank funding of education from the pre-McNamara levels of twenty-one projects and $157 million (1964–68) to ninety-five projects and $800 million between 1972 and 1976 (World Bank 1971, 24). Under McNamara, the World Bank would go on to fund 192 education projects in eighty-one countries, with the bulk of the resources going to the construction of buildings and infrastructure (Haddad, Habte, and Hultin 1980, 7). Between the 1960s and 1990s, higher education consisted of roughly 15 to 25 percent of total education funding (Hopper 2004, 73).

The World Bank's approach to education was publicly formalized three years later in the "Education Sector Working Paper." In the foreword, Mc-Namara writes that the World Bank shared a commitment to universal basic education, expanding access to skills training, and ensuring more "equitable access to education" for marginalized groups as a means to help "developing countries reform and expand their educational systems" in order to "contribute more fully to economic development" (World Bank 1974, i–ii). This report details many policies concerning how education could be better integrated into development strategies, implemented in rural areas, include mass participation and greater equity, and be more successfully administered. Along these lines, the report described its approach as creating "a useful and constructive dialogue" between member countries and the World Bank, resulting in every country exhibiting "a unity of purpose and plan between it and the Bank" (World Bank 1974, 61).

The resulting financial support greatly expanded educational opportunities throughout the Third World. Between 1960 and 1975, the Third World experienced a dramatic increase in the numbers of students enrolled in primary, secondary, and tertiary education, rising from 141.8 million in 1960 to 314.9 million in 1975 (Haddad, Habte, and Hultin 1980, 102–3). The greatest annual increase, however, occurred in postsecondary education, where the number of students rose from 2.2 million to 9.5 million (Haddad, Habte, and Hultin 1980, 102–3). Between 1970 and 1978, roughly 26 to 40 percent of World Bank funding of education went to higher education, much of it for professional, agricultural, and teacher training programs (Heyneman 1999, 185; Jones 2007, 119).

The World Bank's increased funding of higher education took place as countries across the Third World, and Africa in particular, were making considerable new investments in higher education as part of the decolonization process. Prior to the 1940s, only six formal colleges existed in sub-Saharan Africa, each affiliated with European degree-granting universities (Hinchliffe 1987, 34).[11] In 1945, the British government's Asquith Commission concluded that, given the inevitability of decolonization, Britain and other colonial powers should expand higher education in Africa to train an educated, and hopefully politically moderate, ruling elite. The expansion of higher education started during the waning days of colonial rule and was greatly accelerated as newly independent African countries both expanded these Asquith Colleges and built and staffed new institutions of higher learning (Hinchliffe 1987, chapter 3; Ajayi, Goma, and Johnson 1996, chapters 2–4). Consequently, between 1950 and 1962 the number of African universities tripled, and the number of university students in Africa increased six times (Samoff and Bidemi 2004, 77). Between 1960 and 1980, university enrollments increased nearly 11 percent every year, with higher education accounting for, on average, nearly 20 percent of educational spending (Hinchliffe 1987, 1).[12] In East Africa alone, university enrollments skyrocketed from 2,193 in 1964, to 9,818 in 1973, while the number of university teachers increased from 279 to 1,440 during the same period, nearly a third of whom were East African (Court 1974, 8).

Newly independent African governments expanded university education to meet the demand for the skilled workers required for national development, or "manpower requirements" in World Bank–speak. The lack of academically trained professionals left many African countries economically dependent on the former colonial power. For example, when the Democratic Republic of the Congo won independence in 1960, only sixteen Congolese held college degrees (Gilroy 1960). In 1961, East Africa contained only ninety-nine university graduates, and a total population of 23 million (Court 1974, 8). At independence in 1964, Zambia had no universities, thereby ensuring that the National Commission for Development Planning remained dominated by expatriate economists even a decade later (Ake 1996, 19).

While universities in newly independent African countries focused on the immediate demand for a trained labor force, expanded university education also created opportunities for the emergence of pan-African intellectual circles that began to "challeng[e] the imperial narrative" that defined colonial education (Mkandawire 2005, 1). During the 1960s and 1970s, a handful of African universities emerged as "the vanguard" of African intellectual life, and "campus[es] vibrated with debates about fundamental issues of the day—nationalism, socialism, democracy and the party system" (Mazrui 2005, 58–59). The prestigious academic journals—*Transition* (Kampala) and *East Africa Journal* (Nairobi)—became centers of public debate, as were the overflowing lecture halls at the universities of Makerere, Nairobi, and Dar es Salaam (Mazrui 2005, 58–59).[13] With the rapid expansion of African higher education, a large number of foreign-trained African intellectuals returned home to take up academic positions on the continent. In addition, graduate students and young faculty from Europe and North America—many of whom were funded through area and international studies programs—spent time studying and teaching in postcolonial African institutions.

These scholarly migrations had profound impact on whole fields of academic knowledge production. For example, Ngũgĩ wa Thiong'o returned from Leeds University to take a position in the English Department at the University of Nairobi in 1967. Upon his return, Ngũgĩ and two colleagues, Henry Owuor-Anyumba and Taban Lo Liyong, circulated a document calling for replacing the English Department with a Department of African Literature and Languages, claiming that, as it currently existed, the department assumed that "the English [literary] tradition and the emergence of the modern west is the central root of our consciousness and cultural heritage," thereby reducing Africa to "an extension of the west" (Ngũgĩ, Owuor-Anyumba, and Liyong 1972, 146). This challenge—which caused a flurry of activity "at all levels of the university," the press, and parliament—traveled "beyond Nairobi to other universities in Africa and beyond" and became one of "the earliest shots in what later became postcolonial theory" (Ngũgĩ 2012, 9).

Similarly, during the 1960s and 1970s, the University of Dar es Salaam achieved an international reputation as one of the foremost universities on the continent, home to a dynamic intellectual community of scholars from around the world, including Issa Shivji (Tanzania), Walter Rodney (Guyana), Mahmood Mamdani (Uganda), Lionel Cliffe (United Kingdom), Giovanni Arrighi (Italy), Immanuel Wallerstein (United States), David Apter (United States), John Saul (Canada), and Terence Ranger (Britain), among many others. Between 1966 and 1974, the University of Dar es Salaam fostered an environment "of intense intellectual ferment and ideological debates and discussion" (Shivji 1993, 33). There was considerable student activism, including the creation of the University Students African Revolutionary Front, which ran its own student-led ideology classes and published the magazine *Cheche* (Swahili for "spark"; Shivji 1993; Hirji 2010). At times, Tanzanian president Julius Nyerere (1968) regularly attended university events and made education, including higher education, central to his policy of self-reliance. Many of the early theorists of world systems, dependency, and underdevelopment were part of the vibrant intellectual debates taking place within African higher education at that time. Scholars working within African universities often moved between the university, radical political movements, and policy circles, creating modes of academic knowledge that directly concerned themselves with the political, social, and economic questions of African decolonization. Walter Rodney, for example, described in Great Britain (where he was trained) a "scholarly apparatus . . . [based on] whom you footnote. The game is to . . . start with so and so and come down the line and pay your deference to each one of these authorities" (1990, 25–26). He contrasted this with University of Dar es Salaam, which allowed him "the opportunity to grow in conjuncture with the total movement in society," participating in the struggle of a whole society by engaging in the "struggle going on in the university" (Rodney 1990, 35, 37; see also epigraph).

This rapid expansion of higher education across Africa and the Third World, made possible by decolonization and national development policies, as well as financing from the World Bank, helped create a highly heterodox intellectual environment. Consequently, by the 1970s, there existed a large and vibrant ecosystem of concepts, terms, political commitments, and modes of analysis available to understand the economic reworlding of the world. As the economic turmoil of the 1970s brought about by spikes in oil prices, geopolitical instability, and mounting Third World debt unfolded, these problems received considerable attention from intellectuals trained in a wide variety of academic settings around the world. The diversity of worldviews in circulation is clearly observable by comparing the different and often competing imaginaries used to understand the fundamental causes of (and solutions to) the Third World debt crisis.

Contested Imaginaries

By the early 1970s, the world economy had reached its highest levels of productivity since the end of World War II. Much of the Third World saw considerable economic growth, including many of Africa's newly independent countries. However, widespread economic growth put pressure on the American dollar, which was still pegged to gold under the Bretton Woods system. While other countries freely devalued their currencies in relationship to the U.S. dollar to avoid inflationary pressures and to lower the cost of exports, this arrangement meant that American goods became relatively more expensive. In response, on August 15, 1971, Nixon unilaterally delinked the U.S. dollar from the gold standard. This move not only made it possible for the government to devalue the U.S. dollar, but also freed the government to print money to pay its mounting debts. As other countries followed suit, the total supply of money in the world economy grew 40 percent between 1970 and 1973 (Frieden 2006, 364; Prashad 2012, 16). This financial instability was magnified during the 1973 oil crisis, which was caused by the Organization of the Petroleum Exporting Countries' attempts to gain greater sovereignty over the oil markets by raising prices. This price hike converged with an oil embargo organized by the Organization of Arab Petroleum Exporting Countries, retaliating against those countries who supported Israel during the Yom Kippur War (Venn 2002, 7–21). Oil-importing countries were hit especially hard, especially those in the Third World without alternative energy sources and an already delicate balance of payments (Venn 2002, 119). Following the Iranian Revolution in 1979, the second oil crisis caused additional volatility as prices increased from an average of $12.70 to $30 per barrel, reaching $40 at its peak (Venn 2002, 26).

The oil shock crippled the economies of many oil-importing economies, shifting more than $150 billion from oil-importing to oil-exporting economies. American and European banks became the depositories of this deluge of petrodollars, often loaning the money back to energy-importing countries to pay increasingly high fuel costs. High oil prices combined with easy access to credit created an unprecedented combination of hyperinflation and economic stagnation. Lacking a conventional Keynesian response, the U.S. Federal Reserve, headed by Paul Volker, raised interest rates to 20 percent in August 1979 in a dramatic effort to fight inflation. While the Volker Shock eventually brought inflation under control in the United States, it also pushed both the American economy and the world economy into deep recession. The lasting effects of high interest rates and slumping international demand created a precarious situation for many Third World countries, most of which had navigated the economic turmoil of the 1970s with short-term borrowing. These countries were now forced to borrow more money, at much higher interest rates, to make payments on existing debt (see George 1990; Arrighi 2002; Frieden 2006, 367–75; Prashad 2012, chapter 1).

In 1980 and 1981, three major reports sought to explain the causes of this crisis and prescribe possible solutions. Each of the three reports—the Lagos Plan of Action, the Brandt Commission Report, and the Berg Report—contain wildly different approaches to the causes and possible solutions to the Third World debt crisis (cf. Shaw 1983; Ake 1996, chapter 2), each grounded in different ways of imagining the world. The Lagos Plan (see Luke and Shaw 1984) and the Brandt Commission Report bear the intellectual marks of highly heterogeneous intellectual milieus, ones that included liberals, Marxists, Keynesians, Third World intellectuals, and social democrats. The Berg Report, in contrast, was authored under McNamara's replacement at the

World Bank, A. W. Clausen, and presented the debt crisis as simply resulting from the failure of African countries to appreciate the cold realities of the global financial market.

The Lagos Plan of Action, published in 1980, offers an Afro-centric understanding of the crisis, rooted in the history of colonization, neocolonialism, and calls for greater self-reliance and mutual aid among African countries. Written over the course of multiple meetings among African leaders and under the auspices of the Organization of African Unity (OAU), this report was heavily influenced by theories of underdevelopment and dependency circulating within African and Latin American universities.[14] The Lagos Plan of Action argued that "Africa's underdevelopment is not inevitable" but rather the direct result of colonialism and the recent legacy of "exploitation . . . carried out through neo-colonialist external forces" (OAU 1981, 7; see also Eyoh 1998, 284–88). Based on this analysis, the report offered an alternative vision of African countries working together to create greater regional economic integration, mutual assistance, and economic redistribution. It called upon each African country to (1) harness its "huge resources . . . to meet the needs and purposes of its people"; (2) end "Africa's almost total reliance on the export of raw materials"; (3) actively "cultivate the virtue of self-reliance"; (4) "mobilize her entire human and material resources for her development"; (5) "pursue all-embracing economic, social and cultural activities which will . . . ensure that . . . [the efforts and benefits] from development are equitably shared"; and (6) pursue continental economic integration "with renewed determination in order to create a continent-wide framework . . . based on collective self-reliance" (OAU 1981, 8–9). The twin themes of national and regional self-reliance and self-sustained development focus on developing agricultural self-sufficiency (Jamieson 1984). The Lagos Plan situates the economic crisis of the late 1970s as originating from outside Africa, with the solution coming from African countries themselves, through a process of African economies "delinking" from the world system (Shaw 1985, 11).

The Brandt Commission Report, formally titled *North-South: A Programme for Survival* and also published in 1980, describes the debt crisis as culminating within a world imagined as spatially divided between North and South. Recognizing the North as partially culpable in the economic crises in the South, the report suggests that the creation of a North-South dialogue is necessary to achieve the common goal of human survival. Headed by former social democratic West German chancellor Willy Brandt, the report declared North-South relations as the fundamental challenge of the day, arguing that "world citizens everywhere" must work together to collectively address the "many global issues" facing a shared humanity (Brandt et al. 1980, 7). While the report concerns itself with a wide-ranging list of crises—poverty, development, health, housing, education, gender inequality, and so on—the report suggests the need for a North-South dialogue requiring that everyone accept "global responsibility for economic and social development" (Brandt et al. 1980, 8).[15] The Brandt Report became an instant best seller in England, with a provocative cover depicting a world map divided into North and South by a black line (commonly known as "the Brandt Line").[16] The idea for the commission originated with McNamara, who shared an interest in examining the growing economic gulf between North and South (Elson 1982, 110; Prashad 2012, 15), and the report was written by a collection of scholars and politicians that included dependency theorists, neo-institutionalists, and Keynesians, from a wide range of national origins (Kuwait, Colombia, Upper Volta, Chile, U.S., U.K., Tanzania, India, Malaysia, Indonesia, Japan, Canada, Sweden, France, Guyana, and Algeria). The report called for developing institutional mechanisms by which the North could transfer purchasing power to the South, as well as come together to develop common solutions for the "globalization of dangers and challenges—war, chaos, self-destruction" (Brandt et al. 1980, 19). The Brandt Commission imagined the debt crisis as an extension of a world divided into North and South, advocating for a benevolent reordering of the North's economic priorities to more fully incorporate the South into a global and mutually beneficial exchange (Piasecki and Wolnicki 2003).

The following year, the World Bank, now headed by A. W. Clausen, published its own assessment of the debt crisis in Africa. "Accelerated Development in Sub-Saharan Africa: An Agenda for Action" (World Bank 1981a)—often referred to as the Berg Report (after its sole named author, University of Michigan economics professor Elliot Berg)—presented the African debt crisis as a global crisis fundamentally out of the control of individual countries.[17] The only choice available to individual countries was to adapt to the global financial pressures being placed upon them from outside. On the one hand, the report recognized that economic problems in Africa resulted primarily from "domestic policy inadequacies" that required "increased aid *together with policy reform*" in order to achieve conditions for economic growth in Africa (World Bank 1981a, 4, 121, italics in original). While acknowledging that African countries faced many "basic constraints" (including limited human resources, weak institutions, "hostile" climate and geography, and a rapidly growing population), as well as challenging "external factors" (including a deteriorating balance-of-payments problem), the report nonetheless concluded that African countries should adopt a pro-growth economic strategy, one that included developing "more suitable trade and exchange-rate policies," making the public sector more efficient (including the privatization of parastatals), and refocusing the agricultural sector on exports (5). The Berg Report claimed that balance-of-payment problems caused by "internal and global factors" and against "the backdrop of global economic recession" conspired to create a dire economic forecast for sub-Saharan Africa (3, 4). The report claimed that "domestic policy inadequacies" were primarily responsible for intensifying existing economic constraints, namely those "structural" factors existing at the national level (such as those that "evolved from historical circumstances or from the physical environment") as well as global factors beyond the control of individual countries (4).[18] In other words, since geography, climate, (colonial) history, and the global economy cannot be changed, individual nations must make sacrifices to adapt to these external forces. While the report uses the term "global" sparingly, in each case "global" is used to describe external, naturalized forces demanding conformity of national response. This vision of a natural and global financial market demanding that nations sacrifice their development agendas in favor of strict monetary policy would become the guiding vision of the Clausen bank (see chapter 4).

Arriving at the World Bank in 1981 shortly after the second oil crisis and in the immediate aftermath of the Volker Shock, Clausen did not have much input in the writing of the Berg Report, which was well under way when he arrived. However, in his introduction to the report, Clausen wrote that, while the World Bank generally agreed with the vision laid out in the Lagos Plan of Action, it cautioned that African countries must conserve their limited resources by reducing public sector funding and rely instead "on the managerial capacities of private individuals and firms" (World Bank 1981a, v). In subsequent years, however, Clausen's vision of the world as a single, global financial market would become central to shaping the World Bank's response to the debt crisis. Clausen would largely walk away from McNamara's national development agenda, imagining the World Bank instead as simply an apolitical tool for helping struggling countries adapt to the demands of a natural, global financial market. In doing so, he would argue that African countries were largely to blame for failing to adopt policies that recognized the realities of global markets. For example, just a year after its publication, Clausen defended the Berg Report before the Nigerian Institute of International Affairs—arguing that while "global trends" and "external shocks" did conspire to place African economies in a precarious position, "domestic policies" were primarily to blame (Clausen 1982, 1195).

Clausen's policies of structural adjustment would have considerable adverse effects on Third World countries, on Africa, and on higher education around the world. However, before we get there, we must first return to McNamara's alma mater—Harvard Business School—to examine the emerging global imaginary being produced there during the early 1980s. Theodore Levitt's efforts to reimagine the world as a single, global market represented a new way of imagining the world, one fundamentally different from modernization's national development imaginary in which countries developed separately, but toward the same destination.

II Marketing the Global Imaginary

3 "Marketing Can Be Magic"

Theodore Levitt and Globalization as a Market Imaginary

Things don't have to be true to be so.
—THEODORE LEVITT

An *idea* is not responsible for who believes in it.
—THEODORE LEVITT

The idea of globalization became ubiquitous within academic writing during the 1990s because it provided something knowledge consumers needed—a compelling way to frame the rapidly changing post–Cold War world. Over time, the national imaginary became increasingly untenable, tied to a developmental dream being challenged by economic stagnation, recession, and the eventual end of the Cold War. Within this context, it became more and more common for academics, social scientists, and policy makers to talk about the world as global. The increased usage and dissemination of the term "globalization" within academic writing, however, did not simply materialize out of thin air. Globalization was not a term coined in the 1990s by social scientists desperate to find a way to more accurately reflect the world around them. Rather, globalization was already a widely discussed term and concept within the business world as early as the mid-1980s. This helps explain why business leaders and consultants (for example, Ohmae 1991, 1995; Wriston 1992), journalists covering economic issues (Greider 1997; Friedman 1999), and academics defining globalization in terms of the spread of iconic American brands (Ritzer 1993; Barber 1995) authored many of the books heavily cited within the early globalization literature. However, globalization did not simply migrate from the business world into the academy. Rather, the concept of globalization was first actively produced, reproduced, and circulated within the university; not within the social sciences, however, but rather the business schools, and the academic field of marketing in particular. The first widely embraced argument that business practitioners should imagine the world as global arrived in 1983 with the publication of Harvard Business School professor Theodore Levitt's now-canonical article "The Globalization of Markets."

As presented by Levitt, globalization offered a radical break from the dominant conception of markets. For most of the twentieth century, business practitioners—not unlike development agencies and foreign policy analysis—had imagined markets primarily as nationally inscribed entities, possessing their own tastes and characteristics, and shaped by their own internal logics. With markets understood as discrete national entities sutured together by multinational corporations and transnational financial institutions (national markets within an international political economy), firms commonly imagined themselves as developing and selling products tailored to these discrete markets.[1] During the late 1970s and early 1980s, only a small handful of economists and business practitioners used the term "globalization," and did so in a largely unsystematic and underconceptualized way. In fact, the term "globalization" and adjective "global" only appear sporadically throughout marketing journals and business newspapers during this period and are largely confined to discussions of particular industries and sectors.[2] In short, prior to 1983 globalization was "quite novel," both within and outside the business world (Quelch and Deshpande 2004, 9).

In his groundbreaking article, however, Levitt argued that American marketing practitioners should reimagine the world not as a series of individual national markets but rather as a single market. Rather than marketing products tailored to discrete national tastes, businesses should sell the same product to everyone everywhere. Recognizing that consumers might still adhere to national preferences, Levitt nonetheless contended that a convergence of taste—when combined with aggressive marketing campaigns and an overall preference for lower prices—would ultimately privilege global firms. Levitt's argument became widely disseminated within the business world during the 1980s, profoundly changing how business practitioners conceptualized markets.

While scholars have rightly emphasized the important role Levitt's article played in single-handedly popularizing the concept of globalization, I argue that understanding the impact of this article requires taking seriously the fact that Levitt's understanding of globalization was produced within the academic field of marketing.[3] The best marketers, Levitt argued, did not simply survey customers to find what they wanted but instead asked themselves, "What is new?," thereby opening the possibility of "transcending the ordinary and thus reaching imaginatively beyond the obvious or merely deductive" (Levitt 1986b, xxi, xxii). Understood in this context, Levitt's article on globalization does not simply describe the world as it is—namely, as a self-evident global market— but rather enacts the "marketing imagination," imagining the world in ways that encourages new marketing practices and yields strategic advantages. In suggesting that firms imagine the world as global—and therefore act as if it were global—Levitt helped produce the possibilities for making it so.

This chapter approaches Levitt's essay not from the perspective of its rightness or wrongness, but rather from the point of view of reproduction. The fact that "The Globalization of Markets" is a rhetorically flashy and metaphor-laden piece of writing, overflowing with examples and not confined by an expectation of internal consistency, helps explain why this argument traveled so quickly outside the business school and into the hands of business practitioners. It is also important, however, to take seriously the fact that Levitt wrote from within a network of institutions—including the Harvard Business School and *Harvard Business Review*—that gave his imagined global market extra credence, at a time when business education and academic training (especially in the field of marketing) were attaining a privileged position within the business world. As such, it is not inconsequential that Levitt's essay about globalization was rapidly and widely disseminated within business schools, including being codified into Harvard Business School case studies used to train business practitioners across the U.S. and around the world. Levitt also worked tirelessly to advance his global imaginary within the business world, making sure that the top officials at U.S. and international firms had access to his writings. As such, by the 1990s when "globalization" arrived as a buzzword within the social sciences, its appearance could not be read as simply the arrival of the right term at the right time.[4] Rather, by the mid-1990s, globalization had been—for nearly a decade—a very well-marketed marketing concept within the business world.

To understand globalization's rapid popularity within the business world, one must first understand the peculiar intellectual space of the academic field of marketing—a discipline that explicitly works at the intersection of abstract reimaginings of the world and the integration of these reimaginings into applied business practices. The next two sections examine Theodore

Levitt's formulation of globalization, arguing that his concept of globalization needs to be understood within the context of his writing about the "marketing imagination." In doing so, it becomes evident that Levitt's strange article on globalization is not simply a description of the world but rather an exercise in creating the marketing imaginaries needed to give American firms an advantage within the stagnating world economy of the early 1980s. The chapter concludes by looking at the social relations that allowed Levitt to reproduce the global imaginary he did, enabling his imagined global market to travel from the Harvard Business School into the business world more broadly.

Reconceptualizing Markets

It is not coincidental that the term "globalization" was first fully theorized and popularized within the academic field of marketing. Unlike other fields of economic and business scholarship, marketing places a primary interest in the conceptual, imaginative, and creative processes of identifying consumer needs and desires, and designing products and marketing strategies that address these often ephemeral concerns. The academic field of marketing—and the business practices it informs—involves the continual reconceptualization of a business's consumers, products, and even entire markets, making the academic field both theoretical and highly speculative, while also grounded within the problematics of specific companies and industries. Because marketing stylizes itself as a form of outsider knowledge, it remains one part of the business world highly influenced by business school education.[5] Anthropologist of marketing Kalman Applbaum describes marketing as "a systematized set of practices known to and employed by a community of professionals," most of whom "are trained in the field, typically beginning in business school" (2004, 23).

The Disciplinary Field of Marketing

Marketing became a coherent and recognizable academic field only during the second half of the twentieth century. During the first half of the century, marketing research was largely unfocused and scattered throughout the fields of economics and business. The scholarship that did exist focused primarily on developing better understandings of how businesses could adapt to various contemporary trends—such as migration to cities, the growing importance of chain stores and catalog sales, and questions regarding how to advertise successfully in newspapers and magazines—and on understanding the "[marketing] functions" of "particular marketing *institutions*," and how they moved "*commodities* from sources of supply to places of demand" (Shaw and Jones 2005, 242, emphasis in original). Only by the end of the 1940s did marketing have its own professional associations, academic journals, and textbooks (Wilkie and Moore 2003).

During the 1950s, the academic field of marketing experienced its first important "paradigm shift" (Wilkie and Moore 2003, 123; Shaw and Jones 2005, 241–42). A period marked by great economic prosperity within the United States—including growing levels of personal consumption, a stunning increase in the variety of goods and services, and the rise of a new professional management class—gave marketing a new importance. This emergent consumer-driven capitalism meant that American firms were increasingly forced to compete against each other for control of this growing, and highly profitable, market for consumer goods. However, many of these goods—soaps, cereals, light appliances, and so on—had very little to differentiate themselves from one another. Marketing became the practice of differentiating such products, but also inventing new ways of moving goods from producer to consumer. During this period, academic marketers embraced a "managerial perspective," namely "viewing the field from the vantage point of the manager" (Wilkie and Moore 2003, 125). These traditional approaches to marketing were modernized by the incorporation of mathematical modeling developed by the military during World War II. Funded in large part by the Ford and Carnegie Foundations, many scholars of marketing were trained in these new scientific approaches such that by the 1960s there was a large number of books on market research and mathematical modeling (Wilkie and Moore 2003, 126–27).

In addition to a growing professionalization and changing methodologies, many working in the academic field of marketing also engaged in a radical rethinking of what constituted a market. In the 1950s, early marketing theorist Peter Drucker offered the pivotal distinction between "selling" and "marketing," which he explained as the shift from "the sales department . . . sell[ing] whatever the plant produces" to the idea that "it is our job to produce what the market needs" (1954, 38). Drucker argued that businesses should embrace marketing as their core function and that, when they do, marketing ceases being the narrowly defined task of moving product from the factory floor and into the consumer's hands and instead "encompasses the entire business" such that every aspect of the company is managed "from the customer's point of view" (1954, 39). Harry Hansen—another pioneer in the academic field of marketing—explained the distinction as one between the marketer as "a creator of the flow of goods and services" rather than someone who simply manages "that flow as it goes by him" (1956, 7). Rather than placing primary emphasis on the management of production, as was the earlier focus of economists and business practitioners alike, academic marketing theorists began to offer new ways of imagining the corporation itself. In this account, the corporation gathered market research and used this information to design, produce, brand, price, and distribute products designed for the consumer. This new mantra—that business should not sell what a company already produces but rather should identify and produce what the customer wants—rapidly became the core tenet of academic marketing, a contribution commonly referred to as the marketing concept (Applbaum 2004, 29–31, 203–10).

The Marketing Concept

The development and popularization of the marketing concept constituted a radically "new marketing idea" which effectively "burn[ed] the roof and towers that historically limited the marketing imagination" (Applbaum 2004, 208). While prewar marketers understood themselves as marketing goods in order to grow a business, and therefore provide for their workers and shareholders, the marketing concept reimagined corporations as being in "the business of servicing individual human needs and wants, which are infinite" (Applbaum 2004, 209). In his landmark essay in the *Journal of Marketing*, Robert Keith—drawing on his experience as the executive vice president at Pillsbury—called this change in thinking a "marketing revolution" that was firmly in place across the business world. Drawing on an analogy from astronomy, Keith claimed that businesses increasingly place "the man or woman who buys the product" at the "absolute dead center of the business universe," a revolutionary rethinking on par with Copernicus situating the sun at the center of the celestial universe (Keith 1960, 35; see also Houston 1986).

Theodore Levitt's seminal 1960 *Harvard Business Review* essay "Marketing Myopia" went a long way toward popularizing the marketing concept. This piece clearly spells out the basic distinction between selling—which focuses on the seller's need "to convert his product into cash"—and marketing, which fundamentally focuses "on the needs of the buyer" (Levitt 1960b, 50). Marketing, in other words, is predicated on "satisfying the needs of the customer" by attending to not only the product itself but also "the whole cluster of things associated with creating, delivering, and finally consuming it" (50). While most companies focus on selling products they produced, Levitt argues that, in reality, a "truly marketing-minded firm" takes its "cues from the buyer" so that the product itself "becomes a consequence of the marketing effort" (50).

In a classically Levittian style, the piece starts with the provocative claim that "growth industries" do not exist; industries do not gain (or lose) market share simply because the market for their product is growing (or shrinking). Railroads, Levitt argues, did not lose out to automobile and air travel simply because new sectors replaced demand for rail transportation. Instead, railroads lost market share because they defined themselves as in the railroad business, rather than the transportation business. Similarly, Hollywood did not lose out to TV because the movie business declined, but because they defined their business as "product oriented (making movies)" not "customer-oriented (providing entertainment)" (Levitt 1960b, 45). If railroads and movie studios paid attention to what their customers really wanted—not trains and movies but transportation and entertainment—they could adapt their products to satisfy their consumers' needs, whether or not these new products fell outside the company's existing product lines. In this way, selling "concerns itself with the tricks and techniques of getting people to exchange their cash for your product," while marketing envisions "the entire business process" as "a tightly integrated effort to discover, create, arouse, and satisfy customer needs" (Levitt 1960b, 55).

Four months after the publication of "Marketing Myopia," Levitt wrote another *Harvard Business Review* article calling for greater artistic creativity in marketing, pushing back against the prevailing trend toward the science of consumer research. While he understood the power of scientific approaches to market research,[6] he warned that "motivation [i.e., customer] research" often results in "senseless sameness"—as exemplified in Detroit's 1959 rollout of compact cars with names such as Valiant, Corvair and Falcon, immediately followed by the Dart, Comet, Invader, Lancer, Tempest, and Rocket (Levitt 1960c, 76–78). These undifferentiated marketing efforts resulted not from a failure to do consumer research, but by uniformly successful market research; all the major car companies, for example, introduced cars perfectly targeted toward their defined market and, as such, failed to differentiate themselves. The cause of this failure, Levitt argued, lay in a "paralysis of the imagination" that results when management capitulates to highly paid and credentialed consultants who offer homogenized marketing suggestions.[7] In contrast, Levitt (1960c, 83) declared that "the highest form of achievement is always art, never science" and that "business leadership" is an art needing greater respect. All marketing, "whether it comes from a businessman, an artist, a preacher, or a panhandler," is successful when conducted artfully; when it is "clear, distinctive, [and] meaningful" (84).

While diagnosing the need for inventiveness and originality, on the one hand, Levitt also acknowledged that the claims he made in "Marketing Myopia" were themselves not original but instead were drawn from the earlier work of Drucker, McKitterick, Alderson, Howard, and others. He recognized his contribution not as creating the marketing concept but rather in writing a "manifesto" that brought it "to the inner orbit of business policy" (Levitt 1975, 180), bridging the academic field of marketing with the broader business world.[8] In a "Retrospective Comment" included with a republication of "Marketing Myopia," Levitt wrote that the ideas in the essay were

> nothing new. Others preceded me, saying what was original and instructive about *the marketing concept* much more carefully than I, as a latecomer, did. The major purpose of the article was to communicate to a wider audience in a much more provocative way what my predecessors had pioneered. And it sought to emphasize thereby the powerful relationship between marketing and the corporate purpose.... One thing is interesting: why the enormous popularity of the article? What is the hidden message? Is it that concrete illustrations and anecdotal facts communicate better than abstract statements standing in theoretic isolation? ... Is the message that the character of the message is at least as important as its content? (Levitt 1976, 58, emphasis in original)

Levitt's insistence that he was merely summarizing and popularizing the work of others is consistent with his own approach to marketing. While Levitt (1966, 63) sees marketing as pushing the boundaries of what has already been thought, he also argues that "the greatest flow of newness is not innovation at all" but rather imitation. Levitt (1966, 63) points out that most of the companies that popularize an original product—IBM and computers, Texas Instruments and transistors, RCA and televisions, and so on—did not invent the product but rather found more successful ways to market the products invented by others. Through imitation, these companies reap great financial rewards without investing in costly, high-risk research and development. As one literary critic of marketing literature points out, Levitt recognizes that the "communicator of ideas is ... *more* important than ... the composer of ideas"—Levitt is himself "a marketer not a manufacturer of knowledge and, as everyone knows, marketing is everything" (Brown 2005, 27). As such, "Levitt is more than a skillful advocate of the marketing cause; he *is* marketing" (Brown 1999, 5).[9]

If Levitt's ultimate goal was to introduce the marketing concept to a broader, practitioner audience, then "Marketing Myopia" was a stunning success. The piece was an "extraordinarily influential article" (Kennedy 2002, 140). It quickly became one of the most reprinted and circulated pieces in marketing. In 1960, it won the prestigious McKinsey Award for best article published in the *Harvard Business Review*.[10] In the months shortly after its publication, 35,000 reprints were sold by the *Harvard Business Review* to a thousand different companies ("Professor Theodore Levitt" 2006). By 1975, it had been "widely quoted and anthologized, and the HBR ha[d] sold more than 265,000 reprints of it" (Levitt 1975, 26). By 2006, it had sold more than 850,000 reprints, placing it among the top-selling *Harvard Business Review* articles of all time ("Professor Theodore Levitt" 2006). It was twice reprinted in the *Harvard Business Review* in full (Levitt 1975, 2004), and at least twice as lengthy excerpts (Levitt 1986a; 2006, 128–29). "Marketing Myopia" was also republished as a chapter in various editions of Levitt's collected essays (Levitt 1962, chapter 2; 1986b, chapter 8) and more recently as part of a pocket book series published by Harvard Business Press (Levitt 2008). It is still widely taught in business schools around the world and, according to Google Scholar, been cited more than seven thousand times. Levitt's popularizing of the marketing concept within the business world made him "the Copernicus of American business" (Clutterbuck and Crainer 1990, 158). And, based on the success of a piece crafted over the course of one evening, Levitt was promoted from Harvard Business School lecturer to full professor in three short years (Mark 1987, 95).

While the essay was enough to catapult Levitt into the realm of top management gurus (Kennedy 2002, 140–43), two decades later Levitt made another monumental contribution to the academic field of marketing with his 1983 article "The Globalization of Markets." To understand this article, we need to first situate it within Levitt's approach to the marketing imagination.

Theodore Levitt and the Marketing Imagination

Marketing can be magic.
—THEODORE LEVITT

Born in Germany in 1925, Levitt moved as a young boy to Dayton, Ohio, to flee the rise of Nazism. After serving in World War II, he attended Antioch College and later Ohio State University, where he received a PhD in economics in 1951. His first academic job was at University of North Dakota, which he quit in 1955 to become a business consultant (Mark 1987, 55). His 1956 *Harvard Business Review* article "The Changing Character of Capitalism"—an engagement with the work of sociologist David Riesman to rebut the "classical economic theory" that "man is a rational, calculating, self-motivated, acquisitive creature" (Levitt 1956a, 37)—caught the eye of Harvard Business School professor Edward Bursk, who invited Levitt to apply for a vacant lecturer position in marketing (Mark 1987, 94). With a PhD in economics and some business experience, Levitt had no formal training in marketing when he joined Harvard Business School as a lecturer in 1959.

However, based on the success of "Marketing Myopia," Levitt is widely known today as "a founder of modern marketing" (HBR 2006, 127) and remains "the world's best-known marketing thinker" (Clutterbuck and Crainer 1990, 158). However, he has always been an iconoclastic figure, one of "the industry-transforming misfits and mavericks" that he celebrated as the imaginative forces behind good, creative marketing (Brown 2005, 30). With a writing style that contained "congeries of incongruities, oxymorons, [and] paradoxes," Levitt put together a highly productive academic career that defined itself against "the prevailing management orthodoxy" (Brown 2005, 29–30).

Some of his most notorious essays encouraged business leaders to openly defend profit seeking rather than adopting the increasingly popular language of corporate responsibility (Levitt 1958, 44).[11] At the same time that business was worshiping at the feet of "the tribal god *innovation*," Levitt (1966, 63, emphasis in original) counseled companies to spend greater resources imitating the products designed by their competition. His writings are filled with Delphic claims such as, "people buy ¼-inch drills bits but need ¼-inch holes; they buy cosmetics but want 'hope'" (Levitt 1977, 108). He writes, for example, that when a company advertises itself as offering a "tool" that the consumer needs to "fill a need, fix a problem, [or] stop a headache," then it has effectively "invite[d] the user into a world where that need is fulfilled"—at this moment, "advertising is the poetry of becoming" (Levitt 1993, 135). At one point, swept up in an explanation as to why IBM and Revlon are actually doubling-down on—rather than abandoning—the marketing concept, Levitt comes right out and declares: "Marketing can be magic" (1977, 107). While often as catchy as they are head scratching, these phrases are held together by a common commitment to a consumer-centric vision of marketing.

Contrary to much of the economic and management thinking of his time, Levitt's provocative arguments are deeply rooted in a vision of humans not as rational, calculating beings but rather as complicated, psychologically motivated actors who often act in ways that appear irrational from the perspective of a market calculus. While his early work offers a "fairly conventional" (HBR 2006, 127) analysis of the effects of postwar mass consumer society on American economic life, even these pieces portray an intellectual commitment toward understanding humans as complicated economic actors motivated by obscured desires. For example, he predicted that, contrary to economic wisdom of the time, labor disruptions and strikes would become less common during periods of sustained economic prosperity, given the growth in consumer debt (Levitt 1953a). This position faced considerable criticism, most notably for its lack of empirical evidence (Goldner 1953; Weinberg and Weisenfeld 1953; Blitz 1954). Levitt responded by reminding his critics that his primary concern was "with what may be expected in the future, and the broad sweep of the future [could] not be predicted on the basis simply of recent or current aberrations" (Levitt 1953b, 581). As such, he chose to speak the language of "tendencies and likelihoods, not of absolute certainties," and therefore could not be expected to "provide tangible evidence to support a hypothesis about a course of events that [was] not yet worked out" (Levitt 1953c, 127).

This line of thinking led Levitt to find theoretical motivation outside the canonical readings of economics, business, and even marketing. Rather than simply accepting the image of "economic man," Levitt (1956b, 95–96) instead plumbed "the more esoteric wing of the social sciences" for "theories of human behavior" that disrupted "the virgin simplicity" of most economic thought. For example, rejecting the "it's-all-a-matter-of-supply-and-demand and that's-human-nature school of business reasoning," Levitt argued instead that national prosperity was changing national character in negative ways, privileging "acquiescence" and "routine" (1956a, 37, 39). This foundational commitment to appreciating the complexity of consumer motivations meant that Levitt was aware of the profound blind spots in scientific and empiricist approaches to marketing. For example, in a letter addressed to "Cliff," Levitt wrote the anthropologist Clifford Geertz, acknowledging, "Over the years I've had lots of fun, and also frustration pushing thick description as a legitimate way of knowing onto the obsessive metricists" in the business school.[12]

In 1983, Levitt summed up his general approach to marketing in *The Marketing Imagination*, a book he considered his most important contribution (Kennedy 2002, 141). The book consists of a series of essays collected over twenty-five years as well as a title chapter written specifically for this collection. That title chapter synthesizes many of his previous arguments—including the need to avoid myopic thinking and instead approach marketing as an art—while clearly framing these insights in terms of "the marketing imagination." The essay starts with the cryptic claim that "nothing drives progress like the imagination. The idea precedes the deed" (Levitt 1986b, 127). Drawing on examples as far-ranging as Sir Ernest Shackleton's ad seeking polar explorers to GCA's design for its DSW wafer stepper, and Apple's rebranding of the microcomputer as the personal computer, Levitt (1986b, 137) reiterates his now-hallmark observation that how firms imagine (and reimagine) their markets actually creates "meaningful differentiation in their offerings," and therefore the possibility of becoming more competitive. In this chapter he defines his phrase "marketing imagination" by first repeating the now-enshrined definition of "marketing" as a business practice that constantly attends to "get[ting] and keep[ing] a customer" while making sure "existing buyers . . . prefer to do business with you rather than your competitors" but then introducing the imagination as the process of "construct[ing] mental pictures of what is or is not actually present, what has never been actually experienced" (130). Therefore, put together, Levitt introduces the marketing imagination as the art of "combining disparate facts or ideas into new amalgamations of meaning" in ways that—moving beyond "daydreams and fantasies" yet unconstrained by "convention or conviction"—create new products as well as strategies for selling goods and services designed to fulfill a consumer's often unknown wants and desires (130); "To exercise the imagination is to be creative. It requires intellectual or artistic inventiveness" (127).

Levitt argues that individuals can access the marketing imagination when they consciously cultivate the skills of being perceptive, inquisitive, and creative. In a later interview, Levitt describes the process of developing a marketing imagination with the following advice:

> Expose yourself to your environment and ask questions to develop your sensitivity and sensibility. . . . I see things all the time. I go into factories, offices, stores and look out the window and just see things and ask why? Why are they doing that? Why is it this way and not that? You ask questions and pretty soon you come up with answers. When you begin to try to answer your own questions you become much more receptive to reading things which help you to answer questions. . . . Seeing is one thing but perceptiveness requires cognitive efforts and personal involvement. You bring something to what you see. (quoted in Clutterbuck and Crainer 1990, 161)[13]

It is this combination of casual observation and "perceptiveness" that Levitt brings to his analysis of globalization.

A few months before the publication of *The Marketing Imagination*, Levitt published "The Globalization of Markets" in the *Harvard Business Review*. Published the same year that President Reagan denounced the Soviet Union as an evil empire, this essay also quickly became a transformative article in marketing and was included as the second chapter in *The Marketing Imagination*. Applbaum argues that as marketers and firms adopt the notion a single global market, globalization becomes a "social fact in the making . . . an abstraction that is developing thicker institutional moorings in the life world" (2004, 76). Ushered into the business world by Levitt, this global imaginary came to profoundly influence how American corporations act in the world.

Globalization as a Marketing Imagination

As in his previous pieces, "The Globalization of Markets" combines anecdotal examples and personal observation to create a compelling new marketing imagination, one that boldly asserted that the world exists as a single global market. Often overlooked, however, is the fact that Levitt's argument does not rest on the claim that the world is actually global. Rather, in line with his understanding of the marketing imagination, this piece should be read as a sort of manifesto designed to encourage corporations to creatively reimagine themselves as if they were operating in a global market. In other words, the piece does not describe a world Levitt observed but rather imaginatively draws a picture of a world that does not actually exist yet. The editor of the *Harvard Business Review*, Kenneth R. Andrews (1983, 1), introduces Levitt's essay as "assert[ing] a strategy-shaping change in the world economic environment."

The Argument

Largely credited with explaining and popularizing the concept of globalization within the business world, "The Globalization of Markets" proposes that firms operating in multiple countries no longer imagine themselves as multinational but rather as global corporations. Levitt speculates about the existence of "a new commercial reality," one marked by "the emergence of global markets for standardized consumer products on a previously unimagined scale of magnitude" (1983, 92). In this context, multinational corporations can no longer afford to imagine the world as divided into discrete national markets. What defines global corporations for Levitt is that they operate "with resolute constancy—at low relative cost—as if the entire world (or major regions of it) were a single entity." In other words, they make goods cheaper by selling "the same things in the same way everywhere" (Levitt 1983, 98). Drawing on Isaiah Berlin's distinction, the multinational corporation, like a fox, "knows a lot about a great many countries and congenially adapts to supposed differences," while the global corporation, like a hedgehog, "knows everything about one great thing" and, in doing so, is positioned to treat "the world as composed of few standardized markets rather than many customized markets" (Levitt 1983, 96).

Levitt draws this distinction between multinational and global corporations using the example of Hoover, Ltd.'s efforts to sell washing machines in continental Europe. Hoover started its campaign with an extensive study of its potential consumers, including surveying consumers from different countries asking what they wanted in a washing machine. Hoover then retooled its British production facility (at great cost) to make washing machines catering to these national markets. Instead, Levitt argues, Hoover should have offered a "simple, standardized high-quality machine at a low price" all across Europe and heavily advertised this machine with a message that appealed to all potential consumers: "*This* is the machine that you, the homemaker, *deserve*" (Levitt 1983, 98, emphasis in original). He argues that within a global market, national and regional preferences could not weather an "aggressively low price" combined with "heavy promotion" (98). While consumers might express "local preferences," these preferences are themselves largely the result of years of "respectful accommodation" by multinational corporations that "*believe* preferences are fixed" due to "rigid habits of thinking about what actually is" (92, emphasis in original).

For Levitt, Hoover's strategy exemplified the absence of "any kind of marketing imagination": "Such companies are like the ethnocentricists [*sic*] in the Middle Ages who saw with everyday clarity the sun revolving around the earth and offered it as Truth. With no additional data but a more searching mind, Copernicus, like the hedgehog, interpreted a more compelling and accurate reality. Data do not yield information except with the intervention of the mind. Information does not yield meaning except with the intervention of imagination" (1983, 98–99). In other words, the difference between a multinational corporation and a global firm rests on how it imagines the changing world around it. Looking beyond the common sense of national markets, a global company decenters the familiar understanding of these markets. Those firms capable of imagining the world differently will "decimate competitors that still live in the disabling grip of old assumptions about how the world works" (98).

It is important to note that Levitt's argument in "The Globalization of Markets" presents itself primarily as an argument about the need to imagine the world as global, and only secondarily as a description of that world. The essay begins with the bold, futuristic declaration that the world has changed because of recent technological developments that are drawing "the world towards a converging commonality": "The globalization of markets is at hand. With that, the multinational commercial world nears its end, and so does the multinational corporation" (Levitt 1983, 92). These opening prognostics soon give way to an argument that hinges less on the specifics of empirical changes, focusing on how companies should reimagine their environment. For example, in the final section of Levitt's essay, titled "The Earth Is Flat"—a phrase later appropriated by Thomas Friedman (2005) as the title of his best-selling book on globalization (Steger 2008, 180–81)[14]—Levitt reminds his readers that "globalization affirms an ancient dictum of economics," namely "that things are driven by what happens at the margins, not at the core." He argues that, during certain phenomena like the extension of telecommunications, "reality is not a fixed paradigm, dominated by immemorial customs and derived attitudes, heedless of powerful and abundant new forces" (Levitt 1983, 101).

As with his other work on marketing, Levitt is entirely comfortable describing the world in terms of antinomy (Brown 2004). In this essay, Levitt argues that the world is becoming global yet also retains intransigent localized preferences. Globalization is a new reality brought into being by "the liberating and enhancing possibilities of modernity," changes that do not actually replace, but rather coexist alongside, "the inherited varieties of national preferences" and the "persistent differences in the world" (Levitt 1983, 101). These two realities—economic convergence and persistent difference— "often complement rather than oppose each other," just as in physics, "matter and anti-matter" exist "in symbiotic harmony" (Levitt 1983, 101). Within a world defined by the twin realities of economic convergence and persistent difference, Levitt nonetheless argues that business leaders should exclusively privilege the reality of convergence and choose to ignore the reality of persistent difference.

Levitt in effect argues that, while the world is complex, heterogeneous, and diverse, and human consumers make choices for a wide variety of incomprehensible reasons, it is nonetheless important to make marketing decisions based on an imagined world that excludes these complexities. In other words, the world is many, many different things, yet it is important that marketers imagine the world as if it were a single, global thing. Invoking the Copernican metaphor again, Levitt points out that "the earth is round, but for most purposes it's sensible to treat it as flat. Space is curved, but not much for everyday life here on earth" (1983, 101). For Levitt, Copernicus heroically collects data to imagine the world differently and more accurately than everyone else of his time. However, in this essay, Levitt also concedes that one transformative practice for marketers might be to see the world as it isn't—that is, flat.

In this way, Levitt's analysis of globalization vacillates wildly between statements about a changing global reality and the embrace of a highly speculative marketing strategy. However, upon closer examination, it becomes clear that Levitt is actually conceding that this new global reality is itself the effect of practices adopted by companies that imagine themselves as global. For example, the final paragraph of "The Globalization of Markets" reads, "the global company will shape the vectors of technology and globalization into its great strategic fecundity. It will systematically push these vectors toward their own convergence, offering everyone simultaneously high-quality, more or less standardized products at optimally low prices, thereby achieving for itself vastly expanded markets and profits. Companies that do not adapt to the new global realities will become victims of those that do" (Levitt 1983, 102). In other words, technological trends and globalization are two "vectors" not necessarily convergent until "push[ed]" by global companies. Pushing this convergence into reality results in greater corporate profit, which appears to be "the new global realities" that Levitt describes as victimizing those companies that fail to adapt to globalized markets. The reality of globalization being described, it turns out, is itself the effect of corporations that have already imagined themselves—and therefore marketed their products—as global. It is as if Levitt is telling a story about a heroic Copernicus who first imagined a world spinning around the sun, and then—with an Archimedean lever—made it so.

The Effects

Internal inconsistencies aside, Levitt's provocative argument had an immediate and profound impact on the business world. Published as an article in the *Harvard Business Review* and as a chapter in *The Marketing Imagination* during the same year, and written in Levitt's hallmark prose, "The Globalization of Markets" offered a marketing manifesto that elaborated the terms "global markets" and "globalization" in ways that could be easily grasped and quickly deployed by business practitioners (Tedlow and Abdelal 2004).[15] While the term "globalization" had been used before in various ways and contexts, it was Levitt who "first popularized (marketed?) it" within the business world (Hindle 2008, 264). Levitt's article "instantly became the manifesto of global marketing" (Klein 2002, 116; quoted in Quelch and Deshpande 2004, 2) and was widely discussed in the *New York Times*, *Washington Post*, and *Wall Street Journal* (Quelch and Deshpande 2004, 9). Soon after its publication, many multinational corporations engaged in "roundtable discussions, task forces, corporate strategy meetings, or informal studies" aimed at discussing strategies for marketing their products within a global market (Applbaum 2000, 264). And, as a consequence, Levitt's argument about globalization "reverberated in boardrooms around the world" even if, at the time, it looked more like "futuristic fantasy" (Tomkins 2003, 14). This piece would lay "the foundation for the popular depiction of globalization" (Steger and Wahlrab 2017, 31). In short, Levitt's reimagining of markets as global constituted "little short of a revolution," shaping both "how companies organized themselves" and "how they thought about what they were doing" (Tedlow and Abdelal 2004, 13).

Levitt's piece encouraged "hundreds of similar pieces convincing the world's leading companies to 'go global,'" to create "'global brands' by means of global commercial campaigns," and to attach "the words 'world' and 'global' to every conceivable commodity or service" (Steger 2008, 181). For example, Sir Martin Sorrell, then finance director of the advertising firm Saatchi & Saatchi, read Levitt's article and recalls "giving it to Maurice [Saatchi] saying 'this is a key article.'" A copy of Levitt's article was then given to Saatchi's main clientele with the disclaimer that "'this is the way the world's going and this is the way the Saatchi agency will be positioning itself'" (Tomkins 2003, 14). As a result, Saatchi & Saatchi reimagined itself as a global company that would actively engage in developing global advertising campaigns for its numerous clientele—most notably the British Airlines advertising campaign in which Manhattan Island itself flies over a London neighborhood before landing at Heathrow airport (Tomkins 2003, 14). This advertisement for "The World's Favorite Airline"—concluding with an *Earthrise*-esque image of the viewer rounding the moon to look down on an earth below, as lighted trails radiate out from London to all corners of the earth (British Airways 1983)—was broadcast simultaneously in twenty languages and in the world's top thirty-five television markets (Tomkins 2003, 14).[16] Soon after the publication of "The Globalization of Markets," Levitt was asked to join the board of Saatchi & Saatchi (Micklethwait and Wooldridge 1996, 221). Similarly, Edward H. Meyer, chairman and president of the premier New York marketing firm Grey Advertising, wrote Levitt telling him, "We at Grey decided to follow in your distinguished footsteps and publish our own point of view about global marketing."[17] Levitt responded to Grey's "Global Vision with Local Touch" campaign, calling it "a masterpiece—a persuasively argued and beautifully presented statement. . . . You did it again—and you treated me nicely, which I appreciate."[18]

In addition to advertising firms, manufacturers also utilized Levitt's argument to reimagine how they could market goods for international markets. For example, the president of the Stuart McGuire shoe company wrote to Levitt saying, "you really have hit the nail on the head. . . . I called our merchandise people in, gave them copies of it and spent two hours yesterday talking about the concept."[19] He went on to apply the themes of the article to his own industry: "In our business, we need to develop basic shoes that people all over the world will like . . . find the cheapest place to make them on a standardized sizing system and develop the most efficient distribution network. . . . The only shoe today that really is 'global' in design is the Kung-Fu from the People's Republic of China. You stimulated our thinking to figure out a way to make this available to the masses in the world."[20] Similarly, after reading the "Globalization of Markets," the president of the Regina Company, Earl W. Seitz, wrote Levitt asking for advice about how to expand their international vacuum and small appliance business beyond South Africa, Greece, Saudi Arabia, and the Philippines where they already had a presence, asking if Levitt could suggest "any companies that . . . can help us prepare an international marketing plan."[21]

Levitt also leveraged his connections within business to actively and aggressively self-promote his marketing philosophy and vision of global markets. In 1983 Levitt had copies of the newly published *The Marketing Imagi-*

nation sent to presidents, CEOs, vice presidents of marketing, and chairmen of the board at many of the largest corporations in the U.S. and around the world, including American Airlines, Bank of America, Coca-Cola, Firestone, Ford, General Mills, McGraw-Hill, Monsanto, Nabisco, the Washington Post, Woolworths, and many others.[22] George Weissman, chairman of the board at Philip Morris, called *The Marketing Imagination* "a superb book" that "upgrades a changing discipline," while the vice president for marketing at Hallmark Cards appreciated that Levitt has "some interesting thoughts about the world of marketing."[23] The deputy secretary of commerce, Clarence J. Brown, who also received a copy, called the book "very good."[24] In addition, Levitt wrote to his editor at Free Press, Robert Wallace, suggesting a list of "people that might be contacted with suggestions that they buy large quantities of *The Marketing Imagination* for distribution to their clients or employees," and a letter to his associate editor asking that he send copies to people on his list "of influential people whom I feel would be willing to give a statement on the manuscript."[25] Levitt asked his editor to send a copy to the senior editor of *Building Supply News*, who, he said, "is doing an article on me."[26] Reporting back on his presentation at the General Books Sale Conference, Robert Wallace recounted that he "conveyed the theme of 'imagination' as the central focus of your career. The sales reps are excited and think they will get the books in the stores for us."[27]

It might be tempting to explain the profound impact of Levitt's writing about globalization simply in terms of an opportune idea arriving at the right time and place, made all the more powerful because it was penned by an author who possessed an uncanny ability to market his own vision of globalization. An important part of understanding the impact of Levitt's ideas, and therefore what globalization came to mean, requires taking seriously the fact that Levitt's views on globalization did not simply originate in his own head before migrating into the business world. Rather, they were produced, reproduced, and circulated within highly influential apparatuses of knowledge production—most notably the business school, and Harvard Business School in particular. Focusing exclusively on Levitt as the iconoclastic marketer of globalization, in other words, loses sight of—as does most marketing theory more generally—the question of reproduction.

Reproducing the Global Imaginary

Establishing globalization as a prominent marketing imagination did not take place within the vacuum of Levitt's academic writing. Rather, the widespread success of Levitt's global imaginary was possible because it fulfilled a specific need. On the one hand, the American business community felt pressured by the rapid and unexpected success of high-quality, low-cost Japanese automobiles and electronics entering American markets during the 1970s and early 1980s (Takeuchi 2004). This occurred against the backdrop of a decade of economic stagnation, recession, and a crisis of domestic consumption. Levitt's argument also proved timely for managers of large multinationals who, during the 1980s, were "seeking good arguments to restore central headquarters control over their far-flung, decentralized empires" and used the language of "global marketing programs" to recentralize corporate control (Quelch and Deshpande 2004, 2). Levitt's argument was also able to spread so rapidly because of the particular material conditions of knowledge production in which he was writing.

Within the business world during the 1980s business school education, and the knowledge produced within these institutions, played an increasingly important role in shaping corporate practices. By 1983, the number of people receiving an MBA was at an all-time high. More and more business schools were prioritizing academic research, which made its way into curricular offerings. And, finally, ideas produced within business schools were traveling into the business world through the outsized role of management gurus and practitioner-focused academic journals. Levitt not only actively marketed his global imaginary to these large practitioner audiences, as seen in the previous section, but could do so because he wrote from within the context of the Harvard Business School and the vast apparatus of knowledge production the institution constructed around itself. Levitt's writing on globalization not only appeared in the highly influential *Harvard Business Review* but permeated the case studies written at Harvard, which, in turn, were used in business education around the world. It was this particular conjuncture of knowledge production that allowed Levitt's global marketing imaginary to travel far beyond Soldiers Field and influence all corners of the business world.

Business Schools and Gurus

The rise of marketing as an academic field is closely entwined with the rapid expansion of business school education during the second half of the twentieth century, a time in which business school enrollments expanded at an astonishing rate. The first master's degree in business was awarded by Dartmouth College in 1902. By 1922 there were 147 business schools, but demand vastly outpaced supply. Harvard Business School, for example, started in 1908 as a pilot program of fifty-nine students; thirteen years later it capped enrollment at three hundred students per year (Daniel 1998, 70–71). Business schools grew particularly fast after World War II as many older students, returning on the GI Bill, sought more practical and readily applicable education. In 1955, 42,812 students earned BAS and 3,280 earned MAS in American business schools; by 1975 these numbers reached 143,171 (a 334 percent increase) and 42,492 respectively (a 1,299 percent increase) (Starkey and Tiratsoo 2007, 17). By the end of the twentieth century, nearly one in every 250 Americans had an MBA (Daniel 1998, 15). In addition to training ever-larger incoming classes, business schools also established themselves during the second half of the century as sites of rigorous academic knowledge production. Over a short period of time, business schools transformed themselves from institutions for training business managers into highly productive domains of knowledge activity, providing the business world with its own theories, terminologies, expertise, scientific models, trained professionals, and visionary prophets.

During the first half of the twentieth century, business education and curricula remained comparatively unstandardized, often focusing on teaching practical skills. Consequently, business education was rarely a prerequisite for full integration into the business world—which, during this period, could still be accessed largely through personal connections and apprenticeship and, unlike medicine, law, and the clergy, was widely seen as a profession not needing academic training. During the 1950s, however, this view began to change. The Carnegie and Ford Foundations, for example, actively promoted and standardized business education and sought to develop it into a "systematic expert knowledge with a sound theoretical foundations" by improving the "faculty, curricula, students, and research," and equating the training of managers and business professionals as integral to the fight against the Soviet Union (Khurana 2007, 240, 246–47). Both the Carnegie and Ford Foundations published independent reports in 1959 expressing concern that business education "lacks a well-defined base or well-knit internal structure" (Pierson 1959, ix; see also Gordon and Howell 1959). To address these problems, the Carnegie and Ford reports recommended business schools increase their academic rigor and do more to align themselves with the core academic mission of the university.

The Carnegie report, for example, suggested that the "many less gifted students" interested in "secretarial science, elementary bookkeeping, or other routine procedures" should pursue their education "on a part-time basis in evening and extension programs, industry trade schools, and the like" (Pierson 1959, x). In contrast, business schools should establish themselves as rigorous academic programs "concentrate[ing] on the things they are uniquely qualified to do," namely applying "general knowledge and scientific method to significant issues of business policy," including the publication of scientific research (Pierson 1959, x–xi). The Ford Foundation similarly reported that if "the business school belongs in the university, then research belongs in the business school" (Gordon and Howell 1959, chapter 7). The authors argued the business world needed research that is "more analytical," develops "a more solid theoretical underpinning," and utilizes "a more sophisticated methodology" (Gordon and Howell 1959, 377).

These philanthropic foundations placed considerable resources behind standardizing curricular offerings around these principles. Starting in the early 1950s, the Ford Foundation engaged in a robust effort to "infuse scientific theory, methods, and analysis" into "the research agenda, doctoral education, and teaching approaches" in American business education, including experimenting with trial programs at Carnegie Mellon, Harvard, Columbia, Chicago, and Stanford. It also created a year-long training program for business faculty to receive training in advanced statistical methods from MIT mathematics professors, and hosted summer workshops for faculty around the country to learn the latest methodological and statistical developments (Gordon and Howell 1959, 384; Wilkie and Moore 2003, 126). The Ford Foundation encouraged program attendees to leverage their training as a springboard for persuading colleagues to adopt business school curricula that reflected these values (Porter and McKibbin 1988, 57). The success of these programs became evident by the early 1960s when many of the scholars attending Ford Foundation programs wrote the foundational books on the use of statistical modeling in marketing (Wilkie and Moore 2003, 127).

By the early 1980s, business schools had firmly established themselves as the primary gateway into the upper echelons of the business world. However, as this occurred, there was a growing mandarinism among business school faculty. In an unpublished article "The Immiseration of Marketing in the Academy," Levitt observed,

> The world of the marketing academician is a miserable mess. It is filled with irrelevance, triviality, drift, boredom and, worst of all, pretention. It parades with unctuous seriousness concepts without content, theories without context, paradigms without practical value, and methodologies without merit. For what it lacks in intelligence it makes up with ignorance.... The guiding principle of marketing scholarship should be to inform the profession by doing solidly intelligent work that guides and helps practice . . . using tools and concepts from other fields that are usefully appropriate to the world as it is, not what is dreamed as it might be or ought to be, and especially using one's own mind, not just somebody else's computer or a fanciful foreign paradigm. Much clarity and progress will be made if we then attack each problem with the passion of the scientist and the precision of the artist.[28]

As evidence, Levitt points to the split in the American Marketing Association between educators and practitioners. He could have also pointed out that, by the 1980s, most academic business journals, including those in the field of marketing, were targeted almost exclusively toward a scholarly audience, contained few nonacademic contributors, and were steeped in "scientific perspectives" (Wilkie and Moore 2003, 132).

As a counterpoint to this dominant trend within academic scholarship, there also emerged during the 1980s the new figure of the management guru. While business schools rewarded those engaged in grand theorizing and scientific findings, corporate managers were looking for simple ideas that could help them take decisive actions within the business world; rather than abstract analyses about the complexity of the world, managers were looking for "prophets" (Huczynski 2006, 203). Unlike the prototypical business school professor, management gurus have charismatic personalities and are often "bred out of the great business schools" including Harvard, Stanford, and MIT (Kennedy 2002, xi). Marketing gurus began playing an outsized role in the business world starting in the early 1980s, at the same time American businesses were feeling the threat of highly successful Japanese firms. In this context, management gurus offered pithy insights into how individual managers could move complex corporations and cultivate leadership qualities. Often traveling through a life cycle of splashy *Harvard Business Review* articles, a best-selling book, and then very well-compensated speaking and consulting tours, management gurus doled out strategies to managers about how to overcome pressing business problems (Kennedy 2002, xx). The first book in this genre arrived in 1982 when two consultants from McKinsey, Peters and Waterman, published *In Search of Excellence*, which, a year after its publication, had sold more books than any other except the 1972 *Living Bible* (Micklethwait and Wooldridge 1996, 6; Clark and Salaman 1998, 140; Evans 2000, chapter 4). The management gurus embodied a vision of the corporation as an "imagined community . . . integrated through shared beliefs, mutuality, consensus," managed by a heroic leader (who was also a "strategist" and "savior"), and engaged in an "'epic' narrative" of a "perilous journey" through "contested terrain to achieve ultimate salvation" (Clark and Salaman 1998, 154–55).

Theodore Levitt, widely recognized as "Harvard's most respected marketing guru" (Wooldridge 2011, 271; see also Kennedy 2002), is notable for being one of only a very small handful of marketers to reach such status. Levitt follows a formula similar to those of the other gurus of his time—"Globalization of Markets" was first published in *Harvard Business Review*, then included in a best-selling book, which launched Levitt into positions as a consultant and board member. The essay was written by someone with elite business school credentials yet did not assume an academic audience. This piece also valorizes the individual marketer as the one who—by imagining globalization differently—might save the company from the failures of existing marketing strategies. Like other management gurus, Levitt identifies corporate change as occurring when individual business leaders step back and reimagine the world around them.[29]

The rise of American business schools, and the distinctive role they play in both incubating a cadre of business gurus and training professional marketers, is an important part of the story of how Levitt's formulation of globalization spread so rapidly. This story also includes the fact that Harvard Business School is a particularly influential site within which to produce knowledge about the business world. In addition to housing the widely read *Harvard Business Review*, it also develops and publishes the majority of case studies used in business school instruction around the world.

Harvard Business School

Harvard Business School is one of the oldest and most prestigious business schools in the world. A former managing editor of the *Harvard Business Review* went so far as to call it "probably the most powerful private institution in the world" (Ewing 1990, 3)—a demonstration of such impressive hubris and bravado that, facticity aside, demonstrates the kind of deference the institution demands. In addition to a large endowment, impressive faculty, long scholarly tradition, and a widely recognizable brand, Harvard Business School plays an outsized role in producing academic knowledge within the business world. Harvard Business School was early to embrace—and prioritize—academic research as central to its academic offerings. For example, in 1911 the business school established the Bureau of Business Research to collect qualitative data on various businesses and industrial sectors, providing empirical data about distribution patterns and operating expenses. These data were then used in various research projects and classroom activities (Copeland 1958, 208–24). By the mid-1950s, the business school was already adopting steps to encourage its faculty to engage in formal research. Rather than leaving research to the domain of individual faculty interest, Harvard Business School developed mechanisms for funding research (with money coming from the government, philanthropic organizations, or members in the business community) and helped ensure that research was materially supported through the creation of institutional centers, dedicated staff, and reduction of teaching loads (Copeland 1958, chapter 8).

This attention to empirical data collection, and an interest in making business education more empirical, scientific, and readily applicable, gave rise to the case method of business instruction. First introduced in Dean Gay's 1912 Commercial Organization class—precursor to the course later titled "Marketing" (Copeland 1958, 256)—Harvard's case method revolves around specific examples from the business world. Case studies ask students to imagine themselves as business practitioners, taking concepts learned in the classroom and applying them to specific questions facing a corporation—placing students "in the shoes of high-level managers and CEOs" (Datar, Garvin, and Cullen 2010, 240). A case study presents students with a business problem that needs to be solved, providing an overview of the corporation (its history, product lines, and the dilemma it faces) as well as an appendix containing relevant information (profit margins, images of product lines, operational diagrams, etc.). The aim of this method of instruction is not for students to arrive at a predetermined correct answer, but rather to argue and justify their approach to those in the class.[30]

During the first decade of their use at Harvard, most cases were so-called armchair cases, pulled together from published secondary material. However, starting in the 1920s Harvard Business School introduced the "field case."[31] Drawing upon the institution's many connections in the business world, Dean Wallace B. Donham tasked the Harvard Bureau of Business Research with developing cases rooted in firsthand interviews and experiences with specific corporations (Copeland 1958, 227–38). In a demonstration of his commitment to field-based knowledge, Dean Donham sent four researchers to General Electric Company in Schenectady, New York, to conduct interviews and get a working knowledge of the plant before returning to write a series of cases studies (Copeland 1958, 227–38). By the mid-1920s, the case study method had become the pedagogical backbone of a Harvard Business School education (Ewing 1990, 23). For example, future president of the World Bank James Wolfensohn (chapter 4) credits the case study method with shaping his intellectual world while a student at Harvard Business School in the late 1950s:

> I could enter the world of steel, airlines, or banking, express my views and spend billions of dollars on investments or make decisions about marketing programs. This gave all of us the chance to experience business in a compressed way, to test our skills, analytical capacities, negotiating capabilities, and persuasive powers. We had the opportunity to live a life—*albeit an imaginary life*—that covered a wider range of experiences than a person would encounter in decades of business. (2010, 72, emphasis added)

Less than ten years after adopting the case study method, Harvard Business School began publishing and selling case books, which were rapidly adopted in business schools around the country (Copeland 1958, 259). By the 1950s, and with funding from the Ford Foundation, Harvard Business School hosted the Summer Case Writing Program, which not only increased the number of cases being written but improved the methodologies, enhanced distribution, and trained many people from across a variety of institutions in the creation and use of case studies (Copeland 1958, 227–38). By the late 1980s, Harvard Business School had created a vast case-writing enterprise, and was selling roughly 2–2.5 million cases annually (Ewing 1990, 14).[32]

In 1983, the year Levitt published "The Globalization of Markets," the Harvard Business School course catalog described the case method to prospective students in these terms:

> MBA students confront over 800 cases during their two years at HBS. Through daily exposure to cases, the students learn not only to differentiate one situation from another and to recognize important components in each situation,

but also to search out the unique in the situation at hand . . . the case method requires the student to learn by doing, to realize that decision making under real conditions is not an exact science, that decision making under conditions of uncertainty does not produce the precise results that academic theory suggests. This process makes a student's education more of a personal experience: an intense, exciting, absorbing involvement in personal growth.[33]

The aim of Harvard Business School is to produce managers, training them at the very beginning of their study to be decision makers capable of impressing their vision upon the corporate world. In this way, the case method is designed not to emphasize skilled interpretation or theorization of intractable complexity, but rather to instill the tools needed to take action. As a pedagogical method, it assumes that the world can be presented as factually known—as presentable within a brief synopsis—leaving the business students-cum-managers not to debate the meaning of the world but rather to imagine possible solutions to an already knowable and documented problem. The case method trains students, in other words, to take the world as given and develop new ways of acting upon it.[34]

During the 1980s, more and more case studies were written that trained students to think of themselves as managers of global corporations. The first Harvard case on the topic of globalization was published in 1985 and asked students to implement a global marketing strategy for a reticent West German chemical company specializing in adhesive products (Dolan 1985). Since then, more than 160 cases have been written directly on questions of globalization, asking students to examine how companies as varied as General Electric, Eli Lilly, Daewoo, Acer, Swatch, Red Bull, Cargill, Florida orange growers, 7-Eleven, the NBA, and Starbucks should market themselves within a global context. The case "Perspectives on Globalization" provides students a varied collection of writings on globalization—from Fareed Zakaria to Kenichi Ohmae, Theodore Levitt, Dani Rodrik, George Soros, and others—as a venue to discuss the relationship between globalization and democracy, looking specifically at the question of child labor (Huang 2002). Over the past three decades, many of these marketing case studies have encouraged students to enact the part of high-level marketing executives operating within the context of a global market. The self-evident existence of a global market is built into the assumption of these cases, as is a faith that students' cultural and social knowledge, and the ideas learned in business school, are sufficient to develop successful business strategies and marketing campaigns anywhere in the world.

In terms of institutional brand, by the early 1990s Harvard Business School had clearly begun marketing itself as the premier place to train students for management positions within global corporations. For example, the school's newly designed 1992 catalog promises students "opportunities to develop knowledge of contemporary issues through involvement with the school's increasingly international community," while boasting a "global network" of alumni and a faculty and student body that "has significant experience living, working, and studying outside their home country."[35] About its curriculum, the school offers courses that "are informed by research conducted on a global scale and through educational partnerships with institutions in other countries."[36] In 1993, Harvard president Neil Rudenstine described how "changes in the global economy" were making it necessary for the business school to appreciate "the growing importance of international perspectives," and that "the School's publishing organization" was central to "delivering the School's intellectual capital to managers, students, and scholars around the world" (1993, 38).

In addition to the production of case studies and the training of students, the *Harvard Business Review* is another important component of Harvard Business School's extensive apparatus of knowledge production. During the 1980s, the *Review* translated ideas produced within the business school to both academic and practitioner audiences. Started in 1922 as a "little gray magazine" with only a few thousand subscribers (Ewing 1990, 213), the *Harvard Business Review* only became a powerhouse decades later. Between 1947 and 1985, circulation increased from 10,000 to 243,000, reprint sales grew from a few thousand to 2.5 million, and the demand for advertising grew from a few pages to 433 pages, as the publication turned from an economic liability—requiring a $100,000 bailout from the business school in 1949—to a venture that turned $2 million in annual profits for the school by the mid-1980s (Ewing 1990, 214–15). Much of this growth was due not only to the growing role of business schools but also to the specific editorial efforts to make the *Harvard Business Review* accessible and interesting to business practitioners themselves. In the field of marketing, for example, the *Harvard Business Review*, along with other journals including *Chain Store Age*, *Tide of Advertising and Marketing*, *Advertising Age*, *American Marketing Journal*, and others, played a crucial role in conveying new academic thinking about marketing to a wider business audience (Applbaum 2004, 186–87).

Levitt was particularly attracted to *Harvard Business Review*'s dual mission, publishing in this venue extensively and becoming the publication's most-published author (Kennedy 2002, 140).[37] Two years after the publication of "The Globalization of Markets," Levitt was appointed editor, a post he held until 1989. During this time he changed the format of the journal even further, placing the consumer at the forefront of how the journal presented itself.[38] To do so, he introduced shorter articles, covered a wider range of topics, and included a "New Yorker-style cartoon" with the aim of making the journal more "reader-friendly" and "accessible" to a "readership composed of top business leaders" ("Professor Theodore Levitt" 2006). He is quoted as having said, "If people don't read what you write, then what you write is a museum piece" (Hindle 2008, 264).

Given that the term "globalization" was popularized within American business schools, circulated within their journals, and taught in their case studies, it is not entirely surprising that business schools have themselves engaged in their own global marketing strategies. Today, one can attend almost any business school in the world and get a curriculum comparable to the one pioneered at Harvard. In this context, business education has itself become a global commodity. Not only are there more business schools in more countries than ever before, but academic institutions increasingly see themselves as competing against each other in a global market.[39] Within many Western countries, the dramatic cuts in public funding of higher education resulted in universities investing in business schools as a revenue source, with international students playing a key role in offsetting flagging domestic enrollments (Onzoño and Carmona 2007, 25–28). As Levitt would applaud, many schools are placing students and consumers at the center of their curricular reforms and marketing strategies. Rather than exclusively offering two-year degrees designed around a fixed curriculum, many business schools are designing curricula around greater flexibility and online instruction to attract part-time and evening learners. Some schools are competing for students by introducing one-year degrees and offering a wide range of management degrees other than the MBA (Onzoño and Carmona 2007, 23–24, 28). As a result, around the world—"with the possible exception of parts of Africa"— business schools are now found in most countries and have become "woven into higher education, the business system and the culture" (Starkey and Tiratsoo 2007, 15).

Conclusion: Globalization as a Marketing Imagination

It is commonly observed that during the mid-1980s, and thanks to Levitt's provocative article, globalization rapidly became part of the "common vocabulary" of business schools in the United States and around the world (Quelch and Deshpande 2004, 9). Such observations, however, need to be situated within a longer history of business education, the growing cultural and economic importance of business schools, and the role that certain individuals and institutions played in promoting and spreading global-speak throughout the business world (and eventually into the social sciences). Theodore Levitt not only reproduced the concept of globalization but, as an important intermediary between the academic and the business worlds, actively worked to spread globalization as a marketing imagination at a time when larger portions of the business world were being schooled in a common curriculum. While the professionalized practices of marketing, the centrality of the marketing concept, and the facticity of an imagined global market are now widely accepted within the business world, they were not always so.

Yet it is not entirely clear if markets are global in the ways Levitt suggested, or if imagining markets as global is even a useful marketing strategy for corporations. Since the publication of "The Globalization of Markets," a chorus of critics has shed doubt on Levitt's claim that a convergence of preferences is taking place, suggesting that it might not make sense to sell the same products in all markets (see, for example, Quelch 2003; Ghemawat 2004). During the twenty-year anniversary of "The Globalization of Markets," Tomkins observed that rather than a convergence of taste, in actuality people "around the world started demanding more local sovereignty and more protection for their cultural identities" (2003, 14). Some corporations that adopted global strategies have since switched management teams in response to slowing sales. In 2000, for example, the new CEO of Coca-Cola, Douglas Daft, wrote in the *Financial Times* that his company planned to return to its past as a "multi-local" company. He wrote, "We were operating as a big, slow, insulated, sometimes even insensitive 'global' company and we were doing it in a new era when nimbleness, speed, transparency and local sensitivity had become absolutely essential to success" (Tomkins 2003, 14). Similarly, by 1995—just a few years after its Levitt-inspired British Airways campaign—Saatchi & Saatchi saw its stock lose 98 percent of its value and the shareholders pushing out the Saatchi brothers (Micklethwait and Wooldridge 1996, 221).

However, debating whether Levitt was right or wrong about globalization misses the fact that Levitt was himself always somewhat ambivalent about the facticity of globalization. A careful reading of "The Globalization of Markets" reveals considerable confusion about whether Levitt thinks the world is round, flat, or round-imagined-as-flat. In other words, the primary contribution of Levitt's reimagining of markets was the creation of a powerful "heuristic"—one that does not describe the world but rather empowers corporate managers to think about (and therefore act upon) the world differently (Tedlow and Abdelal 2004).

Global markets, as Theodore Levitt describes them, do not actually exist—they must be actively produced and reproduced. The first step in creating global markets, however, is for corporate leaders to imagine the globalization of markets as already under way and inevitable. Levitt's global imaginary, therefore, makes it possible for marketing practitioners to approach the world as if it were already a single market, and already inhabited by individual consumers desiring the products that the global firm is selling (even if these future consumers do not already know it). As such, the global imaginary Theodore Levitt produced is real not because it accurately describes the world but rather is real in its effects.

Take, for example, the 1993 Harvard Business School case that asks students to reflect upon Harlequin Enterprises' efforts to sell romance novels in Poland (Quelch and Laidler 1993; Laidler and Quelch 2000). Rather than creating a series of books with Polish characters and themes—that is, catering to a national market—Harlequin embraced the logic of globalization by deciding to merely translate its already written novels into Polish. In practice, however, the company found that there was little convergence in taste around, or desire for, this particular product. Thus, to sell its romance novels in Poland, the company actively created a global market where none actually existed, a task that included the costly strategies of purchasing ads to run during reruns of *Dynasty* and *The Cosby Show*, creating a Harlequin talk radio show, importing Valentine's Day (which included hanging a gigantic heart from the Palace of Culture), hosting Readers Parties, and sponsoring cultural events. The managing director of the Polish subsidiary described her advertising strategy thus: "We want to be the experts on love. We want to be called upon to judge the best love songs and the beauty contests" (quoted in Applbaum 2000, 266). In short, there was not already a convergence of taste within Poland—that is, a Western consumer market with Western conceptions of love and romance did not already exist. Instead, this market had to be actively created. The aim of Harlequin's marketing team was nothing short of actively working to "influence the entire cultural framework for thinking about love, beauty, and romantic relationships" (Applbaum 2000, 265). While the Harvard Business School case study details Poland's demographics and Cold War history, and overviews Harlequin's product line, distribution strategy, (foreign) competition, advertising strategy, and consumer research the materials do not include a discussion of Poland's indigenous literary culture, its strong Catholic history and social values, or its cultural politics of vibrant anti-Soviet resistance. Instead, the case treats Poland as simply a once-closed market in the process of opening to the global market. At the heart of this case study, students are placed in the middle of a disjuncture between an image of an already existing global market and the reality of the hard work needed to bend markets toward a convergence of taste.

This does not mean, however, that Levitt's argument about globalization is incorrect or misguided (unless, of course, one reads his claims about globalization as merely descriptive). Rather, if one reads his essay as imagining that which does not yet exist, then Levitt's argument becomes important in its effects—namely, helping to train a generation of marketers and managers to be confident that romance novels will inevitably sell in Poland, if only one markets them successfully. Levitt's global imaginary reassures marketing practitioners engaged in the arduous, costly, and economically risky task of creating global markets for their products. He offers a conceptual framework that rejects the "inconvenient theories of disparate cultural traditions" in favor of a framework that assumes the inevitable flattening out of all "obstacles created by political, economic, and cultural differences" (Applbaum 2000, 265). As such, the hard and labor-intensive task of reproducing global markets first requires that marketing managers already possess "a consumption-led universalizing paradigm" in which they strongly "believe in innate universal psychological tendencies that transcend local culture" and that these tendencies "can be tapped safely" in ways that circumvent "particularistic patterns of behavior" that might otherwise threaten "marketing standardization and firm globalization" (Applbaum 2000, 275). Imagining markets as they really are—as highly heterogeneous, hierarchical, exclusionary, and constituted as entwined parochial worlds—would make it difficult to justify the considerable efforts needed to produce a global market where none actually exists.

Levitt's account of globalization is often presented as the first successful attempt to clearly define globalization. Its actual brilliance, however, lies in the conceptual flattening of the world so that it can be imagined as global. Levitt presents lived heterogeneity and contested regimes of meaning making—that is, worldliness—as that which can (and must) be ignored in the ultimate pursuit of a global market that, on its own, does not yet exist.

It is important to note that Levitt's analysis depends upon compartmentalizing the production of meaning exclusively within the economic domain. For Levitt, marketing is about the production of meaning—the creation of imaginaries, campaigns, and products that resonate and speak to the deepest, hidden desires of humans. Marketing gives new meaning to the things around us. Marketing's power lies in its ability to transform cars from "means of transportation" into "symbols of freedom, status and power"; it translates the immediate needs of "food, clothing, transportation, etc." into goods that fulfill "wider social and spiritual needs for belonging and meaning" (Grant 1999, 404). In the hands of a visionary, marketing also transforms contested, heterogeneous, national markets into global ones. However, while Levitt understands himself to be "functioning in this realm of meanings," he nonetheless assumes that the production of new meaning takes place exclusively within a hermeneutically sealed economic domain (Grant 1999, 400). In other words,

> Levitt invokes the standard expedient of neo-classical economics, the isolationist view of business. The focus of business is purely economic, and the economic is sealed off in hermetic isolation from every other area of life. With this, Levitt has the best of both worlds: he can insist that marketing, particularly in its advertising mode, must be seen to occupy the domain of meaning, but, at the same time, he can absolve marketers of responsibility for the meanings they purvey because their focus is only commercial after all. (Grant 1999, 401)

The vast academic literature on globalization that emerged a decade after Levitt's article often contains this very same contradiction. On the one hand, globalization is presented as a self-evident, inevitable reality resulting from changing technology and economic practices. On the other hand, the practice of deploying the term "globalization" allows various practitioners—including those within the business world—to do things to the world that are not otherwise possible. While reproducing the world as global starts in the business world, it rapidly spreads in unforeseen ways. For example, when the term "globalization" first arrived in the social sciences in the 1990s, it was used almost exclusively to describe specific economic and business practices. However, this new way of giving the world meaning could not be contained

FIG. 3.1 Unattributed and untitled illustration (Karen Watson),
Harvard Business Review, May–June 1983, 95.

to scholarship but, for reasons explained in the following chapters, soon shaped the academic world itself.

In conclusion, those interested in examining globalization from the point of view of reproduction should start with the recognition that Levitt's landmark essay, "The Globalization of Markets," is less a description of the world than a very successful marketing imaginary produced within a given conjuncture, for a particular audience and purpose. The practice of imagining the world as consisting of individuals desiring new products, and open to receiving these well-priced and well-marketed goods, became the condition under which marketing professionals, business leaders, and owners of capital actively pursued the hard work of exporting Western-made commercial goods to very different, heterogeneous, and largely unknown markets around the world. Levitt's global imaginary, therefore, is less a description of the world than an artist's sketch about how to fashion a yet nonexistent global market.

To see what this artistic rendition might look like, one can consult the uncredited illustration included alongside the original version of "The Globalization of Markets" published in the *Harvard Business Review* (figure 3.1). The top half of the illustration is an architecturally dense world—a claustrophobic landscape bursting with different iconic buildings from around the world (a pagoda, a Dutch round barn, the Tower of Pisa, two staggered yet identical renderings of New York's Flatiron Building, a thatched Pacific Island structure on stilts, etc.) all against the backdrop of a starry night sky, a half moon, and the satellite Voyager orbiting the earth. Right below this complex, dense, and cosmic world is a stark, geometrically precise world composed of a long hallway of pillars and arches, in the middle of which two businessmen in dark suits and briefcases meet. Their heads are cocked as if in negotiation. This transaction is not possible in the disjointed world above. The meeting of two businessmen instead takes place in a hypothetical subterranean world. Upon a closer look, one realizes that this lower world—with its pillars rising up to support the heterodox world above—actually exists only in the mind of a geometer; each angle is marked (a, b, c . . .), and the lines forming the hallway are actually geometrical abstractions pushing out into the horizon. Unlike the man and woman engaged in neighborly discussion in the shadows of the buildings above the transaction takes place unhindered within an imagined flat world. It is only in a placeless, imagined world that it becomes possible to conduct the business of a global market.

4 "Realities of the Global Economy"

A. W. Clausen and the Banker's Global Imaginary

Indeed, the message of the entire postwar period is abundantly
clear: Markets will be served. And being terribly prejudiced, I have
a personal preference for an active role for the commercial banking industry.
—A. W. CLAUSEN, "The Changing Character of Financial Markets in
the Postwar Period" (1980)

In 1983, Theodore Levitt mailed then president of the World Bank, Alden W.
Clausen, a copy of his most recent book, *The Marketing Imagination*. Clausen
replied to Levitt thanking him for the book, noting that it came at a pivotal
time and saying, "We have just embarked on determining the 'role of the
Bank' for the coming years and identifying our corporate strategy. The book
will help us form our thinking." Clausen went on to observe, "Harvard Business School has certainly produced some thought-provoking books recently,
and I'm pleased to add them to my library."[1] Clausen had only arrived at the
World Bank two years earlier, having left his job as president and CEO of the
world's largest commercial bank, Bank of America.[2] When he replaced Robert McNamara, Clausen's tenure did indeed mark a new corporate strategy
for the World Bank.[3] Clausen governed the institution during a time of considerable transformation in the world economy, exemplified most dramatically by high oil prices, skyrocketing inflation, deep economic recession, and
mounting debt across the Third World. How the Clausen Bank navigated
these changes was shaped by a fundamentally different vision of how the
world fits together. While McNamara enacted policies guided by a national

development imaginary, focusing on geostrategic stability, poverty reduction, and a world organized into a system of interconnected national economies, Clausen came from the world of high finance. A corporate banker who pioneered the rapid international expansion of Bank of America during the 1970s, Clausen brought with him the "strong conviction . . . from his years in business" that the world was now a global financial market, and that the World Bank was uniquely positioned to help countries "cope with the new realities of interdependence" in the world economy (Kraske et al. 1996, 224). In contrast to the vision of the world circulating within the McNamara Bank, Clausen and his people saw the world as a single, global market, with the World Bank tasked with assisting states to adapt to this new reality.

The banker's global imaginary introduced by Clausen meant that the World Bank began to focus less on development and the eradication of poverty, and instead saw peace and stability as resulting primarily from the free movement of money within a vastly interconnected global market. Rather than reengineering national economies to achieve national development, the Clausen Bank developed structural adjustment policies as a mechanism for requiring countries to constrain domestic spending in ways that met the demands of the global market. This chapter argues that the new policies adopted by the World Bank during the 1980s were not inevitable responses to the realities of economic stagnation and the crisis of Third World debt. Rather, structural adjustment, and the rate-of-return accounting it required, was based upon this fundamental reimagining of the world. The policies that followed from this banker's global imaginary had many profound effects, including the imposition of dramatic cuts to African higher education.

Reimagining the World as a Global Financial Market

In August 1980, U.S. presidential election watchers were already forecasting a Reagan victory, and both Carter and Reagan viewed Clausen as an acceptable choice to replace McNamara at the head of the World Bank (Kraske et al. 1996, 214). Robert McNamara visited A. W. "Tom" Clausen in California to encourage him to consider accepting the position. Clausen ultimately accepted the job explicitly planning not to "alter the direction, or redefine the mission" established by McNamara (Kraske et al. 1996, 215). At the time, few observers could predict that the choice of Clausen would prove a transformative moment for the World Bank.

Clausen joined an institution under siege from all sides. On the right, critics—including the Reagan administration—accused the World Bank of financial waste and economic interventionism. Because of McNamara's push to offer large, low-interest International Development Association loans to noncreditworthy nations, critics accused the World Bank of participating in a form of international welfare. Many conservative observers, including in the U.S. Treasury Department, greeted Clausen as a welcome change from McNamara, noting that Clausen's concern "with the bottom line" stood in stark contrast to his predecessor's willingness to "financ[e] socialism," subsidize the nationalization of energy companies, and fund programs focused on birth control, rural irrigation, and other projects (Scheibla 1981, 11). On the left, critics accused the World Bank of supporting authoritarian regimes and lending money for Cold War political calculations (Rowan 1981, 337–38).

Clausen joined this embattled institution from the world of high finance. He had graduated from University of Minnesota Law School in 1949 before taking an entry-level job with Bank of America in Los Angeles. When he started, Bank of America was a California-based operation that loaned almost exclusively to California residents and industries, including agriculture, wineries, real estate, defense, technology, and aerospace (Johnston 1990, chapter 5).[4] Clausen initially worked in the division responsible for lending money to semiconductor and computer companies in Silicon Valley, and quickly moved up to the ranks of vice president (1961) and senior vice president (1965). In 1966, being groomed for higher posts, he enrolled in Harvard Business School's Advanced Management Program, paid for by Bank of America. At Harvard, Clausen cultivated knowledge of international business increasingly required for those seeking to enter the top ranks at Bank of America (Johnston 1990, 76). It is likely that Clausen became familiar with Levitt's work during this time, given Levitt's active engagement with the Advanced Management Program and the fact that Clausen attended Harvard just six years after the publication of "Marketing Myopia."[5] After Harvard, Clausen returned to California and quickly moved through the ranks of executive vice president (1968), vice chairman of the board (1969), and eventually president and CEO in 1970.

During his thirty-year career at Bank of America, including a decade as president, Clausen participated in transforming the institution from a national bank to the largest commercial bank in the world. As early as the mid-1940s, Bank of America established itself as the largest bank in the U.S., focusing almost exclusively on domestic lending and demonstrating very little interest in pursuing overseas markets. For example, in 1947 Bank of America operated exclusively within the U.S., with the sole exception of a single branch in London (Clausen 1980, 90). During the 1960s, however, Bank of America began actively expanding its international presence, acquiring ownership stakes in fifty-seven foreign banks around the world, including in Canada, Brazil, Australia, Italy, and Japan (Mitchell 1970, 9).

Upon taking over the presidency, Clausen accelerated Bank of America's involvement in foreign capital markets, most notably reorganizing the bank's operating structure in ways that made it easier to lend large sums of money to foreign countries. The Bank of America that Clausen inherited was highly hierarchical, with most financial decisions still being hammered out in California. In 1974, however, Clausen established the World Banking Division, which divided the world into four units and tasked regional offices with overseeing lending and borrowing in their regions (Johnston 1990, 86). As investment opportunities within the United States remained largely stagnant or in decline throughout the 1970s, these regional offices gave Bank of America greater flexibility to court the growing supply of petrodollars in the Middle East and loan this money throughout the Third World (Johnston 1990, 87). Under Clausen's leadership, Bank of America continued purchasing foreign banks and financial institutions and, in doing so, gained even greater access to international markets. The purchase of a 30 percent share in the Luxembourg-based Bank for Credit and Commerce International, as well as an 80 percent share of Lebanon's Bank Chartouni, gave Bank of America greater access to capital markets in the Middle East ("Why They're Slowing Growth" 1975, 56). In the early 1970s, Bank of America was the first to loan the Soviet Union money at a variable interest rate, and was actively in contact with the People's Republic of China (Mitchell 1974, 14).

This strategy of internationalization proved so successful that, in the five short years from 1970 to 1975, Clausen had grown Bank of America's assets from $30 billion to $66 billion (Johnston 1990, 96). By the end of the 1970s, Bank of America had over one hundred branches, eight international offices, and sixty-one subsidiaries in seventy-seven countries (Clausen 1980, 90). While the American economy—and many economies around the world— suffered deep economic downturns during the 1970s, for the commercial banking sector this was a time of incredible growth and prosperity, a period of "go-go growth" during which time Bank of America grew "more than 55 percent!" (Clausen 1980, 90).

In his last months as president of Bank of America, Clausen (1980, 86) described his "thirty years as a commercial banker" in terms personifying the postwar economy. He wrote that Bank of America's

> shift toward a more international orientation reflected a profound reordering of the *global financial structure*. In place of compartmentalized national markets, the world was entering an era of highly integrated financial systems that overcame the old limitations imposed by distance and political divisions. This metamorphosis placed the evolving transnational markets on a collision course with some national governments, illustrating once again that changes in the financial environment owe as much to laws, regulations, and similar restraints as to *the basic forces of economics*. (Clausen 1980, 90, emphasis added)

In presenting a "global financial structure" as an extension of basic economic forces, Clausen imagined the world as defined by a conflict between a single global market and the many antiquated "compartmentalized national markets" that had failed to move beyond their "old limitations."

It was this banker's global imaginary that Clausen brought with him to the World Bank. For example, three months into his term, Clausen addressed the board of governors, acknowledging that as president of Bank of America he attended these joint annual meetings "as a guest" (Clausen 1986a, 3). Acknowledging that the "global economic situation has weakened" (3), Clausen nonetheless assured his fellow bankers that the financial health of the World Bank was still strong. He continued, describing the World Bank as a commercial bank largely devoid of a national development mandate. The World Bank was an institution simply facilitating a working relationship between "two fundamental constituencies . . . the borrowing and lending countries" (7). However, with the troubling "realities of the world economic scene today," Clausen recognized that the existing terms of this partnership required reconsideration:

> Many of our developing member countries are going to be confronted in the early years of the decade with the prospect of low rates of economic growth. Their problem is to find ways to *adjust* to those aspects of the *external economic situation — which they cannot change* — by taking actions to improve those *domestic economic factors which they can change*.
>
> Structural adjustment for these countries to *the realities of the global economy* means in practice more appropriate policy responses, more effective price incentives, improved market signals, increased export activity, and overall better use of both material and human resources. . . . The Bank will direct its

project and sector lending, and its wide range of technical assistance, to help our developing member countries make these structural adjustments. (1986a, 8–9, emphasis added)

In advocating for structural adjustment, Clausen defined the "realities of the global economy" as an external force to which national governments must respond, while situating bankers as uniquely capable of steering states through this newly turbulent water. Clausen concluded his presentation by asking all the World Bank's shareholders to "look around this great hall" populated with "the very collection of key economic and financial executives in the world" and saying, "[If] we in this room cannot get those actions underway, then I ask you who can?" (1986a, 20).

In imagining the world as a single global financial market, most effectively managed by bankers, Clausen explicitly rejected earlier visions of a world divided according to political differences, criticizing specifically those who—like the authors of the Brandt Report—saw a "rigid 'North-South' dichotomy" (Clausen 1986b, 39–40). In his 1982 address to the Yomiuri International Economic Society, Clausen expressed disdain for those "vast oversimplifications" that divide the world into regions, especially those that "create a bipolar concept of world economic dynamics" (39–40).[6] For Clausen, such "oversimplifications about global economic models" were particularly troubling given that they focused on politics rather than the rightful purview of the World Bank, namely "the health of the global economy" (39). In a muddled sort of Cold War–speak, Clausen then described the world not as "bipolar" (North-South) but rather "multipolar," containing eight poles—Western Europe, North America, Japan, Eastern Europe, "oil exporting countries in the Middle East," "newly industrialized nations," "great populous countries of Asia," and, finally, the "poverty-stricken countries of sub-Saharan Africa" (43). While acknowledging that nothing is "sacrosanct about the number eight," and welcoming others to complicate his model even further, Clausen nonetheless expressed his conviction that "the world's economic activity is truly global in nature" and "individual national economies are already far more genuinely interdependent than either their governments, or their people, realize" (48). In treating the global financial market as a self-evident fact (if only seen accurately as such by bankers), Clausen further argued that those who read human politics into the economic situation miss what is in fact taking place: "Labels and slogans, and buzz words and battle cries, are very human phenomena—and have their place—but . . . aren't very useful for disentangling complexity . . . [namely] the world economy today: a whole complicated ganglion of interdependent relationships and a very dynamic environment in which they are all interacting" (48). Clausen imagined a global economy of great complexity, but which could not be accurately understood unless one successfully rejects the otherwise human tendency to view the economy as a political phenomenon.[7] The World Bank, therefore, was not only positioned to help nations adapt to global financial markets but was also staffed with bankers and economists uniquely capable of seeing the world as it really is.

This vision of the World Bank as an apolitical institution—simply facilitating the transfer of capital and advising its clients within the context of a global market—became the terrain upon which the World Bank introduced a raft of new policies. At stake in Clausen's presidency, therefore, was not only the spread of neoliberal economic policies and ideologies (see Goldman 2005; Harvey 2005; Chang 2008), but also the grafting of a banker's global imaginary onto the now-mammoth apparatus of knowledge production created by McNamara. As the Clausen Bank reproduced a banker's vision of the world, the image of the world as a global financial market made it possible to fundamentally reshape the institution's knowledge production practices as well as its lending policies.

The World Bank Goes Global

There now is reason to believe that the world of the future will
be shaped as much by commercial and financial statesmen as by
diplomats and politicians.
—A. W. CLAUSEN, "The International Corporation" (1972)

Clausen's vision of the world as a single, global financial market informed all aspects of his presidency. For starters, he was fundamentally skeptical of McNamara's emphasis on national economic development as poverty reduction. Early in his tenure, Clausen confided in Mahbub ul Haq—the World Bank's director of policy planning and leading development economist— that poverty alleviation played little role in shaping his policy agenda and that he considered it a "thin veneer" (Kapur, Lewis, and Webb 1997, 336).[8] Clausen also replaced McNamara's chief economist, Hollis Chenery, with Anne Krueger—a "Milton Friedman neoliberal" who blamed national development failures on domestic causes, such as rent-seeking (Goldman 2005, 91; see also Krueger 1974). The Clausen Bank slowly purged many of the institution's career development economists, favoring economists more in line with a banker's global imaginary.[9]

The Clausen Bank also ramped up and radically redefined the policies of structural adjustment originally introduced by McNamara. During his final year at the World Bank, and shortly following the second oil shock, McNamara conceded that his poverty reduction agenda needed to be accompanied by structural economic changes as well (McNamara 1981b, 617; World Bank 1981b). McNamara used the term "structural adjustment," however, to encompass a wide range of modifications "in both national and international policies" (McNamara 1981b, 621; World Bank 1981b, 1; see also Stern and Ferreira 1997, 541). He argued that structural adjustment involved a "collective effort on the part of the world community" to change the underlying economic dynamics giving rise to the debt crisis, suggesting that a "global adjustment problem" required ensuring that deeply indebted countries reduce imports and expand exports but also, when possible, pursue "import substitution" within "domestic energy production" (McNamara 1981a, 621–22). He called for OPEC and OECD countries to donate more money for Official Development Assistance to help low-income countries "manage the adjustment process" without sacrificing social services (McNamara 1981a, 623). McNamara (1981a, 628) also argued that the World Bank should replace commercial banks as the primary vehicle for "recycling" the profits from oil exports back into developing economies.[10] In other words, for McNamara structural adjustment involved a full-scale transformation of both domestic and international economic policies in ways that could confront "the most fundamental development issue of all: the drive against absolute poverty" (1981a, 628). Along the lines of the Brandt Commission, he recommended a profound reordering of financial commitments between North and South. This proposal, however, gained little political traction, and might have led indebted countries to assume that financial assistance would be forthcoming, thereby contributing to higher levels of debt borrowing (Stern and Ferreira 1997, 542).

The departure of McNamara and Chenery, and the arrival of Clausen and Krueger, greatly changed the way the World Bank imagined structural adjustment. Clausen avoided sweeping discussions of structural adjustment, preferring instead to talk about specific adjustment plans, loans, or policies. Unlike McNamara, Clausen presented structural adjustment as bringing domestic policies in line with an already global market; global financial markets, for Clausen, could not be adjusted—they were facts. Intrinsically, economic policy within the Clausen Bank focused not on national development, or even "macroeconomic stabilization," but rather on helping countries address the "price distortions" resulting from wrongheaded domestic policies and, in doing so, "bring relative domestic producer prices into closer harmony with world prices" (Stern and Ferreira 1997, 543). Signaling a stark shift from a vision of structural adjustment still wedded to a national development imaginary, a banker's imaginary made it possible for the World Bank to see itself as merely encouraging countries to follow the will of an already global market.

In his 1982 presentation concerning the shared mission of the World Bank and commercial banks given before the International Monetary Conference (a convention of the world's top bankers), Clausen described the relatively new "economic policy dialogue" that the World Bank had begun, through what he called "'structural adjustment loans'" (1986c, 88). He reminded his audience that, "at the global level," the World Bank, IMF, and GATT worked together to "build an interdependent global economy," by encouraging "orderly monetary change," eliminating barriers to trade, and "develop[ing] the weaker parts of the global economy" (87). Commercial banks, he argued, were an important part of this work. Not only did "international commercial banking depend[] on the relatively integrated, dynamic, and peaceful world economy," but the "complementary relationship between the World Bank and commercial banks [was] a fact of global economic life" (87–88).

World Bank officials working on the issue of education shared this vision of the world as a global financial market that (when freed from price manipulation) could settle upon a natural global price. As the World Bank reorganized lending policies according to a banker's global imaginary, they found themselves needing to better understand the actual market price of education. To answer this question, they drew upon a concept developed within the American academy—human capital—as a means for measuring the rate of return on education. Human capital calculation made it possible, in other words, to measure whether education was accurately priced or needed greater exposure to market pressures in order to arrive at its price equilibrium. The application of rate-of-return accounting on education would result in dramatic cuts to universities across the formerly colonized world, including unleashing the devastation of structural adjustment upon African higher education.

Human Capital and the Rate of Return on Education

Structural adjustment policies introduced by the World Bank during the early 1980s required that governments cut expenditures to state services that did not demonstrate substantial economic return. This required determining the rate of return on all different kinds of aid programs, including funding for education. While the World Bank had long used the language of human capital to describe the general value of education, it was the Clausen Bank that developed new ways of calculating a specific monetary return on education, which could then be contrasted against its cost.

The language of human capital is found throughout World Bank publications corresponding with the institution's earliest interest in education. For example, in 1960—and in response to President Black's declaration about the economic importance of education—Staff Director Leonard Rist asked for a briefing on the latest academic debates about the economic benefits of education. His staffers provided him with "a synopsis of recent articles by Schultz, Lewis, Harbinson, Becker, and Renshaw" (Jones 2007, 34). However, under McNamara, economists within the World Bank used the term "human capital" as a placeholder for the general consensus that education yielded a positive, often long-term (and therefore largely unquantifiable) return on investment (Vawda et al. 2003, 645–47; Jones 2007). During the 1970s, the World Bank also used human capital analysis to explain examples of national economic decline and growing social inequality (Jones 2007, 247–48). Underperforming economies, for example, could be explained by a lack of human capital.

While human capital had an evolving and relatively loose meaning within the World Bank, in the decades after World War II a number of academics began developing an increasingly technical understanding of education's monetary value as human capital. Starting in the 1950s, neoclassical economists began returning to Adam Smith's brief references to education. In doing so, they sought to reimagine education not in terms of national development objectives but rather as individually owned fixed capital that, like machinery in a factory, yielded private returns for those risking the investment.[11] Economists at the University of Chicago and the Labor Workshop at Columbia University developed the concept of human capital in the late 1950s and 1960s. The Labor Workshop drew together leading labor economists including Jacob Mincer, Gary Becker, H. Gregg Lewis, Melvin Reder, and others who aspired to transform the academic field of labor economics from its "dominant Keynesian paradigm" into a discipline stocked with neo-classical economists (Heckman 2003). The project of remaking the discipline of labor economics around neoclassical premises drew from Jacob Mincer's seminal study using the concept of human capital to explain income inequality (Mincer 1958, 1962, 1974; see also Polachek 2008). Mincer's colleague Gary Becker further refined the relationship between formal education and human capital in his influential 1964 book, *Human Capital: A Theoretical and Empirical Analysis, with Special Emphasis on Education*, developing a theoretical model for calculating the relative human capital gained during on-the-job training, general life experience, and formal schooling.[12] In addition to Becker, Theodore Schultz—the University of Chicago economist who would go on to win the Nobel Prize in 1979 for his work in development economics—played an important role popularizing the concept in his 1960 presidential address at the American Economic Association (Schultz 1961). By 1971, he expanded his analysis to include calculating the rate of return on education (Schultz 1971). In the case of higher education, Schultz argued that driving down the cost of education, and therefore making the rate of return more favorable, required providing more consumer information about different institutions, increasing the consumer base by increasing access to student loans, expanding the numbers of private institutions, and generally encouraging an entrepreneurial relationship to higher education. He argued that such steps would help the education market more naturally establish the price of education (Schultz 1971, chapter 10). During the 1960s and 1970s, arguments about education as human capital spread rapidly within the academy and quickly entered the realms of economic and social policy (Jones 2007, 33).[13] On the one hand, human capital theory dovetailed with development and modernization theory in explaining how, within decolonizing countries, Western-inspired institutions could not only shape "the personal attributes—values, attitudes and dispositions—of individuals capable of leading their societies out from backwardness to progress," but also plant the seeds of economic growth (Jones and Coleman 2005, 32). The key difference, however, rested on a different conception of whether the state or individual should make the investment, and therefore yield the reward.

By the time Clausen replaced McNamara at the World Bank, there was growing concern over how much money Third World countries, and African governments particularly, were spending on higher education. In a ground-breaking study, the World Bank calculated that in sub-Saharan Africa the per-pupil cost of a university degree averaged one hundred times the cost of primary education, compared with twice the cost in industrialized countries (World Bank 1980, 46). To better calculate the rate of return on higher education, Clausen brought in George Psacharopoulos in 1981. Psacharopoulos's approach of measuring human capital in terms of wage differential would quickly "emerge[] triumphant" within the World Bank (Jones 2007, 93). Psacharopoulos—a University of Chicago–trained economist on faculty at the London School of Economics—had written extensively about the use of human capital analysis to calculate the rate of return on education, measured as the difference between the costs of education (either private costs borne by the individual or the public costs of government spending) compared to the benefits of education (either private benefit of increased wages or public benefit of increased tax income on higher wages) (Psacharopoulos with Hinchliffe 1973, chapter 2).[14] Psacharopoulos's own work aggregated the vast academic scholarship calculating the rate of return on education within national economies to develop an average rate of return across countries.

Working as a consultant for the World Bank in 1980, Psacharopoulos (1980a, 3) authored *Higher Education in Developing Countries: A Cost-Benefit Analysis*, which found that higher education offers a 15 percent return on investment, with personal incomes differing dramatically depending upon the degree earned.[15] With the addition of Psacharopoulos to the World Bank staff the following year, the institution began churning out a large number of reports (for example, Psacharopoulos, Tan, and Jimenez 1986; Kelly 1991; Noss 1991) that collectively called for "drastic reduction of higher education in Africa" in the "name of higher efficiency and a more egalitarian distribution of education resources" (Caffentzis 2000, 3).

In particular, the 1986 World Bank report *Financing Education in Developing Countries* famously calculated the relative rate of returns on primary, secondary, and tertiary education, concluding that primary education returns 28 percent, compared to 17 percent for secondary education, and 13 percent for higher education (Psacharopoulos, Tan, and Jimenez 1986, 7). Psacharopoulos et al. argued that, despite higher returns on primary education, developing countries tended to "heavily subsidize higher education at the expense of primary education" (1).[16] Drawing the calculation of relative rates of return from Psacharopoulos's 1985 academic article "Returns to Education: A Further International Update and Implications," this report called for "recovering the public cost of higher education" through increased tuition and redirecting government revenue toward primary and postprimary schooling (Psacharopoulos, Tan, and Jimenez 1986, 8).[17]

Whereas the McNamara Bank prioritized human capital in terms of training "manpower"—that is, a government developing a national workforce (imagined as masculine)—Psacharopoulos viewed education as simply a private, personal investment. In drawing this distinction between manpower planning and his preferred labor market analysis, Psacharopoulos argued that manpower planning requires first predicting the number of various experts a country needs and then building enough "redbrick universities" to train enough people with the "higher qualifications and university degrees" to fill these roles, even as the "majority of the population remained illiterate" (1991b, 461).[18] Labor market analysis, in contrast, emphasizes the efficiency of providing education, examines the cost of provision against its market benefit, encourages a transition from academic to "firm-based" training, rejects the claim that education is a "free good," and encourages the general privatization of education (Psacharopoulos 1991b). In other words, education becomes a commodity functioning within a market and with a measurable rate of return. As such, within a world imagined as a single global market, the World Bank came to treat higher education as an individual—rather than national—investment.

It should be noted that this reconceptualization of higher education as a private investment was also developed, within different yet parallel academic sites, as the cornerstone of a right-wing counterrevolution seeking to prevent the kind of social turmoil displayed on American campuses during the 1960s. Members of libertarian academic, policy, and philanthropic circles—including those closely tied to Irving Kristol, Charles Koch, John Olin, and the Scaife family—argued for slashing state university budgets and requiring students to pay for their own education. Doing so would recalibrate the students' "incentive structures" by making education a private investment rather than a public good (MacLean 2017, 104). This strategy sought to transform "state universities into dissent-free suppliers of trained labor, run with firm managerial hands and with little or no input from faculty, and at the lowest possible cost to taxpayers" (105).

The Effects of a Banker's Imaginary
on National Universities

One of the abiding impressions ... is the sense of loss, amounting
almost to grief, of some of the most senior professors in the older
African universities as they compare the present state of their
universities with the vigor, optimism and pride which the same
institutions displayed twenty or thirty years ago.
—TREVOR COOMBE, *A Consultation on Higher Education in Africa*
(1991)

The move toward calculating the rate of return on education encouraged the
World Bank to demand a substantial defunding of higher education as part
of structural adjustment policies imposed upon African countries. Countries
that experienced three or more structural adjustment loans between 1980
and 1986 saw per capita spending on education fall 11 percent, compared with
nonadjusting countries, where per capita expenditures on education doubled
during the same time (Caffentzis 2000, 11).

The World Bank criticized African countries for treating universities as
"sacred cows" that consumed "an undue amount of limited resources" and
demanded that African governments cut subsidies (Caffentzis 2000, 4). At
a 1986 meeting of African university vice chancellors in Harare, for example, World Bank officials announced that higher education in Africa "was a
luxury" and that many African countries would be "better off closing universities at home and training graduates overseas" (Mamdani 1993, 10). The
World Bank also claimed that it was "foolish" to fund universities unless
they could be made "profitable" (Mamdani 1993, 10). The emphasis on rate of
return also meant that the arts, humanities, and social sciences were hit particularly hard, as the World Bank characterized these disciplines as "market
unfriendly" and therefore largely "irrelevant" (Olukoshi and Zeleza 2004, 2).
By the mid-1990s, only 7 percent of the World Bank's education funding went
to higher education, compared to 50 percent a decade earlier (Polgreen 2007;
see also Coombe 1991). For African higher education, World Bank–imposed
austerity measures resulted in nothing short of a "starvation diet" (Ajayi,
Goma, and Johnson 1996, 144).

The structural adjustment of higher education, justified on the grounds
of human capital analysis, had a number of catastrophic effects on African
higher education. Spiraling inflation caused by currency devaluation made

education materials—including textbooks, journals, computers, and other basic infrastructure—prohibitively expensive and out of reach for most African universities (Caffentzis 2000, 4). As a result, the 1980s and 1990s became known as a time of "book famine," marked by a sharp decline in the "material intellectual base" needed to do academic work (Assié-Lumumba 2006, 10; see also Lawal 2007, 67). For example, Ghana's adoption of structural adjustment in the mid-1980s resulted in students living and studying in crowded living quarters and classrooms, a nationwide lack of professors, libraries reduced to "moribund, neocolonial scholarship of the 1950s and 1960s," low morale among students and teachers, continual student protests and state counterrepression, and curricula driven by a "creeping Westernism" containing "neocolonial thinking," alongside a "mushrooming of private colleges and universities" (Akurang-Parry 2007, 44–53). Once known as the Harvard of Africa, Makerere University followed the World Bank's proposals and engaged in a full-scale commercialization of the institution, which included dramatic cuts to government funding, followed by the rapid expansion of the fee-paying student body, the prioritization of professional programs, bone-cutting cuts in faculty wages and research infrastructures, and a system whereby individual departments competed against each other for students' tuition revenue.[19] As a result, Makerere was transformed from a university containing both "academic Faculties" and "professional Schools" into an institution almost entirely reduced to "vocationalisation" (Mamdani 2007, 42).

The failing and overcrowded infrastructure, limited access to teaching and research material, large class sizes, low pay, and dependency on foreign donors also affected the kinds of academic knowledge produced within African universities. Many African scholars lacked access to the materials required to produce academic work, leaving them dependent upon international agencies to "determine what can be studied, written, and voiced in the continent" (Federici 2000, 19).[20] The result has been more than two decades of a marketized model of African higher education, which "opened the door to a galloping consultancy culture" and "the NGO-ization of the university" (Mamdani 2011, 3–4). The most prominent senior African academics have largely been hired away by American and European institutions, leaving African universities "with young, inexperienced and insufficiently trained staff" and lacking in senior leadership and mentorship (Ajayi, Goma, and Johnson 1996, 152).[21] Furthermore, African universities remain heavily dependent on foreign aid, tuition from foreign students studying abroad, and philanthropic donors. Collaborations between African universities and the Euro-American academy tend to be "externally driven" and focus on establishing thin "institutional partnerships" rather than incorporating "local researchers into an externally driven project" (Mamdani 2011, 6–7). The structural adjustment of African universities has also meant that graduate training and academic publishing remain centralized in core universities, such that curricular and research priorities within African countries continue to be driven by major universities within the North (Altbach 2007), leaving many African academics largely excluded from "global-knowledge circuits" (Koehn and Obamba 2014, 5).

It is not coincidental that Clausen's tenure at the World Bank corresponded with a radical transformation of higher education across Africa. By imagining the world as a single financial market, it became normalized to develop policies that treated education as a private good, owned by individuals and purchased on an open market. Whereas a national development imaginary contained room for the cultivation of robust, well-funded national universities, the banker's imaginary reproduced a world in which education is little more than a consumer good—one that is competitively produced, and priced, by only a limited number of providers.

This global imaginary that Clausen grafted onto the World Bank had effects far beyond his presidency. Clausen unceremoniously left the World Bank after just one five-year term, returning to lead a struggling Bank of America. He was replaced by the equally short and largely ineffectual tenures of Barber Conable (1986–91) and Lewis T. Preston (1991–95). Throughout the tenures of Conable and Preston, the World Bank maintained an aggressive commitment to structural adjustment and further reproduced a vision of the world as a single financial market requiring concessions from national governments. One long-term effect of these policies was the continued structural adjustment of African universities, gutting institutions that in previous decades had served as radical sites for imagining the world differently.

The Knowledge Bank

By the mid-1990s, after fifteen years of structural adjustment, the World Bank faced widespread criticism from governments, nongovernmental organizations, and civil society. In 1995, James Wolfensohn assumed the presidency of the World Bank and, in an effort to rebuild the bank's image, embraced a slightly different global imaginary than the one permeating the Clausen Bank. Wolfensohn returned to the prodevelopment and antipoverty language of McNamara, but with a new focus on economic development as taking place within a global knowledge economy. In reimagining the world not only as a circulation of finance capital, but also including the production and exchange of knowledge, Wolfensohn oversaw the World Bank's revalorization of education, and especially higher education, as essential for economic development.

After graduating from Harvard Business School in 1959, Wolfensohn enjoyed a successful career in finance, which included rising to senior positions at Salomon Brothers and, in 1979, negotiating the deal that saved Chrysler from bankruptcy (Wolfensohn 2010, chapter 9). Throughout his career, Wolfensohn was a great admirer of McNamara and made a point of attending the World Bank's annual meetings throughout the 1970s. He was even known to tear up while listening to McNamara speak about the eradication of poverty (Wolfensohn 2010, 209). In 1980, McNamara put Wolfensohn's name forward for consideration as his replacement, causing Wolfensohn to begin the process of revoking his Australian citizenship in preparation. He only learned about Clausen's nomination in the newspaper (Mallaby 2006, 37–40).

Upon becoming World Bank president, a decade and a half later than expected, Wolfensohn prioritized "getting into the field" and "meet[ing] our real clients" (2010, 274). Only fifteen days after his appointment, Wolfensohn left on a five-country tour of Africa. Over the subsequent years, his public addresses were densely populated with examples and anecdotes from these and other travels. For example, in his first address to the board of governors, Wolfensohn offered an overview to his agenda for the World Bank by recounting experiences meeting "government leaders, businesspeople, activists in NGOs, farmers, trade unionists, students, mothers and children" (2005b, 29–30). He routinely tied these anecdotes together with sweeping language of globalization. For example, in his 1999 address to the board of governors, Wolfensohn unveiled the *Voices of the Poor* study, which involved interviewing sixty thousand poor men and women in sixty countries. Following a list of assembled quotes from interviewees—for example, "An old woman in Africa: 'A better life for me is to be healthy, peaceful, and to live without hunger'"—Wolfensohn concluded that "globalization can be more than the unleashed forces of the global market. It can also be the unleashing of our combined efforts and expertise to reach global solutions" (2005a, 157, 162–63).

While Wolfensohn shared an antipoverty focus, he approached development very differently than McNamara. Rather than focusing on national development, Wolfensohn used his travels—and the litany of anecdotes they produced—to describe the individual recipients (the "clients") of development and antipoverty programs.

This individualized, rather than national, approach to development also involved reimagining the world not as an externally imposed financial market but rather as a collaborative global knowledge economy, which included a renewed emphasis on the centrality of education. Explicitly laid out in the influential 1998–99 World Development Report *Knowledge for Development*, the Wolfensohn Bank argued for paying greater attention to knowledge as part of the development process. In the introduction, Wolfensohn wrote that placing "knowledge at the center of our development efforts" has two benefits: "increased social benefits" and "better-functioning markets" (World Bank 1998–99, iv).[22] Wolfensohn also applied the language of the global knowledge economy to the task of re-creating the bureaucracy of the World Bank itself, seeking to transform the institution into a "Knowledge Bank" which operated in a more open institutional style while also promoting knowledge-based development (Jones 2007, 201).

The following year, the Task Force on Higher Education and Society created by the World Bank and the United Nations Educational, Scientific and Cultural Organization (UNESCO) released an influential report on higher education. *Higher Education in Developing Countries: Peril and Promise* framed the importance of higher education in terms of economic development within a global knowledge economy, arguing that higher education "has never been as important to the future of the developing world as it is right now" owing to the fact that, without it, "developing countries will find it increasingly difficult to benefit from the global knowledge-based economy" (World Bank 2000, 19, 9).[23] While briefly referencing the bank's previous policy of defunding higher education, *Peril and Promise* neither explicitly acknowledged the devastating effects of these policies nor explicitly marked its proposals as a substantial revision. Rather, the report described the previous period of imposed austerity as a result of "many national governments and international donors" who, since the 1980s, had "assigned higher education a relatively low priority." The report called this a

> narrow—and, in our view, misleading—economic analysis [that] has contributed to the view that public investment in universities and colleges brings mea-

ger returns compared to investment in primary and secondary schools.... As a result, higher education systems in developing countries are under great strain. They are chronically underfunded, but face escalating demand.... Quite simply, many developing countries will need to work much harder just to maintain their position, let alone catch up. There are notable exceptions, but currently, across most of the developing world, the potential of higher education to promote development is being realized only marginally. (World Bank 2000, 10)

While this report offered a "radical re-thinking" of the "anti-university orientation" that defined the World Bank's previous stance, it still affirmed the bank's "strong market-instrumentalist logic" (Olukoshi and Zeleza 2004, 3). In tying higher education to development, the World Bank reimagined global markets as knowledge-based but also placeless. For example, the World Bank recommended that countries promote world-class universities and the creation of global partnerships to link developing countries into an already global knowledge economy.[24] Rather than developing universities as generators of political, cultural, or economic knowledge rooted within the particularities of their home nation, the World Bank identifies higher education as valuable to the degree that it encourages "economic growth and global competitiveness" in a world market already "driven by knowledge" (Salmi 2009, 1; see also Altbach and Salmi 2011).[25]

Several important effects of placing higher education squarely at the center of the World Bank's agenda followed (King and McGrath 2004, 60). First, the World Bank continued to establish itself as the single largest producer of knowledge about the economic benefits of higher education. Between 2000 and 2012, the bank published more than 1,900 documents examining education, including more than 550 on higher education specifically. In fact, the World Bank has published more articles on the economics of education than all of the fourteen highest-ranked universities, with only Harvard coming anywhere close (World Bank 2011, 54; also Ravallion and Wagstaff 2012). In addition, just two months after the release of *Peril and Promise*, the Carnegie Corporation, Ford Foundation, MacArthur Foundation, and Rockefeller Foundation launched the Partnership for Higher Education in Africa, pooling their resources to "turn 'the funding tide' in favor of higher education in Africa" (Bloom and Rosovsky 2004, 79). Consequently, while greater levels of education aid began to pour into African higher education, such funding often comes attached to the terms and imaginaries of education as a marketable commodity, in which students and faculty are valued insofar as they generate potential economic returns within a global knowledge economy.

Starting in the 1990s, this marketization of higher education, and the reconceptualization of universities as value generators within a global knowledge economy, was also taking a firm hold within American higher education. In no place was this more evident than in area studies, where changes in funding and research priorities of philanthropic organizations were encouraging a retrenchment of Cold War geostrategic vestiges in favor of academic research that more specifically addressed global problems.

III Reproducing the Global University

5 "Stakeholders and Co-investors . . . Have 'Reform' on Their Mind"

Kenneth Prewitt and the Defunding of Area Studies

In 2000, the World Bank's Task Force on Higher Education and Society released its sweeping report, *Higher Education in Developing Countries: Peril and Promise*. The report marked a profound shift in the World Bank's approach to higher education, distancing the institution from its nearly two-decade focus on education's rate of return and instead creating an argument for the centrality of higher education to economic development (Bloom, Altbach, and Rosovsky 2016; Salmi 2016). Building upon World Bank president James Wolfensohn's vision of higher education as a cornerstone of economic development within an increasingly global economy, *Peril and Promise* concluded that "without more and better higher education, developing countries will find it increasingly difficult to benefit from the global knowledge economy" (World Bank 2000, 9). The report quickly became a touchstone document for philanthropic and corporate funders, many of which began shifting funding and attention back to higher education. In a dramatic change from its position in the 1960s and 1970s, the World Bank's justification for greater investment in higher education no longer relied upon claims about the importance of education for national development but rather hinged on human capital and the production of research deemed necessary to generate value within a global knowledge economy. The shift in thinking exemplified in *Peril and Promise* did not spontaneously arise within the World Bank but evolved in relationship to academic debates already taking place within the world of higher education.

Within the social sciences, one such debate concerned the relative merits of producing social scientific knowledge within traditional social science disciplines versus within interdisciplinary area studies centers and programs. While traditional disciplinary fields were more comfortable making universalizable knowledge claims about the world, by the 1980s—and within the context of the declining attraction of modernization theory—many interdisciplinary area studies programs evolved into academic spaces that prioritized understanding, and appreciating, the internal complexity and uniqueness of specific, geographically defined worlds. However, under conditions of funding scarcity at the end of the Cold War, the academic debate concerning what counted as proper social science research became tied to funding decisions—with area studies in its crosshairs. While area studies had initially been created in the decades after World War II to provide a strategic reserve of knowledge about the non-Western world, the demand for such knowledge changed substantially by the mid-1990s. By this time, area studies had also largely repositioned itself in relationship to the security apparatus, becoming more critical and theoretical and therefore less "useful" to its original patrons. Within this context, philanthropic funders that once served as the backbone of area studies in previous decades began rethinking their commitments. As the future of area studies waned under shifting budget and epistemic priorities, global studies began to flourish, with many scholars tying their futures to its rising tide.

The transition from area studies to global studies is exemplified in the 1996 watershed moment when the Social Science Research Council (SSRC)—historically one of the most significant supporters of area studies—announced it was decommissioning its area committee structure, and publicly called for scholars to produce social scientific research deemed more global in nature. At the center of this decision was SSRC president Kenneth Prewitt, a political scientist whose research career focused primarily on developing widely generalizable findings about the functioning of American political institutions. Four years after overseeing the decommissioning of the SSRC's joint committee structure, Prewitt would serve as vice chair on the World Bank task force that wrote *Peril and Promise*.

This chapter examines the academic debates within the SSRC concerning the reorganization of the social sciences. These debates took place within the context of growing resource scarcity that hit American higher education at the end of the Cold War. Within this context, globalization emerged as a unique object of study within the American academy. This chapter first examines the SSRC's thirty-year history organizing area studies as a distinctive form of academic knowledge production. Historically located within well-funded programs and centers at major research universities, area studies produced considerable academic knowledge about the non-Western world, firmly rooted in a commitment to understanding the particularity and specificity of nations and regions. The second section examines the academic debates concerning the SSRC's decision to defund area studies. This decision was driven by two intersecting considerations: first, a renewed emphasis on a vision of the social sciences as primarily responsible for developing universally generalizable findings, and, second, financial pressures that encouraged the SSRC to adapt its priorities to meet those of its stakeholders. By the 1990s, declining federal funding of higher education meant universities increasingly depended upon private donors and philanthropic organizations for funding, many of which were now steeped in the language of globalization. The final section examines the effect the SSRC's decision had on area studies, and particularly African studies. Within this conjuncture, globalization emerged as a particularly useful object of study, one that articulated an object of universalizable knowledge and appealed to both these private funders.

The SSRC and the Production of Area Studies

As described in chapter 1, the post–World War II American academy was fundamentally transformed in many ways, including by the creation and expansion of interdisciplinary area studies scholarship. In this context, the SSRC served as an influential node for bringing together federal and philanthropic funding, academic institutions, and individual scholars. Under the SSRC's tutelage, area studies developed into an interdisciplinary form of knowledge production, bridging the humanities and social sciences, and dedicated to an understanding of the complexity and particularity of individual nations and regions. While not necessarily a major funder of research in terms of total dollars—by 1974, for example, the SSRC contributed one-half of 1 percent of the total spending on social science research (Sibley 1974, 2)—the SSRC's considerable influence stemmed from bringing scholars from different disciplinary backgrounds together to collaborate on specific research agendas organized around semipermanent topical and regional committees. Each committee was responsible for distributing grants, organizing conferences and workshops, and collaborating on publications.

Established in 1923, the ssrc was the brainchild of Charles E. Merriam—former president of the American Political Science Association (1921) and chair of political science at the University of Chicago—and Beardsley Ruml, director of the Laura Spelman Rockefeller Memorial foundation. During a time when the social sciences were beginning to embrace the methodologies and epistemologies of the natural sciences, Merriam and Ruml envisioned the ssrc as assisting this development by funding otherwise prohibitively costly statistical and experimental studies. As such, the ssrc was designed to bring together academic expertise, the American government's demand for scientific management, and the vast financial resources of philanthropic organizations to transform traditional social studies into "academic social sciences" by encouraging "cooperative scientific research that would attack 'real' social problems" (Fisher 1993, 27). In a tension that would define the institution for decades to come, the ssrc remained internally conflicted between those who saw the council's primary role as pursuing research on issues of urgent policy concern and those who envisioned it as primarily responsible for strengthening scientific methodology within the social sciences, including expanding mathematical and statistical training and data collection (Sibley 1974).[1]

During World War II, the fledgling ssrc put much of its energy into organizing academics to assist the war effort. Headquartered in New York, the council opened a branch office in Washington, DC, to connect social scientists with government agencies (Sibley 1974, 5). Working with the American Council of Learned Societies (acls), the National Research Council, and the Smithsonian Institution, the ssrc created the Ethnographic Board in 1942, providing the military much-needed information about "foreign regions" of the world (Ward and Wood 1974, 54). The ssrc's Committee on World Regions, created in 1943, was among the first academic efforts to advocate for permanently harnessing the social sciences to provide the U.S. government with information about the non-Western world (Sibley 1974, 87). In the years immediately following World War II, the ssrc actively promoted the creation of permanent area studies programs on university campuses. To advance this agenda, its World Area Research Committee published a number of highly influential reports developing the intellectual and policy arguments for such efforts.[2] The World Area Research Committee not only funded Robert Hall's survey of area studies programs, but also published a number of committee reports on the importance of area studies, organized national conferences on the topic, and created the Committee on Area

Research Training Fellowships to administer Carnegie-funded area studies research grants (Ward and Wood 1974, 55). While the SSRC terminated the Committee on World Area Research in 1953, this change did not signify waning interest in area studies but rather the initial stages in restructuring and expanding its support. In 1954, the SSRC launched the Committee on Comparative Politics, which sought to reorganize "a major field within the discipline of political science," that is, the subfield of comparative politics, in ways that combined the council's "strong interest in the politics of the developing non-Western nations as a whole" and its focus on "political modernization" and "political development" in particular (Ward and Wood 1974, 56).[3] The SSRC also created committees dedicated to the study of the Soviet Union, Eastern Europe, and East Asia. The passage of the National Defense Education Act in 1958, and the subsequent creation of Title VI area studies programs with sustained philanthropic support (most notably from the Ford Foundation), encouraged the SSRC to greatly expand the number of area-specific committees it sponsored. By the early 1970s, the SSRC had established joint area committees on the "Slavic area" (established 1948), Asia (1949), the Near and Middle East (1951), China (1959), Africa (1960), Japan (1967), Korea (1967), and Eastern Europe (1971) (Sibley 1974, 89).

The SSRC approached area studies from a "whole-culture approach," which involved bringing together scholars in the languages, humanities, and social sciences to develop academic knowledge capable of understanding the entirety of "an alien society and culture" (Sibley 1974, 89). To facilitate this interdisciplinary approach, the SSRC collaborated with the humanities-focused ACLS to create joint committees, dividing funding and administrative duties between the two organizations.[4] In addition to providing grants to individual researchers, these joint committees cultivated professional connections and collaborations within regional fields of research, hosted conferences and seminars, published regular assessments of the field, and engaged in other "activities of general and basic utility to the field" (Sibley 1974, 90).

The postwar decades witnessed considerable expansion of area studies within the United States. By 1970, for example, there was a total of 312 programs—up from fourteen total programs in 1947, and twenty-five in 1951 (Lambert 1973b, 15).[5] The SSRC was at the center of this expansion. Between August 1980 and January 1983, for example, the SSRC hosted two hundred "area-based meetings, conferences, seminars and workshops" on a wide range of topics from Eastern European film, economic development in Kenya and Ivory Coast, and Malaysian and Indonesian legal reforms (Worcester

2001, 77). The ssrc's role in shaping area studies was so profound that, between the 1960s and early 1990s, the identity of the ssrc "substantially overlap[ped] with area studies itself" (Worcester 2001, 77).

African studies also benefited greatly from the ssrc's support. Prior to World War II, the study of Africa was largely absent from most American institutions of higher education, with the notable exception of historically black colleges and universities (see chapter 1). However, the growing governmental and philanthropic support for area studies during the second half of the twentieth century included considerable interest in African studies, which primarily took the form of funding interdisciplinary centers, programs, and scholars at large research universities. The result was the reproduction of a very particular form of knowledge about Africa, and therefore the world.

The Case of African Studies

By the mid-1960s, African studies was spreading through the American academy "like wildfire in the bush during the dry season" (Vansina 1994, 111). For more than thirty-five years, the ssrc's Joint Committee on African Studies helped shape, fund, and fuel this academic study of Africa, funding hundreds of dissertations and research projects and launching the careers of some of the most prominent scholars of Africa (Worcester 2001, 82). For example, the Joint Committee on African Studies, in combination with the African studies section of the ssrc's Foreign Area Fellowship Program (FAFP), funded Yale history graduate student Alison Des Forges's field research in Rwanda, Burundi, Belgium, and Italy (ssrc 1967b, 33; 1968, 32; 1970, 32); MIT political science graduate student Robert Bates's research in England and Zambia (including language training in ChiBemba) (ssrc 1966, 36; 1968, 32); University of Wisconsin history graduate student Allen Isaacman's dissertation research on colonial estates in Mozambique (ssrc 1969, 39); Catherine Newbury's dissertation research on colonial political integration in Rwanda (ssrc 1971, 32); and Michael Watts's dissertation research on drought in Nigeria (ssrc 1976, 25).[6]

The Joint Committee on African Studies also funded midcareer scholars as well as established luminaries in the field, including assistant professor James Mittelman's research on socialist transition in Mozambique and Tanzania (ssrc 1977, 20), associate professor Crawford Young's research on agricultural politics in Uganda (ssrc 1967a, 9), and professor Jan Vansina's work on the colonial history of Congo's Lower Kasai states (ssrc 1965b, 13). During a time when research on Africa focused almost exclusively on rural populations, the joint committee hosted the agenda-setting workshop on urbanization in Africa (SSRC 1965a, 23), the proceedings from which were later published as *The City in Modern Africa* (Miner 1967).[7] The committee hosted a 1967 conference on the relationship between labor and leisure in African societies (Jones 1968), a 1969 conference on historiographical and anthropological methodologies for studying African intellectual history (Curtin 1970), a 1975 conference on inequality in Africa (Berry 1976), and a 1976 workshop on understanding cultural change in Africa (Fernandez 1977), among many others.[8] During the 1990–91 academic year alone, the Joint Committee on African Studies funded a subcommittee researching African agriculture, a research project on African archives and museums, and ten predissertation and twelve dissertation fellowships, as well as eight postdoctoral fellowships; distributed five grants to scholars working on agriculture and health; hosted two workshops and a seminar; and commissioned original research pertaining to African agriculture (SSRC 1990–91, 61–63; 104–5, 123–25).

Given its importance in establishing and cultivating African studies, it must be noted that during this period the SSRC funded almost exclusively white American scholars at major research universities, often overlooking African and African American scholars and institutions. Within the context of the Cold War, African studies within "the *World* of U.S. Research Universities" was separated by an "enormous resource gulf and racial divide" from the study of Africa taking place within either America's historically black colleges and universities or African universities (Robinson 2004, 119, 132, emphasis in original). The explosion of funding for area studies during the Cold War primarily benefited white scholars working within a handful of prestigious research universities. If one scans the lists of award recipients in the SSRC's newsletter, *Items*, it becomes quickly evident that those receiving grant funding, as well as those serving on the fellowship committees, were located within an American research (R1) university—and especially those institutions known for their well-funded African studies programs.[9]

This hierarchical construction of African studies was a product of the American research university after World War II, in which every major element of African studies' Cold War "architecture"—the FAFP, Title VI programs, the African Studies Association (ASA), and the SSRC's Joint Committee on African Studies—"carried resource endowments that were largely denied to these earliest advocates of African Studies" (Robinson 2004, 139). Howard University, for example, was denied funding to create a Title VI African studies program, and the ASA originally operated as a closed insider network with membership depending upon a Roster of Fellows vouching for an applicant's "academic achievement and experience in the African field" (Robinson 2004, 139). As a result, African studies within the Cold War university remained largely "de-link[ed]" from the early scholarship on Africa produced within historical black institutions, such that African studies became sort of "a *World* unto itself" (Robinson 2004, 139, emphasis in original).

In this way, African studies—as a specific institutionalized form of knowledge production—emerged as a uniquely American creation. This meant that, on the one hand, it was able to avoid the "colonial, settler, and missionary paradigms" that defined earlier European scholarship of Africa (West and Martin 1997, 313). On the other hand, however, it reproduced its own epistemic assumptions, developed within the context of a close working relationship with the needs of the American state and philanthropic funders. Often excluded from these circles were African and African American scholars who had long studied Africa in ways that drew historical, cultural, and intellectual connections between Africa, the African diaspora, and the rest of the world. Du Bois argued as early as 1946 that fully understanding World War II as a "crisis of civilization" required attending to "the African point of view" and the "history of the Negro as part of the world which now lies about us in ruins" (Du Bois 1965, vii–viii). In contrast, African studies, as practiced within the Cold War American university, instead produced knowledge about Africa as a collection of peoples and nations largely separate and distinct from each other and the rest of the world. The "U.S. Africanists' paradigm" made Africa appear as an isolated place, populated by distinct and independent nations (West and Martin 1997, 313). While African studies often viewed Africa outside the tether of European empire, it nonetheless sought to replace this imperial imaginary with a vision of the world as a strategic terrain of competing nation-states. No longer studying "competing colonial systems and boundaries that had sustained . . . colonial and settler rule," African studies instead studied "new world regions" with boundaries "defined by the U.S. government—and filled with pro- or anticommunist independent states" (West and Martin 1997, 313).

While area studies—and African studies in particular—was initially closely aligned with modernization theory and American foreign policy objectives (see chapter 1), by the 1970s and 1980s space had opened up to substantially change the utilitarian relationship between African studies and the American security apparatus. The legacy of a close relationship with the humanities, as exemplified in the ssrc's joint committee structure developed with the ACLS, enabled area studies to evolve into an intellectual space in which it was possible to examine "other times, places, cultures, and societies," and to appreciate the existence of "local knowledges" that often remained "initially unintelligible to externally based observation" (Karp 1997, 284). This level of appreciation, which might be summarized as a commitment to "knowing otherness," was built up on extensive field research and required time and proximity to cultivate (Karp 1997, 284). This epistemic approach often meant that area studies scholars increasingly found themselves aligned with decolonization, civil rights, and other struggles for political and economic self-determination.

Despite being initially funded to engage national security concerns, area studies had unevenly evolved into a site in which developing critiques of American imperialism and advocating "radical, race-based multiculturalism" became increasingly possible (Schueller 2007, 50). However, and especially in comparison to intellectual work taking place in decolonizing African universities, this critical gaze remained fairly limited in its political imagination. Area studies became "a style of knowing" that developed its critique of "the conjuncture of corporate funding, state support, and the flexible managerial systems of university governance" yet retained a commitment to "liberal pluralism" (Rafael 1994, 91). Consequently, area studies often remained committed to an "egalitarian union of men" that effectively "reproduced the liberal ideal of managed pluralism that would bind the diversity of the world within the flexible authority of experts and practitioners" (Rafael 1994, 95).

On the one hand, this meant that by the mid-1990s the unifying vision of knowledge production previously espoused by modernization theory was in retreat across area studies. Theoretical developments originating from the humanities, such as those offered by post-structural and postcolonial theory, further privileged the creation of particularized, area-specific knowledge, developed through the attainment of language proficiency, extended field research, and full immersion into one's area of study. The visions of the world being produced, reproduced, and widely circulated within area studies were largely possible because of considerable investments by the SSRC. However, during the last decades of the twentieth century, area studies as a form of academic knowledge production became seriously challenged—both intellectually and materially. Fine-tuned understandings of plurality and difference found themselves prone to skepticism about their ability to develop universalizable knowledge. Such criticisms largely took the form of debates concerning methodology, and specifically from those "advocating science in the face of interpretation"—a methodological debate that also played out along the "axis" of the "global-local debates" (Karp 1997, 282). This debate was also of particular interest to funders of the social sciences.

Debating Area Studies within the Context of Funding Scarcity

By the 1970s, the world of American higher education, which had enjoyed "an economy of abundance" for decades, began entering "an economy of scarcity" (Lambert 1973b, 2). Within this context, questions emerged about the economic and academic viability of area studies. Many "Western-based scholars"—the majority of whom worked on their native societies using analyses rooted in disciplines and subfields characterized as the "most behavioral, quantitative, ahistorical, and acultural"—began vocally questioning the intellectual merit of area studies, especially given its proximity to the humanities (Lambert 1973b, 3). At individual universities, hiring began shifting back to the disciplines, leaving area experts not only with fewer dedicated tenure track positions but now also required to speak directly to the core social science disciplines. These material challenges were compounded by the fact that area centers and programs often operated in "the chinks and crevices" between disciplines, departments, and the administration, and often depended upon "ad hoc arrangements" of "personnel, teaching time, office space, and library resources" (Lambert 1973b, 2–3). As resource scarcity became more prevalent, area studies programs found themselves competing with department chairs—"the original academic entrepreneur"—for increasingly scarce resources (Lambert 1973b, 3). And a major warning bell was heard in 1974 when the U.S. Congress just barely avoided canceling Title VI funding altogether (Nugent 2010, 25).

The changes in funding priorities took place at a time when philanthropic organizations were also reassessing their commitment to funding higher education. While philanthropic donors had increased their contributions to American universities between 1970 and 1978 from $25.1 to $46.9 billion, by the end of the decade declining foundation revenue and increasing university operating costs—a result of high inflation—led philanthropic organizations to focus on strategically maximizing the "effectiveness of their diminishing contributions" (Cheit and Lobman 1979, 5). To this end, philanthropic organizations funded more research grants but at smaller amounts, so as to prioritize the development of new programs rather than sustaining already existing institutional capacity. This shift toward short-term, exploratory grants gave philanthropic agencies "greater budget flexibility," while leveraging their shrinking overall funding to focus on developing "something new" (Cheit and Lobman 1979, 30).

The 1980s saw considerable retrenchment of funding for higher education at both the federal and state levels. The gradual winding down of the Cold War, the success of Reagan's antitax message, the culture wars, and the reconceptualization of higher education as a private good (as "human capital"; see chapter 4) made public funding of higher education increasingly unpopular. The Carnegie Foundation for the Advancement of Teaching (CFAT) warned that, in this environment, the "forty-year tradition of bipartisan consensus" about the importance of funding higher education had ended, as evidenced in the dramatic cuts being made to student aid, Fulbright fellowships, and other programs (Newman 1985, 3). The percentage of the federal budget dedicated to higher education shrank from nearly 3 percent in 1975 to less than 2 percent a decade later (Newman 1985, 4). Funding cuts, however, were not evenly distributed. While federal funding continued to flow into research with direct marketability, especially the life sciences, cuts primarily targeted the humanities and social sciences.[10] The culture wars became a political cudgel in the hands of antitax crusaders to further delegitimize the public university, and the humanities in particular (Newfield 2008). In response to these changes, CFAT suggested that those championing renewed federal support to higher education should focus on competitiveness in a "new economy" by arguing that higher education was essential for technological advancement, international competition, and the training of a flexible workforce (Newman 1985, chapter 2).

As federal and state governments withdrew public funding for higher education, colleges and universities sought additional revenue sources and cost reductions, including the patenting and marketization of research, higher tuition revenues, and the outsourcing and privatization of campus and student services.[11] Private and corporate philanthropy was increasingly called upon to fill the vacuum. The humanities—which, after the Cold War, now "lack[ed] something to sell" (Newfield 2008, 19)—found cost savings in converting departments previously organized around national languages into amalgamated departments of modern or world literatures. This condition of resource scarcity renewed academic discussion about the proper role of area studies within the increasingly embattled social sciences. Renewed focus on making social sciences more scientific, and therefore less closely aligned with the humanities, had a profound effect on area studies, which had forged its intellectual identity around bringing political, economic, and social analyses together with cultural understandings. By the 1990s, the academic world of area studies was being targeted by scholars, administrators, and funders who increasingly expressed interest in research of a more global nature. For those advocating greater emphasis on disciplinary knowledge production, the language of globalization came closely aligned with certain premises about the universality of knowledge—claims only possible by deemphasizing cultural specificity.

Kenneth Prewitt arrived at the SSRC in 1995 fully immersed within these debates. His decision in 1996 to decommission the SSRC's area joint committee structure is consistent with his broader vision of the social sciences, developed over decades of scholarship committed to the disciplinary social sciences. For Prewitt, social sciences should construct widely generalizable—or global—knowledge that transcends location, rather than focus on the complexity and particularity of certain area-specific worlds. He argued that widely generalizable knowledge is best produced within the disciplinary social sciences that take the economy, society, and politics—rather than area or region—as their object of study. For Prewitt area studies offer an auxiliary to the universalizable knowledge produced within the established disciplines. Prewitt conceptualized knowledge production within the academic disciplines as containing the possibility of a global vantage, while calling upon those with area-specific knowledge to confirm and translate these universal findings into particular contexts. This vision of knowledge production would guide the SSRC as it reorganized its distribution of academic resources.

Kenneth Prewitt and the Area Studies Debates

The long and varied academic career of Kenneth Prewitt, a self-described "card-carrying political scientist" (2004, 783), is defined by the deployment of political science methodologies to explain how political institutions shape individual behavior. For example, as a graduate student he studied the motivations of local politicians in the San Francisco Bay area and, four decades later as head of the U.S. census, explored the history and political ramifications of how racial categories are built into the census instrument (see Prewitt 2013).[12] After receiving a PhD from Stanford University in 1963, Prewitt joined the faculty of the University of Chicago, eventually becoming full professor. In 1976 he headed the National Opinion Research Center, one of the nation's largest collectors of survey research. Three years later, in 1979, he became president of the SSRC, where he served until he left to accept the position of senior vice president at the Rockefeller Foundation in 1985. He returned to head the SSRC in 1995. While the topical focus of his research shifted over time, Prewitt consistently advanced a vision of the social sciences as committed to identifying generalizable findings about political behavior.

Prewitt's early research focused on developing the concept of political socialization—a contribution to modernization theory that sought to explain why individuals identify with particular parties, ideologies, nations, and political groupings, and therefore how these groupings become politicized.[13] He argued that this approach to political behavior was increasingly important during a time when "national self-determination, coupled with forces of modernization and democratization" were demonstrating that "traditional theories of politics" were insufficient, largely because they assumed the "familiar territory of Western Europe and North America" (Dawson and Prewitt 1969, 3–4). Political socialization, Prewitt argued, focused on politicization within institutions, including the family, peer groups, the media, and schools. Within schools, for example, students became socialized not only through the curriculum (which often includes civics training), but also through the ordering of ritual life within the classroom, the interaction with authority figures, and the social constitution of the school itself, as well as organized participation in extracurricular activities (Dawson and Prewitt 1969, chapter 9). Prewitt and his coauthor drew their evidence for the political socialization process from studies and examples from schools located in the United States, New Zealand, Uganda, the Soviet Union, South Africa, imperial Japan, rural France, an Israeli kibbutz, and post–World War II Germany, and a hypothetical American comparison between a black urban school and a middle-class, white suburban school (Dawson and Prewitt 1969, chapter 9).

For Prewitt, political socialization was a concept describing how a generalizable social process takes place across a multitude of different places. For example, he brought the concept of political socialization within him to East Africa, first as a visiting lecturer at University of East Africa (Makerere) in Uganda (1965–66) and later as a Rockefeller Foundation Visiting Research Fellow at University of Nairobi's Institute for Development Studies (1970–73).[14] Prewitt used his theory of political socialization to explain how "religious identity" among Tanzanian students shaped "nationalistic political culture" (Prewitt, von der Muhll, and Court 1970, 220), and how limited access to higher education—combined with a curriculum dominated by Western-style modernization theory—made Makerere students less politically engaged (Prewitt 1971c; see also Prewitt 1966).[15] Based on a survey of 280 adult education students in Uganda, Prewitt explored the contours of political socialization in "new" nations that, he argued, previously lacked "general, systematic pattern[s] of political norms" (1968, 56). In doing so, he drew out the complicated connections between "political identity" and "nation building" (Prewitt 1971b, 199). His 1971 edited volume examined how schooling shapes what "a nation's people believe about themselves as citizens" (Prewitt 1971a, vii).[16]

Taken in total, Prewitt's writings on political socialization in East African universities contain assumptions about the ability of social science research to understand universal political behavior. Prewitt presented himself not as an Africanist specializing in Uganda or Tanzania, but rather as a social scientist testing a theory of political socialization on one part of the (non-Western) world—with which he had only passing familiarity. In fact, after returning from East Africa, Prewitt returned his research attention to American political institutions, developing increasingly sophisticated quantitative methods for understanding American political behavior (SSRC 1979, 1).[17]

As Prewitt assumed various administrative roles within the SSRC and the Rockefeller Foundation, he began writing more broadly about the function of American social sciences. In a 1984 article, for example, he argued that the social sciences should adopt a more "global vantage." He expressed concern that American social science had little to say about how global issues affect the Third World—a problem he blamed on the fact that "problem-focused researchers, students of international processes, and area scholars" all "inhabit separate domains" (Prewitt 1984, 89). He argued that while area studies scholars enjoyed a "well-established infrastructure," including centers, programs, library collections, grant funding, and scholarly exchanges, the area-specific knowledge they produced often lacked international context. In contrast, the branch of the social sciences best positioned to study the international connections, namely international studies, remained mired in the prism of American security concerns. As such, scholars examining global issues often forget to ask how these issues "originate in, and return to haunt, the households and villages of Third World countries" (87). At the same time, Prewitt argued, scholars who have "dedicated a lifetime of research to understanding those households and villages" rarely connect their findings to questions of a global nature (87). Prewitt saw this problem as compounded by the fact that "discipline-based research communities," which employ cutting-edge scientific methodologies to address specific domestic policy concerns, only "brush against" area studies and international studies on rare occasions. Few scholars, as a result, are capable of applying social scientific "tools and theories" to questions about "improving the human condition" outside the United States. Social scientific knowledge produced within the American university, Prewitt worried, tends to examine the non-Western world from the perspective of American foreign policy and national interest rather than from a global perspective.

Prewitt used the term "global" to denote a spatial reach. His preferred global vantage, in other words, involved the application of disciplinary social science methods to the study of global issues, which he defined as "phenomena transcending and spilling across linguistic, cultural, and political boundaries," such as "the international divisions of labor, capital flows, nuclear proliferation, resource depletion, biosphere damage, and so forth" (Prewitt 1984, 86). Unfortunately, American disciplinary social scientists, he contended, rarely tackle global issues, and the closest they come to engaging the Third World "is when they insert the names of countries in their computer models," thereby ensuring that "global issues are studied" with "only passing reference to the histories and cultures hidden behind such place-names as China, Nigeria, or Mexico" (86). The role of area experts, Prewitt argued, should be to resquare this circle—to ensure that social scientific research on global issues truly engages the particularity of Third World countries. In this analysis, however, Prewitt ends up advocating a form of academic knowledge that sees social scientific methods as capable of identifying global issues, and then asks area experts to confirm that these generalizable findings apply to the non-Western world. Therefore, area studies become conceptualized as the receiver of social scientific knowledge, which is then tasked with translating such knowledge back into areas of expertise.

Prewitt again articulated his desire for area studies to focus more directly on issues of global relevance in an article critiquing area studies as out of touch with the major issues of policy concern, arguing that security issues—including the threat of nuclear conflict—were altogether missing from the research agendas laid out by area studies scholars. Examining 2,500 dissertation and 5,000 postdoctoral funding applications received by the SSRC during the early 1980s, Prewitt argued that only a small fraction "take up international peace and security issues" (1985, 14). Of the 724 applications received by the Joint Committee on African Studies, for example, only seven dealt with questions of security (14). Prewitt, in other words, remained concerned that area studies scholars were compelled primarily by problematics driven by their specialized worlds of expertise—and not by what the disciplines and policy makers deemed issues of global importance.

Upon returning to the SSRC in 1995, Prewitt inherited an institution engaged in reassessing its support for area studies. Within these discussions, Prewitt clearly sided with those articulating a vision of the social sciences as providing widely universalizable findings and, in doing so, privileging the global as the spatial area of analysis.

The SSRC and the Debate over Area Studies

Within the SSRC, discussions about the relative merit of area studies in relation to the disciplinary social sciences played out in the pages of the newsletter *Items* long before Prewitt returned in 1995. For example, an institutional account of the SSRC's commitment to area studies, written by two scholars with long histories of working within the institution, expressed concern that even though the SSRC was largely responsible for the "initial establishment and subsequent expansion" of area studies, the current utility of such research remained up for debate (Ward and Wood 1974, 58). This criticism remained rooted in the claim that area studies serves two primary functions within the social sciences: providing the raw data needed for disciplinary social scientists to test universalizable theories, and unearthing parochial assumptions embedded within social scientific inquiries. While acknowledging the value of area studies in addressing these concerns, critics expressed skepticism that area studies was able to provide its own universalizable findings:

> It has long been obvious that area-specific knowledge by itself is not enough.... It is an unfortunate fact that a large proportion of the raw data available to social scientists is American in provenance. As a consequence, both the methodologies and the theories of contemporary social science have to an unrealistic and perhaps critically unsound degree been built on bases that are predominantly or exclusively derived from American practice and experience. Thus while we recognize in principle the importance of culture as a determinant of social attitudes, values, and behavior, in practice we have too often proceeded along lines that may prove to be disastrously culture-bound.
>
> From the *social science viewpoint*, the initial value and essentiality of area studies and of the Council's role in their development derives from the limita-

tions of American experience. Area studies are calculated to restore a measure of cultural equilibrium to an otherwise American-biased endeavor, to *supply basic data* from a rich variety of cultural contexts, and to add thereto orderly *descriptions, analyses, and interpretations* of economic, political, and social systems other than our own.

By themselves these are valid and valuable contributions, but they are not in the long run sufficient. A further effort must be made *to transcend the limits of particular cultures* and to formulate and synthesize these expanded and enriched data in cross-cultural and comparative terms. (Ward and Wood 1974, 58, emphasis added)

These early calls for area studies to "transcend the limits of particular cultures" and instead provide insights beyond the geographical regions of individual scholarly expertise became even more pronounced within the context of resource scarcity.

By the early 1990s, the SSRC was fully engaged in a reassessment of the future of area studies within the post–Cold War academy. For example, Stanley Heginbotham—then the vice president of the SSRC—authored essays and speeches questioning the value of area studies (Ludden 2000, 5). In one instance, he suggested that in light of current developments, social scientists should take the initiative "to articulate a persuasive rationale for the support" of area studies "among funders," especially given that the "major traditional U.S. funders of international scholarship" were themselves in the process of "reassessing their priorities and redirecting their resources in the wake of the end of the cold war" (Heginbotham 1994, 34).[18] Rather than articulating regions and nations as unique objects of study, Heginbotham suggested that "political, social, cultural, and economic dynamics" should become the objects of study—as situated within "a local context." He suggested that a reconstituted area studies capable of attracting financial support would, in turn, focus on corroborating those universal findings developed within the disciplinary social sciences by applying them to the "local" setting. To this end, Heginbotham suggested that all graduate training take place within a discipline, while encouraging students to receive additional training in a selected region of the world. This training, Heginbotham argued, would be "sufficient" to confirm the generalizability of otherwise scientific findings within a particular context.

Sitting SSRC president David Featherman was similarly skeptical of area studies, arguing that "disciplinary social sciences were more universally applicable, globally useful, and more worthy of support than area studies" (Ludden 2000, 5). In 1994, he commissioned a task force to assess the relative merits of the joint area committee structure. While the task force did not ultimately advocate for the dissolution of funding along regional divisions, it did recommend that the council place greater emphasis on "problem-driven research agendas" (Worcester 2001, 89). Internal conversations within the SSRC raised the objection that the joint committee structure facilitated scholarship that largely stood outside the "core social science disciplines" (Worcester 2001, 89; see also Bendix 2003, 46).

Between 1993 and 1994, more than one hundred internal memoranda were written and circulated by SSRC staff discussing how to reorganize the joint committees (Worcester 2001, 120n149). But for outside observers, the academic discussion about the changing role of area studies took a dramatic turn in 1996 when—like a "bolt from the blue" (Worcester 2001, 88)—the SSRC announced it was abandoning its joint area committee structure.

Reorganizing the Joint Committee Structure

The official policy concerning the decommissioning of the joint area committees was unveiled in 1996 over the course of two issues of *Items*. The first installment made the academic argument for the change, and the second laid out what would replace the joint committee structure. Taken together, these pieces merge Prewitt's intellectual commitment to the universality of the social sciences with a pragmatically administrative concern for the economic viability of continued support for area studies in their current form.

In the first piece, Prewitt justified the changes based on two conditions. First, area studies were not capable of studying an increasingly global world:

One of the frequently remarked consequences of the globalization accelerated by new information technologies and post-1989 market forces is that "areas" are more porous, less bounded, less fixed than we previously assumed.... Area studies traditionally had a fairly clear grasp of what was meant by "here" and what was meant by "there." But when areas, from remote villages to entire continents, are caught up in processes which link them to events that, though geographically distant, are culturally, economically, politically, strategically, and ecologically quite near, the distinction between "here" and "there" breaks down.... The global-local notion is not a methodological metaphor invented by social theorists; it is the lived experience of billions of people. And it is being lived today in ways unanticipated even a decade ago. (Prewitt 1996c, 15–16)

Prewitt argued that the shape of scholarship around the world was also chang-ing such that academic knowledge production was now more widely dis-persed: "one's colleague in the study of Uganda, Chile, India, or China is as likely to be a scholar from that country—or from Europe or from elsewhere in Africa, Latin America, Asia" (1996c, 16–17). As such, the "international production of knowledge" was not area based but "discipline-based" (Pre-witt 1996c, 17). Prewitt argued that the SSRC therefore needed to support re-search agendas driven by the disciplinary social sciences, which were global in scope, but also incorporated "area-based knowledge." Unlike area studies, which assumed a "single, fixed referent," Prewitt saw the reality of globaliza-tion as requiring "a system in which region and discipline and theme vary according to the research question at hand" (1996b, 37).

In consultation with "the leadership and staffs of the Councils" as well as "scholars, practitioners, and funders" (Prewitt 1996b, 37), Prewitt an-nounced that the SSRC would replace the joint area committees with five interrelated components. The first component, the Collaborative Research Networks, would include project-specific and semipermanent networks cre-ated to examine issues of "pressing theoretical and substantive concern" and link "scholars separated by boundaries of discipline, region, and method-ological tradition" (37). The Regional Advisory Panels, the closest of the five components to the joint committees, would meet once a year to advise the Collaborative Research Networks to ensure that area coverage of the research networks was diverse and inclusive, and to "identify how global issues im-pact and are influenced by" local histories, cultures, political arrangements, and so on (38). These panels, however, would remain advisory and exercise no direct "authority over research and training" (38). The third component, the Human Capital Committee, centralized the role of coordinating and distributing dissertation and postdoctoral research fellowships. The fourth component, the Committee on Engagement, existed as an ad hoc committee designed to bring together academics and nonacademics to "articulate and demonstrate the multiple ways in which contemporary societies will benefit from international knowledge grounded in an understanding of local condi-tions" (39). And, finally, the Field Development Working Group supported "language training, field research and/or academic infrastructure" for those studying "under-studied world regions" (39).

Prewitt conceded that these five components, while conceived of as an "integrated system," were nonetheless "open-ended and multi-directional" (1996b, 40). It was designed to make sure "many things . . . happen simultaneously": "Area-based knowledge" should more deeply engage the disciplines, and that "U.S. perspectives will be challenged through sustained interactions with non-U.S. academic communities. Discipline-bound certainties will encounter the local knowledge of area specialists. Academic agendas will be exposed to the concerns of practitioners" (40). Prewitt acknowledged the "messiness inevitable in an open-ended structure with multiple tasks," but argued that such an approach is necessary to study a complex global world.[19]

At its core, Prewitt called for a move from area studies to a widely distributed form of knowledge production that is simultaneously global and area specific. Unlike area studies—which took "regions in their totality as its primary unit of analysis"—Prewitt defined "area-specific knowledge" as starting "with knowledge about an area, but then appl[ying] that knowledge to processes, trends, and phenomena that transcend any given area" (1996b, 31–32). Unlike area studies, area-specific knowledge might start locally but arrive at conclusions that transcend location.

While framed as a necessary academic response to the realities of globalization, Prewitt's refiguring of area studies took place against the background of funding difficulties for the joint committee structure. Prewitt argued that reorganizing area studies into area-specific knowledge, and sheltering area experts within traditional social science disciplines, would make it easier to secure funding:

> Because area studies remains disturbingly vulnerable to shifts in funding trends, and to changes in the intellectual climate within the academy, it is worth emphasizing that the repositioning herein recommended is an effort by the Councils to insure a durable place in intellectual life for area studies. Methods of inquiry developed by and for area studies will continue to have a central role in the international program structure of the Councils. We will continue the effort to integrate an area-based epistemology into discipline-based studies, and vice versa. Just as one would not expect the disciplines to advance in the absence of methodologies of quantification, they cannot advance in the absence of methodologies which reveal the varieties of human experience in the larger world. (1996b, 32)

While funding concerns make an appearance in Prewitt's public justification for the defunding of area studies in the SSRC's newsletter, the annual report from the same year expresses these funding concerns even more candidly. Here Prewitt acknowledges that higher education was increasingly under "heightened public scrutiny" and says, "Many are asking about the efficiencies/

inefficiencies of university education" and "its links to those parts of the society for which its graduates and its knowledge are intended" (1996a, 13). As such, many of the "stakeholders and co-investors (parents, legislative committees, industrial consumers, taxpayers, employers) have 'reform' on their mind" (13). Prewitt acknowledges that higher education in the United States "has become a large, heterogeneous, and costly industry" such that "new stresses" including "resource constraints, increased public scrutiny, demographic transformations, new information technologies, competition from non-traditional suppliers of educational services, and demands for higher return on investment" are placing higher education under considerable "pressure to raise productivity, improve accountability, and to set and realize priorities that serve not only higher education, but society and the economy as well" (15–16). Within the context of heightened scrutiny, and more pronounced market-based incentives undergirding academic knowledge production, Prewitt acknowledges the difficulty of justifying the costly funding of intensive language training, extensive field research, and the writing of seemingly esoteric monographs of parts of the world no longer at the forefront of American geopolitical interests.

Conversations similar to those taking place within the SSRC during the mid-1990s were occurring across the world of higher education, and specifically within the governmental, philanthropic, and institutional organizations that historically supported area studies. The result was a considerable sense of epistemic and institutional crisis within area studies.

The Crisis of Area Studies
(and the Rise of Global Studies)

Given the SSRC's history as the "national think-tank for area studies" (Ludden 2000, 4), its decision to move away from the joint area committee structure profoundly affected the production of academic knowledge across the social sciences. As early as the mid-1980s, MacArthur, Mellon, and a few smaller foundations had already begun reassigning funds from area studies, favoring instead the study of globalization and the creation of cross-regional programming (Hall and Tarrow 1998, 25; Nugent 2010). The SSRC's 1996 decision to disband the area studies committee structure, however, signaled a clear shift in momentum away from area studies in favor of research deemed more global in focus (West and Martin 1997; see also Cumings 1998,

178; Mirsepassi, Basu, and Weaver 2003, 3–6). For example, in 1996 the Ford Foundation also unveiled its $25 million Crossing Borders program (Ludden 2000, 6). Organized under the subtitle Revitalizing Area Studies, the Crossing Borders initiative gave out Phase I funding to thirty colleges and universities, funding programs that privileged the *"movement"* of "peoples, ideas, commodities," and "problems and processes," such as migration, transnationalism, globalization, and democratization (Nugent 2010, 27–29, emphasis in original). Similarly, when Congress reauthorized Title VI funding in 1998, they amended the program to prioritize globalization, defending the training of area experts as central to the purpose of preserving the "security, stability, and economic vitality of the United States in a complex global era" (quoted in Wiley 2001, 15).

The new prioritization of global problems among philanthropic and government funders resulted in considerable outcry among area studies practitioners. By the mid-1990s, scholars were widely aware that area studies—and African studies in particular—were in crisis. A number of academic forums debated the future of area studies, often acknowledging the paralyzing effects of limited funding on the possibilities for field research and language acquisition.[20] Some scholars observed that "academic policy makers, foundation executives, and researchers" were attracted to the topic of globalization as if it had "a natural allure, offering new mysteries to be unraveled and new ways of packaging or organizing research" (Hall and Tarrow 1998, cited in Mirsepassi, Basu, and Weaver 2003, 6). Others vocalized the concern that area studies was being sacrificed because the federal government no longer required a standing reserve of area experts and instead preferred scholars whose training reflected foreign policy priorities that emphasized expanding markets and free trade organizations, including NAFTA, Asia-Pacific Economic Cooperation (APEC), and the World Trade Organization. As such, policy-relevant scholarship became that which discussed "a world without borders, increasing globalization, [and] the wonders of the Internet and the World Wide Web" (Cumings 1998, 180). Others commented that it remained difficult to discern whether the "structural changes" in area studies funding were "driven by 'real world changes'" or originated with funders "enamored with sloppy notions of a global village and new programming opportunities" (Watts 1997, 187). In this way, "the globalization of knowledge production . . . look[ed] suspiciously like a speedup of the production line"—scholars were simply required to "do[ ] more with less"—with the SSRC "hitching" itself to "the globalization mantra" based not on intellectual merit but rather because "in an era of growing academic corporatism" there was greater demand for "a more lean and mean research enterprise" (Watts 1997, 187–88).

Within area studies, the language of crisis became more prevalent. And in no place was this felt more acutely than in African studies.

The Case of African Studies

While acknowledging that the austerity felt by African studies scholars paled in comparison to the experience of "African peasants and workers," West and Martin nonetheless described African studies during the 1990s as undergoing a crisis akin to the structural adjustment policies imposed on African countries a decade before. They argued that "declining government, private and, indeed, academic institutional support ha[d] serious implications for Africanists and their craft" (1995, 3). This concern was subsequently confirmed when the ASA published its report on the state of the discipline. The document was prefaced by past and present ASA presidents highlighting the ways in which the end of the Cold War meant that "foundation priorities have turned from area studies" and, as a result, "the African continent risks becoming increasingly marginalized in [American] academic life" (quoted in Guyer 1996, vii). In her report, Jane Guyer compared scholars working on development issues, who were lavishly funded to travel "back and forth to Africa for regular visits," with Africanists who increasingly found it "difficult and competitive to fund a research trip" (1996, 7). Resource scarcity and higher publishing pressures created a condition in which Africanists shied away from intensive fieldwork, turning instead to more theoretically grounded arguments (7).

It quickly became clear that African studies faced increasingly limited resources, even while globalization and global studies experienced considerable resource expansion. As West and Martin wrote at the time, "One need only to examine universities' current investment and strategic plans" to see where new opportunities were being had: "the creation of new global programs and centers" (1997, 318). Shifting scholarly focus to globalization meant the subject matter could be studied from any location, and from a more theoretical perspective, without requiring costly and time-intensive field research and language specialization. In this context, area experts often reframed their work in ways that spoke to global issues. Greater emphasis was also placed on justifying how the study of Africa was central to the core academic disciplines (for example, Bates, Mudimbe, and O'Barr 1993).

The proverbial structural adjustment of African studies, however, took place a decade after the actual structural adjustment of African higher education (see chapter 4). During the 1980s and into the 1990s, universities across Africa experienced profound economic pressures, including "overcrowded classrooms, under-equipped laboratories, empty library shelves, dwindling research grants, falling real wages, and plummeting morale," that forced many African scholars to leave for positions in the U.S. and Europe, and prevented African doctoral students trained in the West from returning home (Zeleza 1997a, 13). This movement of people—which began a decade earlier—not only "reflected and reinforced Africa's intellectual underdevelopment and dependence" (Zeleza 1997a, 20), but magnified the increasingly fractured nature of African studies.[21] While Western scholars traveling to Africa now routinely did so on a short-term basis, African scholars migrating for work in American universities often found themselves "valued only as a source of cheap, docile labour" (Zeleza 1997a, 15). This migration only magnified the existing hierarchies concerning where academic knowledge about Africa was being produced, and the substantial decline in the production of academic knowledge within African universities.[22]

Conclusion

By the 1990s, the language of globalization, which had already circulated widely within the business world during the previous decade, as discussed in chapters 3 and 4, became an increasingly popular term within the academy as well.[23] It might be tempting to ascribe the growing usage of the term "globalization" to its descriptive accuracy; namely, crediting the term's widespread usage accompanying a world that was simply, in fact, becoming more global. As this chapter demonstrates, however, the turn toward globalization as an object of study needs to be understood from the perspective of reproduction, including the economic reorganization of higher education taking place during the 1990s. Changing funding priorities became one important dimension of the overdetermined material relations giving rise to new ways of imagining the world as global. Funding previously available for interdisciplinary area studies programs, which prioritized understanding the internal logics of various worlds, either dried up or was rechanneled toward disciplinary knowledges or global studies. These changes were made in response to stakeholders now less concerned with either Cold War security questions or issues of national development, and instead enamored with the language of globalization.

Philanthropic funders of higher education, such as the SSRC, saw a focus on global issues as involving a reprioritizing of disciplinary knowledge production, treating disciplinary social sciences as better positioned to examine global trends. Many scholars trained in area studies also adopted the language of globalization, often as a strategy for adapting to changing funding streams and institutional priorities.

Many scholars also adopted global studies as a conceptual language for pushing back against calcified, Cold War–era disciplinary practices within the social sciences.[24] As such, the discourse of globalization was used to open more critical lines of study, emphasizing a need to expand what counted as global. For example, prominent Africanist James Mittelman argued for a critical globalization studies that assumed "a *polymorphous world*" that can only be examined incompletely from one's particular "standpoint" (2004b, 221, emphasis in original). Such a critical perspective requires taking seriously "whose words and voices are represented" and who is allowed to "speak"; the "critic must listen, remain open, and make ample room for an array of voices from various zones, in a vertical and horizontal sense, in the globalization matrix" (Mittelman 2004b, 224). In warning against "entrapping ourselves in worlds of our own making," Mittelman used the example of globalization scholars focusing on the "antiglobalization movement" as exemplifying how a "social-*movement* filter" becomes reproduced in ways that ignore other forms of resistance that might not be recognizable to Western social scientists (2004b, 223, emphasis in original).

However, even with such warnings about narrative entrapments, globalization remained the object of study—even as critical scholars sought to pluralize what globalization means.[25] While critical approaches to globalization, many written by area studies and interdisciplinary scholars, examined a global world in terms of polymorphic plurality, multiplicity, and fluidity, these accounts often failed to acknowledge how the incentives to produce academic knowledge about the world as global were themselves shaped by a changing world of higher education.

It is not surprising, therefore, that the repurposing of area studies and the rise of global studies occurred at a time when debates within the social sciences also became more intensely focused on methodological and epistemological concerns. For example, in 2000, the growing hegemony of behavioralism, statistical analyses, and game theoretical approaches within the discipline of political science received the ire of "Mr. Perestroika," whose anonymous email titled "On Globalization of the APSA and APSR: A Political Science Manifesto" questioned, among other things, why many scholars of comparative politics steered clear of the American Political Science Association (APSA) in favor of regional associations and journals (Perestroika 2005). Mr. Perestroika's missive touched off a lively discussion within the discipline concerning the tendency for political scientists to prioritize the "singularity of truth" over "multiplicity of truths," "certainty" over "contingency," "universal" over "contextual," and "homogenous" over "heterogeneous" approaches to knowledge (Rudolph 2005, 18). Within these disciplinary debates, globalization played a particular role:

> While globalization can claim expounders on both the scientific and the interpretivist sides of the line, the concept resides more comfortably with universalizing/homogenizing phenomena. Globalization is, among other things, a theory of history, a theory that features convergence and the erasure of difference. It has in common with its predecessor, modernization theory, the not-so-hidden implications that convergence entails cultural, economic, and political assimilation of the other to the Atlantic world. . . . On the homogeneity-heterogeneity continuum the logical academic counterplayers to globalization are area studies. Area studies were crafted during the cold war to stockpile area experts who could guide American policy makers through the exotic linguistic and cultural byways of the other. But the unofficial ideology of area studies was always more subversive. It provided an arena in which difference could be not only explored but celebrated. Area studies worked within an episteme . . . in which the heterogeneity . . . was valued. (Rudolph 2005, 18–19)

However, the debates over the relationship between globalization and area studies, as well as between positivist and interpretivist understandings of globalization, are often read as heated epistemic, methodological, and disciplinary debates, concerned with the contours of how scholars describe an already existing world. This chapter shows, however, that the disputes over the nature of social science knowledge as well as the meaning of globalization are themselves symptoms of a rapidly shifting political economy of higher education. Viewed in this context, Prewitt's remaking of the SSRC's joint committee structure might be understood as one small but significant moment that helped remake the world of higher education in ways that facilitated the production of knowledge about the world as global. In this way, while many of the debates concerning global knowledge versus area studies (which often included debates about the relative merits of postmodernism, post-structuralism, and the influence of the humanities in general) appeared as disciplinary skirmishes, they were fundamentally also about the reallocation of resources within a changing political economy of higher education. Within a condition of economic scarcity, there were no longer enough resources to maintain the university as a well-funded strategic reserve in which a thousand flowers might bloom.

It should be noted that the prioritization of scientific, universal, and global knowledge was not limited to Prewitt and the SSRC but reappeared in various iterations across different institutional contexts. For example, the World Bank's *Higher Education in Developing Countries: Peril and Promise* projected an image of the world as a single knowledge economy, with economic development tied to the production of skilled knowledge workers and proprietary (scientific?) research (World Bank 2000). Treating higher education as driving economic growth in a global knowledge economy assumes knowledge is universally transactional, rather than multiple, contingent, heterogeneous, and worldly.

However, the reorganization of academic knowledge production to favor knowing the world as global expands beyond disciplinary debates or the funding (and defunding) of specific academic fields. In recent decades, many administrators at American colleges and universities have embraced the global imaginary as a vision for remaking whole institutions of higher education. Seeing a world drawn together by an ever-faster circulation of universalizable knowledge, one college after another has moved toward branding, rebranding, and marketing itself as global. Using the example of New York University, the following chapter examines what happens when a search for a global vantage becomes not only an argument about how to organize the funding of social scientific research, but also the guiding vision for remaking an entire academic institution.

6   "An Opportunity to Transform the University and, Frankly, the World"

John Sexton and the Global Networked University

In November 2005, Graduate Student Organizing Committee (GSOC)/United Auto Workers Local 2110, representing graduate student workers at New York University (NYU), went on strike. The iconic Washington Square Park became a picket line, as graduate employees protested in front of the Bobst Library housing the offices of President John Sexton on the top floor. The student committee had been organizing at NYU since the late 1990s, and even won National Labor Relations Board (NLRB) recognition in 2000. In 2002, GSOC negotiated the first graduate assistant contract at a private university, a three-year deal that included substantial pay increases for most workers, health care, and an institutionalized dispute resolution process. However, in 2005 the NLRB—now stacked with Bush appointees—revoked the legal requirement that private universities recognize graduate employee unions, emboldening NYU's administration to cease renegotiating the now-expired contract. In response to this position, 85 percent of GSOC voted to strike. The strike began on November 9, 2005, and lasted until the end of the school year. Over the course of seven months, twenty striking graduate workers were fired, protestors were arrested, and striking workers suffered numerous forms of retaliation. Throughout the strike, however, GSOC members and their student and faculty supporters drew clear connections between their strike and the broader problem of the corporatization of NYU, and higher education more generally (see Krupat and Tenenbaum 2002; Buchsbaum et al. 2006; Raza 2006; Palm 2007; Krause et al. 2008b).[1] This strike can be read as a symptom not only of the transformation of NYU but also of the world economy of higher education overall.

Albert Gallatin founded NYU in 1831 as a university "in and of the City" (McDonald, et al. 2013, 579). For much of its history, NYU existed as a commuter school focusing on educating residents of New York City and the surrounding area. By the mid-twentieth century, NYU was attracting an eclectic and "nontraditional student body, matriculated 'all comers,'" and enjoyed a "middling academic reputation" (Dreifus 2014). During the mid-1970s, amid the international financial crisis, NYU—like the city of New York itself— barely avoided bankruptcy. During subsequent decades, and most notably under the presidency of John Sexton (2002–15), the school began aggressively pursuing a strategy of institutional growth and transformation, enlarging its downtown footprint, increasing its student body, poaching top academics from a number of prestigious institutions, embarking on a capital campaign netting $2.5 billion (a rate of $1 million per day for six years), expanding its institutional reach abroad, and drawing increasingly close to New York's political, cultural, and economic elite (Krause et al. 2008a, 2; NYU 2008, 3–5). Under Sexton, NYU established itself as an internationally recognized brand, a school known for its academic quality, and the university receiving the highest number of college applications (Krause et al. 2008a, 2).

The rise of NYU in terms of prestige, rankings, and endowment during this period required an enormous amount of spending, much of which was financed by student tuition. Many NYU students graduate with high levels of debt, even while taking courses taught either by a vast army of poorly paid graduate workers or by contingent faculty (Krause et al. 2008a, 2). By driving down labor costs for a majority of its workforce, NYU used the savings to aggressively recruit high-profile "academic star[s]," thereby reproducing a workforce defined by "enormous differentials in pay, workload, and benefits" (Krause et al. 2008a, 2).[2] The GSOC strike, therefore, took place within an institution experiencing staggering growth in resources and reputation, much of which was possible because of the labor provided by a vast, overworked and underpaid workforce. Even as NYU used its newfound wealth to become one of the largest landowners in New York, it routinely paid its contingent faculty less than $3,000 per course (McGee 2008, 102)—in many cases, barely enough to cover one month's rent in New York City. In this way, the GSOC strike was symptomatic of the deep contradictions NYU found itself embodying during the first decades of the twenty-first century.

The story of NYU is therefore more than a story about transformation at a certain institution; it speaks to broader changes taking place within the world economy. On the one hand, Sexton described NYU's transformation as emblematic of economic changes taking place within New York, as the economy transitioned from a focus on the financial, insurance, and real estate (or FIRE) sectors to the intellectual, cultural, and educational (ICE) sectors (Sexton and Lackman 2005; Sexton 2007). Clever acronyms aside, I argue that NYU exemplifies the ways in which colleges and universities now fully imagine—and work to embody—the academic world as a global market. Rather than globalization existing simply as an object of study, it has become the organizing principle, and a taken-for-granted fact, among college and university administrators, guiding how schools market themselves, distribute resources, and prioritize initiatives. This is a radical break from previous eras, in which students, faculty, administrators, and the broader public imagined colleges and universities as national assets—producing strategic knowledge and training a national workforce (see chapters 1 and 2). However, from the beginning of the twenty-first century through the present, colleges and universities increasingly imagine themselves as firms competing against each other in a strongly competitive higher education market—a market imagined as already global. In this context, institutions brand themselves and their strategic principles as more successful competitors in a global market of "education services"—a market now worth $2 trillion (Ross 2009, 190).

In this context, the story of NYU—and the presidency of John Sexton in particular—can be read as a tale of how the global imaginary not only is reproduced within higher education but becomes fully embraced as the organizing logic of universities themselves. Sexton's reimagining of NYU as a "global network university" is a highly emblematic, if verging on hyperbolic, example of how most American colleges and universities have adapted to post–Cold War financial constraints. As sources of state and philanthropic funding dry up, and post–baby boom demographics no longer ensure a steady stream of tuition-paying students, many colleges and universities have begun reimagining (and remaking) themselves as global institutions. In doing so, they market themselves to parents and students around the world, as well as to corporate and philanthropic funders, not as national economic and security assets but rather as sites for the reproduction of knowledge, skills, experience, expertise, and capital within a global market.

As exemplified in NYU, efforts to globalize American universities often reproduce a vision of global colleges as cosmopolitan institutions, enabling students and faculty to follow their passions, in a spirit of cooperation, and working toward the collective improvement of the world through the creation of new knowledges. This global imaginary, what I call the edu-theological global imaginary,[3] makes it difficult to see and fully appreciate the highly asymmetrical and exclusionary political and economic practices that still undergird the world of higher education. The reproduction of a highly market-oriented vision of a transcendent global university—one imagined as existing outside political constraints and market demands, and for the betterment of all humanity—forecloses the spaces from which to appreciate universities as worldly institutions. In this context, the desire to become a global university functions as a powerful heuristic whereby schools—embedded within particular worlds—are able to reimagine themselves as transcending their very real constraints: imagining themselves instead sailors upon a frictionless market already teeming with new customers and boundless opportunity.

This edu-theological global imaginary is evident in the evolution of NYU's rebranding, from being "in and of the city" to being "in and of the world." Despite New York City being the home of dozens of educational institutions (Columbia University, twenty branches of the City University of New York, State University of New York, the New School, Pace University, Fordham, etc.), NYU's reimagining of itself as global requires redefining the institution as existing within the pantheon of the world's most elite educational institutions. However, to compete against these elite institutions, many of which enjoy centuries of accumulated endowment wealth, NYU has pursued additional revenue streams from around the world, including remaking NYU into a global network university. Rather than a university singularly located in New York City's Washington Square, branch campuses in Abu Dhabi and Shanghai serve as portals that—together with a vast catalog of study abroad locations—allow students, faculty, knowledge, and money to circulate freely from location to location, while remaining within the same institution. The GSOC strike took place during the time Sexton was in secret negotiations to establish the first branch campus in Abu Dhabi (NYUAD), which came with a $50 million gift to the school. Sexton defended the NYUAD venture, claiming that "the world that is emerging" would include "eight or 10 idea capitals," each anchored "by research universities"; as such, Abu Dhabi was not simply entering a financial partnership with NYU, but rather engaging in "a deep investment in creating an idea capital . . . a magnet for the whole region and the whole world" (quoted in Krieger 2007, 54).

This chapter first briefly historicizes the general shift colleges and universities have made in marketing themselves as global—demonstrating a move away from the Cold War treatment of study abroad and the recruitment of foreign students as closely tied to state security interests. I then examine NYU's transformation into a global network university, looking specifically at Sexton's edu-theological global imaginary undergirding this project. I conclude by juxtaposing this vision of the global university with the reality of profound labor abuse and exploitation involved in building the NYUAD campus. As with the GSOC strike, NYU's reimagining of itself as a global network university fails to appreciate the numerous ways in which institutions of higher education reproduce very real hierarchies and asymmetries within the world economy.

The Evolution of Global Education as a Revenue Stream

As described in chapter 5, the decline of government funding at the end of the Cold War created a context in which many institutions of higher education found themselves scrambling to secure different sources of funding, including new pools of tuition-paying students. Efforts to diversify funding streams often involved colleges and universities rebranding themselves as global, with the expansion of study abroad and the recruitment of foreign students as central to this strategy. While colleges and universities have long sent students abroad and recruited foreign students, prior to the 1990s the federal government and philanthropic foundations largely funded these efforts for geostrategic reasons. Today, however, the massive expansion of study abroad and recruitment of foreign students within American higher education is commonly driven by the need for revenue generation and justified using the language of globalization.

Study Abroad

Prior to World War I, only a small handful of American students studied abroad. Those who traveled did so primarily to Europe on nonaccredited academic adventures or as part of prestigious postgraduation fellowships, such as the Rhodes (Hoffa 2007, 30–35). While study abroad was temporarily halted during World War II, it was actively expanded and formalized during the Cold War. The U.S. Department of State, for example, became increasingly supportive, believing that American students "could serve as unofficial goodwill ambassadors on behalf of the American way of life" (Hoffa 2007, 112–13; see also Twombly, Salisbury, and Tumanut 2012, 17–20).[4] During the 1940s and 1950s, the State Department and the Office of Public Information spearheaded study abroad, including the launch of the Fulbright program in 1946, in response to the "pro-Communist culture campaign" initiated by the Soviet Union (Keller and Frain 2010, 39).[5] Study abroad opportunities expanded even further after the passage of the 1958 National Defense Education Act and the 1961 Fulbright-Hays Act, which funded study abroad on the grounds that it "contributed to national security" (Keller and Frain 2010, 22; also Hoffa 2007, 117–18). During this period, study abroad received considerable support from philanthropic foundations including Carnegie and Ford (Hoffa 2007, 112–13).

By the early 1990s, however, the expansion of study abroad became increasingly tied to institutional concerns over revenue. While colleges and universities grew rapidly during the higher education boom of the 1950s and 1960s, by the late twentieth century "gloomy demographic forecasts" began predicting larger institutional capacity than available students, putting in motion a "struggle for bodies" between institutions (Goodwin and Nacht 1988, 21). Study abroad become one way for institutions, especially smaller rural schools, to market themselves as "glamorous, cosmopolitan, and up-to-date" (Goodwin and Nacht 1988, 21). Study abroad programs were also used to recruit tuition-paying foreign students, to harness "the entrepreneurial drives of faculty," and to increase the size of the student body by housing students at locations with lower overhead (Goodwin and Nacht 1988, 21–29).

Study abroad mushroomed during the next two decades. While a little more than 48,000 American students were studying abroad in 1985, this number more than quadrupled by 2005 (Guruz 2008, 185; Keller and Frain 2010, 39). In 2000, 65 percent of American higher education institutions offered study abroad; six years later this number reached 91 percent (Hoffa and DePaul 2010, 2). During the 1990s, the growing popularity of study away was driven by a sense that going abroad would prove attractive to potential employers. As "the term 'globalization' began to take root in the American consciousness," it played "an important role in the mindsets of students, administrators and faculty," and their interest in study abroad (Keller and Frain 2010, 39). No longer motivated by the "diplomatic, foreign policy, and national security purposes" of previous decades, students' decisions to study abroad became increasingly driven by a desire to acquire "the knowledge and skills to function in a global world" (Twombly, Salisbury, and Tumanut 2012, 23). The end of the Cold War, therefore, meant that universities increasingly found themselves marketing to parents and students, positioning themselves as institutions that provided skills needed to "navigate a flat world" (Keller and Frain 2010, 41).

These changing economic demands inform how study abroad is commonly marketed.[6] Zemach-Bersin, for example, demonstrates that while many study abroad programs claim to promote "global citizenship and cross-cultural understanding," they are nonetheless advertised to students in ways that "endorse attitudes of consumerism, entitlement, privilege, narcissism, and global and cultural ignorance" (2009, 303). The commercialization of study abroad, which "parallel[s] the commodification of higher education," presents students as the consumers of a particular global experience: "Students are told that they can purchase not only international travel itself, but also cross-cultural understanding, global citizenship, personal advancement, and adventure" (Zemach-Bersin 2009, 305).[7]

Recruiting Foreign Students

In addition to sending students abroad, American colleges and universities also have a long history of recruiting foreign students. During the late nineteenth and early twentieth centuries, few foreign students studied in the United States—those who did were primarily educated in American evangelical missionary schools and supported in the United States by Christian organizations (Bu 2003, chapter 1). After World War I, however, U.S. universities found themselves inundated with applications from foreign students displaced by war. In response, the Carnegie Endowment for International Peace funded the Institute of International Education (IIE), established a framework for placing international students in various schools, created programs to make U.S. campuses more hospitable, published informational booklets and pamphlets, provided legal assistance, and connected students with scholarship assistance (Bu 2003, 51–66; Hoffa 2007, 67). With the beginning of the Cold War, the U.S. government placed even greater importance on training foreign students for, in the words of George Kennan, "combatting the negative impressions" of the United States (Bu 1999, 393). The State Department, Ford Foundation, and IIE worked together to recruit, fund, and place students in host institutions, together "form[ing] a trio that dominated the entire range of [student] exchanges" (Bu 1999, 403). As early as 1950 the National Security Council, assisted by the U.S. Information Agency, operated centers in 138 countries recruiting politicians, journalists, and business leaders to attend educational activities organized by the State Department (Tsvetkova 2008, 206–7). By the mid-1960s, however, student recruitment shifted to focus on college-age students, placing them in American universities where they "would be exposed to the American liberal democratic and capitalist ideology" in "the formal curriculum" as well as the "extracurricular activities organized by the institutions or the government" (Tsvetkova 2008, 207). Assistant Secretary of State George Allen pointed out, "these students will return to positions of responsible leadership in their own countries," and therefore their lasting views of the United States would be the most valuable thing they learn (quoted in Bu 1999, 398).[8] Approximately 600,000 foreign citizens studied in the United States during the Cold War as part of these programs (Tsvetkova 2008, 208).

By the end of the Cold War, however, mounting economic pressures on American colleges and universities meant that foreign students were increasingly seen as a potential revenue source. Today, approximately half a million foreign citizens study in the United States, many of whom pay their own expenses and therefore contribute $11 billion annually to the U.S. economy in the form of tuition payments and other expenses (Altbach 2002, 7).[9] In recent decades, branch and satellite campuses have become the latest front in the growing competition for tuition-paying foreign students. Motived in part by visa and travel restrictions imposed after September 11, 2001, branch and satellite campuses allow American schools to meet potential consumers in their home country. This possibility has been facilitated by international trade agreements, including the World Trade Organization's General Agreement on Trade in Services, that established the legal frameworks protecting higher education as an export service (Ross 2009, 190). In addition, the Department of Commerce's Commercial Services program actively promotes higher education exports and assists U.S. universities wishing to expand into overseas markets (Ross 2009, 196). The result has been an "unabated stampede to set up branches and programs overseas" with all the "hallmarks of high-risk investment"—namely, the desire "to reduce costs, to build their 'brands' in 'emerging markets,' and to spread their assets" to avoid risk (Ross 2011, 11).[10]

Today, numerous American universities and colleges have set up shop in the Middle East and Asia, often in "free-trade industrial zone[s]" and with the assistance of "lavish package[s] of tax holidays, virtually free land, and duty-free privileges" (Ross 2008, 213). For example, the Qatar Foundation built the 2,500-acre Education City, housing branches of the Weill Cornell Medical Center, Texas A&M's College of Engineering, Georgetown's School of Foreign Services, Northwestern University's School of Journalism, and Virginia Commonwealth University's School for the Arts (Noori 2016, 66–67; Wildavsky 2010, 53–55). Whereas the Qatar Foundation underwrites much of Education City, including providing free tuition to Qatari citizens, Knowledge Village in Dubai rents space to "a range of British, Iranian, Russian, Indian, and Australian institutions," geared toward providing educational services to the expatriate "residents from South Asia and the Middle East" otherwise excluded from public universities in their home countries (Noori 2016, 66).

A pioneer in study abroad and recruiting foreign students, NYU is now a path blazer in establishing branch campuses. Starting in the 1950s, NYU created a large portfolio of study-away programs, operating and staffing NYU sites in Accra, Berlin, Buenos Aires, Florence, London, Madrid, Paris, Prague, Shanghai, and Tel Aviv. From their inception, each study-away site developed a "distinct academic identity" with, for example, the Ghana program focusing on development and public health and Berlin focusing on arts and sciences (Sexton 2010).[11] Even prior to the opening of NYU's Abu Dhabi campus, roughly a quarter of NYU students were abroad at any given time, making it possible to expand class enrollments without the constraints of having to house students in the expensive Manhattan real estate market (Ross 2009, 194).

John Sexton's Global Imaginary and the Remaking of NYU

Mythology, salesmanship, branding—it's all the same thing. . . .
The greatest power of a university president is to be the Homer
of the community.
—JOHN SEXTON, quoted in Krieger, "The Emir of NYU" (2003)

Under the presidency of John Sexton (2002–15), New York University engaged in a dramatic effort to transform itself into one of the world's foremost research universities. The core of this strategy involved transforming the institution from a university located in New York, with scattered outposts around the world, into a newly imagined global network university with portal campuses in Abu Dhabi and Shanghai. This vision of NYU as a network, rather than an institution located within a specific place, draws from Sexton's edu-theological global imaginary—grounded in his Jesuit training—and rebrands NYU as a transcendent, cosmopolitan, apolitical, and global institution engaged in the selfless betterment of the entire world. This vision, however, contains profound tensions. Sexton and others are quick to acknowledge that NYU's global qualities originate with its "locational endowment" of being situated within a global city. However, for Sexton, truly fulfilling the school's ecumenical and pluralist global promise requires no longer limiting the institution to New York. Instead, Sexton imagines NYU as a space of networks and flows, with peers no longer defined by its neighboring institutions but rather a small handful of world-class institutions scattered around the globe.

Sexton attended a Jesuit high school in Brooklyn, before receiving a bachelor's degree in history and a master's and doctorate in religion from Fordham University. After graduating from Harvard Law School, he clerked for Justice Warren Burger and, in 1981, accepted a faculty position at the NYU School of Law. In 1988 he became dean of the law school, where his hallmark achievement was the creation of the Hauser Global Law School Program.[12] He was appointed president of NYU in May 2001.

As president, his signature project has been the controversial decision to open a branch campus in Abu Dhabi. Sexton (2010) remained critical of how other institutions set up branch campuses as academic outposts, with only "loose connections to the core of the university, its faculty, and its student body," and therefore with varying degrees of quality control. Therefore, rather than merely offering a small selection of professional programs, NYU's Abu Dhabi campus is imagined as a portal campus, offering a full liberal arts curriculum, providing campus community, and awarding degrees indistinguishable from those offered by the New York campus. The Abu Dhabi and Shanghai campuses are designed to serve as "point[s] of primary affiliation and activity," such that students can earn their degrees entirely at these campuses or move between different portal campuses and study-away sites.[13] For example, undergraduate business majors in the Stern School can participate in Stern World—which includes five semesters in New York, and one semester at each of the London, Shanghai, and Abu Dhabi campuses (Sexton 2010).

This vision of NYU as a global network university is the outgrowth of Sexton's edu-theological global imaginary. Laid out most coherently in "Global Network University Reflection," Sexton (2010) speaks of NYU in world-historic terms: "The joy of discovering new worlds and new peoples is as old as Herodotus; and such encounters always have shaped our world and world-view. Today, globalization in its many forms washes like a flood over cultures and economies. Floods can be destructive; but they can also bring blessings, as the annual floods of the Nile sustained the brilliant civilization of ancient Egypt. . . . Great universities—and especially those that reshape themselves as what I call 'global network universities'—can influence globalization positively and, thereby, foster the advancement of humankind in special ways." Sexton argues that today "*the* defining element" is globalization, which he explains, quoting John Coatsworth, as "what happens when the movement of people, goods, or ideas among countries and regions accelerates" (2010, emphasis in original).[14] Sexton then proceeds to construct his argument about the need to transform NYU into a global network university by drawing from a collection of eclectic source material: theories of ecumenicalism drawn from the Roman Catholic scholar of comparative religion Raimon Panikkar, the Sufi philosopher Ibn al-'Arabi, and Martin Buber; the concept of cosmopolitanism as exemplified in Confucius, Socrates, Petrarch, and Kant; Kwame Anthony Appiah's notion of the "cosmopolitan patriot"; a speech delivered by British Prime Minister Gordon Brown that draws heavily upon references to JFK; Diogenes's claim to be "a citizen of the world"; the writings of Nigel Thrift (the vice chancellor of Warwick) and Rick Levin (president of Yale); the NYU bioethicist Troy Duster; and an editorial from an Abu Dhabi newspaper, among other sources. Sexton's central claim, that the world is currently undergoing a world-historic transformation, is drawn from the theologian (and his Fordham mentor) Ewert Cousins. Sexton writes, "we—humanity—find ourselves at an inflection point, a critical threshold" that, in many ways, mirrors the Axial Age. Cousins develops the concept of the Axial Age (800–200 BCE) from Karl Jaspers, who defined it as the epoch in which humanity developed all the world's greatest religions as well as the most important practices of individual consciousness and social meaning making (Sexton 2010; see also Sexton 2005). Sexton (2010) argues that the new millennium of globalization represents a "Second Axial Period" marked by, quoting Cousins, the emergence of "not a mere universal, undifferentiated, abstract consciousness" but rather a "complexified global consciousness," one that is "global through the global convergence of cultures and complexified by the dynamics of dialogic dialogue" most exemplified in cosmopolitanism.

In this treatise, Sexton presents NYUAD "as evidence of [this] concept"—situating the global network university as part of the remaking of the human species in ways defined by cosmopolitan connectivity and unity. Sexton (2010) notes that while some have responded to globalization "out of fear" or following "the powerful pull of nativism" (as exemplified in the "clash of civilizations"), others embrace globalization as "a tremendous opportunity in the process of global evolutions." Those who approach the world with a "spirit of openness and an appreciation of community" recognize that the world is entering a period of "sympathetic and symbiotic interconnection of peoples"—"an age of cultural and intellectual ecumenism (to use the term in a secular sense)" (Sexton 2010).

Sexton (2010) argues that universities are uniquely positioned to serve as the handmaidens of this Second Axial Period, having historically been "the homes of thought, creativity, understanding and progress," the "instruments" for "resisting isolation and divisiveness," which are "comfortable with difficult dialogues" and continue to be "incubators of new approaches" that transform the human condition. Sexton concludes his reflection with a quote from comments delivered by NYU history professor David Levering Lewis at the opening celebration of the Abu Dhabi campus: "the words of Archimedes . . . are a perfect expression of the complementary visions of President John Sexton and Sheikh Mohammed bin Zayed Al Nahyan: 'Give me a place to stand and I'll move the Earth'" (Sexton 2010).

This vision of NYU—and the research university more generally—as a radically ecumenical, cosmopolitan, and deeply apolitical institution ravenously pursuing a better world pervades all of Sexton's writings and public speeches, predating his articulation of a global network university. For example, in a 2004 speech at the University of Amsterdam, Sexton explores the question of what stance universities should take toward those who are not "like us." He starts by drawing the historical connections between the global cities of New York and Amsterdam via the story of Henry Hudson who "sailed into New York Harbor for the Dutch East India Company in 1609," establishing what would become the "prototype of the American experiment itself: open to immigrants, enriched by different cultures, and upwardly mobile . . . remarkably restless, ambitious, and polyglot" (Sexton 2004b; see also Sexton 2010). This cosmopolitanism Sexton points to, of course, requires remaining silent about the native populations already existing in the area and the violent and imperial history of Hudson's Dutch East India Company, choosing instead to reimagine European colonialism as simply the spreading of European enlightenment.[15] Sexton (2004b) then argues that NYU and the University of Amsterdam are bound together by a common DNA stemming from their shared "'locational endowment' in global cities": they both contain "a density and concentration of mind and matter, an entrepreneurial spirit, an embrace of complexity and an openness to the 'other.'" He argues that, as members of a shared community, these "great cosmopolitan research universities" have the indispensable role of "probing the unknown" and "identifying the connections that constitute the fabric of human knowledge and understanding" (Sexton 2004b). Sexton's imagined cosmopolitan university, therefore, not only ignores the history of settler colonialism and land theft, but also projects a curious, revisionist institutional history. While the University of Amsterdam has been a national center of teaching and research for centuries, Sexton's binding of NYU to this imagined community of elite research institutions serves to rewrite NYU's recent history as a trade school "for the city."

Elsewhere Sexton routinely blends his ahistorical vision of NYU as an ecumenical global institution with explicitly theological imagery. For example, Sexton (2004c) describes universities as a "sanctuary" and "the pursuit of knowledge" as "theological," while criticizing those who would politicize academic knowledge. Elsewhere Sexton (2004a) advocates a "common enterprise university" inhabited by faculty dedicated to both scholarship and teaching, and committed to the community, rather than the "bidding wars" that take place in the "market for faculty talent." Despite making this statement at the same time NYU was actively pursuing (and winning) numerous high-priced bidding wars for top academic talent, Sexton nonetheless insists upon an imagined NYU as a monastic community of scholars disinterested in the material world around them. Quoting Ewert Cousins again, this time in a speech at Catholic University (KU) Leuven, Sexton (2005) declares himself an "unabashed Teilhardian optimist," after the French Jesuit Pierre Teilhard de Chardin, who argued that growing complexity and organization was enabling humans to evolve toward the highest stage of unified consciousness—the Omega Point.[16] Sexton uses this reference to argue for the transcendent qualities of the research university:

> In Ewert's eyes, this Second Axial Age . . . requires a new and broader ecumenical dialogue which entirely and joyfully pursues mutual insight and enrichment. . . . The claim is that we are at an important juncture in the ongoing Teilhardian

process of emergence, divergence, and convergence. The First and Second Axial Ages taken together will have seen emergence of a new form, its divergence into a multiplicity of forms, and finally a convergence towards a Point Omega. The attainment of that point will mark a vital passage across a critical threshold to a new form. . . . In the life I lead today, both as a person of faith and as a university president, the lens through which I view things is different from Ewert's; still, I often see connections between his thoughts on transcendent issues and both the nature of my daily work and the role of research universities such as the one that I serve. (Sexton 2005)

While Sexton routinely insists that research universities are secular institutions, he nonetheless understands his work as university president through the theological imagery of transcendence.[17] For Sexton, research universities such as NYU are vessels endowed with the world-historic duty of helping humanity transcend itself and thereby enter a new era of human flourishing. Sexton describes NYU as an "ecumenical gift" (quoted in Krieger 2008b). This gift, however, becomes fulfilled only when the unique and exceptional institution of NYU leaves its particular (yet already global) moorings in New York to establish itself as one of the top-ranked research universities in the world.

This aspiration to give itself as an ecumenical gift for the world, however, comes up against the harsh reality that NYU historically lacks many of the resources needed to become a school with a worldwide reach. As described in the institutional master plan, *NYU Framework 2031*, NYU is an outsider institution lacking many of the financial resources enjoyed by many of the world's most elite schools. However, harnessing the school's "entrepreneurial," attitudinal, and "locational" endowments can help overcome this lack. An entrepreneurial spirit, as well as a prime location in Manhattan, offers the opportunity for NYU to adopt a different financial model: "In the next quarter century, there will be two or three dozen truly great research universities in the world. NYU, first and foremost, must secure its place in that group, not simply by mimicking what other great research universities are doing, but by building on its own unique strengths, assets, and ambitions. NYU's entrepreneurial spirit, attitudinal and locational endowments, and global reach, *imaginatively deployed*, can create this future" (NYU 2008, 2, emphasis added). The institution reimagined as a global network university not only fulfills the selflessly humanitarian, ecumenical, and transcendent goals Sexton believes define a global university, but (it just so happens) also makes it possible to secure much-needed financial resources:

The society of this century is increasingly global. . . . This global society will grapple with worldwide problems in health, environment, population, poverty, economy, education, politics, and the complex relationships among cultures. The welfare and even the very existence of the world's inhabitants will depend upon the solutions found. . . . One of these challenges is how, as the University extends its locational endowments to sites across the world, to be *in and of these places*, while being *in and of the whole*. . . . Located in one of the world's key intellectual, cultural, and educational [i.e., ICE] capitals, [NYU] is positioned, perhaps uniquely well, to lead this transformation. It is fortunate in that over time, it has developed a rich lineup of global study and research sites, specifically tailored programs, and institutional international relations that engage the community in New York and also attract international faculty and students. Given its valued and time-proven entrepreneurial spirit and tradition of offering higher education within an international university that is "in and of the city," NYU clearly can exploit opportunities to deliver education that is "in and of the world." . . . As it looks to the future, NYU must make room explicitly for the *unimagined*. . . . NYU's paramount goal must be to secure its place among those top-ranked research institutions, not by imitating what others are doing, but by capitalizing on its own unique strengths, assets, character, and ambitions. (NYU 2008, 10–12, emphasis added)

The transcendent goal of becoming "of the whole," a task that requires overcoming the lack of centuries of an accumulated endowment, involves strategically rethinking the university itself as globally networked, with the Abu Dhabi campus (NYUAD) as its crown jewel. As Hilary Ballon, the vice chancellor of NYUAD, admitted, "NYU can't compete with Harvard in terms of endowment or basic resources. . . . For NYU to become a great world institution of higher education, it has to *imagine* itself in a different paradigm" (quoted in Krieger 2008b, emphasis added).[18] Of course, the primary objective is to become a top-ranked world-class university . . . the same goal as all other large research institutions today.

Becoming a global university not only attracts wealth from Abu Dhabi, but simultaneously enables an escape from the constraints that accompany the institution's physical location. Being in a global city remains foundational to NYU's self-identity, but this also comes with considerable financial constraints. For one, the expensive Manhattan real estate market—combined with pressure from community groups, politicians, and others pushing back at NYU's territorial aspirations—has limited NYU's expansionist tendencies.

Community activists have painted NYU the "Villain of the Village," repeatedly sparring with administrators over its building projects, including the Twelfth Street dorms (Dawson and Lewis 2008, 23–24). Expansion of the law school also came in conflict with those who demanded preservation of the Edgar Allan Poe house on West Third Street.[19] Many have criticized the expansion of NYU, a private institution with tax-exempt status, with causing the loss of $7 billion in property taxes, money that might otherwise be funding the city's public institutions, including the chronically underfunded City University of New York system (Duncombe and Nash 2008, 77). It does not go unnoticed that the very qualities that made Greenwich Village a center for arts and culture during the early and mid-twentieth century are being undermined by the "studentification" of the neighborhoods, rising rents, and the treatment of the arts as a commercial enterprise—a vector for the information, culture, and education (ICE) economy (Duncombe and Nash 2008, 78). In this context, NYU's aspiration to become a global network university, as exemplified in its Abu Dhabi campus, cannot be disaggregated from the contradictions that occur when a tuition-driven academic business model—based on the expansion of the student body—comes into conflict with soaring land and rent costs, strong unions, high wages, bureaucratic permitting processes, and neighborhood opposition. In this context, going global becomes a way to free the institution from these very real, and worldly, constraints.[20]

The Limits of Sexton's Edu-theological Global Imaginary

The edu-theological vision of NYU as a global network university also contradicts many of the realities lived by those whose labor makes NYU possible. This section, focusing on the construction of the Abu Dhabi campus, highlights the disjuncture between Sexton's vision of NYU as a global network university bearing ecumenical gifts and the very real political and economic marginalizations and asymmetries needed to reproduce NYU in Abu Dhabi. Far from being an ecumenical node in an emergently interconnected human species, NYUAD reproduces stark inequalities and exclusions, even while imagining itself as enabling a world where "faculty and students . . . move seamlessly through the network," creating a "kaleidoscopic interaction with deep connectivity" (Sexton 2010).

From its inception, NYUAD brought together Sexton's edu-theological global imaginary with a vast pool of petrodollars. Sexton negotiated the Abu

Dhabi campus with the crown prince of the United Arab Emirates, Sheikh Zayed bin Sultan Al Nahyan, at his $3 billion palace, complete with gold-leafed chairs, crystal chandeliers, and Justin Timberlake setting up for a concert outside (Krieger 2008b). Publicly announced in October 2007, the deal included NYU providing the "immaterials"—the brand, curriculum, managerial know-how, and faculty—in exchange for a $50 million gift upfront, and an agreement that the government of Abu Dhabi would cover faculty salaries and student financial aid, and build a state-of-the-art campus "complete with athletic facilities, student dorms, and so forth" (Wildavsky 2010, 47; see also Krieger 2008a; Noori 2016, 70–71).[21] Sexton describes the negotiation of this agreement in quasi-spiritual terms, detailing his first meeting with Sheikh Zayed bin Sultan as "electric," and recounting how the crown prince told him that they shared a deep "connection" that was apparent, he said, "in my handshake, in my eyes, in my aura" (quoted in Krieger 2008b).

The NYUAD campus opened in 2008 in downtown Abu Dhabi. During the first two years, NYUAD offered a limited number of seminars, conferences, workshops, and performances designed to establish the school's presence in the country. To signal NYUAD campus as an academic priority, Sexton regularly flew thirteen hours from New York (first class on Emirates) to teach one of his undergraduate seminars, "The Relationship of Government and Religion," to a group of sixteen Sheikh Mohamed bin Zayed University scholars (Wildavsky 2010, 46–49). Accompanied by two teaching assistants (also flown in from New York), Sexton introduced his students to the American Constitution, including the notion of a separation of church and state. He asked his students to think about how they might "embrace all the ways of looking," asking them whether "your century" will be defined by "a clash of civilization[] or interconnected elements of a watch where we have a whole that's greater than the sum of its parts" (quoted in Wildavsky 2010, 49–50).[22]

The first class of 150 students was admitted to NYUAD in 2010. In 2014, students began taking classes on the newly built main campus on Saadiyat Island. Translated from Arabic as Happiness Island, the entire twenty-seven-square-kilometer $22–27 billion island development project was overseen by the government-owned development company Tourism Development and Investment Company (TDIC). The NYU campus, designed by Rafael Viñoly, who combined design elements from Washington Square and a traditional Islamic village, sits alongside prestigious cultural institutions similarly recruited to Abu Dhabi and housed in buildings also designed by top architects—Louve-AD by Jean Nouvel, the Guggenheim by Frank Gehry, and a new performing arts center by Zaha Hadid—all nestled alongside a maritime museum, a marina, luxury apartments, and two golf courses (Krieger 2008b).

The construction of Saadiyat Island, including the NYU campus, is a predictably sordid tale of labor abuse and exploitation, existing alongside incredible profit-making for the well-connected economic elite. The prevalence of politically and legally accepted labor abuse in UAE is well documented, even prior to NYU's pursuit of its Abu Dhabi campus. For example, the 2006 Human Rights Watch report found that behind the "glittering skyline" and "profusion of luxury resorts" live half a million migrant workers who face considerable exploitation due to the government's systematic failure to enforce labor laws. The result has been "extremely low wages, typically withheld by employers for a minimum of two months along with the passports, as 'security' to keep the workers from quitting. Having incurred large debts to recruitment agencies in their home countries . . . the workers feel compelled to remain in these jobs, despite the low—and in some cases, more protractedly unpaid—wages. . . . Workers [also] face apparently high rates of injury and death with little assurance that their employers will cover their healthcare needs" (Human Rights Watch 2006, 2, 6). Migrant workers, approximately 80 percent of the country's population, do most of the construction and menial jobs in the UAE. Most workers come into the country as part of the *kafala* system, which often involves forfeiting passports and thereby linking employment status directly to one's ability to enter and exit the country. Many migrant workers pay recruiters in their home countries hundreds, if not thousands, of dollars for work in the UAE, often ending up in conditions of hyperexploitation and unable to return home (see Human Rights Watch 2009, 28–31; Noori 2016, 75).

Aware of the labor abuse in the UAE, and under political pressure from faculty and students, NYU officials negotiated commitments that workers building and staffing the Abu Dhabi campus would receive some degree of labor protection. Codified in the "Statement of Labor Values," contractors in Abu Dhabi agreed to guarantee fair pay, a maximum forty-eight-hour work week, paid overtime, safe accommodations, freedom from harassment, and the ability to retain one's passport, among other guarantees.[23] However, in 2009, Human Rights Watch once again reported profound labor abuses taking place in UAE. This report, focusing on Saadiyat Island, found that exploitation of migrant workers remained the norm. Laborers were still recruited through the kafala system, working long hours, in dangerous conditions, without overtime, while receiving wages much lower than promised, subject to various arbitrary pay deductions, without days off, proper health care, legal recourse to challenge these abuses, or the ability to form a union or strike, all while facing the continual threat of deportation (Human Rights Watch 2009, 28–72; 2015, 20–24). Despite these concerns, NYU continued with campus construction, breaking ground in October 2010.

The NYU administration undoubtedly felt protected by its pledge from the Executive Affairs Authority and various statements from the TDIC, reassuring NYU that labor protections would be enforced. However, these assurances lacked any enforcement mechanisms or transparency (Human Rights Watch 2012, 24). In fact, the firm tasked with auditing the Statement of Labor Values, Mott MacDonald, refused to answer basic questions about "the nature of monitoring methodology, or the measures to be taken if violations are found" (Human Rights Watch 2012, 35; 2015, 32–34). Investigative reporting by the *Guardian* and *New York Times* found that workers building the NYUAD campus faced conditions nearly identical to those across Saadiyat Island, and lived in "filthy, overcrowded camp housing" located "at the heart of the polluted, industrial Musaffah area":

> There the men, hired to paint the campus, complained of being trapped by recruitment fees that exceeded a year's salary and of the high cost of even the most basic healthcare. Some, hired from myriad unregulated subcontractors, had to pay for their own work clothes on a salary of £149 a month.
>
> The men were crammed nine or 10 to a windowless room measuring 13×14ft, and had to put up a sheet over the corridor toilet for privacy. All said they hated the camp and had been tricked by their recruiters. One man said: "Look how we live. We are no better than animals. That is all we are to them. Sheep that are to be sold, and nobody in the world is listening." (Carrick and Batty 2013)

Wages were commonly half the promised amount and, after the considerable cost of food, housing, cell phones, and other expenses were deducted, most workers found themselves trapped by crushing debt (Kaminer and O'Driscoll 2014). Many contractors refused to pay workers, leaving them stranded in UAE without money for the expensive exit fees and airfare necessary to return home. Workers who attempted to strike were dragged away by police, beaten, and summarily deported (Kaminer and O'Driscoll 2014). The failure to monitor and enforce labor standards is not entirely surprising given that the chairman of Mubadala Development Company—the government-run construction company contracted to build NYU's campus—was Khaldoon Khalifa Al Mubarak, a member of the NYU board of trustees, an advisor to the crown prince, and also the overseer of Tamkeen, the agency tasked with enforcing the Statement of Labor Values and for hiring Mott MacDonald (Stripling 2014).[24] A 2018 report found that, in addition to the forced labor employed during the construction of the NYUAD campus, safeguards and adequate monitoring have not been put in place making it impossible to ensure that forced labor is not currently being used on campus (Gill 2018).

Without making a false equivalency, it is relevant to note that the same kafala system governing migrant construction workers also applies to migrant academics, including those working at NYUAD. Foreign academics across the Gulf Cooperation Council states experience incredible employment precarity and often acknowledge a host of constraints on their academic freedom (Noori 2016, 71–72). While many professors at NYUAD enjoy greater protection because they often have tenure protection from the New York campus, considerable concern remains about how the campus's location within an illiberal society seriously compromises academic freedom. Many students and faculty acknowledge that NYUAD operates as an autonomous bubble—a guest in a foreign country—with academic freedom enjoyed only within the comfort of an opulent campus, largely disconnected from the rest of the country (Lindsey 2012). This includes more than a few political reprisals against outspoken critics of labor conditions in Abu Dhabi, including a 2015 incident in which Andrew Ross was denied entry when he sought to conduct field research in labor camps (Mangan 2015; Ross 2017, 8).[25]

Furthermore, rather than drawing humanity closer together, the English and math skills required for admittance to NYUAD exclude most regional high school students, and those who are admitted often graduate without the Arabic skills necessary to contribute to their local communities. The result is a highly stratified, isolated, and insular global university (Mills 2010).

In 2013, NYU faculty in the Colleges of Arts and Science, the Steinhard School of Culture, Education, and Human Development, the Gallatin School of Individualized Study, and the Tisch School of Arts passed resolutions of no confidence in President Sexton. Faculty pointed to grievances over the corporatization of the institution (guided by what one faculty member called an "expand or die" mentality), the constant undermining of faculty governance, the creation of branch campuses without faculty input, and plans to expand even further into Greenwich Village (Kiley 2013).

Conclusion

The harsh working conditions faced by those building the NYUAD campus, and those teaching at the New York campus, stand in sharp contrast to the vision of an ecumenical global university espoused by President Sexton. Rather than a story of people and ideas moving freely from location to location, with faculty and students collaborating to expand human potential, the story of NYUAD as lived by those building its infrastructures is a story of a largely invisible and coerced circulation defined by considerable exploitation. While the exploitation of labor was predictable, Sexton's edu-theological global imaginary—as exemplified in his vision of a global network university— could not appreciate the lived worlds of migrant construction workers and striking graduate workers. This is because a global network university means a very specific thing: an institution not constrained by the very real limitations imposed by the land, labor, and politics. Sexton imagines the university as not of this world. For a university to become a global network, it must transcend the worlds inhabited by others.

Conclusion

Reworlding the Global

The production of academic knowledge about globalization necessarily involves imagining the world as global. Global imaginaries, however, do not simply emerge from thin air but are themselves produced and reproduced within diverse worlds. While it might be just as accurate to say "we have always lived in a plurality of worlds" or we live in "a complex political reality embedded within a constellation of complexities" (Kamola 2017, 84), within recent decades it has become increasingly common to simply say "we live in a global world."

This book argues that the reproduction of the global imaginary exists in relation to profound transformations taking place within the world of higher education. *Making the World Global* examines the ways in which American and African universities serve as important sites within which the world became imagined and reimagined, produced and reproduced, worlded and reworlded. These worlds of higher education are not discrete locations but rather are constituted by academic institutions, philanthropic foundations, government agencies, professional associations, and international financial organizations, all of which form an overdetermined conjuncture that shapes the contours of academic knowledge production. This book demonstrates how the second half of the twentieth century saw a fundamental shift in the way in which the world was imagined within American higher education. In the decades immediately following World War II, the American university was reorganized to produce knowledge about the world—including the contemporary non-Western world—as composed of discrete nation-states, operating within an international system, and all seen from the perspective of U.S. strategic interests. Universities became strategic reserves capable of assisting the security apparatus navigate this postimperial and decoloniz-ing world. The federal government and philanthropic organizations injected unprecedented levels of funding into fields such as area studies, international studies, and International Relations, in order to produce knowledge about modernization and national development.

However, the crisis of accumulation in the 1970s, and the remaking of the world economy during the 1980s and 1990s, demanded the creation of new imaginaries. It also placed increasing financial strain on higher educa-tion. Within this context, colleges and universities adapted, turning toward funders and marketers that encouraged reimagining the world as global, and higher education became reimagined as a product sold (and consumed) within a global market.

While the book ended up focusing on the production of national and global imaginaries by white males within elite spaces, it is fundamentally motivated by a prior set of questions: What knowledges, institutions, and subjects are silenced and foreclosed upon when imagining the world as global? How do these foreclosures make certain kinds of knowledge pos-sible? And how might the world be imagined otherwise if academic knowl-edge production was organized differently? The fact that this book focuses on the production of certain global imaginaries, rather than their possible alternatives, is a product of being written within a particular conjuncture: a time in which the inevitability of globalization seemed unquestionable. The political questions being asked during the first decades of the 2000s—with the help of hindsight—might be crudely summarized thus: Given that there is no alternative to globalization, what are the possible alternatives? I there-fore originally envisioned this book as an effort to chip away at the seemingly impermeable faith in a world that has been indisputably and already viewed as global. In doing so I hope I have begun to open a space from which to ask: What changes are possible if we do not assume that the world is self-evidently global, but rather imagined as such? What new political terrains are possible if one understands academic knowledge as reproductive rather than merely descriptive? What if we understand global imaginaries as parochial rather than universal?

While *Making the World Global* examines the structured conjuncture that gave rise to the global imaginary, the book does not answer the more fundamental questions about possible alternatives. This is indeed a limita-tion of the book. However, I'd like to think that this limitation is an honest acknowledgment—one developed through the writing of this book—that

efforts to produce alternative imaginaries are fundamentally political questions and material struggles. This book seeks to raise the possibility that
academic answers are not themselves sufficient to answer political questions.
In other words, if global imaginaries are not the spontaneous products of human minds but rather always produced, reproduced, and circulated within
unique, heterogeneous, and contradictory worlds, then new ways of imagining the world must also entail changing how the production of knowledge is
organized. If we take seriously the claim that the worlds of higher education
do not exist as isolated sites, inhabited by monkish scholars, then statements
such as "the world is global" always contains the markings of the apparatuses that made such claims possible. While the language of globalization
often insists upon its own universality and a-worldliness, this book demonstrates that such claims are produced, reproduced, and circulated within
particular worlds. Universities—as well as the World Bank, the federal government, and philanthropic organizations—organize the production of
academic knowledge and in doing so reproduce material asymmetries and
hierarchies.

I remember a conversation I had with an African scholar a few years into
the writing of this project. After I described the premise, he replied, "Globalization? You mean modernization theory repackaged?" If the core argument of this book is right—namely, that how the world became imagined as
global cannot be disaggregated from the material apparatuses in which such
knowledge is produced, reproduced, and circulated—then this observation
does indeed contain the crux of my argument. Just as modernization and development theories came to permeate American universities in the decades
immediately following World War II, it is similarly possible to think of globalization—and its cognates (global governance, global knowledge economy,
global development, global war on terror, etc.)—as also constructed within
many of the same colleges, universities, and foundations that produced
modernization theory (albeit, as this book demonstrates, under changing
conditions). We might think of the differences between modernization and
globalization theories, therefore, as epistemic refractions of structured yet
changing relations of knowledge production. The many similarities and differences between modernization and globalization—including the fundamental
shift from the national to the global as the primary object of study—can
be explained by examining how the conditions of knowledge production
changed or remained the same. The academic gaze embodied within both
modernization and globalization theories, after all, are still firmly rooted

in the worlds of American higher education, even as these worlds change, evolve, and adapt over time.

Writing now—during a time in which the language of globalization and its assumed inevitability are under question—it becomes even more important, however, to ask this book's still unanswered question: How might we imagine the world otherwise? This question is especially important given that the current alternative imaginaries being unleashed, ones driven by nationalism, isolationism, and white supremacy, often view the world in terms of economic carnage, omnipresent terror, and unending national, racial, and civilizational conflict. It might be tempting to respond to this "What is to be done?" question by developing newer academic articulations; for example, by crafting an even more inclusive theory of cosmopolitan globalization. In doing so, we might expand our academic vernacular to include terms like "world," "worldliness," "cosmos," or "pluriverse." We might advocate bringing excluded parts of the world "back in" to conversations about globalization, insisting that unions, activist groups, indigenous peoples, and other protagonists are also global (and thereby empowered to disrupt globalization in its status quo form). Or we might search out different epistemological structures and cosmologies to identify the germs of an alternative future. Such strategies, however, fundamentally assume that new global imaginaries can be produced within existing sites of knowledge production—that students and scholars might make the world different simply by imagining it differently, from within the universities that already exist.

However, if the argument of this book is correct, imagining the world otherwise requires first asking what kinds of institutions are necessary to cultivate such possibilities. This project asks that we embrace a politics of worldliness (introduction, this volume; see also Mignolo 2000, 39–41; Mbembe and Nuttall 2008, 1) and, in doing so, treat institutions of higher education not as towers unto themselves, or as satellites orbiting a world down below, but rather as worldly sites of knowledge production. In doing so, the "abstract univeralism" undergirding the global imaginary and its practices might give way to the cultivation of "an alternative totality conceived as a network of local histories and multiple local hegemonies" (Mignolo 2000, 22). Within new organizations of knowledge production, globalization might cease being a self-evident fact but rather become a "*grounded* theory" designed to navigate "the epic and the everyday, the meaningful and the material" (Comaroff and Comaroff 2011, 48, emphasis in original). The epic, everyday, meaningful, and material realities of globalization would no longer reference a far-off world, but would rather mark the adaptations, concessions, appropriations, and resistances taking place within the changing conditions of academic knowledge production itself. Taken to its logical conclusion, this book insists that imagining the world otherwise is not strictly an academic question, but rather a political question. Such a problematic involves the intentional creation, maintenance, and defense of institutional arrangements designed to develop, cultivate, and curate new kinds of knowledges about the world.

Such spaces, of course, already exist. While this book tells the story of the reproduction of the global imaginary, it does so primarily from the point of view of capital, structure, and hegemony. As such, this book demands that we also envision a compendium project: one written from the point of view of living academic labor. Such a project would examine both worlds that already exist and ones not yet created (or even imagined), for the purpose of constructing a broader cartography and ecology of knowledge production—academic and otherwise. This compendium might start by exploring the "undercommons," namely those alternative practices of study that exist alongside the dominant organization of academic knowledge production (Edu-factory Collective 2010; Harney and Moten 2013). While these under-commons make appearances throughout this book (as student protestors, area studies programs transformed into spaces for anti-imperial struggle, circles of African anticolonial scholars, unionized graduate students walking the picket line, etc.), their presence is fleeting and contrapuntal. In the compendium, however, Nkrumah's story would overshadow McNamara's and the authors of the Lagos Plan would push out Theodore Levitt.

In terms of its organizing characters, this compendium would include a much broader population of thinkers—across lines of gender, race, religion, orientation, and class. It might start by examining those interesting spaces existing within the cracks and contradictions of traditional institutional and disciplinary spaces.[1] But it would quickly move to the many radical interdisciplines, black studies, and indigenous studies, as well as the long histories of political struggle that made these sites possible. It would take inspiration from the student and faculty struggles to create Third World studies at San Francisco State in 1968 (Okihiro 2016). This compendium would also focus on the many exciting academic spaces flourishing across Africa and the Global South, such as the Makerere Institute of Social Research at Makerere University in Kampala, the Council for the Development of Social Science Research in Africa in Dakar, the Wits Institute for Social and Economic Research at University of the Witwatersrand, and the Centre for Humanities

Research at the University of the Western Cape. It would examine networks that bring together scholars to produce knowledge in collaboration with social movements, such as the newly formed Tricontinental: Institute for Social Research.[2] The compendium would chronicle the political and epistemological work done by South African students in the #RhodesMustFall and #FeesMustFall movements, following the circuits of decolonial scholarship, the occupied university space, the autonomous seminars, lectures, and research, and how this struggle inspires students around the world. We will need to carefully read the work of those who continue to think, write, and teach despite being pushed out of the academy, as well as those who have slammed the door in disgust. This compendium project should not be limited to a book, even an edited book, but rather should become a corpus of political work—many chapters of which are already being written.

During the current conjuncture, one marked by debilitating attacks on higher education, there exists a strong impulse to look outside the academy for inspiration on how to imagine the world otherwise. However, for those whose life and work revolves around the university, the political task of answering the question "How might the world be imagined otherwise?" remains closely bound to our shared world within the academy. As such, the academic practices of imagining the world differently must also include imagining universities differently. It requires engaging the institutions, making demands upon them and upon each other. Some might argue that the real fight lies elsewhere. They might be right. However, it seems strange to write and teach about making the world in more just, equitable, and democratic ways yet watch our own academic institutions remain immune to such transformations. Pushing back against the privatization, corporatization, colonization, segregation, and militarization of higher education, therefore, requires contestation, organization, and political engagement. Unfortunately, such labor cannot take place solely, or even primarily, through the creation of new ideas or concepts, new books and articles, or different classroom experiences. Rather, remaking, reworking, and reimagining the university requires a different kind of academic work.

How might the world be imagined otherwise? There is no single answer, given the particularity of the different worlds we inhabit. But I am interested in continuing to find ways to cultivate, invent, create, curate, and defend those intellectual spaces within which such questions might still be answerable.

Notes

Preface

1   The dissertation has since been published as a series of articles and book chapters (Kamola 2011, 2012, 2013, 2014b, 2016).

2   This annual measure of globalization, published by ETH University, Zurich, Switzerland, can be found online (http://globalization.kof.ethz.ch). Other quantifications of globalization, with similar lists of global measures, can be found in "Measuring Globalization" (2001), Heshmati (2006), "The Globalization Index" (2007), and Vujakovic (2009).

3   In 2005 the University of Minnesota Board of Regents adopted a strategic plan declaring: "The University of Minnesota's vision is clear—to transform this great institution into one of the world's top three public research universities within a decade" (University of Minnesota 2007, 3). The institution measured its progress in meeting this goal by compiling a list of ten "comparative group institutions" (e.g., University of California, Los Angeles; University of Michigan; University of Wisconsin; Ohio State) and four "pillars" of comparison—"Exceptional Students," "Exceptional Faculty and Staff," "Exceptional Organization," and "Exceptional Innovation." The institution then compiled qualitative and quantitative data to measure how well Minnesota compared to its peer institutions along these four categories. The number of students studying abroad, international students enrolled, and international scholars on campus were all considered metrics used to establish the category of "Exceptional Students" (University of Minnesota 2007, 35–41).

4   See, for example, Pason (2008), Kamola and Meyerhoff (2009).

5   These quotes are taken from the OIP website. By the time I was finishing my degree in the late 2000s, OIP officially announced that, as part of broader institutional transformations, its new focus to be "preparing global citizens." OIP, last accessed in 2009, http://www.international.umn.edu/ (no longer active). OIP has since become the Global Programs and Strategy Alliance, or GPS (Kamola 2014b, 528). GPS

currently defines its mission as being "the driving force for the University of Minnesota in globalizing teaching, learning, research, and engagement." See "About the GPS Alliance," GPS Alliance, University of Minnesota, Minneapolis, accessed October 9, 2018, https://global.umn.edu/about/.

Introduction

1   These programs ranged from Kaplan University's certificates in terrorism and national security management to Syracuse University's Institute for National Security and Counterterrorism, Stanford's Center for International Security and Cooperation, the Center on Terrorism at John Jay, and "homeland security programs at Johns Hopkins, MIT, and so on" (Martin 2005, 29).

2   In introducing the Minerva Consortium, Secretary Gates (2008) stated quite explicitly that this project was based "on the success we had in the Cold War. During that period, we built up the Department of Defense's—and the nation's—intellectual capital with new research centers such as RAND and new mechanisms like . . . the National Defense Education Act."

3   Prior to the mid-1990s, only a handful of academic books and articles took globalization as their object of study. However, between 1993 and 1996 the yearly output of articles on globalization quadrupled and saw a "steep upwards trend" stabilizing at "about 1,000 to 1,200 publications per year" (Busch 2007, 23; see also Busch 2000; Guillén 2001, 241; James and Steger 2014a, 418–19). Of articles listed within the Factiva database, the usage of globalization rose from two mentions in 1981 to 57,235 references in 2001 (Chanda 2008, x, 246, cited in Steger 2008, 179). Only 0.4 percent of all the material with the search term "global" was published between the years 1906 and 1989—the remaining 99.6 percent was published since 1989 (according to a search of the ABI/INFORM database, covering newspapers, journals, magazines, and other documents, conducted March 2013). The Proquest Dissertations and Theses index similarly shows that the annual number of dissertations on globalization increased from single digits in the 1990s to 140 by 2007 (Kamola 2010, 23). For similar results calculated using Google Ngram and JStor searches, see Steger and Wahlrab (2017, 26, 58).

4   Of the colleges examined, schools preferred "global" over "international," "linked global learning with diversity and multiculturalism," and focused on "responsible citizenship, social justice, and leadership." Many schools opted for "global" over "international" because it was deemed "trendier" (Hovland 2006, 12).

5   For a discussion of how concepts are understood in the social sciences, see Goertz (2006) and Sartori (1970).

6   *Earthrise* is officially known as NASA photograph AS08-14-2383.

7   *Earthrise* was taken a few hours before the crew of Apollo 8 televised grainy live images of the lunar surface to an international audience of more than one billion

viewers. This broadcast, the most-viewed broadcast of the time, was accompanied by the three Apollo astronauts reciting the first twelve lines from Genesis (Zimmerman 1998, xi; Maher 2004, 526).

8   Similarly, the image used for the 1969 Earth Day flag took the *Earthrise* photo but added an artistic rendering of swirling clouds to make the earth circular (Weir 2007, 106).

9   It is useful to draw a distinction between "earth," "world," and "globe." According to Cosgrove, each possesses a "distinct resonance": earth "is organic; the world denotes rootedness, nurture, and dwelling for living things"; world "has more of a social and spatial meaning" and "implies cognition and agency . . . humans go 'into the world,' they may become 'worldly'; they create life-worlds or worlds of ideas, worlds of meaning"; and globe "associates the planet with the abstract form of spherical geometry, emphasizing volume and surface of material constitution or territorial organization. Unlike the earth and the world, the global is distanciated as a concept and image rather than directly touched or experienced" (Cosgrove 2001, 7–8).

10 Starting in the mid-1960s, there was growing public demand for pictures of earth from space. During the early years, NASA discouraged astronauts from taking pictures that were not part of the operation (Poole 2008, 67–71). However, the public began clamoring for pictures of earth. Most notably, Stewart Brand, "after ingesting Haight-Ashbury hallucinogens in February of 1966," began to publicly ask "why we as a culture had not yet seen a photograph of the entire planet" (Maher 2004, 529). He believed that if a "color picture of the whole Earth" existed "no one would ever perceive things in the same way" (Maher 2004, 529). He produced hundreds of buttons with the simple question, "Why Haven't We Seen a Photograph of the Whole Earth Yet?" He sold them to "college students at Berkeley, Stanford, Harvard, and MIT. He also mailed them to members of Congress, United States and Russian scientists, and to Marshall McLuhan and Buckminster Fuller. Soon, Brand's buttons were visible on shirt collars and lapels around Washington, D.C., and at NASA" (Maher 2004, 529).

11 Benedict Anderson (2002), of course, argued that the rise of print culture played a critical role in the nation becoming an imagined community. This book argues that changes in academic print culture during the 1990s and early 2000s might similarly explain the rise of the global imaginary.

12 Boggs and Mitchell (2018, 434) have criticized this line of argument as the "crisis consensus," namely, the common claim that the university is "a good in itself" that nonetheless finds its progressive social function hindered by increased exposure to corrosive external and market threats. Calls to save the university from crisis, the authors argue, ignore the fact that for many the university has always been in crisis.

13 Within the field of International Relations (IR), for example, there is also a growing and fast-accelerating interest in postcolonial theory, decoloniality, global IR,

and the politics of worlding and world making. The 2015 ISA conference was called "Global IR and Regional Worlds: A New Agenda for International Studies," with a presidential speech (Amitav Acharya) and program chairs (Pinar Bilgin and L. H. M. Ling) who have written extensively on the need to examine the hierarchies and asymmetries involved in the academic production of knowledge. This interest is further evidenced in the success of Routledge's *Worlding beyond the West* series (Tickner and Waever, eds.). Vitalis's stunning book, *White World Order, Black Power Politics* has renewed interest in critical archaeologies of the discipline, demonstrating how the history of International Relations is intertwined with the maintenance and reinforcement of racial and colonial orders (Vitalis 2015; see also Oren 2003; Guilhot 2011b; Hobson 2012; Parmar 2012).

14 "Fast Facts: Educational Institutions," National Center for Education Statistics, U.S. Department of Education, accessed October 2015, http://nces.ed.gov/fastfacts/display.asp?id=84.

15 For example, in his analysis of Jane Austen's *Mansfield Park*, Said hones in on a few scattered passages that hint at Mr. Bertram's Caribbean plantations and the slave labor making the idyllic British manor possible. In juxtaposing the slave plantation against the prim and proper Victorian morality vigorously defended within the novel, Said (1993, 84–97) highlights the imperial conditions making the novel, and therefore imperial culture, possible. Said not only helps understand how texts might be understood as worldly, but also how one can see structural tendencies within a careful study of particular works.

16 Symptomatic reading is a method of reading that pays careful attention to understanding how a text was produced within a particular set of social relations. Althusser argues that Marx's most significant theoretical innovation was conceptualizing knowledge as production. For Marx (and Althusser), knowledge does not simply reflect an already existing world but is itself an effect of social reproduction taking place within a particular conjuncture. Contradictions and tensions existing within these social relations can be read as embodied within a text itself (Althusser and Balibar 1999; Kamola 2012).

17 The social whole, or (global) structure, is the totality of social relationships and their effects. For Althusser, the social whole is the mode of production, and can be analytically divided into different registers that overdetermine one another. The social whole, however, cannot be seen or known in itself because the production of knowledge about the social whole is itself reproduced within the very overdetermined structures being studied.

1. "Creative Imagination" Is Needed

Epigraph: This passage concludes Max Millikan and W. W. Rostow's 1957 book *A Proposal: Key to an Effective Foreign Policy*, which argues that the U.S. government should use expanded foreign aid to combat communism across the so-called underdeveloped world (Millikan and Rostow 1957, 151). The use of transcendentalist poetry to conclude a book of hard-nosed Cold War strategy might seem downright farcical had the book's author not been Walt Whitman (W. W.) Rostow, son of Russian Jewish socialists and brother of Eugene "Gene" V. Debs and Ralph Waldo Rostow. Gene Rostow would later also serve in the Johnson administration, as undersecretary for political affairs, and would found the neoconservative Committee on the Present Danger during the 1970s (Milne 2008, 18–19).

1 The proposal affirmed the stance that the "fundamental contributions to human knowledge are seldom collective products." Therefore, CENIS is unique because it does not "impose too logical a pattern on the activities of its members," but rather regards itself as a group "of individual scholars bound by no mechanical classification of common programs, each free to pursue his independent interests by whatever techniques seem to him fruitful" (CENIS 1958, 7).

2 In one year alone, the Ford Foundation funded CENIS scholars to develop training programs to improve plans for development in Chile; complete a three-volume set examining "elite attitudes in Venezuela"; study the "psychological and cultural attitudes and predispositions" responsible for national development in Asia; conduct preliminary research on the relationship between Indian voting patterns, economic development, and social change; study defense planning and the budgeting effect of withdrawing from Southeast Asia; research the group identity of Chinese citizens living in the U.S.; and research "the development and interactions of Communist parties and states throughout the world." In addition to philanthropic funding, scholars at the center received federal funding from the Office of Naval Research to study how "attitudinal and behavioral dimensions of the modernization process" affect development; the Department of Defense to develop computer simulations of information diffusion within the Soviet Union and China; and the NSF to research possible uses of the ADMINS "computerized file-handling system" and "tape-punch-card" readers in social science research. Hayward Alker received funding from the NSF to complete research into cybernetic "models of political systems." Federal funding also came from the Center for Space Research to study how "the international system" is reorganized by technological advancements; and from the U.S. Arms Control and Disarmament Agency for studies on the development of "political simulations ('games')" aimed at reducing violence; the effects of conventional arms transfers in developing countries; the "impact of defense expenditures on economic development"; and expanding the "computerization of data on local conflicts" (CENIS 1969, 3, 5–6).

3 Heidegger argues that modern technology seeks to transform nature into a "standing-

reserve": like a dam that constrains a river to create the possibility for energy generation in the future, or an "airliner that stands on the runway . . . ready for takeoff" (1993, 322). For Heidegger, this represents a change in how humans understand their relationship to the world; we become less concerned with thinking about the world than enframing it—that is, developing "the mode of ordering, as standing-reserve" (1993, 325). See also Mitchell (1991, 1–21).

4   I capitalize International Relations—while leaving other disciplines, including area studies and international studies, in lowercase—to mark the incredible effort that has gone into conceptualizing, historicizing, and critiquing IR as a coherent academic discipline: a discipline that examines a specific object (international relations) using specific methods and theoretical perspectives. This compulsion toward disciplinary narration, self-identification, and reification should be read as a symptom of IR's unique formation within the Cold War university. Undifferentiated for most of the twentieth century, the split between International Relations and the more interdisciplinary field of international studies only becomes relevant as academic studies of international relations became less interdisciplinary and more clearly aligned with those theoretical and methodological commitments (e.g., realism) deemed particularly useful for the security apparatus.

5   As this chapter demonstrates, many colleges and universities receive considerable funding from the federal government, yet exist as private or state institutions. The only higher education institutions that operate as part of the federal government itself are the five academies dedicated to training commissioned military officers: the U.S. Military Academy (West Point, NY), Naval Academy (Annapolis, MD), Air Force Academy (Colorado Springs, CO), Coast Guard Academy (New London, CT), and Merchant Marine Academy (Kings Point, NY). American University, Gallaudet University, Georgetown University, Howard University, and George Washington University are all private universities but chartered by the federal government (due to their location in Washington, DC).

6   Philanthropic organizations (rather than the federal government) played the central role creating coherence across different American institutions of higher education. During the late nineteenth century, the country's vast banking, railroad, utility, and manufacturing conglomerates sought workers able to manage complex corporate bureaucracies. During this period, however, American colleges and universities were primarily regional institutions providing classical training to children of the elite. By displacing clergy, local politicians, and agriculturalists on the governing boards of major American colleges and universities, leaders of industry leveraged their newfound positions to impose scientific management on higher education (Barrow 1990, chapter 2). Drawing on the work of Frederick Taylor and others, the Carnegie Foundation for the Advancement of Teaching (CFAT) and the Rockefeller Foundation's General Education Board (GEB) used their considerable economic influence to rationalize American higher education in ways that met corporate labor demands (Barrow 1990, chapter 3). During the first decades of the

twentieth century CFAT and GEB undertook a series of national surveys of higher education institutions, using these data to establish the very terms and categories still widely used within American (and world) higher education. They introduced, for example, the distinction between college and university, between private and public, defined who counts as a professor, and introduced the concept of the credit hour as the measurable product of university education (Barrow 1990, chapter 3).

7   Land grant institutions being the notable exception to direct investment. But even in this case, the federal government gave federal land to states for "the endowment, support, and maintenance of at least one college . . . in such manner as the legislatures of the States may respectively prescribe" ("Transcript of Morrill Act" 1862).

8   In June 1940, President Roosevelt established the National Defense Research Council (NDRC) based on advice from Vannevar Bush, MIT vice president, president of the Carnegie Institution, and founder of American Appliance Company (now known as Raytheon). By 1941, the NDRC was folded into the Office of Scientific Research and Development (OSRD), which oversaw the Manhattan Project and other military scientific research projects (Cole 2009, 86). By the end of World War II, the OSRD had spent $325 million to support university research (Lowen 1997, 44).

9   McNamara, for example, was tasked with developing the most efficient ways to transport people and material to the Pacific front, determining which bombers would be most effective for different tactical operations, and calculating how to maximize the number of civilian casualties in the firebombing of Japanese cities (Byrne 1993, chapter 3; Morris 2003).

10   Catalog cards were the modern technology for storing, organizing, and retrieving data.

11   The government's various wartime security agencies became "informal postgraduate schools where the country's brightest minds mentored young talent in research methods" (Oren 2003, 13). For example, many of the scholars who would become the pillars of postwar political science (Gabriel Almond, Heinz Eulau, Alexander George, Abraham Kaplan, Daniel Lerner, Ithiel de Sola Pool, Edward Shils, and many others) worked with Harold Lasswell during World War II (Oren 2003, 13). Lasswell was himself a scholar of technocracy and propaganda who had studied at University of Chicago under Charles Merriam, "the chief U.S. propagandist in wartime Italy" during World War I (Oren 2003, 10). Merriam had served as president of the American Political Science Association (1925) and cofounded the SSRC.

12   Gendzier identifies three pivotal moments in 1945 that signaled the commitment to cementing closer working relationships between academic, military, and philanthropic institutions: the SSRC's creation of the Committee on Political Behavior, which funded and facilitated the behavioral revolution within the social sciences; the Air Force's launch of Project RAND; and Columbia University's creation of the Russian Institute with $250,000 from the Rockefeller Foundation (Gendzier 1998,

71). Originally a collaboration between the Air Force and the Douglas Aircraft Company, Project RAND harnessed the private sector for military research and development. In 1947, Project RAND separated from Douglas and, with funding from the Ford Foundation, established itself as an independent corporation.

13   There is no family relationship between Vannevar Bush and the war profiteer Prescott Bush.

14   For an overview of the policy debates behind the founding of the NSF and the SSRC's role in shaping the NSF to include the social sciences, see Solovey (2013, chapter 1). In 1951, the NSF budget was $100,000; by 1961 it had grown to $100 million—85 percent of which ended up in university research (Lewontin 1997, 12–18; Cole 2009, 86–106).

15   The GI Bill provided tuition for ten million students over seven years, costing a total of $5.5 billion during a time when the annual federal budget stood at $100 billion. The GI Bill is credited with training "450,000 engineers, 240,000 accountants, 238,000 teachers, 91,000 scientists, 60,000 physicians, 17,000 journalists," and many other highly skilled professionals (Hoffa 2007, 111).

16   One way the humanities became an adjunct of the Cold War effort was through the CIA-funded Congress for Cultural Freedom, which supported artists, writers, musicians, critics, journalists, international exhibitions, conferences, and more than twenty cultural magazines in an organized effort to promote the image of "a pax Americana, a new age of enlightenment . . . called The American Century" (Saunders 2000, 2).

17   I thank Robert Vitalis for making this important clarification.

18   Nkrumah never completed his dissertation, but records show he was working on two different thesis projects: one on the philosophy of imperialism in Africa and a second on group life in Africa. While drafts of both dissertation projects exist in state archives in Ghana, there is no record that Nkrumah submitted either of his manuscripts to his advisors at the University of Pennsylvania. One explanation is that he was accepted into the PhD program with a proposal for the relatively conventional project on group life but dedicated his time and energy to the project of the philosophy of colonialism, resulting in conflict with his committee (Sherwood 1996, 61–65).

19   For a stunning account of the role historically black colleges and universities played in shaping area and international studies, and the discipline of political science in particular, see Vitalis (2015).

20   The Columbia report argues that graduate students should still be trained in traditional disciplines, but should receive additional expertise in "general knowledge of a region": "An appropriate image would be that of a mine with numerous lateral shafts and one deep vertical shaft" (quoted in Wallerstein 1997, 197).

21   The report demonstrated how, by 1947, area studies programs occupied "a permanent place in higher education" and could be found in fifty-two undergraduate and thirty-seven graduate programs (Hall 1947, 7). Latin America was the most popular

region of study, followed by the Far East, the United States (American civilization and American studies), and Russia, but still lacked coverage in "the Near East, Africa, the Indian World, or Southeast Asia" (Hall 1947, 9).

22 Robert Hall was an intelligence officer in World War I, received his PhD in geography from the University of Michigan in 1927, became a leading Japanologist, and later served with the oss in the Pacific during World War II. After the war, he returned to the academy, where he helped create the Center for Japanese Studies at the University of Michigan and served as president of the Association for Asian Studies and as chairman of the ssrc's board. See "Faculty History Project," University of Michigan, accessed June 2018. Searchable under "Faculty Histories" at http://um2017.org.

23 Hall laments, however, that "a great deal more is known about the Greek and Roman world than about China," because of long-term academic interest in classical fields. In addition, the world of antiquity is "an essential part of our heritage" and therefore "student and teacher alike . . . have a better chance of understanding them" than, say, the "life and problems of India or the Arab world" (Hall 1947, 12).

24 The first Committee on African Studies was created in 1941 at University of Pennsylvania. Working for the oss, Pennsylvania history professor Conyers Read became keenly aware of how little information was available about Africa. The committee was one initiative that brought together political scientists, economists, linguists, geographers, earth scientists, and botanists to create a graduate program that included language training (in Swahili and Fanti) and also recruited African students—including future Ghanaian president Kwame Nkrumah. Read would also recruit Howard University professor Ralph Bunche to the oss (Robinson 2004, 134–35).

25 For biographical accounts of what it was like to live during this expansionist heyday of area studies, see Vansina (1994) and Anderson (2016).

26 Government officials argued, in a December 5, 1964, working paper, that the U.S. government could offer "assistance and advice" to "indigenous governments" in conducting "counterinsurgency operations." However, these efforts were hampered by a "poverty of knowledge" owing to the fact that "social science resources ha[d] not yet been adequately mobilized to study social conflict and control" (reprinted in Horowitz 1967, 51–52).

27 Secretary of Defense Robert McNamara shut down Project Camelot in 1965 after Professor Johan Galtung leaked sensitive documents to Chilean colleagues who began denouncing the project. While Project Camelot was shuttered before it had produced its behavioral model, many of its main supporters continued to argue that the merger between policy and science—including psychology and other social sciences—would help spread American liberal values around the world and make it possible to "prosecute the Cold War efficiently and nonviolently" and in ways consistent with "the democratic values embedded in U.S. policy" (Herman 1998, 107; see also Horowitz 1966, 1967; Lowe 1966; Rohde 2013). The project was

funded by the Special Operations Research Organization, whose "work included providing the army with dozens of country-specific handbooks on psychological operations, case studies of Southeast Asia focusing on the exploitation of psychological vulnerabilities, and a comprehensive data bank called the Counter-Insurgency Information Analysis Center" (Herman 1998, 102).

28 During the Vietnam War, counterinsurgency operations "required the kind of information about Vietnamese society that only social scientists could provide" (Gendzier 1998, 86). In 1967, Samuel Huntington estimated that more than 90 percent of social scientific research on Vietnam was funded by the U.S. government (Huntington 1967, 505). Between 1966 and 1970, the Department of Defense spent between $34 million and $48 million on "behavioral and social-science research" (Nader 1997, 123).

29 I would like to thank an anonymous reviewer for making this connection.

30 The same year, Dunn published an article in the first issue of *World Politics* arguing that IR "should be regarded as a separate branch of learning" rather than "a miscellany of materials and methods drawn from existing subjects" (Dunn 1948, 142). The following year, Dunn published a follow-up article overviewing the committee's findings, offering a highly "interdisciplinary vision of the field" (Guilhot 2011, 19; see also Dunn 1949).

31 Dean Rusk served in World War II, returned from war to work in the War Department and the State Department, and as president of the Rockefeller Foundation (1952–61). He later served as secretary of state under Presidents Kennedy and Johnson (1961–69) and finished his career teaching international law at the University of Georgia School of Law (Schoenbaum 1988; Rusk 1990).

32 George Kennan, Herbert Butterfield, and Raymond Aron were also invited but could not attend the meeting.

33 These included, for example, the American Committee for International Studies, the Council on Foreign Relations, the Foreign Policy Association, and Institute of Pacific Relations, among many other professional organizations and academic and policy forums (Parmar 2012, chapter 3).

34 Georgetown's Center for Strategic and International Studies, which opened just weeks before the Cuban missile crisis, was originally named the Center for Strategic Studies. The absence of "International" in the center's original name indicates the centrality of "cold war strategic issues" to its founding (Smith 1993, 1). The founders, however, shared a more nuanced understanding of strategic studies than come from simply focusing on national military power. They instead advocated conceptions of security that drew from classical theories (rather than systems analysis) and resisted focusing exclusively on military weaponry and nuclear arsenals (Smith 1993, 3). The inclusion of "International" in the title evolved as a means to acknowledge this more nuanced understanding of security. In its early years, and under the leadership of executive secretary David M. Abshire, the center established a whole series of new "councils, boards, and working groups," in-

cluding the International Research Council (IRC). The IRC brought together an interdisciplinary and transatlantic group of high-powered scholars, which quickly become the center's intellectual hub. Six years later, the growing status of the IRC encouraged the board to officially change the center's name to the Center for Strategic and International Studies (Smith 1993, 39–40).

35 The Center for International Studies is commonly abbreviated CIS. However, I use the abbreviation CENIS not only in recognition of Rostow's preferred acronym, but also because of the internal disagreements raised by this acronym. As one CENIS member and institutional historian wrote, "many Center members . . . found the acronym [CENIS] unattractive and misleading in its subtle suggestion that the Center was akin to a governmental institution" (Blackmer 2002, xvii–xviii). While not claiming that the center is the same as a governmental institution, I nonetheless think that the acronym CENIS marks the uncomfortably close working and intellectual relationship that actually existed between the center and the American security apparatus.

36 This articulation of his intellectual history appeared to be a strong guiding point in Rostow's thinking as he presented a nearly identical autobiographical narrative a decade earlier at the annual meeting of the Economic History Association (Rostow 1947).

37 Even at this point in his career, Rostow's decision to study British industrialism was undertaken with an eye toward the refutation of Marxist economic explanations of economic growth: "Like Marx, Rostow came to believe that it was possible to trace through the ages a number of inevitable stages through which all nations passed. The British industrial revolution was the linchpin of modern history: the event that all nations had to emulate in order to expand and mature" (Milne 2008, 27).

38 A number of these articles were republished in Rostow's first book, *British Economy of the Nineteenth Century* (1948), which establishes distinct periods of economic change between 1790 and 1914. This book argues that the rise of the British industrial economy was not simply attributable to changing economic processes and the centralization of capital, but also to particular political and social developments. In the years between the end of World War II and his appointment at CENIS, Rostow wrote on questions concerning European reconstruction (Rostow 1949, 1950a, 1950c), gave a speech at Oxford regarding the history of American diplomacy (Rostow 1946), and authored a number of theoretical pieces examining how economic historians might better understand the complex relationship between internal characteristics—such as "short-run fluctuations in income, output, and employment"—and the nation's "rate of economic progress" (Rostow 1951b, 316; see also Rostow 1950b, 1951a).

39 The manuscript was nearing completion in 1941, but Gayer was killed in a car accident and the book was not published until 1953. This book, however, served as a reservoir of data that Rostow drew from in subsequent works on British industrialization.

40 For a history of the extensive role this text played in laying the intellectual foundation of CENIS, see Gilman (2003, 160–63).

41 Max Millikan described this book as using "the resources of the academic community" to address "problems of action confronting the United States in its relationship with the rest of the world" and, thereby, aiding "the harried official who must plot daily moves in the chess game" as well as the "worried citizen who must decide whether to support or oppose the general national strategy" (Rostow 1952a, ix).

42 During World War II, Kluckhohn demonstrated that nonexperts on Japan could nonetheless make "careful use of social science methods" in order to achieve "a substantially higher level of understanding, precisely in the areas most relevant to policy" (Parsons and Vogt 1962, 146–47).

43 While the CENIS monographs on the Soviet Union and China involved considerable collaboration within CENIS, Rostow is listed as the sole author of each book. This stems from CENIS's policy concerning authorship, based on a concern about the fundamental difficulty that arises when presenting a clear and coherent view of a "whole society in motion"; it is the "general conviction of the Center for International Studies (CENIS)" that "a unified view" of China can only be "the responsibility of one person" (Rostow 1954b, vi). In this way, Rostow claims to offer a "unified view" of China, but one that is by no means "definitive," since "other scholars charged with this task would have emerged with a synthesis somewhat different in emphasis" and "substance" (1954b, vi). Both books list Rostow as the sole author, but name other collaborators on the title page (Alfred Levin, Richard W. Hatch, Frank A. Kierman, and Alexander Eckstein), along with the acknowledgment that the books were written with the "assistance of others at the Center for International Studies, Massachusetts Institute of Technology."

44 Coming from a well-connected New England family, McGeorge Bundy served as an army intelligence officer in World War II, including time as aide to Rear Admiral Alan G. Kirk. After the war, he took a position at the Council on Foreign Relations, and in 1949 a lectureship in Harvard's government department, receiving tenure in 1951. A decade later President Kennedy appointed him national security advisor, a position he held in the Johnson administration. From 1966 to 1979, he served as president of the Ford Foundation (Bird 1998). Between 1979 and 1989, he taught history at New York University.

45 I thank an anonymous reviewer for this.

46 While area studies, including African studies, were largely created as extensions of the Cold War university, it is important to note that Africana, black, and African studies centers within institutions of higher education were often created as the result of demands and protests from students and faculty (Vitalis 2015, 15). However, starting in 1968 and in the face of increasingly radical student protests, the Ford Foundation, under the leadership of McGeorge Bundy, began heavily funding African American studies programs in an effort to exert moderating influence over them (Rooks 2006).

47 Descriptions of these activities can be found in the MIT student newspaper, *The*

Tech (Staff 1967, 1969a; Ashe 1968; Elkin 1969; Kunin 1969; Makowski and McRoberts 1969; Makowski 1970; Feirtag 1971).

48 The Instrumentation Laboratory played a key role in developing multiple independently targeted reentry vehicle (MIRV) missile technology, while the Lincoln Laboratory conducted research on antiballistic missiles and moving target indicator technologies. For an overview of the MIT faculty and student protests targeting the science laboratories, see Leslie (1993, 233–41).

49 The aim of this "one-day takeover" was to gather incriminating documents from CENIS, an action modeled on a previously successful occupation at Harvard in which students took documents from the president's office and published them in a newspaper, *The Old Mole*, which became the primary research for the study *How Harvard Rules* (Albert 2006, 98–101).

50 The project on Communist Communication (Com-Com), directed by Ithiel de Sola Pool, mapped to the Soviet internal communication system and developed computer simulations of the possible effects of pro-Western messaging. The International Communism Project developed assessments of revolutionary movements around the world, which were used by governmental security agencies to externally corroborate intelligence findings. The Cambridge Project (Project CAM) was funded by the Department of Defense to "develop general theory" of revolutionary activity (Old Mole 1969).

2. "The World's Largest . . . Development Institution"

Epigraph: From McNamara's inaugural keynote speech to the board of governors (McNamara 1981a, 3).

1 One of the common criticisms of the term "Third World" is that it spatially fixes the world in ways that make it impossible to appreciate the world as actually global.

2 The World Bank consists of the IBRD and the International Development Association (IDA), created in 1960. The IBRD borrows capital from international bond markets and loans it to governments for use in public development projects. The IDA receives money from donor nations for the purpose of making low-interest, debtor-friendly loans to countries otherwise deemed not creditworthy by international bond markets. The World Bank is also a constitutive member of the World Bank Group, which includes the IBRD, IDA, International Financial Corporation (IFC; created 1956), the International Center for Settlement of Investment Disputes (ICSID; created 1966), and the Multilateral Investment Guarantee Agency (MIGA; created 1988). The IFC facilitates investment in the private sector in developing countries, while ICSID seeks to resolve legal disputes between international investors and debtor nations and MIGA insures private investors against losses suffered in developing countries due to noneconomic risk, such as political instability (World Bank 2003, 10–23; Marshall 2008, 9).

3   The early World Bank loans went to France, Netherlands, Luxembourg, and Denmark.

4   In his first presentations as president of Ford Motor Company in November 1960, McNamara gave a corporate overview to the company's senior executives at the Greenbrier Hotel in West Virginia. In this talk, he drew from the work of Harvard Business School professor Theodore Levitt, arguing that Ford should consider manufacturing different parts in different countries to reduce the cost of labor (Byrne 1993, 362).

5   This trend only continued after McNamara's tenure. By the mid-1990s, the World Bank employed roughly eight hundred economists and controlled a research budget of approximately $25 million, "resources [that] dwarf those of any university department or research institution working on development economics" (Stern and Ferreira 1997, 524).

6   Those present at this meeting remember looking out the window as McNamara talked and seeing a darkening sky that they thought portended an imminent thunderstorm. Only later did they discover that large parts of Washington, DC, were on fire as rioters torched buildings in the wake of the Martin Luther King Jr. assassination (Clark 1981, 168).

7   Prior to McNamara's tenure, the World Bank was considered a "reluctant Bank" and capitalized at $5.5 billion—only $3.5 billion of which was borrowed on financial markets. By the time McNamara left, the World Bank had collected $4.7 billion from national treasuries and an astonishing $99 billion from bond markets (Clark 1981, 168).

8   In this book, Ferguson distinguishes between the "development discourse" of the World Bank and the "academic discourse," thereby setting up the academic discourse as a measure against which to adjudicate the inaccuracies in the World Bank's discursive production. However, it is important to note that Ferguson is aware that the academic discourse is itself always situated within its own institutions, which shape what academics do and say. He writes,

> Academic discourse on Lesotho has of course its own rules of formation and responds to its own ideological and institutional constraints, which could well be the subject of another analysis. Like "development" discourse, academic discourse deals not simply with "the facts" but with a constructed version of the object. This does not imply, of course, that the two versions are somehow equally true or equally adequate to any given purpose. Indeed, the reader will see in the analysis to follow that I write from within academic discourse, and that I unreservedly accept the academic judgment that much of "development" discourse on Lesotho is widely inaccurate. *But that judgment is not itself the point of this analysis.* Rather, I take the incompatibility of "development" discourse and academic norms as a point of departure for an exploration of the distinctly different way that "development" discourse is structured. (Ferguson 1994, 29, emphasis in original)

In drawing a connection between the World Bank's national development policies and their effects on higher education, this chapter argues that development and academic discourses might not be as distinct as Ferguson depicts here.

9   During this period, member countries of the Organization for Economic Cooperation and Development were spending $1.1 billion in bilateral aid for education (about half of which was coming from France to Francophone Africa); the USSR, China, and the Eastern Bloc spent $200 million; international organizations such as the World Bank, Inter-American Development Bank, the United Nations Development Programme (UNDP), the United Nations Children's Fund (UNICEF), and the United Nations Educational, Scientific and Cultural Organization (UNESCO) spent roughly $582 million; nonprofit organizations spent another $400 million; and philanthropic organizations were spending $45 million (Phillips 1976, 1–2).

10   Today the World Bank is the largest nongovernment funder of education, a surprising fact given that during its first decades of operation education did not even register as an area of focus. The World Bank provides roughly 20 percent of the total nongovernmental funds for education worldwide (Jones 2007, xiv). Since 1962, the World Bank has spent more than $69 billion on more than 1,500 projects (World Bank 2011, 1). The World Bank first publicly expressed an interest in funding education projects in 1960, when President Eugene Black observed a connection between economic development and much-needed education opportunities in newly independent Africa (Vawda et al. 2003, 646; Jones 2007, 30–31). Black's successor, George Woods, made the first World Bank loan for an education project in 1962, a $5 million IDA credit to build six secondary schools and a teacher training college in Tunisia (Jones 2007, 45).

11   These institutions include Fourah Bay College (Sierra Leone), Makerere College (Uganda), Gordon Memorial College (Sudan), Kitchener School of Medicine (Sudan), Achimota College (Gold Coast), and Yaba College (Nigeria).

12   This took place within the context of a general increase in all education spending. For example, in 1960, total expenditure of education stood at $2 billion (in 1976 dollars), or 2.4 percent of GNP. By 1976, African countries were spending $38 billion (4 percent of GNP) on education (World Bank 1980, 46).

13   *Transition* was one of the many journals created by the Council of Cultural Freedom, operated by the CIA (Saunders 1999, 334).

14   Unlike the World Bank response, which was written for the World Bank by an American economist, the Lagos Plan of Action was preceded by three conferences—in Dakar, Monrovia, and Addis Ababa—and was itself "a culmination of a long intensive process of discussion and preparation by African scholars, experts and Government officials, principally through the umbrella of the OAU and the ECA" (Bujra 1982, i; see also Shaw 1985, 8).

15   Brandt takes a slight detour in the text "to make some remarks on my own behalf." He writes, "As a young journalist opposing dictatorship, I was not blind to the problems of colonialism and the fight for independence. During the Second World War,

I also gave thought to the problem of decolonization and development in terms of a new world order. I met Nehru, Nasser, Tito, and other leaders, at a time when most people, at least in my part of the world, had not even heard about a Third World or the beginning of a non-aligned movement" (Brandt et al. 1980, 8–9).

16   While the Brandt Report was an immediate best seller in Britain, problems translating and distributing the report meant that "six months after its release there was very little first-hand knowledge of the contents of the Report among public opinion makers in the South" (Elson 1982, 126n1).

17   The Berg Report was the product of a 1979 request by the World Bank's African governors to McNamara to study the causes of the economic problems facing Africa. It was written over the course of two years "on the basis of memoranda from a range of invited commentators, a basic consultancy drafted by Elliot Berg and a series of in-house papers and review committee meetings." It was "the first comprehensive ideological and programmatic manifesto setting out the post-McNamara Bank's response to lagging development" (Green and Allison 1986, 62).

18   African nations have been unable to adapt to the global crisis because they have "overprotected industry, held back agriculture, and absorbed much administrative capacity," paid "too little attention . . . to administrative constraints" allowing "public sectors [to] frequently become overextended," and, finally, show "a consistent bias against agriculture in price, tax, and exchange-rate policies" (World Bank 1981a, 4; see also Berg 1986). The same concerns were echoed in Robert Bates's (1981) highly influential book *Markets and States in Tropical Africa*.

3. "Marketing Can Be Magic"

Epigraphs: (1) From a handwritten note archived with Levitt's working paper draft of "The Globalization of Markets," found in Theodore Levitt, "You can observe a lot just by watching . . . ," 1982(?), 3, Theodore Levitt Papers, HBS Archives, Baker Library Historical Collections, Harvard Business School, hereafter cited as Theodore Levitt Papers. (2) From a list of thoughts typed on a yellow note card and included with the letters and drafts pertaining to the writing of the "Author's Note" for the republishing of "Marketing Myopia" in Howard A. Thompson's *The Great Writings of Marketing*. Found in Theodore Levitt, "Mehidabell—Don Marquis' cockroach . . . ," 1974, Theodore Levitt Papers.

1   An understanding of the world as comprising a series of national markets is, of course, not limited to marketing practitioners. As described in chapter 2, development practitioners during this period also imagined a world in which economic gains could be achieved by managing "national economic growth, with trade as a stimulus," within the context of "a clear range of national political-economics" and under the "macroeconomic goal" of consolidating "national welfare, through a context of stable monetary relations" (McMichael 1996, 26; see also Ferguson 1994).

2   For example, in 1982 very few business publications used the word "globalization." The term appears in only twenty-four articles listed in EBSCO Business Abstracts (a number inflated by the fact that a search returns articles given the subject heading "insurance and globalization," despite the fact that "globalization" does not appear in the article itself), accessed August 2015. A search of ABI/Inform Complete turns up five articles in 1982 that use the word "globalization" (accessed August 2015). There were considerably more articles containing the word "global"; a total of 312 listed on EBSCO Business Abstracts. Many of these articles describe particular changes in specific industries that are "going global," including insurance (Dowling 1982), reinsurance (Jannai 1982), banking (Forsyth 1982), and security manufacturing (Hitchler 1982). Other articles review such moves at particular firms—such as AT&T (Adam 1982), American International Group (Campanella 1982), Arco (Emond 1982), and General Motors (Walsh 1982). Other articles use the term "global" to refer generally to climate change, energy policy, the recession, trade talks, the economic threat posed by Japanese companies, competition faced by American manufacturers, American fiscal policy, changing retail and purchasing habits, concerns about the competitiveness of American workers, and changing computer technologies and communications, among other topics (accessed August 2015).

3   Steger writes that Levitt's article "spawned hundreds of similar pieces convincing the world's leading companies to 'go global.' The advertising industry, in particular, set about creating 'global brands' by means of global commercial campaigns" (2008, 181).

4   One could say that globalization was not simply "a particular new object" that arrived "like an unexpected guest at a family reunion," but rather the production of a new problematic that ends up transforming "the *entire* terrain and its *entire* horizon" (Althusser and Balibar 1999, 24, emphasis in original).

5   For example, between 1910 and 1930 basic marketing terms such as "brands," "comparison shopping," "durable goods," "market segmentation," "marketing research," "markup," "product differentiation," and dozens of others were developed first by academics in business schools before being "passed into common managerial use," where they "adhered to a wider field of action among manufacturers, sellers, and eventually consumers who integrated this vocabulary" into all aspects of their practice (Applbaum 2004, 184–85).

6   Levitt applied the scientific approach himself, conducting a mail-in survey of *Harvard Business Review* subscribers concerning their views on the Cold War and military spending (Levitt 1960a).

7   Levitt points out that market researchers were not only all trained by the same small pool of people but were fundamentally worried "about the trustworthy quality of their" recommendations, and therefore offered as definitive their own "common sense" marketing suggestions backed by data drawn from interviews conducted on a hypothetical customer "in his living room or an isolation booth" (Levitt 1960c, 78, 82–83).

8   An example of the ways in which business leaders are the intended audience for the 1960 article is evident in the textbox that directs "executives concerned with increasing marketing effectiveness" to other articles published by the *Harvard Business Review* (Levitt 1960b, 54).

9   In many ways, the success of "Marketing Myopia" owes a lot to Levitt's "ability to string pithy, punchy, pacy phrases, paragraphs and papers together" (Brown 2005, 27; see also Aherne 2006) as well as his ability to portray himself "as a practical man, an ordinary Joe, one of the guys" (Brown 1999, 5). His writing comes across as natural and his claims self-evident. As such, Levitt is "virtually alone among the discipline's intelligentsia" as "the voice, personification, and apotheosis of marketing and the marketing concept" (Brown 1999, 5).

10   Levitt would go on to win this prize three more times over the course of his career, along with numerous prestigious academic awards, and remains the most published author in the *Harvard Business Review* (Brown 2004, 211).

11   Levitt argued that "in some respects" talk about social responsibility "*is* merely talk" but can become "dangerous" because "what people say, they ultimately come to believe if they say it enough, and what they believe affects what they do." In this case, he predicted that "with all its resounding good intentions business statesmanship may create the corporate equivalent of the unitary state," turning "the corporation into a twentieth-century equivalent of the medieval Church" (Levitt 1958, 44).

12   Letter from Theodore Levitt to Clifford Geertz, June 6, 1983, Theodore Levitt Papers.

13   Levitt uses the term "marketing imagination" to refer to an individual's ability to imagine markets anew. I would argue, however, that this approach assumes that individuals—especially those possessing unique capabilities of thought—are the primary producers of new knowledge. From the point of view of reproduction, however, Levitt is both someone of unique capabilities and also someone working within a conjuncture, and set of material apparatuses, that make it possible not only to imagine markets differently but also to reproduce a global imaginary. For a discussion of the differences between imagination and imaginary, and how one might theorize the imaginary in relation to the global imaginary, see Kamola (2010).

14   This debt to Levitt, however, goes unacknowledged by Friedman. In the first scene of *The World Is Flat*, Friedman claims instead to have discovered the flatness of the world while playing golf in Bangalore. Describing the trip to Bangalore as his "own Columbus-like journey of exploration," Friedman claims to arrive at this insight by combining anecdotal observations gathered during an afternoon playing golf surrounded by buildings bearing the logos for Microsoft, IBM, Goldman Sachs, HP, and Texas Instruments with the fairly pedestrian observation offered by the Indian CEO Nandan Nilekani that communications technology is leveling the economic "playing field" (Friedman 2005, 4, 7).

15	In addition to the twin 1983 publications in *Harvard Business Review* and *The Marketing Imagination*, this essay was also highly anthologized (see Kantrow 1985; Aliber and Click 1993; Buzzell, Quelch, and Bartlett 1995; Ghauri and Brasad 1995).

16	For an overview of the importance of the *Earthrise* photo in shaping the global imaginary, see the introduction.

17	Letter from Edward H. Meyer to Theodore Levitt, September 19, 1984, Theodore Levitt Papers.

18	Letter from Theodore Levitt to Edward H. Meyer, September 25, 1984, Theodore Levitt Papers.

19	Letter from Cabell Brand to Theodore Levitt, May 17, 1983, Theodore Levitt Papers.

20	Letter from Cabell Brand to Theodore Levitt, May 17, 1983, Theodore Levitt Papers.

21	Letter from Earl W. Seitz to Theodore Levitt, May 9, 1983, Theodore Levitt Papers.

22	Others on the list include Bank of Boston, Barclay's, Barnett Bank, Boston Globe, Carnation, Carter Hawley Hale Stores, Chemical Bank, Ciba-Geigy (Basle, Switzerland), Citibank, Continental Bank, csx, Deloit Haskins & Sells, Estée Lauder Companies, Dun & Bradstreet, Equitable Life Assurance, First International Bank, First Mississippi Corporation, Gulf Oil, Heinz, Highland Resources, IBM, International Executive Service Corporation, Irving Trust, Knight Ridder, LEX Service, Lockheed, Loews, MacMillan Bloedel, Matsushita School of Government and Management, McCann-Erickson Worldwide, McKinsey & Co., Goodyear Tire, Merloni Elettrodomestici, Mohawk Rubber, Motion Pictures Association, Motorola, NEC, Nestlé, Nomura Research Institute, Northfolk Southern, Northrop, Royal Bank of Canada, Scientific Atlanta, Shawmut Bank, chancellor of Vanderbilt University, csx, and Union Pacific. This list is compiled based on the letters received by John H. McArthur, dean of Harvard Business School, recognizing the receipt of *The Marketing Imagination* as well as an alphabetized list of seventy-four individuals and companies, including an indication whether the book should be sent to the "CH" or "COB" (chairman of the board), "CEO," "Pres," "VP-Mrtg," and so on. Theodore Levitt Papers.

23	Letter from George Weissman to Dean McArthur, December 14, 1983, Theodore Levitt Papers; letter from E. D. Disborough to Dean McArthur, December 14, 1983, Theodore Levitt Papers.

24	Letter from Clarence J. Brown to Dean McArthur, November 25, 1983, Theodore Levitt Papers.

25	Letter from Theodore Levitt to Robert Wallace, November 18, 1983, Theodore Levitt Papers. This list includes top executives at General Foods, American Express, Consolidated Natural Gas, Grey Advertising, MGM Entertainment, New York Magazine, Twentieth Century Fox, and Wyse Advertising, as well as academics at University of Toronto, Stanford, MIT's Sloan School of Management, Northwestern's Kellogg School of Management, and the Wharton School at University of Pennsylvania. Letter from Theodore Levitt to Megan E. Keller, March 3, 1983, Theodore Levitt Papers.

26   Letter from Theodore Levitt to Robert Wallace, June 29, 1983, Theodore Levitt Papers.

27   Letter from Robert Wallace to Theodore Levitt, May 13, 1983, Theodore Levitt Papers.

28   Theodore Levitt, "The Immiseration of Marketing in the Academy," c. 1979, 1, 14, Theodore Levitt Papers.

29   Even while eschewing the lifestyle of the management guru ("I prefer playing tennis or writing" to "travel[ing] the world preaching" a "particular gospel"), he nonetheless pronounces, with a sage-like quality, that "what really counts is thinking—thinking with energy and courage" (Clutterbuck and Crainer 1990, 162).

30   Cases do, however, come with teaching notes and are explicitly designed to elicit certain kinds of responses. As one Harvard professor announced in his class, "There may not be any 'right' answers to these cases, but I sure as hell know a 'wrong' answer when I hear one" (Mark 1987, 23).

31   The connections Theodore Levitt enjoyed with the private sector meant that he would become particularly useful in "turn[ing] an armchair case into a field case" with a single phone call (Mark 1987, 23).

32   These numbers have only increased in subsequent years. By the mid-2000s, Harvard Business Publishing was selling eight million cases, or 80 percent of the world's business cases, with faculty and staff creating 250 new cases a year (Datar, Garvin, and Cullen 2010, 240, 250). Case writing is organized according to a highly stratified division of labor. During the 1980s, much of the work took place on the top floor of the Baker Library, in a cubicle-filled room—Baker 400—inhabited by some forty to sixty researchers. Most of those writing cases are Harvard DBA students who write cases for credit, postdocs, junior faculty, and paid research staff. Cases are overseen by faculty—usually junior faculty—who do so to curry favor with the dean, for promotion, or as a favor to senior colleagues. Primary authorship is often attributed to the faculty supervisor, even if others did the vast majority of the work. Once written, the company featured vets the study. Based on their feedback, cases are accepted, accepted but with key details disguised, scrapped altogether, taught once then discarded, or taught only in the presence of a company representative. If successfully taught, cases become part of the curriculum. Successful cases are sent to the Division of Case Services, which has them edited, typeset, printed, marketed, and distributed (Mark 1987, 19–28). Eric Richtmeyer should be credited with the idea of looking at how Harvard case studies have changed over time.

33   Graduate School of Business Administration, "Harvard Business School: MBA Program, 1983," AB5.2, 7, HBS Archives, Baker Library Historical Collections, Harvard Business School.

34   Case writing is also commonly used to draw closer connections between Harvard Business School and potential corporate donors. Some have noted that the brilliance of the case method "lies not in pedagogical effectiveness, but rather in its

business-generating power" (Mark 1987, 76). When asked, executives are usually eager to have Harvard Business School use their corporation as the topic for a case study. The company gets not only hundreds of the brightest students examining their business strategies but also an opportunity to draw closer connections with the school and possibly even recruit Harvard MBAs in the future. In return, the business school often leverages the personal and institutional relationships developed during the case-writing process to fund-raise, with a smaller subset of cases written specifically to solicit endowed chairs (Mark 1987, 77–79). The year Levitt wrote "The Globalization of Markets," for example, Harvard Business School spent $150,000 writing cases on Korean companies as an explicit attempt to attract the $1.5–2 million needed for an endowed chair. When the chairman of Daewoo arrived on campus, he was not only treated to lavish meals and limousine rides to and from the airport, but also invited into a classroom discussing the Daewoo case study, a private screening of a movie on Daewoo Corporation produced for the AMP program, and numerous opportunities to meet with senior faculty (Mark 1987, 80–84).

35 "Harvard Business School: Masters in Business Administration," 1992, AB5.2, 11–12, Masters in Business Administration Catalogue and Accompanying Material, HBS Archives, Baker Library Historical Collections, Harvard Business School.

36 "Harvard Business School: Masters in Business Administration," 1992, AB5.2, 12.

37 "The Globalization of Markets" was Levitt's twenty-third article published in the *Harvard Business Review.*

38 Levitt described his approach to editorship of the *Harvard Business Review* as starting from the question "Who are the customers?" and from there trying "to understand the customers and the competitive environment and the customer's own internal environment, their cognitive systems and what pressures they work under. . . . This has been reflected in the kind of articles we run, the design and the editing of the magazine" (quoted in Clutterbuck and Crainer 1990, 162–63).

39 As of 2007, five hundred business schools in thirty countries were accredited by the Association to Advance Collegiate Schools of Business (Hay 2007, 371).

4. "Realities of the Global Economy"

Epigraph: From an essay written just prior to joining the World Bank and published in *The American Economy in Transition* (ed. Martin Feldstein, 1980) alongside contributions from Harvard professor Benjamin M. Friedman and Milton Friedman.

1 Letter from A. W. Clausen to Dean McArthur, November 22, 1983, Theodore Levitt Papers, HBS Archives, Baker Library Historical Collections, Harvard Business School.

2 It should be noted that Clausen was, more precisely, president and CEO of Bank-

America Corporation, the holding company that owns and operates Bank of America along with a host of other subsidiaries. However, because Bank of America is the most important, and best known, of these entities, I use it throughout the chapter as colloquial shorthand for BankAmerica Corporation.

3   I thank Vijay Prashad for recommending I spend time fleshing out the key differences between McNamara and Clausen.

4   Bank of America started as Bank of Italy, a small San Francisco institution that survived the 1906 earthquake and fire, and made its profits loaning money to Bay Area residents for reconstruction (Clausen 1971). Clausen took over Bank of America from its founder, Amadeo Peter Giannini.

5   I have been unable to confirm that Clausen took classes with Levitt while at Harvard Business School, due to the fact that the pertinent archival material remains sealed. However, the possibility that a personal connection developed while at Harvard might help explain why Levitt sent Clausen a copy of *The Marketing Imagination*.

6   The Yomiuri International Economic Society is a monthly social gathering and lecture event bringing together business leaders, think tank professionals, scholars, and diplomats stationed in Japan. The Yomiuri Research Institute—a think tank run by Japan's largest newspaper, the center-right *Yomiuri Shinbun*—runs this speaker series. Many thanks to Reo Matsuzaki for this explanation.

7   This is a view Clausen held prior to his tenure at the World Bank. As president of Bank of America, he addressed a meeting of top executives from the world's 116 largest banks, arguing that growing levels of nationalism and regionalism threatened the global market, while urging international bankers to do more to advocate for increased free trade and movement of capital (Hummer 1977, 24).

8   Munir Benjenk, one of the "closet conservatives" in the McNamara Bank, who was eventually promoted to vice president for external relations under Clausen, urged his new boss to "signal a break" from his predecessor and follow the "more conservative public opinion" (Kapur, Lewis, and Webb 1997, 336).

9   This process culminated when Clausen's successor, Barber Conable, imposed a full-scale reorganization of the World Bank in 1987 that purged the remaining Keynesians within the World Bank (George and Sabelli 1994; Goldman 2005, 92).

10   The amount of money borrowed by middle-income developing countries from commercial banks had grown $221 billion over the decade, from $30 billion in 1970 to $251 billion in 1979, compared with a $40 billion growth in borrowing from the World Bank ($7 to $47 billion). McNamara worried that commercial banks would eventually become unwilling to continue lending at levels high enough to offset losses resulting from domestic adjustment (McNamara 1981a, 627–28).

11   Adam Smith observed that fixed capital also includes "the acquired and useful abilities" such as those received through "education, study, or apprenticeship" (Smith [1776] 1999, 377). In his 1962 book *Capitalism and Freedom*, Milton Friedman builds on this argument but advances the claim that, unlike primary and

secondary education, higher education lacks a "neighborhood effect." While government-funded primary and secondary education might have broad social benefits, investment in higher education constitutes human capital, an investment that, like fixed capital, benefits primarily those making the prudent investment in the form of higher wages (Friedman 1962, chapter 6; for a brilliant critique, see Adamson 2009b). Psacharopoulos writes, "The view that education is a form of investment is at least as old as the economics profession itself. Adam Smith put it loud and clear in his *Wealth of Nations* that the creation of labor skills entails an expense that is later paid off by increased productivity. The basic principle, almost forgotten for nearly two centuries, took on new vigor in the late 1950s with the work of T. W. Schultz, Gary Becker, and Jacob Mincer at the University of Chicago and Columbia University" (1991a, 7).

12 In calculating the rate of return on college education in the United States, Becker found that, while there was considerable variation depending upon "sex, race, urban or rural, and graduate and dropout status," the rate of return on higher education for "white male college graduates" was "considerable even after adjustment for differential ability"—and even "college dropouts, nonwhites, women and rural persons" saw rates of return that were "far from negligible" (Becker 1993, 195).

13 For a more detailed overview of human capital theory, see Thurow (1970).

14 Before and during his tenure at the World Bank, Psacharopoulos published numerous academic studies comparing national levels of investment in education and the differing spending levels on primary, secondary, and tertiary education, and calculating the rates of return on these investments (Psacharopoulos with Hinchliffe 1973; Psacharopoulos 1981, 1985, 1994).

15 The data, in fact, find that students graduating with college degrees in social sciences and arts have nearly the same earning potential as those with degrees in engineering, and greater earning potential than those with degrees in sciences and agriculture—despite the fact that liberal arts degrees cost the government half as much (Psacharopoulos 1980a, 3). Pointing out that "the sample of countries is extremely small" and focuses on urban populations, Psacharopoulos explains away these findings as resulting from high levels of public sector hiring. As such, he warns governments not to use these data to justify a switch "from basic to higher education, or from engineering and agronomy to liberal arts" (Psacharopoulos 1980a, 4).

16 Citing the "untapped willingness of households to pay for education," especially higher education, the authors argue that it was unjustifiable during a time of "adverse macroeconomic conditions" for taxpayers to subsidize university education (Psacharopoulos, Tan, and Jimenez 1986, 1).

17 The journal article (Psacharopoulos 1985) was part of a long succession of academic articles, books, and dissertations examining the comparative rate of return on education across different countries and regions (for an overview of this literature, see Psacharopoulos 1985, 584). The first empirical national studies of human capi-

tal drew upon national censuses, surveys, and other data to calculate the rate of return on education in individual countries, including the United States (Hanoch 1967), Great Britain (Blaug 1967), India (Gounden 1967), and Mexico (Carnoy 1967). Subsequent studies drew upon these national surveys to create cross-national comparisons of rates of return. For example, Psacharopoulos's book, *Returns to Education: An International Comparison* (Psacharopoulos with Hinchliffe 1973) compared previously published data from across thirty-two countries. The 1985 article expanded his initial analysis to forty-five countries (Psacharopoulos 1985, 584). In this article, he concludes that the social rate of return on primary education is "several percentage points" higher than those of secondary and higher education, and therefore "remains the number-one priority" (Psacharopoulos 1985, 591). As such, he recommends that governments cut subsidies to higher education and invest these resources in primary education. The rate of return on education in African countries was calculated by drawing upon a diverse number of annual surveys, spanning more than two decades (1960–83) and including countries under colonial or settler rule when the studies were completed. The African countries included in Psacharopoulos's study were Botswana, Ethiopia, Ghana, Kenya, Lesotho, Liberia, Malawi, Morocco, Nigeria, Rhodesia, Sierra Leone, Somalia, Sudan, Tanzania, Uganda, and Upper Volta (Psacharopoulos 1985, 598).

18 Elsewhere, Psacharopoulos argues that one major limitation of education planning, relative to cost-benefit analysis, is the lack of information, especially in developing countries. For Psacharopoulos (1980b), "education decision-makers"—ministers of education, local technocrats, students and families, and employers—often operate within an "information gap" that makes it incredibly difficult to set educational policy.

19 At Makerere, the commercialization of the university created a perverse set of internal market incentives whereby entrepreneurial departments remade themselves to attract larger numbers of fee-paying students. For example, the Department of Geography contorted itself into the School of Geography, which included the Department of Tourism and Leisure Management, Meteorology and Water Resource Management, Urban and Regional Planning, Physical Geography, and Environmental Sciences—areas where few faculty had specific disciplinary training (Mamdani 2007, 143). Such departments then hired an army of poorly paid, part-time lecturers (many with very limited qualifications) and poached faculty from cash-strapped departments.

20 In the decades since the World Bank's push for defunding higher education, most of the research conducted in African universities is commissioned by "foreign institutions, agencies, or individuals, who thus determine and control its content and gain credit for it," a practice that creates serious hierarchies between those African academics with access to foreign donors and those without (Federici 2000, 21).

21 The exodus of scholars and the slashing of funding also caused many African publishing houses and journals to shut down or move outside the country. For

example, the academic and literary journal *Transition*—started in Uganda in 1961 with funding from the Congress for Cultural Freedom—had become one important site for academic debate among African academics. In 1991, facing economic and political challenges, it was moved to Harvard University's Hutchins Center for African and African American Research.

22 While the report affirmed knowledge and learning as necessary for development, it focused on primary and secondary education, lifelong learning initiatives, and vocational and technical training—with little to say about higher education. When mentioned, emphasis was placed on encouraging private higher education. The report saw the private sector as a source for otherwise limited governmental funding and advocated "decentralizing administration, increasing school autonomy, switching to demand-side financing, increasing information about individual education institutions, and fostering competition among private, nongovernmental, and public providers" (World Bank 1998–99, 9).

23 The report was written with relative independence from its sponsoring institutions and was cochaired by Henry Rosovsky, a former dean of Harvard University, and Mamphela Ramphele, the vice chancellor of the University of Cape Town (1996–2000). After the publication of *Peril and Promise*, Ramphele was invited by Wolfensohn to take the position of managing director at the World Bank. Retired from the World Bank and serving as a member of the Greek parliament, George Psacharopoulos critiqued the report for arriving at vague findings and called the World Bank's discourse of "a global knowledge-based economy" something one would be more likely to find in "a term paper by a student in international education" than one should expect as the conclusions of "intensive discussion and hearings over a 2-year period by a group of eminent task force members" (2004, 76).

24 Within the World Bank, the list of world-class universities is often the same as those topping international rankings. Historically, world-class status was conferred simply by reputation—with schools like Harvard, Yale, Columbia, Oxford, and Cambridge widely regarded as "among the exclusive group of elite universities" (Salmi and Liu 2011, ix). On the other hand, as the number of higher education institutions increased, reputational rankings were largely insufficient. In this context, "the proliferation of league tables" has been assumed to offer "more systematic ways of identifying and classifying world-class universities" (Salmi and Liu 2011, x). Such an understanding of world class, however, imagines higher education as existing within a zero-sum competitive market whereby advances at one institution devalue another.

25 See Kamola (2011, 2016) for an analysis of how the language of global knowledge economy worked against efforts to remake postapartheid South African universities into sites of Africanization, economic redistribution, and democratization.

5. "Stakeholders and Co-investors"

1   In 1925, for example, the central governing committee—the Committee on Problems and Policy—recommended "setting up research committees on five fields of public concern: effects of the Eighteenth Amendment [Prohibition], the negro problem, crime, agricultural economics, and 'certain significant phases of social and industrial relations.' The daily newspaper headlines of the time might have yielded a similar list of current social problems" (Sibley 1974, 9).

2   As discussed in chapter 1, the most notable report was Robert Hall's (1947) "Area Studies: With Special Reference to Their Implication for Research in the Social Sciences." Other key reports advocating for area studies published by the SSRC's Committee on World Area Research included Wagley (1948), Steward (1950), and Bennett (1951).

3   The Committee on Comparative Politics alone, chaired by Gabriel Almond and later Lucien Pye of MIT's Center for International Studies, published three hundred reports, hosted five summer workshops, and sponsored or cosponsored twenty-nine conferences en route to establishing itself as a central site for the "development and refinement of modernization theory" (Worcester 2001, 31).

4   As its name implies, the American Council of Learned Societies, established in 1919, brings together more than five dozen scholarly organizations—including the Modern Language Association, the American Political Science Association, the African Studies Association, and others—to facilitate collaboration across the humanities and social sciences, including the funding of fellowships and grants. As described in the acknowledgments, funding from the ACLS helped make this book possible.

5   This included 73 area studies programs focusing on East Asia, 70 on Latin America, 58 on Eastern Europe, 36 on the Middle East, 34 on Africa, 26 on South Asia, and 15 on Southeast Asia. These numbers are based on a robust definition of area studies. For Lambert, an area studies program must be officially recognized by its home university, have "adequate library resources both for teaching and research," possess "competent instruction in the principal languages of the area," offer "at least five pertinent subjects in addition to language instruction," include an "area research program," and focus on "the contemporary aspects of the area" (Lambert 1973, 14–15; see also Bennett 1951).

6   The FAFP, funded by the Ford Foundation, was administered by the SSRC independently of the area joint committees. However, in 1972, an ad hoc committee recommended that the FAFP be folded into the joint committee structure to facilitate the relationship between the SSRC, ACLS, and Ford Foundation, with the objective of making it easier to align graduate training with the vision of the area committees (Thompson 1972, 56; Ward and Wood 1974). By 1972, the FAFP had already funded 2,050 doctoral students in area studies research (Szanton 2004, 11). Isaacman's book would win the ASA's Melville J. Herskovits award in 1972. Herskovitz created the first African studies program in the United States at Northwestern University,

with initial funding from the Carnegie Foundation and later the Ford Foundation (Gershenhorn 2004). As an associate professor at the University of Minnesota, Isaacman also received a Joint Committee on African Studies research grant in 1971–72, to study "resistance movements in central Mozambique" (SSRC 1973, 21) and again in 1976 for the study of the "social and economic history of precolonial South Central Africa" (SSRC 1976, 28). The names included here are just a small sampling of the many prominent Africanists receiving SSRC funding during this period. I highlighted these individuals because they were either my teachers (as in the case of Allen Isaacman) or otherwise exerted considerable influence over my own academic work.

7   A follow-up conference in 1971 focused specifically on "urbanization for national development in Africa" (Deshler 1971, 25).

8   The results of the 1969 conference were published as *Africa and the West: Intellectual Responses to European Culture* (Curtin 1972).

9   The distinction between higher education institutions—such as R1—was developed in 1970 by the Carnegie Commission on Higher Education, and categorizes institutions based on the highest degrees they award (PhD, MA, BA, AA, or other training degrees). For example, institutions in which MA's are the highest degree awarded are ranked on a scale from M1 to M3 (largest to smallest). Institutions granting doctoral degrees are similarly ranked R1 to R3 based on the intensity of research outputs. "The Carnegie Classification of Institutions of Higher Education," Center for Postsecondary Research, Indiana University School of Education, accessed December 2016, http://carnegieclassifications.iu.edu/classification_descriptions /basic.php. Between 1990 and 1995, the field research fellowships awarded by the SSRC joint committees went almost exclusively to major research universities, with UC Berkeley receiving 61, University of Michigan 49, Columbia 41, University of Chicago 39, Harvard 35, Yale 33, Stanford 31, Cornell 25, UCLA 25, University of Wisconsin 22, University of Washington 19, University of Indiana 17, Princeton 15, MIT 12, University of Pennsylvania 12, NYU 11, Northwestern 10, University of Illinois 10, and single digits awarded to scholars at 43 additional schools—none of which was a historically black institution (Worcester 1996, 12–13).

10 At the beginning of the twenty-first century, the federal government was still the largest funder of academic research—$21 billion in 2003. However, the overall percentage of funding fell from 73.5 percent in the mid-1960s to 60 percent four decades later. During this period, money going to the life science doubled between 1978 and 1998, and again between 1998 and 2003, constituting 70 percent of total federal research funding. All other disciplines, including the social sciences, have seen considerable cuts (Washburn 2005, 8).

11 Within the hard and applied sciences, academics began turning themselves into producers of proprietary intellectual property, as "technoscience and market-related fields" became potential sources of institutional "wealth creation" (Slaughter and Leslie 1997, 37). The 1980 passage of the Bayh-Dole Act set the groundwork

for this intellectual property gold rush by making it legal for universities to patent research findings developed using federal research funding (Newfield 2008).

12 Prewitt's early research argued that individuals become political leaders not because of personal attributes or social networks, but rather because of the political socialization they experience at a young age. He found that certain individuals become "overexposed to politics" by living in political households, participating in student governance, serving in the Peace Corps, campaigning for civil rights, or being employed in sectors with close proximity to "the political world" (Prewitt 1965, 109). His early publications, drawn from interviews of city council members collected as a graduate student at Stanford, expand this argument to also examine how elected officials learn to relate to interest groups and adapt to incumbency (Zisk, Eulau, and Prewitt 1965; Prewitt, Eulau, and Zisk 1966; Prewitt and Nowlin 1969; Prewitt 1969, 1970). Prewitt also engaged questions of race and racism throughout his entire career. For example, in 1967–68 he cofacilitated a "'work-study' seminar" through the Mid-Peninsula Christian Ministry—"a white, church-funded, urban-oriented organization that took seriously the problem of white racism." Seminar members provided community services, attended political meetings, facilitated discussions, and participated in political advocacy, all with the intent of developing a "political understanding of black power and white institutions" (Knowles and Prewitt 1969, v). The seminar sought to "utilize the resources of the university toward a different goal," by making time, access, and materials available to community partners, but also by critically engaging the "white institutions for which a Stanford degree was presumably preparing us" and, in doing so, "mak[ing] our education work against, rather than for, racist institutions" (Knowles and Prewitt 1969, vii–viii). The seminar culminated with the publication of a book aimed at explaining racism to a white audience, describing racism "not as Negro Pathology, but as White and Institutional and all too American" (Knowles and Prewitt 1969, viii).

13 His coauthored book *Political Socialization: An Analytical Study* was published in the Little, Brown Series on Comparative Politics, edited by Gabriel Almond, James Coleman, and MIT's Center for International Studies professor Lucian Pye. Half the monographs in the series were included under the heading Country Studies (*Politics in the USSR, Politics in Venezuela, Politics in West Germany*, etc.) and the other half under Analytic Studies, which, in addition to *Political Socialization*, included Pye's influential work *Aspects of Political Development* (Dawson and Prewitt 1969, v–vi; Dawson, Prewitt, and Dawson 1977, back cover).

14 Established in 1963, the University of East Africa served all of Britain's East African colonies. With national independence, the institution was divided three ways in 1970, into Makerere University, University of Nairobi, and University of Dar es Salaam.

15 While 122,000 Ugandans enrolled in primary school in 1966, only 397—or 0.003 percent of the student population—would attend university. Since those who re-

ceive higher education are on track to join "the governing elite," Prewitt (1971c, 154–55) found that few students were interested in jeopardizing this position of privilege.

16   Prewitt concluded that newly independent Uganda would have difficulty using the classroom for "diffusing a nationalist ideology" not only because primary and secondary education was underfunded, poorly administered, and geographically dispersed, but because top-down socialization only works when the classroom mirrors socialization taking place within the "family, church, friendship group, media, leisure activities, associational life, and so forth" (Prewitt and Oculi 1971, 15, 22). The article was previously published in Roberta Sigel's (1970) reader *Learning about Politics: A Reader in Political Socialization*. This edited collection examines different areas of political socialization, including discussions of childhood development, the family, peer groups, and other forms of political, cultural, and religious socialization. Several chapters focus on the role of education in political socialization—including how students learn to be patriotic and the role of extracurricular activities in shaping political outlooks. Other essays examine colleges and universities in particular, including two studies based on the survey of the student body at Bennington College and other essays discussing the causes of student radicalism.

17   During this period, he cowrote a massive book examining qualitative data relating to local and urban politics (Eulau and Prewitt 1973) and cowrote a study of the power of elites in American democracy (Prewitt and Stone 1973). As president of the SSRC, he defended the public utility of the social sciences in advocating for continued NSF funding for the social sciences (Prewitt 1980a, b). He also argued that social scientific knowledge should not be produced for advocacy, but it should include audiences beyond the academy (Prewitt 2004). He similarly saw his work at the U.S. Census in terms of using social scientific knowledge to help American politics function more democratically (Prewitt 2000, 2003).

18   Heginbotham, for example, pointed out that "Clinton administration deficit reduction budgets put educational and international exchange agencies under far more pressure than did the budgets of the Reagan and Bush administrations," compounded by the fact that universities "are under severe budgetary pressures, and private foundations face program cutbacks resulting from current and projected declines in returns on investments" (1994, 34).

19   The funding to implement this reorganization was provided by a Ford Foundation grant (Prewitt 1996b, 40).

20   For example, in 1995, *Issue* published a special issue on the crises facing African studies (23 [1], winter/spring), and in 1997 *Africa Today* had a special issue titled "The Future of Regional Studies" (44 [2], April/June). Other debates raged about the degree to which area studies were becoming less regionally focused and overly theoretical. For example, *World Politics* (1996) published the proceedings of a symposium at Princeton University titled "The Role of Theory in Comparative Poli-

tics," focusing on the turn toward interdisciplinarity, postmodernism, and global research agendas within the field of comparative politics.

21 During the 1980s, for example, an average of 23,000 African faculty members left Africa each year (Mkandawire 2005, 28).

22 For instance, between 1982 and 1992, only 24 percent of articles (and 15 percent of book reviews) in the most prominent African studies journals were written by Africans—and only 15 (and 10) percent were written by Africans working in African institutions of higher education (Zeleza 1997a, 56; 1997b, 199; see also Briggs and Weathers 2016).

23 See note 1 in the introduction.

24 Within the field of International Relations, for example, globalization was used as an opening to talk about the world in ways not limited to a zero-sum international system defined by a condition of anarchy.

25 Some defined globalization as a multiplicity (Gills 2004; Peterson 2004), as friction between global and local (Tsing 2005), as a discourse (Robertson and Khondker 1998), as competing ideologies (Rupert 2000; Kellner 2002; Steger 2002; Mittelman 2004a), and as occurring across different "-scapes" (Appadurai 1996). Some referred to this as the third wave of globalization, one that treats globalization not as a single phenomenon with causal power but rather as a material effect of various heterogeneous, cultural, and locally driven factors (Hay and Marsh 2000, 5; see also Hopper 2007; Martell 2007). Frederick Cooper similarly describes this as the "Dance of the Flows and the Fragments," a "style of talking about globalization" that followed the "Banker's Boast" and the "Social Democrat's Lament" (Cooper 2005, 93–94; 2001).

6. "An Opportunity to Transform the University"

1 While the strike ended in May 2006, GSOC continued to organize and engage the administration. In 2013, NYU graduate employees, in a 620-to-10 vote, approved a referendum reaffirming GSOC-UAW as their representative in collective bargaining. The union came to terms with the administration for a contract, in 2015, ten years after their previous contract expired. In April 2016, the NLRB under Obama overturned its 2004 Brown decisions, which had defined graduate employees at private colleges as primarily students, and not workers, and therefore ineligible for union representation. It appears that the NLRB under Trump will once-again refuse to recognize graduate student unions at private colleges.

2 In a meeting with AAUP activists, Sexton is reported to have divided the NYU faculty into the "blue team"—"who could get jobs at the drop of a hat at any of the top five universities in the country"—and the "gray team," who included everyone else (Kirp 2003, 85; cited in McGee 2008, 102).

3 The term is a play on Jean-Luc Nancy's argument that globalization entails an

onto-theological perspective. Unlike the French term *mondialisation*, or world making, which captures how worlds are collectively fashioned as places of shared meaning, coconstituted through the lived practices of mediating social relations and creating collective standards of meaning and value, for Nancy globalization rests upon the ontological claim that social life constitutes a "unitotality." To say the world is global assumes it already exists as an established, spatially defined, and singularly knowable thing. Claiming the world is global, therefore, assumes an onto-theological perspective from which the immanent world becomes understood as a single thing. An onto-theological perspective—a human articulation of Godlike omniscience—makes the plurality of worlds appear to have only a singular meaning. Treating the world as global, in other words, forecloses the possibility of world making, since the global imposes the meaning of the world from outside, that is, from the assumed givenness of globalization.

4   For example, in 1959, the federal government's Bureau of Educational and Cultural Affairs provided financial support for universities to establish study abroad programs in Latin America as an attempt "to counter the growing influence of the Soviet Union throughout much of Latin America," believing that American students "could contribute toward the building of a more positive U.S. image" (Hoffa 2007, 123).

5   While the Fulbright program is the most widely known example, in the decades after World War II the U.S. government supported many different forms of American academic presence abroad. For example, the government's early support for UNESCO helped "promote cultural relations, educational exchange programs, and the development of education and technical assistance programs"; in 1948, the State Department established the Advisory Committee on Educational Exchange for Students, which worked closely with Carnegie and Ford to increase the number of American students studying abroad as "unofficial goodwill ambassadors"; the 1954 Agricultural Trade Development and Assistance Act made it possible to use the profits from the sale of American agricultural surpluses to fund "educational exchange, American studies abroad, libraries and community centers, and the translation, publication, and distribution of books abroad"; and in 1959, the Bureau of Educational and Cultural Affairs gave grants for universities to set up study abroad programs (Hoffa 2007, 111–23).

6   It should be acknowledged that study abroad has provided—and continues to provide—many students (including this author) intellectually rich and life-changing experiences. In fact, most study abroad providers are mission oriented—seeking to provide quality educational and pedagogical experiences to students (Cressey and Stubbs 2010, 255). The pedagogical intentions, however, cannot be disaggregated from the economic function and constraints that come along with study abroad being treated as a revenue stream. While the economic returns on study abroad remain relatively mixed, many institutions—especially those with high tuition that charge full tuition for study abroad programming—often see

study abroad generating considerable revenue from placing students in lower-cost overseas programs (Cressey and Stubbs 2010, 286). If not directly yielding tuition dollars, study abroad is often central to how institutions market themselves to potential students (Bolen 2001), with study abroad being overly represented on college websites and campus tours (Twombly, Salisbury, and Tumanut 2012, 24).

7   This trend is compounded by the fact that rapid growth in study abroad owes much to the popularity of "prepackaged programs" with little differentiation from any other "consumer experiences: housing, food, adventure, tours, orientation, with courses added" (Twombly, Salisbury, and Tumanut 2012, 24). In response to pressures to provide more study abroad opportunities to larger numbers of students, schools and independent vendors develop shorter and shorter summer, January term, and spring break programs. These programs often promise "instant culture without students having to sacrifice too much or work too hard"—basically "a consumable, more like educational tourism" (24).

8   Between 1951 and 1956, the Ford Foundation provided 52 percent of the IIE's funding (Bu 1999, 402).

9   Most foreign students are from China (31.2 percent), India (13.3 percent), South Korea (6.5 percent), Saudi Arabia (6.1 percent), Canada (2.8 percent), Brazil (2.4 percent), Taiwan (2.2 percent), Japan (2.0 percent), Vietnam (1.9 percent), and Mexico (1.7 percent). The top ten hosting institutions include NYU (13,178 students), University of Southern California (12,334), Columbia (11,510), Arizona State (11,330), University of Illinois Urbana-Champaign (11,223), Northeastern University (10,559), Purdue (10,230), UCLA (10,209), Michigan State (8,146), and University of Washington (8,035) (OpenDoors 2015, 1).

10 The number of branch campuses has increased 60 percent, from 100 to 162, since June 2005 (Wildavsky 2010, 61).

11 In addition to these sites, the school also operates more than sixty summer programs marketed to non-NYU students (Ross 2009, 194).

12 The creation of this program was predicated on Sexton's observation that "few significant legal or social problems today . . . are purely domestic," and therefore students should study law in an "international (global is the better word) program" (1996, 331, 335). However, rather than studying a codified body of international law, Sexton describes NYU's global law program as examining how "the rule of law permeates the emerging global village" and the outsized role, in particular, "American law and its lawyers" play in the "emerging global community" (1996, 329). He points out that law and education have become two of America's "most coveted exports" and that NYU is uniquely well situated to offer this program because of its "cosmopolitan student body" and well-traveled faculty (330–31).

13 Sexton (2010) points to the example of one student who completed her BA having studied abroad five semesters and predicts a future in which courses might be taught in "sixteen sites simultaneously" or "orchestras located on two continents directed by a single conductor, might perform a symphony together."

14 The essay from which Sexton takes this definition is much more ambivalent about globalization. While Coatsworth argues that productivity—and eventually standard of living—increased during each of the four cycles of globalization (which he defines as 1492 through mid-1600s, late 1600s through European colonialism, the expansion of capitalist economies through the Great Depression, and World War II to the present), he also acknowledges that "the initial gains" in each cycle were "unequally distributed. Short-term benefits generally went to tiny minorities" and caused "immense suffering over many generations." While globalization ultimately made societies "more productive and wealthier," they did so only once "those who had lived through the onset of globalization and paid the heavy price were long dead" (Coatsworth 2004, 39).

15 Elsewhere I have demonstrated that the absence of attention to colonialism and imperialism is central to the production of knowledge about globalization (Kamola 2012, 192–95).

16 For Teilhard de Chardin, the Omega Point is the final endpoint of evolutions, a "universal synthesis" that can be known only upon its emergence. He argues that the universe is constantly evolving, with humans increasingly leaving behind their individualized and material forms as they progress toward a spiritual unity. He writes that "the universe . . . is continually building itself above our heads in the opposite direction of matter that vanishes: a universe that is the collector and conserver not of mechanical energy as we thought, but of persons. One by one, like a continual exhalation, 'souls' breaking away around us, carrying their incommunicable charge of consciousness towards what is above. One by one, yet not in isolation. . . . By the very nature of Omega, there can only be one possible point of definitive emersion"—that is, a point that "collectively reaches its point of convergence—at the 'end of the world'" (Teilhard de Chardin 1999, 194). For more on Teilhard, see Castillo (2012) and Browning, Alioto, and Farber (1973), and for other efforts to use Teilhard to think about globalization, see Camdessus (2006) and Boissonnat (2006).

17 Sexton does not limit his theological imagery to higher education, but applies it to baseball in very similar terms. In *Baseball as a Road to God*, Sexton describes a class he taught at NYU for more than a decade. Sexton starts the course by writing "ineffable" and "hierophany" on the board—the first word used to capture "the truth known in the soul" and the second the "heightened sensitivity" that occurs when one recognizes "the sacred in ordinary life," constituting "a sharp divergence in feeling and awareness, space and time" than what is usually experienced in "our profane experience" (2013, 211). In focusing almost exclusively on the game's epic moments, Sexton's account of baseball remains blind to baseball as a corporate business, with strong player unions, and dependent upon a steady pipeline of young men from Latin America and the Caribbean trained, from a very young age, to exclusively play baseball—with only a small fraction ever making it to the big leagues. Sexton's vision of baseball is that of a swooning fan in a corporate box

at Yankee Stadium, not the lived world of baseball as presented in movies such as *Sugar* (dir. Anna Boden and Ryan Fleck, 2008) or *Pelotero* (dir. Ross Finkel and Trevor Martin, 2012).

18   In 2017, Harvard's $35.7 billion endowment (Powell 2017) was greater than the GDP of thirty-six sub-Saharan African countries. Data on national GDP are available at International Monetary Fund, *World Economic Outlook Database*, 2017, https:// www.imf.org/external/pubs/ft/weo/2017/01/weodata/index.aspx.

19   After public protest, including by high-profile artists and authors, NYU finally agreed to incorporate the Poe house into its new construction. In practice, this resulted in "an interpretive reconstruction" of the Poe house, located behind locked doors and security checkpoints, and named for its donors: Honorable Frank J. Guarini and Caroline L. Guarini Study Lounge (Duncombe and Nash 2008, 80).

20   I want to thank Samantha Majic for this observation.

21   The total value of this agreement has not been made public. However, one top NYU official let slip at a cocktail party that the deal is likely worth somewhere around $2 billion (Dreifus 2014). Abu Dhabi is the wealthiest of the emirates, with oil wealth estimated at $3 trillion. While John Sexton claimed that he was attracted by the emirate's ambition, in reality NYU originally approached Dubai but the agreement fell through when they balked at the price tag (Krieger 2008a).

22   He ended class by telling his students, "For Thanksgiving, I want to thank the Lord for the gift of you people" (Sexton quoted in Wildavsky 2010, 50).

23   Human Rights Watch contacted NYU in September 2007 expressing concern over labor abuses in Abu Dhabi. In 2009, NYU finally responded. At an April meeting, NYU officials shared the agreement they worked out with the Abu Dhabi Executive Affairs Authority (EAA). These officials stated that NYU is committed to being "a model of best practices in Abu Dhabi," and that "we believe them [the EAA] that labor issues are a top priority for them and that they have room to improve" (Human Rights Watch 2009, 10). Human Rights Watch, however, criticized these standards for being "vague" and failing to address their "fundamental concerns." For example, NYU's Statement of Labor Values requested that those building the campus be "paid wages and benefits which comply with all applicable UAE laws and regulations and which provide for their essential needs and living standards," despite no minimum wage standards in the UAE (Human Rights Watch 2009, 11).

24   After the *New York Times* reported on the construction of the NYUAD campus, Tamkeen and NYU hired an independent investigator to examine allegations made by the *Times*, the *Guardian*, Human Rights Watch, and the activist group Gulf Labor Coalition. Nardello and Co.'s report found that Mubadala had extended exemptions from labor standards to subcontractors and interpreted the Statement of Labor Values in ways that minimized protections, resulting in a third of the workforce, or ten thousand people, to be excluded from oversight (Nardello and Co. 2015; Saul 2015).

25   In addition to Ross, researchers from Human Rights Watch and Amnesty In-

ternational, artists Ashok Sukumaran and Walid Raad, and a former NYU student studying labor abuses in Abu Dhabi were all denied access to Abu Dhabi. It also came to light that a private investigator was hired to "interrogate academic acquaintances" of Ross as well as *New York Times* investigative journalist Ariel Kaminer. Prodemocracy activists, including Ahmed Mansoor and Sorbonne lecturer Nassar bin Ghaith, have also been arrested for their public statements (Ross 2017, 8–9).

Conclusion

1   I am thinking here of my own graduate program at the University of Minnesota that long stood out as producing a distinct form of International Relations scholarship—deeply informed by the strong political and critical theory traditions within the department as well as the close relationships between cultural studies and geography scholars and graduate students across campus. It has proven difficult to maintain the Minnesota School, however, during times of profound budgetary crisis and when following the money incentivizes disciplinary mainstreaming.

2   Drawing inspiration from the 1966 Tricontinental Conference in Havana, Cuba, the Tricontinental: Institute for Social Research is funded by social movements and labor unions in Latin America, Africa, and Asia, and links academics together with research agendas driven by the needs of these movements (see https://www .thetricontinental.org/).

References

Adam, Nigel. 1982. "America's Bell System Goes Global." *Euromoney*, November, 81–85.

Adamson, Morgan. 2009a. "The Financialization of Student Life: Five Propositions on Student Debt." *Polygraph: An International Journal of Culture and Politics* 21:107–20.

Adamson, Morgan. 2009b. "The Human Capital Strategy." *Ephemera: Theory and Politics in Organization* 9:271–84.

Afoláyan, Michael O. 2007. *Higher Education in Postcolonial Africa: Paradigms of Development, Decline and Dilemmas*. Trenton, NJ: Africa World Press.

Aherne, Aedh. 2006. "Exploit the Levitt Write Cycle." *Journal of Strategic Marketing* 14:77–87.

Ajayi, J. F. Ade, Lameck K. H. Goma, and G. Ampah Johnson. 1996. *The African Experience with Higher Education*. Accra: Association of African Universities.

Ake, Claude. 1996. *Democracy and Development in Africa*. Washington, DC: Brookings Institution.

Akurang-Parry, Kwabena O. 2007. "Problems of Seeding and Harvesting Higher Education in Postcolonial Ghana: Historical Antecedents and Contemporary Trends." In *Higher Education in Postcolonial Africa: Paradigms of Development, Decline and Dilemmas*, edited by Michael O. Afoláyan, 39–55. Trenton, NJ: Africa World Press.

Albert, Michael. 2006. *Remembering Tomorrow: From sds to Life after Capitalism*. New York: Seven Stories.

Aliber, Robert Z., and Reid W. Click, eds. 1993. *Readings in International Business: A Decision Approach*. Boston: Massachusetts Institute of Technology.

Altbach, Philip G. 2002. "Perspectives on International Higher Education." *International Higher Education* 27:6–8.

Altbach, Philip G. 2007. "Globalization and the University: Realities in an Unequal World." In *International Handbook of Higher Education*, edited by James J. F. Forest and Philip G. Altbach, 121–39. New York: Springer.

Altbach, Philip G., Liz Reisberg, and Laura E. Rumbley. 2009. *Trends in Global Higher Education: Tracking an Academic Revolution.* Paris: UNESCO.

Altbach, Philip G., and Jamil Salmi. 2011. *The Road to Academic Excellence: The Making of World-Class Research Universities, Directions in Development: Human Capital.* Washington, DC: World Bank.

Althusser, Louis. 1999. *Machiavelli and Us.* Translated by Gregory Elliott. London: Verso.

Althusser, Louis. 2001a. "Ideology and Ideological State Apparatus (Notes towards an Investigation)." In *Lenin and Philosophy and Other Essays*, translated by Ben Brewster, 85–126. New York: Monthly Review Press.

Althusser, Louis. 2001b. "Lenin and Philosophy." In *Lenin and Philosophy and Other Essays*, translated by Ben Brewster, 11–43. New York: Monthly Review Press.

Althusser, Louis. 2003. "The Humanist Controversy." In *The Humanist Controversy and Other Writings (1966–67)*, edited by François Matheron, 221–305. London: Verso.

Althusser, Louis. 2007. *Politics and History.* Translated by Ben Brewster. London: Verso.

Althusser, Louis, and Étienne Balibar. 1999. *Reading Capital.* London: Verso.

Anderson, Benedict. 2002. *Imagined Communities: Reflections on the Origin and Spread of Nationalism.* London: Verso.

Anderson, Benedict. 2016. *A Life beyond Boundaries.* London: Verso.

Andrews, Kenneth R. 1983. "From the Editor." *Harvard Business Review* 3:1.

Appadurai, Arjun. 1996. *Modernity at Large: Cultural Dimensions of Globalization.* Minneapolis: University of Minnesota Press.

Appadurai, Arjun. 2000. "Grassroots Globalization and the Research Imagination." *Public Culture* 12:1–19.

Appadurai, Arjun. 2001. "Grassroots Globalization and the Research Imagination." In *Globalization*, edited by Arjun Appadurai, 1–21. Durham, NC: Duke University Press.

Applbaum, Kalman. 1998. "Sweetness of Salvation: Consumer Marketing and the Liberal-Bourgeois Theory of Needs." *Current Anthropology* 39:323–49.

Applbaum, Kalman. 2000. "Crossing Borders: Globalization as Myth and Charter in American Transnational Consumer Marketing." *American Ethnologist* 27:257–82.

Applbaum, Kalman. 2004. *The Marketing Era: From Professional Practice to Global Provisioning.* New York: Routledge.

Aronowitz, Stanley. 2000. *The Knowledge Factory: Dismantling the Corporate University and Creating True Higher Learning.* Boston: Beacon.

Arrighi, Giovanni. 2002. "The African Crisis: World Systemic and Regional Aspects." *New Left Review* 15:5–36.

Ashe, Reid. 1968. "Sala Sanctuary Established; O'Conner Waits for Feds." *The Tech* 88 (41, November 1): 1, 3. http://tech.mit.edu/V88/PDF/V88-N41.pdf.

Ashworth, Lucian M. 2002. "Did the Realist-Idealist Great Debate Really Happen? A Revisionist History of International Relations." *International Relations* 16:33–51.

Assié-Lumumba, N'Dri T. 2006. *Higher Education in Africa: Crises, Reforms and Trans-*

formation. Dakar, Senegal: Council for the Development of Social Science Research in Africa (CODESRIA).

Axt, Richard G. 1952. *The Federal Government and Financing Higher Education: The Commission on Financing Higher Education.* New York: Columbia University Press.

Barber, Benjamin R. 1995. *Jihad vs. McWorld: How Globalism and Tribalism Are Reshaping the World.* New York: Ballantine.

Barrow, Clyde W. 1990. *Universities and the Capitalist State: Corporate Liberalism and the Reconstruction of American Higher Education, 1894–1928.* Madison: University of Wisconsin Press.

Bassett, Roberta Malle, and Alma Maldonado-Maldonado. 2009. *International Organizations and Higher Education Policy: Thinking Globally, Acting Locally?* New York: Routledge.

Bates, Robert H. 1981. *Markets and States in Tropical Africa: The Political Basis of Agricultural Policies.* Berkeley: University of California Press.

Bates, Robert H., V. Y. Mudimbe, and Jean O'Barr. 1993. *Africa and the Disciplines: The Contributions of Research in Africa to the Social Sciences and Humanities.* Chicago: University of Chicago Press.

Becker, Gary S. 1993. *Human Capital: A Theoretical and Empirical Analysis, with Special Reference to Education.* 3rd ed. Chicago: University of Chicago Press.

Bendix, John. 2003. "Past Imperfect and Future Tense: Language and Area Studies Programmes in the US." *Journal of Contemporary European Studies* 11:35–51.

Bennett, Wendell C. 1951. *Area Studies in American Universities.* New York: Social Science Research Council.

Berg, Elliot. 1986. "The World Bank's Strategy." In *Africa in Economic Crisis,* edited by J. Ravenhill. New York: Columbia University Press.

Berger, Mark T. 2004. "After the Third World? History, Destiny and the Fate of Third Worldism." *Third World Quarterly* 25:9–39.

Berger, Mark T. 2007. "Keeping the World Safe for Primary Colors: Area Studies, Development Studies, International Studies, and the Vicissitudes of Nation-Building." *Globalizations* 4:429–44.

Bernhardt, Greg. 1969. "150 Students Peacefully Disrupt CIS." *The Tech* 89 (October 14): 1, 11. http://tech.mit.edu/V89/PDF/V89-N36.pdf.

Berry, Joe. 2005. *Reclaiming the Ivory Tower: Organizing Adjuncts to Change Higher Education.* New York: Monthly Review Press.

Berry, Sara S. 1976. "The Study of Inequality in African Societies." *Items* 30:10–11.

Bérubé, Michael, and Cary Nelson. 1995. *Higher Education under Fire: Politics, Economics, and the Crisis of the Humanities.* New York: Routledge.

Bird, Kai. 1998. *The Color of Truth: McGeorge Bundy and William Bundy, Brothers in Arms: A Biography.* New York: Simon and Schuster.

Blackmer, Donald L. M. 2002. *The MIT Center for International Studies: The Founding Years, 1951–1969.* Cambridge, MA: MIT Center for International Studies.

Blaug, Mark. 1967. "The Private and the Social Returns on Investment in Education: Some Results for Great Britain." *Journal of Human Resources* 2:330–46.

Blitz, Rudolph C. 1954. "Prosperity versus Strikes Reconsidered." *Industrial and Labor Relations Review* 7:449–51.

Bloom, David E., Philip G. Altbach, and Henry Rosovsky. 2016. "Looking Back on the Lessons of 'Higher Education and Developing Countries: Peril and Promise'—Perspectives on China and India." *International Journal of African Higher Education* 3:19–42.

Bloom, David, and Henry Rosovsky. 2004. "Has the Report Made a Difference?" *Comparative Education Review* 48:78–81.

Boggs, Abigail, and Nick Mitchell. 2018. "Critical University Studies and the Crisis Consensus." *Feminism Studies* 44 (2): 432–63.

Boissonnat, Jean. 2006. "Teilhard and Globalization." In *Teilhard and the Future of Humanity*, edited by Thierry Meynard, 89–106. New York: Fordham University Press.

Bok, Derek. 2003. *Universities in the Marketplace: The Commercialization of Higher Education.* Princeton, NJ: Princeton University Press.

Bolen, Mell. 2001. "Consumerism and U.S. Study Abroad." *Journal of Studies in International Education* 5:182–200.

Bousquet, Marc. 2008. *How the University Works: Higher Education and the Low-Wage Nation.* New York: New York University Press.

Brandt, Willy, Abdlatif Y. Al-Hamad, Rodrigo Botero Montoya, Antoine Kipsa Dakoure, Eduardo Frei Montalva, Katharine Graham, Edward Heath, et al. 1980. "North-South: A Program for Survival, Report of the Independent Commission on International Development Issues." Cambridge, MA: MIT Press.

Briggs, Ryan C., and Scott Weathers. 2016. "Gender and Location in African Politics Scholarship: The Other White Man's Burden." *African Affairs* 115:466–89.

British Airways. 1983. "Manhattan." YouTube, 1:30. Posted by Hall of Advertising. https://youtu.be/vZuoy-D6BMs.

Brown, Stephen. 1999. "Marketing and Literature: The Anxiety of Academic Influence." *Journal of Marketing* 63:1–15.

Brown, Stephen. 2004. "Theodore Levitt: The Ultimate Writing Machine." *Marketing Theory* 4:209–38.

Brown, Stephen. 2005. *Writing Marketing: Literary Lessons from Academic Authorities.* London: SAGE.

Browning, Geraldine O., Joseph L. Alioto, and Seymour M. Farber. 1973. *Teilhard de Chardin: In Quest of the Perfection of Man.* Cranbury: Associated University Presses.

Bu, Liping. 1999. "Educational Exchange and Cultural Diplomacy in the Cold War." *Journal of American Studies* 33:393–415.

Bu, Liping. 2003. *Making the World Like Us: Education, Cultural Expansion, and the American Century.* Westport, CT: Praeger.

Buchsbaum, Jonathan, Penny Lewis, Michael Palm, Asad Raza, Tricia Lawler, and Elena

Gorfinkel. 2006. "Interview: Student Strike Organizers at NYU." *Cinema Journal* 45:86–97.

Bujra, Abdalla. 1982. "Editorial Note: Special Double Issue on the Berg Report and the Lagos Plan of Action." *African Development* 7:v–vi.

Bull, Hedley. 1977. *The Anarchical Society: A Study of Order in World Politics*. New York: Columbia University Press.

Busch, Andreas. 2000. "Unpacking the Globalization Debate: Approaches, Evidence and Data." In *Demystifying Globalization*, edited by Colin Hay and David Marsh, 21–48. Hampshire: Palgrave.

Busch, Andreas. 2007. "The Development of the Debate: Intellectual Precursors and Selected Aspects." In *Globalization: State of the Art and Perspectives*, edited by Stefan A. Schirm, 22–39. London: Routledge.

Bush, George W. 2001. "Address to a Joint Session of Congress and the American People." White House, September 20. https://georgewbush-whitehouse.archives.gov/news/releases/2001/09/20010920-8.html.

Bush, Vannevar. 1945. *Science: The Endless Frontier*. Washington, DC: National Science Foundation.

Buzzell, Robert D., John A. Quelch, and Christopher A. Bartlett, eds. 1995. *Global Marketing Management: Cases and Readings*. 3rd ed. Reading, MA: Addison-Wesley.

Byrne, John A. 1993. *The Whiz Kids: Ten Founding Fathers of American Business—and the Legacy They Left Us*. New York: Currency Doubleday.

Caffentzis, George. 2000. "The World Bank and Education in Africa." In *A Thousand Flowers: Social Struggles against Structural Adjustment in African Universities*, edited by Silvia Federici, George Caffentzis, and Ousseina Alidou, 3–18. Trenton, NJ: African World Press.

Camdessus, Michel. 2006. "Teilhard, Globalization, and the Future of Humanity." In *Teilhard and the Future of Humanity*, edited by Thierry Meynard, 71–88. New York: Fordham University Press.

Campanella, Frank. 1982. "Global Insurer: American Int'l Group's Heavy Foreign Stake Proves Sound Policy." *Barron's National Business and Financial Weekly*, September 27, 50–52.

Canagarajah, A. Suresh. 2002. *A Geopolitics of Academic Writing*. Pittsburgh: University of Pittsburgh Press.

Carnoy, Martin. 1967. "Rate of Return to Schooling in Latin America." *Journal of Human Resources* 2:359–74.

Carrick, Glenn, and David Batty. 2013. "In Abu Dhabi, They Call It Happiness Island. But for the Migrant Workers, It Is a Place of Misery." *Guardian*, December 21. https://www.theguardian.com/world/2013/dec/22/abu-dhabi-happiness-island-misery.

Carvalho, Edward J., and David B. Downing. 2010. *Academic Freedom in the Post-9/11 Era*. New York: Palgrave Macmillan.

Castillo, M. 2012. "The Omega Point and Beyond: The Singularity Event." *American Journal of Neuroradiology* 33:393–95.

CENIS. 1953. "A Program of Research in Economic and Political Development." AC 0236 (Box 2.f1). Center for International Studies, MIT. Institute Archives and Special Collections, MIT Libraries, Cambridge, Massachusetts.

CENIS. 1954. "Proposal for Completion of the Economic and Political Development Research Program: July 1, 1954–June 30, 1957." AC 0236 (Box 2.f2). Center for International Studies, MIT. Institute Archives and Special Collections, MIT Libraries, Cambridge, Massachusetts.

CENIS. 1958. "A Proposal for Long-Term Financial Support of the Center for International Studies." AC 0236 (Box 2.f3). Center for International Studies, MIT. Institute Archives and Special Collections, MIT Libraries, Cambridge, Massachusetts.

CENIS. 1969. "Major Current Research Projects." AC 0236 (Box 2.f3). Center for International Studies, MIT. Institute Archives and Special Collections, MIT Libraries, Cambridge, Massachusetts.

Chalou, George C. 1992. *The Secret War: The Office of Strategic Services in World War II.* Washington, DC: National Archives and Records Administration.

Chanda, Nayan. 2008. *Bounded Together: How Traders, Preachers, Adventurers, and Warriors Shaped Globalization.* New Haven, CT: Yale University Press.

Chang, Ha-Joon. 2008. *Bad Samaritans: The Myth of Free Trade and the Secret History of Capitalism.* New York: Bloomsbury.

Chatterjee, Piya, and Sunaina Maira. 2014. *The Imperial University: Academic Repression and Scholarly Dissent.* Minneapolis: University of Minnesota Press.

Cheit, Earl F., and Theodore E. Lobman. 1979. "Foundations and Higher Education: Grant Making from Golden Years through Steady State." Berkeley: Ford Foundation and Carnegie Council on Policy Studies and Higher Education.

Chenery, Hollis, Montek S. Ahluwalia, C. L. G. Bell, John H. Duloy, and Richard Jolly. 1975. *Redistribution with Growth: Policies to Improve Income Distribution in Developing Countries in the Context of Economic Growth.* Development Research Center (World Bank) and the Institute of Development Studies (University of Sussex). London: Oxford University Press.

Chou, Meng-Hsuan, Isaac Kamola, and Tamson Pietsch. 2016a. "Introduction: The Transnational Politics of Higher Education." In *The Transnational Politics of Higher Education: Contesting the Global/Transforming the Local,* edited by Meng-Hsuan Chou, Isaac Kamola, and Tamson Pietsch, 1–20. New York: Routledge.

Chou, Meng-Hsuan, Isaac Kamola, and Tamson Pietsch, eds. 2016b. *The Transnational Politics of Higher Education: Contesting the Global/Transforming the Local.* New York: Routledge.

Chowdhry, Geeta. 2007. "Edward Said and Contrapuntal Reading: Implications for Critical Interventions in International Relations." *Millennium: Journal of International Studies* 36:101–16.

Clark, Timothy, and Graeme Salaman. 1998. "Telling Tales: Management Gurus' Narratives and the Construction of Managerial Identity." *Journal of Management Studies* 35:137–61.

Clark, William. 1981. "Robert McNamara at the World Bank." *Foreign Affairs* 60:167–84.

Clausen, Alden W. 1971. "The Largest Bank Was Once a Plank on the Waterfront." *Nation's Business* 59:54–55.

Clausen, Alden W. 1972. "The International Corporation: An Executive's View." *Annals of the American Academy of Political and Social Science* 403:12–21.

Clausen, Alden W. 1980. "The Changing Character of Financial Markets in the Postwar Period: A Personal Perspective." In *The American Economy in Transition*, edited by Martin Feldstein, 86–99. Chicago: University of Chicago Press.

Clausen, Alden W. 1982. "Looking towards a Brighter Future." *West Africa*, May 3, 1194–99.

Clausen, Alden W. 1986a. "Address to the Board of Governors: Washington, DC, September 29, 1981." In *The Development Challenge of the Eighties: A.W. Clausen at the World Bank, Major Policy Addresses 1981–1986*, edited by World Bank, 1–20. Washington, DC: World Bank.

Clausen, Alden W. 1986b. "Global Interdependence in the 1980s: Address to the Yomiuri International Economic Society." In *The Development Challenge of the Eighties: A.W. Clausen at the World Bank, Major Policy Addresses 1981–1986*, edited by World Bank, 37–54. Washington, DC: World Bank.

Clausen, Alden W. 1986c. "The World Bank and International Commercial Banks: Partners for Development." In *The Development Challenge of the Eighties: A.S. Clausen at the World Bank: Major Policy Addresses 1981–1986*, edited by World Bank, 79–95. Washington, DC: World Bank.

Clowse, Barbara Barksdale. 1981. *Brainpower for the Cold War: The Sputnik Crisis and the National Defense Education Act of 1958*. Santa Barbara, CA: Praeger.

Clutterbuck, David, and Stuart Crainer. 1990. *Makers of Management: Men and Women Who Changed the Business World*. London: Macmillan.

Coatsworth, John H. 2004. "Globalization, Growth, and Welfare in History." In *Globalization: Culture and Education in the New Millennium*, edited by Marcel M. Suáez-Orozco and Desirée Baolian Qin-Hilliard, 38–55. Berkeley: University of California Press.

Cole, Jonathan R. 2009. *The Great American University: Its Rise to Preeminence, Its Indispensable National Role, and Why It Must Be Protected*. New York: Public Affairs.

Comaroff, Jean, and John L. Comaroff. 2011. *Theory from the South: Or, How Euro-America Is Evolving Toward Africa*. New York: Paradigm.

Connell, Raewyn. 2007a. "The Northern Theory of Globalization." *Sociological Theory* 25:368–85.

Connell, Raewyn. 2007b. *Southern Theory: The Global Dynamics of Knowledge in the Social Sciences*. Cambridge: Polity.

Coombe, Trevor. 1991. *A Consultation on Higher Education in Africa: A Report to the Ford Foundation and the Rockefeller Foundation*. London: London University Institute of Education. https://files.eric.ed.gov/fulltext/ED371652.pdf.

Cooper, Frederick. 2001. "What Is the Concept of Globalization Good For? An African Historian's Perspective." *African Affairs* 100:189–213.

Cooper, Frederick. 2005. *Colonialism in Question: Theory, Knowledge, History*. Berkeley: University of California Press.

Copeland, Melvin T. 1958. *And Mark an Era: The Story of the Harvard Business School*. Boston: Little, Brown.

Cosgrove, Denis. 2001. *Apollo's Eye: A Cartographic Genealogy of the Earth in the Western Imagination*. Baltimore, MD: Johns Hopkins University Press.

Côté, James E., and Anton L. Allahar. 2007. *Ivory Tower Blues: A University System in Crisis*. Toronto: University of Toronto Press.

Court, David. 1974. "Rockefeller Foundation Assistance to Higher Education in East Africa, 1961–1973: An Evaluation." New York: Rockefeller Foundation.

Cressey, William, and Nancy Stubbs. 2010. "The Economics of Study Abroad." In *A History of U.S. Study Abroad: 1965–Present*, edited by William W. Hoffa and Stephen C. DePaul, 253–94. Carlisle, PA: Frontiers Journal.

Cumings, Bruce. 1998. "Boundary Displacement: Area Studies and International Studies during and after the Cold War." In *Universities and Empire: Money and Politics in the Social Sciences during the Cold War*, edited by Christopher Simpson, 159–88. New York: New Press.

Cumings, Bruce. 2002. "Boundary Displacement: The State, the Foundations, and Area Studies during the Cold War." In *Learning Places: The Afterlives of Area Studies*, edited by Masao Miyoshi and H. D. Harootunian, 261–302. Durham, NC: Duke University Press.

Curtin, Philip D. 1970. "Intellectual History and Comparative Studies: An Experimental Approach by the Joint Committee on African Studies." *Items* 23:6–8.

Curtin, Philip D. 1972. *Africa and the West: Intellectual Responses to European Culture*. Madison: University of Wisconsin Press.

Curtis, John W. 2011. "Persistent Inequity: Gender and Academic Employment." Washington, DC: American Association of University Professors. https://www.aaup.org/NR/rdonlyres/08E023AB-E6D8-4DBD-99A0-24E5EB73A760/0/persistent_inequity.pdf.

Daniel, Carter A. 1998. *MBA: The First Century*. Lewisburg, PA: Bucknell University Press.

Datar, Srikant M., David A. Garvin, and Patrick G. Cullen. 2010. *Rethinking the MBA: Business Education at a Crossroads*. Boston: Harvard Business Press.

Dawson, Ashley, and Penny Lewis. 2008. "New York: Academic Labor Town?" In *The University against Itself: The NYU Strike and the Future of the Academic Workplace*, edited by Monika Krause, Mary Nolan, Michael Palm, and Andrew Ross, 15–29. Philadelphia: Temple University Press.

Dawson, Richard E., and Kenneth Prewitt. 1969. *Political Socialization: An Analytic Study*. Boston: Little, Brown.

Dawson, Richard E., Kenneth Prewitt, and Karen S. Dawson. 1977. *Political Socialization: An Analytic Study*. 2nd ed. Boston: Little, Brown.

Deshler, Walter W. 1971. "Urbanization in Africa: Some Spatial and Functional Aspects." *Items* 25:25–29.

Diouf, Mamadou, and Mahmood Mamdani. 1994. *Academic Freedom in Africa*. Dakar: CODESRIA.

Dolan, Robert J. 1985. "Henkel Group: Umbrella Branding and Globalization Decisions." Cambridge, MA: Harvard Business School.

Donoghue, Frank. 2008. *The Last Professors: The Twilight of the Humanities in the Corporate University*. New York: Fordham University Press.

Dowling, Jay W. 1982. "Insurance Industry Goes Global." *Business America*, November 1, 9–10.

Downing, David B. 2012. "World Bank University: The War on Terror and the Battles for the Global Commons." In *Terror, Theory and the Humanities*, edited by Jeffrey R. Di Leo and Uppinder Mehan, 66–89. Ann Arbor, MI: Open Humanities Press.

Dreifus, Claudia. 2014. "NYU Eats World." *Chronicle of Higher Education*, September 29. https://www.chronicle.com/article/NYU-Eats-World/148979.

Drucker, Peter F. 1954. *The Practice of Management*. New York: Harper and Brothers.

Du Bois, W. E. Burghardt. 1965. *The World and Africa: An Inquiry into the Part Which Africa Has Played in World History*. New York: International Publishers.

Dugdale, Antony, J. J. Fueser, and J. Celso de Castro Alves. 2011. "Yale, Slavery and Abolition." http://www.yaleslavery.org/YSA.pdf.

Duncombe, Stephen, and Sarah Nash. 2008. "ICE from the Ashes of FIRE: NYU and the Economy of Culture in New York." In *The University against Itself: The NYU Strike and the Future of the Academic Workplace*, edited by Monika Krause, Mary Nolan, Michael Palm, and Andrew Ross, 71–82. Philadelphia: Temple University Press.

Dunn, Frederick S. 1948. "The Scope of International Relations." *World Politics* 1:142–46.

Dunn, Frederick S. 1949. "The Present Course of International Relations Research." *World Politics* 2:80–95.

Edu-factory Collective. 2009. *Toward a Global Autonomous University: Cognitive Labor, the Production of Knowledge, and Exodus from the Education Factory*. New York: Autonomedia.

Edu-factory Collective. 2010. "The Double Crisis: Living on the Border." *EduFactory Webjournal*, 4–9. https://issuu.com/piebbaa/docs/edufactory-journal-0.

Elkin, Robert. 1969. "Rally, Sit-in Protest War Research; SACC-NAC Rally Begins Afternoon Research Protest." *The Tech* 89 (November 7): 1, 5. http://tech.mit.edu/V89/PDF/V89-N43.pdf.

el-Malik, Shiera S., and Isaac Kamola. 2017. *Politics of African Anticolonial Archive*. London: Rowman and Littlefield International.

Elson, Diane. 1982. "The Brandt Report: A Programme for Survival." *Capital and Class* 6:110–27.

Emond, Mark. 1982. "Alaskan Crude Oil Advantage: Global Implications in Arco's Street Moves?" *National Petroleum News*, December, 20–21.

Esteva, Gustavo, and Madhu Suri Prakash. 1998. *Grassroots Post-modernism: Remaking the Soil of Cultures*. London: Zed.

Eulau, Heinz, and Kenneth Prewitt. 1973. *Labyrinths of Democracy*. Indianapolis: Bobbs-Merrill.

Evans, David. 2000. *Management Gurus*. London: Penguin.

Ewing, David W. 1990. *Inside the Harvard Business School*. New York: Crown.

Eyoh, Dickson. 1998. "African Perspectives on Democracy and the Dilemmas of Postcolonial Intellectuals." *Africa Today* 45:281–306.

Fabricant, Michael, and Stephen Brier. 2016. *Austerity Blues: Fighting for the Soul of Public Higher Education*. Baltimore, MD: Johns Hopkins University Press.

Farr, James, and Raymond Seidelman. 1993. *Discipline and History: Political Science in the United States*. Ann Arbor: University of Michigan Press.

Federici, Silvia. 2000. "The Recolonization of African Education." In *A Thousand Flowers: Social Struggle against Structural Adjustment in African Universities*, edited by Silvia Federici, George Caffentzis, and Ousseina Alidou, 19–23. Trenton, NJ: African World Press.

Feirtag, Michael. 1971. "Battering Ram: The Occupation of the President's Office, January 15, 1970." *The Tech* 91 (December 7): 5–8. http://tech.mit.edu/V91/PDF/V91-N53.pdf.

Fenton, William Nelson. 2008. "Area Studies in Amerian Universities." In *American Higher Education Transformed, 1940–2005: Documenting the National Discourse*, edited by Wilson Smith and Thomas Bender, 263–66. Baltimore, MD: Johns Hopkins University Press.

Ferguson, James. 1994. *The Anti-politics Machine: "Development," Depoliticization, and Bureaucratic Power in Lesotho*. Minneapolis: University of Minnesota Press.

Ferguson, James. 2006. *Global Shadows: Africa in the Neoliberal World Order*. Durham, NC: Duke University Press.

Ferguson, Roderick A. 2012. *The Reorder of Things: The University and Its Pedagogies of Minority Difference*. Minneapolis: University of Minnesota Press.

Fernandez, James W. 1977. "African Cultural Transformations." *Items* 31:10–14.

Finnemore, Martha. 1997. "Redefining Development at the World Bank." In *International Development and the Social Sciences: Essays on the History and Politics of Knowledge*, edited by F. Cooper and R. Packard, 203–27. Berkeley: University of California Press.

Fisher, Donald. 1993. *Fundamental Development of the Social Sciences: Rockefeller Philanthropy and the United States Social Science Research Council*. Ann Arbor: University of Michigan Press.

Forsyth, Randall. 1982. "More Shadow Than Substance? A Modest Proposal for Handling Global Bank Failures." *Barron's National Business and Financial Weekly*, September 20.

Frieden, Jeffry A. 2006. *Global Capitalism: Its Rise and Fall in the Twentieth Century*. New York: Norton.

Friedman, Milton. 1962. *Capitalism and Freedom*. Chicago: University of Chicago Press.

Friedman, Thomas L. 1999. *The Lexus and the Olive Tree: Understanding Globalization*. New York: Anchor.

Friedman, Thomas L. 2005. *The World Is Flat: A Brief History of the Twenty-First Century.* New York: Farrar, Straus and Giroux.

Fukuyama, Francis. 1989. "The End of History?" *The National Interest* 16:3–18.

Fukuyama, Francis. 1992. *The End of History and the Last Man.* New York: Avon.

Gardner, Hall. 2010. "Global War on Terrorism." In *A Companion to American Military History,* edited by James C. Bradford, 298–317. Malden, MA: Blackwell.

Gates, Robert. 2008. "Secretary of Defense Speech: Association of American Universities (Washington, D.C.)." Washington, DC: U.S. Department of Defense. http:// archive.defense.gov/Speeches/Speech.aspx?SpeechID=1228.

Gayer, Arthur D., W. W. Rostow, and Anna Jacobson Schwartz. 1953. *The Growth and Fluctuation of the British Economy, 1790–1850.* Vols. 1 and 2. Oxford: Clarendon.

Gendzier, Irene L. 1985. *Managing Political Change: Social Scientists and the Third World.* Boulder, CO: Westview.

Gendzier, Irene L. 1998. "Play It Again Sam: The Practice and Apology of Development." In *Universities and Empire: Money and Politics in the Social Sciences during the Cold War,* edited by Christopher Simpson, 57–95. New York: New Press.

George, Susan. 1990. *A Fate Worse Than Debt: The World Financial Crisis and the Poor.* New York: Grove Weidenfeld.

George, Susan, and Fabrizio Sabelli. 1994. *Faith and Credit: The World Bank's Secular Empire.* Boulder, CO: Westview.

Gershenhorn, Jerry. 2004. *Melville J. Herskovits and the Racial Politics of Knowledge.* Lincoln: University of Nebraska Press.

Ghauri, Pervez N., and S. Benjamin Brasad, eds. 1995. *International Management: A Reader.* London: Dryden.

Ghemawat, Pankaj. 2004. "Global Standardization vs. Localization: A Case Study and a Model." In *The Global Market: Developing a Strategy to Manage across Borders,* edited by J. A. Quelch and R. Deshpande, 115–45. New York: Jossey-Bass.

Ghemawat, Pankaj. 2017. "Globalization in the Age of Trump." *Harvard Business Review,* July/August. https://hbr.org/2017/07/globalization-in-the-age-of-trump.

Giguere, Lee. 1972. "Sit-In Obstructs CIS Entry." *The Tech* 92 (April 28): 1. http://tech .mit.edu/V92/PDF/V92-N21.pdf.

Gill, Sahiba. 2018. "Forced Labor at NYU Abu Dhabi: Compliance and the Cosmopolitan University." New York: Coalition for Fair Labor.

Gills, Barry K. 2004. "The Turning of the Tide." *Globalizations* 1:1–6.

Gilman, Nils. 2003. *Mandarins of the Future: Modernization Theory in Cold War America.* Baltimore, MD: Johns Hopkins University Press.

Gilroy, Harry. 1960. "Lumumba Assails Colonialism as Congo Is Freed." *New York Times,* July 1, 1.

Ginsberg, Benjamin. 2013. *The Fall of the Faculty: The Rise of the All-Administrative University and Why It Matters.* Oxford: Oxford University Press.

Giroux, Henry A. 2007. *The University in Chains: Confronting the Military-Industrial-Academic Complex.* Boulder, CO: Paradigm.

Giroux, Henry A. 2008. "The Militarization of US Higher Education after 9/11." *Theory, Culture and Society* 25:56–82.

Giroux, Henry A. 2014. *Neoliberalism's War on Higher Education*. Chicago: Haymarket.

Glenn, David. 2007. "Anthropologists in a War Zone: Scholars Debate Their Role." *Chronicle of Higher Education* 54 (November 30): A1.

"The Globalization Index." 2007. *Foreign Policy*, no. 163:68–76.

Goertz, Gary. 2006. *Social Science Concepts: A User's Guide*. Princeton, NJ: Princeton University Press.

Golden, Daniel. 2017a. "The CIA's Favorite College President: How the CIA Secretly Exploits Higher Education." *Chronicle of Higher Education* 64 (October 20): 1.

Golden, Daniel. 2017b. *Spy Schools: How the CIA, FBI, and Foreign Intelligence Secretly Exploit America's Universities*. New York: Henry Holt.

Goldman, Michael. 2005. *Imperial Nature: The World Bank and Struggles for Social Justice in the Age of Globalization*. New Haven, CT: Yale University Press.

Goldner, William. 1953. "Strikes and Prosperity." *Industrial and Labor Relations Review* 6:579–81.

Gonzalez, Roberto J. 2014. "Militarizing Education: The Intelligence Community's Spy Camp." In *The Imperial University: Academic Repression and Scholarly Dissent*, edited by Piya Chatterjee and Sunaina Maira, 79–98. Minneapolis: University of Minnesota Press.

Goodwin, Craufurd D., and Michael Nacht. 1988. *Abroad and Beyond: Patterns in American Overseas Education*. Cambridge: Cambridge University Press.

Gordon, Robert Aaron, and James Edwin Howell. 1959. *Higher Education for Business*. New York: Columbia University Press.

Gounden, A. M. Nalla. 1967. "Investment in Education in India." *Journal of Human Resources* 2:347–58.

Grant, Colin. 1999. "Theodore Levitt's *Marketing Myopia*." *Journal of Business Ethics* 18:397–406.

Green, Reginald Herbold, and Caroline Allison. 1986. "The World Bank's Agenda for Accelerated Development: Dialectics, Doubts and Dialogues." In *Africa in Economic Crisis*, edited by J. Ravenhill, 60–84. New York: Columbia University Press.

Greider, William. 1997. *One World, Ready or Not: The Manic Logic of Global Capitalism*. New York: Touchstone.

Guilhot, Nicolas. 2008. "The Realist Gambit: Postwar American Political Science and the Birth of IR Theory." *International Political Sociology* 2:281–304.

Guilhot, Nicolas. 2011a. "Introduction: One Discipline, Many Histories." In *The Invention of International Relations Theory: Realism, the Rockefeller Foundation, and the 1954 Conference on Theory*, edited by Nicolas Guilhot, 1–32. New York: Columbia University Press.

Guilhot, Nicolas. 2011b. *The Invention of International Relations Theory: Realism, the Rockefeller Foundation, and the 1954 Conference on Theory*. New York: Columbia University Press.

Guillén, Mauro F. 2001. "Is Globalization Civilizing, Destructive or Feeble? A Critique of Five Key Debates in the Social Science Literature." *Annual Review of Sociology* 27:235–60.

Guillory, John. 1993. *Cultural Capital: The Problem of Literary Canon Formation.* Chicago: University of Chicago Press.

Guruz, Kemal. 2008. *Higher Education and International Student Mobility in the Global Knowledge Economy.* Albany: State University of New York Press.

Gusterson, Hugh. 2017. "Homework: Towards a Critical Ethnography of the University." *American Ethnologist* 44:435–50.

Guyer, Jane I. 1996. *African Studies in the United States: A Perspective.* Atlanta: African Studies Association Press.

Haddad, Wadi D., Aklilu Habte, and Mats Hultin. 1980. "Education: Sector Policy Paper." Washington, DC: World Bank.

Hall, Peter A., and Sidney Tarrow. 1998. "Globalization and Area Studies: Where Is Too Broad Too Narrow?" *Chronicle of Higher Education*, January 23, B4–B5.

Hall, Robert B. 1947. "Area Studies: With Special Reference to Their Implications for Research in the Social Sciences." New York: Social Science Research Council.

Hamer, Jennifer F., and Clarence Lang. 2015. "Race, Structural Violence, and the Neoliberal University: The Challenges of Inhabitation." *Critical Sociology* 41:897–912.

Hanoch, Giora. 1967. "An Economic Analysis of Earnings and Schooling." *Journal of Human Resources* 2:310–29.

Hansen, Harry L. 1956. *Marketing: Texts, Cases, and Readings.* Homewood, IL: Richard D. Irwin.

Harney, Stefano, and Fred Moten. 2013. *The Undercommons: Fugitive Planning and Black Study.* Wivenhoe: Minor Compositions.

Harootunian, H. D. 2002. "Postcoloniality's Unconscious/Area Studies' Desire." In *Learning Places: The Afterlives of Area Studies*, edited by Masao Miyoshi and H. D. Harootunian, 150–74. Durham, NC: Duke University Press.

Hart, Gillian. 2002. *Disabling Globalization: Places of Power in Post-apartheid South Africa.* Berkeley: University of California Press.

Harvey, David. 2005. *A Brief History of Neoliberalism.* Oxford: Oxford University Press.

Harvie, David. 2004. "Common and Communities in the University: Some Notes and Some Examples." *The Commoner* 8. http://www.commoner.org.uk/08harvie.pdf.

Hay, Colin, and David Marsh. 2000. "Introduction: Demystifying Globalization." In *Demystifying Globalization*, edited by Colin Hay and David Marsh, 1–17. Hampshire: Palgrave.

Hay, Michael. 2007. "Business Schools: A New Sense of Purpose." *Journal of Management Development* 27:371–78.

HBR. 2006. "What Business Are You In? Classic Advice from Theodore Levitt." Editor's Note. *Harvard Business Review* 84 (10): 126–38.

Heckman, James J. 2003. "Some Brief Remarks on the Life and Work of Jacob Mincer." *Review of Economics of the Household* 1:245–47.

Heginbotham, Stanley J. 1994. "Rethinking International Scholarship: The Challenge of Transition from the Cold War Era." *Items* 48:33–40.

Heidegger, Martin. 1993. "The Question Concerning Technology." In *Martin Heidegger: Basic Writings*, edited by David Farrell Krell, 311–41. New York: HarperCollins.

Herman, Ellen. 1998. "Project Camelot and the Career of Cold War Psychology." In *Universities and Empire: Money and Politics in the Social Sciences during the Cold War*, edited by Christopher Simpson, 97–133. New York: New Press.

Heshmati, Almas. 2006. "Measurement of a Multidimensional Index of Globalization." *Global Economy Journal* 6 (2): 1–28.

Heyneman, Stephen P. 1999. "Development Aid in Education: A Personal View." *International Journal of Educational Development* 19:183–90.

Hinchliffe, Keith. 1987. *Higher Education in Sub-Saharan Africa*. London: Croom Helm.

Hindle, Tim. 2008. *Guide to Management Ideas and Gurus*. London: Economist/Bloomberg Press.

Hines, Ralph. 2001. "An Overview of Title VI." In *Changing Perspectives on International Education*, edited by Patrick O'Meara, Howard D. Mehlinger, and Roxana Ma Newman, 6–10. Bloomington: Indiana University Press.

Hirji, Karim F., ed. 2010. *Cheche: Reminiscences of a Radical Magazine*. Dar es Salaam: Mkuki na Nyota.

Hitchler, Ron. 1982. "Security Manufacturing: A Global View." *Security Management* 26:99–101.

Hobson, John M. 2012. *The Eurocentric Conception of World Politics: Western International Theory, 1760–2010*. Cambridge: Cambridge University Press.

Hoffa, William W. 2007. *A History of US Study Abroad: Beginnings to 1965*. Lancaster, PA: Whitmore.

Hoffa, William W., and Stephen C. DePaul. 2010. "Introduction." In *A History of U.S. Study Abroad: 1965–Present*, edited by William W. Hoffa and Stephen C. DePaul, 1–13. Carlisle, PA: Frontiers Journal.

Hoffmann, Stanley. 1977. "An American Social Science: International Relations." *Daedalus* 106:41–60.

Holmwood, John. 2011. *A Manifesto for the Public University*. London: Bloomsbury.

Holsti, Ole R. 2014. "Present at the Creation." International Studies Association. http://www.isanet.org/Portals/0/Documents/Institutional/Holsti_ISA_West.pdf.

Hopper, Paul. 2007. *Understanding Cultural Globalization*. Cambridge: Polity.

Hopper, Richard. 2004. "The Impact of the Task Force within the World Bank." *Comparative Education Review* 48:70–88.

Horowitz, Irving Louis. 1966. "The Life and Death of Project Camelot." *American Psychologist* 21:445–54.

Horowitz, Irving Louis. 1967. *The Rise and Fall of Project Camelot: Studies in the Relationship between Social Science and Practical Politics*. Cambridge, MA: MIT Press.

Houston, Franklin S. 1986. "The Marketing Concept: What It Is and What It Is Not." *Journal of Marketing* 50:81–87.

Hovland, Kevin. 2006. *Shared Futures: Global Learning and Liberal Education*. Washington, DC: Association of American Colleges and Universities. http://archive
.aacu.org/SharedFutures/documents/Shared_Futures.pdf.

Huang, Yasheng. 2002. "Perspectives on Globalization." Cambridge, MA: Harvard Business School.

Huczynski, Andrzej. 2006. *Management Gurus*. Rev. ed. London: Routledge.

Human Rights Watch. 2006. *Building Towers, Cheating Workers: Exploitation of Migrant Construction Workers in the United Arab Emirates*. New York: Human Rights Watch.

Human Rights Watch. 2009. *"The Island of Happiness": Exploitation of Migrant Workers on Saadiyat Island, Abu Dhabi*. New York: Human Rights Watch.

Human Rights Watch. 2012. *The Island of Happiness Revisited: A Progress Report on Institutional Commitments to Address Abuses of Migrant Workers on Abu Dhabi's Saadiyat Island*. New York: Human Rights Watch.

Human Rights Watch. 2015. *Migrant Workers' Rights on Saadiyat Island in the United Arab Emirates*. New York: Human Rights Watch.

Hummer, William B. 1977. "As World Bankers Assess Outlook Now." *Business Monthly Magazine*, June 15, 22–31.

Huntington, Samuel. 1967. "Introduction: Social Science and Vietnam." *Asian Survey* 7:503–6.

James, Paul, and Manfred B. Steger. 2014a. "A Genealogy of 'Globalization': The Career of a Concept." *Globalizations* 11:417–34.

James, Paul, and Manfred B. Steger. 2014b. "Interview: Saskia Sassen." *Globalizations* 11:461–72.

Jamieson, Barbara. 1984. "Agricultural Development and Self-Reliance." In *Continental Crisis: The Lagos Plan of Action and Africa's Future*, edited by D. F. Luke and T. M. Shaw, 13–31. Lanham, MD: University Press of America.

Jannai, Shlomo. 1982. "Global Reinsurance." *Best's Review* 83:96.

Johnson, Benjamin, Patrick Kavanagh, and Kevin Mattson. 2003. *Steal This University: The Rise of the Corporate University and the Academic Labor Movement*. New York: Routledge.

Johnston, Moira. 1990. *Roller Coaster: The Bank of America and the Future of American Banking*. New York: Ticknor and Fields.

Jones, Phillip W. 2007. *World Bank Financing of Education: Lending, Learning and Development*. 2nd ed. New York: Routledge.

Jones, Phillip W., and David Coleman. 2005. *The United Nations and Education: Multilateralism, Development and Globalization*. London: RoutledgeFalmer.

Jones, William O. 1968. "Labor and Leisure in Traditional African Societies." *Items* 22:1–6.

Kaldor, Mary. 2000. "'Civilising' Globalization? The Implications of the 'Battle in Seattle.'" *Millenium: Journal of International Studies* 29 (1): 105–14.

Kaldor, Mary. 2003. *Global Civil Society: An Answer to War*. New York: Polity.

Kaminer, Ariel, and Sean O'Driscoll. 2014. "Workers at N.Y.U.'s Abu Dhabi Site Faced Harsh Conditions." *New York Times*, May 19, A1, A8.

Kamola, Isaac. 2010. "Producing the Global Imaginary: Academic Knowledge, Globalization and the Making of the World." PhD diss., University of Minnesota.

Kamola, Isaac. 2011. "Pursuing Excellence in a 'World-Class African University': The Mamdani Affair and the Politics of Global Higher Education." *Journal of Higher Education in Africa* 9:147–68.

Kamola, Isaac. 2012. "Reading the Global in the Absence of Africa." In *Thinking International Relations Differently*, edited by Arlene B. Tickner and David L. Blaney, 183–204. London: Routledge.

Kamola, Isaac. 2013. "Why Global? Diagnosing the Globalization Literature within a Political Economy of Higher Education." *International Political Sociology* 7:41–58.

Kamola, Isaac. 2014a. "Steve Biko and a Critique of Global Governance as White Liberalism." *African Identities* 13 (1): 62–76.

Kamola, Isaac. 2014b. "US Universities and the Production of the Global Imaginary." *British Journal of Politics and International Relations* 16:515–33.

Kamola, Isaac. 2016. "Situating the 'Global University' in South Africa." In *The Transnational Politics of Higher Education: Contesting the Global/Transforming the Local*, edited by Meng-Hsuan Chou, Isaac Kamola, and Tamson Pietsch, 42–62. New York: Routledge.

Kamola, Isaac. 2017. "Amilcar Cabral and a Politics of Realism without Abstraction." In *Politics of African Anticolonial Archive*, edited by Shiera S. el-Malik and Isaac Kamola, 83–99. London: Rowman and Littlefield International.

Kamola, Isaac, and Eli Meyerhoff. 2009. "Creating Commons: Divided Governance, Participatory Management, and the Struggle against the Enclosure of the University." *Polygraph* 21:15–37.

Kantrow, Alan M., ed. 1985. *Sunrise . . . Sunset: Challenging the Myth of Industrial Obsolescence*. New York: John Wiley.

Kapur, Devesh, John P. Lewis, and Richard Webb. 1997. *The World Bank: Its First Half Century*. Vol. 1. Washington, DC: Brookings Institution.

Karp, Ivan. 1997. "Does Theory Travel? Area Studies and Cultural Studies." *Africa Today* 44:281–96.

Katzenstein, Josh. 2009. "U to Help Africa, Water with Global Spotlight." *Minnesota Daily*, February 9. http://www.mndaily.com/article/2009/02/u-help-africa-water-global-spotlight.

Keith, Robert J. 1960. "The Marketing Revolution." *Journal of Marketing* 24:35–38.

Keller, John M., and Maritheresa Frain. 2010. "The Impact of Geo-political Events, Globalization, and National Policies on Study Abroad Programming and Participation." In *A History of U.S. Study Abroad: 1965–Present*, edited by William W. Hoffa and Stephen C. DePaul, 15–53. Carlisle, PA: Frontiers Journal.

Kellner, Douglas. 2002. "Theorizing Globalization." *Sociological Theory* 20:285–305.

Kelly, Michael J. 1991. "Education in a Declining Economy: The Case of Zambia, 1975–1985." Washington, DC: World Bank.

Kennedy, Carol. 2002. *Guide to the Management Gurus: The Best Guide to Business Thinkers.* London: Random House.

Keohane, Robert O., and Joseph S. Nye. 1977. *Power and Interdependence: World Politics in Transition.* Boston: Little, Brown.

Keohane, Robert O., and Joseph S. Nye. 2001. *Power and Interdependence.* 3rd ed. New York: Longman.

Kerr, Clark. 2001. *The Uses of the University.* 5th ed. Cambridge, MA: Harvard University Press.

Khurana, Rakesh. 2007. *From Higher Aims to Hired Hands: The Social Transformation of American Business Schools and the Unfulfilled Promise of Management as a Profession.* Princeton, NJ: Princeton University Press.

Kiley, Kevin. 2013. "'No Confidence' in the System." *Inside Higher Ed,* March 18. https://www.insidehighered.com/news/2013/03/18/new-york-university-vote-no-confidence-raises-debate-about-ambitions-and-governance.

King, Kenneth, and Simon McGrath. 2004. *Knowledge for Development: Comparing British, Japanese, Swedish and World Bank Aid.* Cape Town: HSRC Press.

Kirp, David L. 2003. *Shakespeare, Einstein, and the Bottom Line: The Marketing of Higher Education.* Cambridge, MA: Harvard University Press.

Klein, Naomi. 2002. *No Logo.* New York: Picador.

Knowles, Louis L., and Kenneth Prewitt. 1969. *Institutional Racism in America.* Englewood Cliffs, NJ: Prentice Hall.

Koehn, Peter H., and Milton O. Obamba. 2014. *The Transnationally Partnered University: Insights from Research and Sustainable Development Collaborations in Africa.* New York: Palgrave Macmillan.

Kraske, Jochen, William H. Becker, William Diamond, and Louis Galambos. 1996. *Bankers with a Mission: The Presidents of the World Bank, 1946–91.* Oxford: Oxford University Press.

Krause, Monika, Mary Nolan, Michael Palm, and Andrew Ross. 2008a. "Introduction." In *The University against Itself: The NYU Strike and the Future of the Academic Workplace,* edited by Monika Krause, Mary Nolan, Michael Palm and Andrew Ross, 1–11. Philadelphia: Temple University Press.

Krause, Monika, Mary Nolan, Michael Palm, and Andrew Ross. 2008b. *The University against Itself: The NYU Strike and the Future of the Academic Workplace.* Philadelphia: Temple University Press.

Krieger, Zvika. 2007. "New York U. Plans to Open a 'Comprehensive Liberal-Arts Campus' in Abu Dhabi." *Chronicle of Higher Education,* October 26. https://www.chronicle.com/article/New-York-U-Plans-to-Open-a/19465.

Krieger, Zvika. 2008a. "An Academic Building Boom Transforms the Persian Gulf." *Chronicle of Higher Education,* March 28. https://www.chronicle.com/article/An-Academic-Building-Boom/20922.

Krieger, Zvika. 2008b. "The Emir of NYU." *New York Magazine*, April 13. http://nymag
.com/news/features/46000/.

Krueger, Anne O. 1974. "The Political Economy of the Rent-Seeking Society." *American
Economic Review* 64:291–303.

Krupat, Kitty, and Laura Tenenbaum. 2002. "A Network for Campus Democracy: Reflections on NYU and the Academic Labor Movement." *Social Text* 20 (1): 27–50.

Kuklick, Bruce. 2006. *Blind Oracles: Intellectuals and War from Kennan to Kissinger.*
Princeton, NJ: Princeton University Press.

Kunin, Jay. 1969. "March 4 Activities Fill Kresge, but Research Goes on as Usual." *The
Tech* 89 (March 7): 1, 5. http://tech.mit.edu/V89/PDF/V89-N8.pdf.

Laidler, Nathalie, and John A. Quelch. 2000. "Harlequin Romances—Poland (A)." Case
594-17. Cambridge, MA: Harvard Business Publishing.

Lambert, Richard D. 1973a. "Language and Area Studies Review." *Items* 28 (2): 17–20.
https://items.ssrc.org/print-archive/.

Lambert, Richard D. 1973b. *Language and Area Studies Review.* Philadelphia: American
Academy of Political and Social Sciences.

Latham, Michael E. 2000. *Modernization as Ideology: American Social Science and "Nation Building" in the Kennedy Era.* Chapel Hill: University of North Carolina Press.

Lawal, Adebayo A. 2007. "Adding a Historical Dimension to the Dilemmas of Higher
Education in Post-colonial Nigeria." In *Higher Education in Postcolonial Africa:
Paradigms of Development, Decline and Dilemmas,* edited by Michael O. Afoláyan,
57–73. Trenton, NJ: Africa World Press.

Leslie, Stuart W. 1993. *The Cold War and American Science: The Military-Industrial-
Academic Complex at MIT and Stanford.* New York: Columbia University Press.

Levitt, Theodore. 1953a. "Prosperity versus Strikes." *Industrial and Labor Relations Review* 6:220–26.

Levitt, Theodore. 1953b. "Reply." *Industrial and Labor Relations Review* 6:581–83.

Levitt, Theodore. 1953c. "Reply." *Industrial and Labor Relations Review* 7:127–28.

Levitt, Theodore. 1956a. "The Changing Character of Capitalism." *Harvard Business
Review* 34:37–47.

Levitt, Theodore. 1956b. "The Lonely Crowd and the Economic Man." *Quarterly Journal
of Economics* 70:95–116.

Levitt, Theodore. 1958. "The Dangers of Social Responsibility." *Harvard Business Review*
36:41–50.

Levitt, Theodore. 1960a. "Cold-War Thaw." *Harvard Business Review* 38:6–8, 10–16, 156–62.

Levitt, Theodore. 1960b. "Marketing Myopia." *Harvard Business Review* 38:45–56.

Levitt, Theodore. 1960c. "M—R Snake Dance." *Harvard Business Review* 38:76–84.

Levitt, Theodore. 1962. *Innovation in Marketing: New Perspectives for Profit and Growth.*
New York: McGraw-Hill.

Levitt, Theodore. 1966. "Innovative Imitation." *Harvard Business Review* 44:63–70.

Levitt, Theodore. 1975. "Marketing Myopia." *Harvard Business Review* 53:26–28, 33–34,
38–39, 44, 173–81.

Levitt, Theodore. 1976. "Marketing Myopia." In *The Great Writings in Marketing: Selected Readings Together with the Authors' Own Retrospective Commentaries*, edited by H. A. Thompson, 23–49. Plymouth, MI: Commerce Press.

Levitt, Theodore. 1977. "Marketing When Things Change." *Harvard Business Review* 55:107–13.

Levitt, Theodore. 1983. "The Globalization of Markets." *Harvard Business Review* 61:92–102.

Levitt, Theodore. 1986a. "Excerpts from Marketing Myopia." *Harvard Business Review* 64:128.

Levitt, Theodore. 1986b. *The Marketing Imagination.* 2nd ed. New York: Free Press.

Levitt, Theodore. 1993. "Advertising: 'The Poetry of Becoming.'" *Harvard Business Review* 71:134–37.

Levitt, Theodore. 2004. "Marketing Myopia." *Harvard Business Review* 82:138–49.

Levitt, Theodore. 2006. "What Business Are You In? Classic Advice from Theodore Levitt." *Harvard Business Review* 84:126–38.

Levitt, Theodore. 2008. *Marketing Myopia.* Boston: Harvard Business Press.

Lewontin, R. C. 1997. "The Cold War and the Transformation of the Academy." In *The Cold War and the University: Toward an Intellectual History of the Postwar Years*, edited by Noam Chomsky, Ira Katznelson, R. C. Lewontin, Laura Nader, David Montgomery, Richard Ohmann, Immanuel Wallerstein, Ray Siever, and Howard Zinn, 1–34. New York: New Press.

Lindsey, Ursula. 2012. "NYU–Abu Dhabi Behaves Like Careful Guest in Foreign Land." *Chronicle of Higher Education*, June 8. https://www.chronicle.com/article/A -Careful-Guest-in-a-Foreign/132075.

Liptak, Eugene. 2009. *Office of Strategic Services 1942–45: The World War II Origins of the CIA.* Oxford: Osprey.

Lowe, George E. 1966. "The Camelot Affair." *Bulletin of the Atomic Scientists* 22:44–48.

Lowen, Rebecca S. 1997. *Creating the Cold War University: The Transformation of Stanford.* Berkeley: University of California Press.

Ludden, David. 2000. "Area Studies in the Age of Globalization." *Frontiers: The Interdisciplinary Journal of Study Abroad* 5:1–22.

Luke, David Fashole, and Timothy M. Shaw, eds. 1984. *Continental Crisis: The Lagos Plan of Action and America's Future.* Lanham, MD: University Press of America.

MacLean, Nancy. 2017. *Democracy in Chains: The Deep History of the Radical Right's Stealth Plan for America.* New York: Viking.

Maher, Neil. 2004. "Neil Maher on Shooting the Moon." *American Society for Environmental History* 9:526–31.

Makowski, Alex. 1970. "Rally Endorses Strike Call." *The Tech* 90 (May 5): 1, 6. http:// tech.mit.edu/V90/PDF/V90-N23.pdf.

Makowski, Alex, and Duff McRoberts. 1969. "Rostow Defends Policies in Kresge Confrontation." *The Tech* 89 (April 11): 1, 8. http://tech.mit.edu/V89/PDF/V89-N15.pdf.

Mallaby, Sebastian. 2006. *The World's Banker: A Story of Failed States, Financial Crises, and the Wealth and Poverty of Nations.* New York: Penguin.

Mamdani, Mahmood. 1993. "University Crisis and Reform: Reflection on the African Experience." *Review of African Political Economy* 58:7–19.

Mamdani, Mahmood. 2007. *Scholars in the Marketplace: The Dilemmas of Neo-liberal Reform at Makerere University, 1989–2005.* Dakar: CODESRIA.

Mamdani, Mahmood. 2011. "The Importance of Research in a University." Presented at Makerere University Research and Innovations Dissemination Conference. Hotel Africana, Kampala. https://www.pambazuka.org/resources/importance-research-university.

Mangan, Katherine. 2015. "U.A.E. Incident Raises Questions for Colleges That Open Campuses in Restrictive Countries." *Chronicle of Higher Education*, March 18. https://www.chronicle.com/article/UAE-Incident-Raises/228565.

Mark, J. Paul. 1987. *The Empire Builders: Power, Money and Ethics inside the Harvard Business School.* New York: William Morrow.

Marshall, Katherine. 2008. *The World Bank: From Reconstruction to Development to Equity.* Edited by T. G. Weiss and R. Wilkinson. New York: Routledge.

Martell, Luke. 2007. "The Third Wave in Globalization Theory." *International Studies Review* 9:173–96.

Martin, Randy. 1998. *Chalk Lines: The Politics of Work in the Managed University.* Durham, NC: Duke University Press.

Martin, William G. 2005. "Manufacturing the Homeland Security Campus and Cadre." *ACAS Bulletin* 70:1.

Mazrui, Ali A. 2005. "Pan-Africanism and the Intellectuals: Rise, Decline and Revival." In *African Intellectuals: Rethinking Politics, Language, Gender and Development*, edited by T. Mkandawire, 56–77. Dakar: CODESRIA.

Mbembe, Achille, and Sarah Nuttall. 2008. "Introduction: Afropolis." In *Johannesburg: The Elusive Metropolis*, edited by Sarah Nuttall and Achille Mbembe, 1–33. Durham, NC: Duke University Press.

McCaughey, Robert A. 1980. "In the Land of the Blind: American International Studies in the 1930s." *Annals of the American Academy of Political and Social Science* 449:1–16.

McDonald, Joseph P., Myrrh Domingo, Jill V. Jeffery, Rosa Riccio Pietanza, and Frank Pignatosi. 2013. "In and Of the City: Theory of Action and the NYU Partnership School Program." *Peabody Journal of Education* 88 (5): 578–93.

McGann, James G., and Richard Sabatini. 2011. *Global Think Tanks: Policy Networks and Governance.* New York: Routledge.

McGee, Micki. 2008. "Blue Team, Gray Team: Some Varieties of the Contingent Faculty Experience." In *The University against Itself: The NYU Strike and the Future of the Academic Workplace*, edited by Monika Krause, Mary Nolan, Michael Palm, and Andrew Ross, 97–112. Philadelphia: Temple University Press.

McGettigan, Andrew. 2013. *The Great University Gamble: Money, Markets, and the Future of Higher Education.* London: Pluto.

McKie, Robin. 2008. "The Mission That Changed Everything." *Guardian*, November 29. https://www.theguardian.com/science/2008/nov/30/apollo-8-mission.

McMichael, Philip. 1996. "Globalization: Myths and Realities." *Rural Sociology* 61:25–55.

McNamara, Robert. 1968. *The Essence of Security: Reflections in Office.* New York: Harper and Row.

McNamara, Robert. 1973. *One Hundred Countries, Two Billion People: The Dimensions of Development.* New York: Praeger.

McNamara, Robert. 1981a. "To the Board of Governors, Washington, DC, September 30, 1968." In *The McNamara Years at the World Bank: Major Policy Addresses of Robert S. McNamara 1968–1981,* edited by World Bank, 1–15. Baltimore, MD: World Bank and Johns Hopkins University Press.

McNamara, Robert. 1981b. "To the Inter-American Press Association: Buenos Aires, October 18, 1968." In *The McNamara Years at the World Bank: Major Policy Addresses of Robert S. McNamara 1968–1981,* edited by World Bank, 17–30. Baltimore, MD: World Bank and Johns Hopkins University Press.

McNamara, Robert. 1995. *In Retrospect: The Tragedy and Lessons of Vietnam.* New York: Random House.

"Measuring Globalization." 2001. *Foreign Policy,* no. 122:56–65.

Menand, Louis. 2010. *The Marketplace of Ideas: Reform and Resistance in the American University.* New York: W. W. Norton.

Mettler, Suzanne. 2014. *Degrees of Inequality: How the Politics of Higher Education Sabotaged the American Dream.* New York: Basic Books.

Micklethwait, John, and Adrian Wooldridge. 1996. *The Witch Doctors: Making Sense of the Management Gurus.* New York: Random House.

Mignolo, Walter D. 2000. *Local Histories/Global Designs.* Princeton Studies in Culture/Power/History. Princeton, NJ: Princeton University Press.

Mignolo, Walter D. 2011. *The Darker Side of Western Modernity: Global Futures, Decolonial Options.* Durham, NC: Duke University Press.

Millikan, Max F., and W. W. Rostow. 1957. *A Proposal: Key to an Effective Foreign Policy.* New York: Harper and Brothers.

Mills, Andrew. 2010. "NYU Populates a Liberal-Arts Outpost in the Middle East." *Chronicle of Higher Education,* April 11. https://www.chronicle.com/article/NYU-Populates-a-Liberal-Arts/65018.

Milne, David. 2008. *America's Rasputin: Walt Rostow and the Vietnam War.* New York: Hill and Wang.

Mincer, Jacob. 1958. "Investment in Human Capital and Personal Income Distribution." *Journal of Political Economy* 66:281–302.

Mincer, Jacob. 1962. "On the Job Training: Costs, Returns, and Some Implications." *Journal of Political Economy* 70:50–79.

Mincer, Jacob. 1974. *Schooling, Experience, and Earnings.* New York: Columbia University Press.

Miner, Horace. 1967. *The City in Modern Africa.* Praeger Library of African Affairs. London: Frederick A. Praeger.

Mirsepassi, Ali, Amrita Basu, and Frederick Weaver. 2003. "Introduction: Knowledge, Power, Culture." In *Localizing Knowledge in a Globalizing World,* edited by Ali

Mirsepassi, Amrita Basu, and Frederick Weaver, 1–21. Syracuse, NY: Syracuse University Press.

Mitchell, Gordon. 1970. "Colossus of the West: Bank of America Is Busily Seeking New Worlds to Conquer." *Barron's National Business and Financial Weekly*, July 13, 9, 17, 19.

Mitchell, Gordon. 1974. "Beyond Bretton Woods? Floating Currencies, Says Bank-America, Work Fine." *Barron's National Business and Financial Weekly*, November 11, 5, 14, 16, 18–20.

Mitchell, Timothy. 1991. *Colonising Egypt*. Berkeley: University of California Press.

Mittelman, James H. 2004a. "Ideologies and the Globalization Agenda." In *Rethinking Globalism*, edited by Manfred B. Steger, 15–26. Lanham, MD: Rowman and Littlefield.

Mittelman, James H. 2004b. "What Is Critical Globalization Studies?" *International Studies Perspectives*, no. 5: 219–30.

Mittelman, James H. 2018. *Implausible Dream: The World-Class University and Repurposing Higher Education*. Princeton, NJ: Princeton University Press.

Mkandawire, Thandika. 2005. "Introduction." In *African Intellectuals: Rethinking Politics, Language, Gender and Development*, edited by Thandika Mkandawire, 1–9. Dakar: CODESRIA.

Mohanty, Chandra Talpade. 2003. "'Under Western Eyes' Revisited: Feminist Solidarity through Anticapitalist Struggles." *Signs* 28:499–535.

Morris, Errol. 2003. *The Fog of War: Eleven Lessons from the Life of Robert S. McNamara*. DVD. Los Angeles: Sony Classics.

Mullen, Anna L. 2010. *Degrees of Inequality: Culture, Class, and Gender in American Higher Education*. Baltimore, MD: Johns Hopkins University Press.

Nader, Laura. 1997. "The Phantom Factor: Impact of the Cold War on Anthropology." In *The Cold War and the University: Toward an Intellectual History of the Postwar Years*, edited by Noam Chomsky, Ira Katznelson, Laura Nader, David Montgomery, Richard Ohmann, Immanuel Wallerstein, Ray Silver, and Howard Zinn, 107–46. New York: New Press.

Nardello and Co. 2015. "Report of the Independent Investigation into Allegations of Labor and Compliance Issues during the Construction of the NYU Abu Dhabi Campus on Saadiyat Island, United Arab Emirates." April 16. http://www.nardelloandco.com/wp-content/uploads/insights/pdf/nyu-abu-dhabi-campus-investigative-report.pdf.

National Research Council. 2005. "Frameworks for Higher Education in Homeland Security." Washington, DC: National Academies Press.

Needell, Allan A. 1998. "Project Troy and the Cold War Annexation of the Social Science." In *Universities and Empire: Money and Politics in the Social Sciences during the Cold War*, edited by Christopher Simpson, 3–38. New York: New Press.

Negroponte, John D. 2006. "The US Intelligence Community's Five Year Strategic

Human Capital Plan." Washington, DC: Office of the Director of National Intelligence. http://www.dtic.mil/dtic/tr/fulltext/u2/a468882.pdf.

Nelson, Cary. 1997. *Manifesto of a Tenured Radical.* New York: New York University Press.

Nelson, Cary. 2004. "The National Security State." *Cultural Studies* ↔ *Critical Methodologies* 4:357–61.

Nelson, Cary. 2010. *No University Is an Island: Saving Academic Freedom.* New York: NYU Press.

Nemfakos, Charles, Bernard D. Rostker, Raymond E. Conley, Stephanie Young, William A. Williams, Jeffrey Engstrom, Barbara Bicksler, Sara Beth Elson, Joseph Jenkins, Lianne Kennedy-Boudali, and Donald Temple. 2013. *Workforce Planning in the Intelligence Community: A Retrospective.* Santa Monica: RAND.

Newfield, Christopher. 2003. *Ivy and Industry: Business and the Making of the American University, 1880–1980.* Durham, NC: Duke University Press.

Newfield, Christopher. 2008. *Unmaking the Public University: The Forty-Year Assault on the Middle Class.* Cambridge, MA: Harvard University Press.

Newfield, Christopher. 2016. *The Great Mistake: How We Wrecked Public Universities and How We Can Fix Them.* Baltimore, MD: Johns Hopkins University Press.

Newman, Frank. 1985. *Higher Education and the American Resurgence.* Princeton, NJ: Carnegie Foundation for the Advancement of Teaching.

Ngũgĩ, James, Henry Owuor-Anyumba, and Taban Lo Liyong. 1972. "On the Abolition of the English Department." In *Homecoming: Essays on African and Caribbean Literature, Culture and Politics,* edited by James Ngũgĩ, 145–50. London: Heinemann.

Ngũgĩ wa Thiong'o. 2012. *Globalectics: Theory and the Politics of Knowing.* New York: Columbia University Press.

Noori, Neema. 2016. "The Political Economy of International Higher Education and Academic Labor in the Persian Gulf." In *The Transnational Politics of Higher Education: Contesting the Global/Transforming the Local,* edited by Meng-Hsuan Chou, Isaac Kamola, and Tamson Pietsch, 63–84. London: Routledge.

Noss, Andrew. 1991. "Education and Adjustment: A Review of the Literature." Washington, DC: World Bank.

Nugent, David. 2010. "Knowledge and Empire: The Social Sciences and United States Imperial Expansion." *Identities: Global Studies in Culture and Power* 17:2–44.

Nussbaum, Martha C. 2010. *Not for Profit: Why Democracy Needs the Humanities.* Princeton, NJ: Princeton University Press.

Nyerere, Julius K. 1968. "Education for Self-Reliance." In *Tanzania: Revolution by Education,* edited by I. N. Resnick. Arusha: Longmans of Tanzania.

NYU. 2008. "NYU Framework 2031." New York: New York University. https://www.nyu.edu/content/dam/shared/documents/NYU.Framework2031.Final.pdf.

OAU. 1981. "Lagos Plan of Action for the Economic Development of Africa: 1980–2000." Organization of African Unity. Geneva: International Institute for Labor Studies.

Odin, Jaishree K., and Peter T. Manicas. 2004. *Globalization and Higher Education*. Honolulu: University of Hawai'i Press.

Office of Public Relations. 1959. "The Ford Foundation Is Releasing Today (July 21) a Story on All Grants." AC 0236 (Box 2.f3). Center for International Studies, MIT. Institute Archives and Special Collections, MIT Libraries, Cambridge, Massachusetts.

Ohmae, Kenichi. 1991. *The Borderless World: Power and Strategy in the Interlinked Economy*. 2nd ed. New York: HarperBusiness.

Ohmae, Kenichi. 1995. *The End of the Nation State*. New York: Free Press.

Ohmann, Richard. 1976. *English in America: A Radical View of the Profession*. New York: Oxford University Press.

Ohmann, Richard. 2003. *Politics of Knowledge: The Commercialization of the University, the Professions, and Print Culture*. Middletown, CT: Wesleyan University Press.

Okihiro, Gary Y. 2016. *Third World Studies: Theorizing Liberation*. Durham, NC: Duke University Press.

Old Mole, The. 1969. "Why Smash MIT?" In *The University Crisis Reader: The Liberal University under Attack*, edited by Immanuel Wallerstein and Paul Starr, 240–43. New York: Random House.

Olukoshi, Adebayo, and Paul Tiyambe Zeleza. 2004. "Introduction: The Struggle for African Universities and Knowledges." In *African Universities in the Twenty-First Century*, edited by Paul Tiyambe Zeleza and Adebayo Olukoshi, 1–18. Dakar: CODESRIA.

Onzoño, Santiago Iñiguez de, and Salvador Carmona. 2007. "The Changing Business Model of B-Schools." *Journal of Management Development* 26:22–32.

OpenDoors. 2015. "2015 Fact Sheet." Institute of International Education. http://www .iie.org/Research-and-Publications/Open-Doors.

Oren, Ido. 2003. *Our Enemies and US: America's Rivalries and the Making of Political Science*. Ithaca, NY: Cornell University Press.

Palm, Michael. 2007. "Beyond the Picket Line: Academic Organizing after the Long NYU Strike." *Workplace: A Journal for Academic Labor* 14:1–8. http://ices.library .ubc.ca/index.php/workplace/article/view/182198/182208.

Parmar, Inderjeet. 2011. "American Hegemony, the Rockefeller Foundation, and the Rise of Academic International Relations in the United States." In *The Invention of International Relations Theory: Realism, the Rockefeller Foundation, and the 1954 Conference on Theory*, edited by Nicolas Guilhot, 182–209. New York: Columbia University Press.

Parmar, Inderjeet. 2012. *Foundations of the American Century: The Ford, Carnegie, and Rockefeller Foundations in the Rise of American Power*. New York: Columbia University Press.

Parsons, Talcott, and Evon Z. Vogt. 1962. "Clyde Kay Maben Kluckhohn, 1905–1960." *American Anthropologist* 64:140–61.

Pason, Amy. 2008. "We Are All Workers: A Class Analysis of University Labour Strikes." *Ephemera* 8:322–30.

Peck, Jim. 1968. "Reflections on the Implications of the Vietnam Caucus." *Bulletin of Concerned Asian Scholars* 1:2–4. http://criticalasianstudies.org/assets/files/bcas /v01n0s1.pdf.

Perestroika. 2005. "The Idea: The Opening of Debate." In *Perestroika! The Raucous Rebellion in Political Science*, edited by Kristen Renwick Monroe, 9–11. New Haven, CT: Yale University Press.

Peterson, V. Spike. 2004. "Plural Processes, Patterned Connections." *Globalizations* 1:50–68.

Phillips, Herbert Moore. 1976. "Higher Education: Cooperation with Developing Countries." New York: Rockefeller Foundation.

Piasecki, Ryszard, and Miron Wolnicki. 2003. "The Evolution of Development Economics and Globalization." *International Journal of Social Economics* 31:300–314.

Pierson, Frank Cook. 1959. *The Education of American Businessmen: A Study of University-College Programs in Business Administration*. New York: McGraw-Hill.

Pietsch, Tamson. 2013. *Empire of Scholars: Universities, Networks and the British Academic World 1850–1939*. Manchester: Manchester University Press.

Pietsch, Tamson. 2016. "Between the Local and the University: Academic Worlds and the Long History of the University." In *The Transnational Politics of Higher Education: Contesting the Global/Transforming the Local*, edited by Meng-Hsuan Chou, Isaac Kamola, and Tamson Pietsch, 21–41. New York: Routledge.

Polachek, Solomon W. 2008. "Earnings over the Life Cycle: The Mincer Earnings Function and Its Application." *Foundations and Trends in Microeconomics* 4:165–272.

Polgreen, Lydia. 2007. "Africa's Storied Colleges, Jammed and Crumbling." *New York Times*, May 20, A1.

Poole, Robert. 2008. *Earthrise: How Man First Saw the Earth*. New Haven, CT: Yale University Press.

Porter, Lyman W., and Lawrence E. McKibbin. 1988. *Management Education and Development: Drift or Thrust into the 21st Century?* New York: McGraw-Hill.

Powell, Farran. 2017. "10 Universities with the Biggest Endowments." *U.S. News and World Report*, September 28. https://www.usnews.com/education/best-colleges /the-short-list-college/articles/2017-09-28/10-universities-with-the-biggest -endowments.

Prashad, Vijay. 2007. *The Darker Nations: A People's History of the Third World*. New York: New Press.

Prashad, Vijay. 2012. *The Poorer Nations: A Possible History of the Global South*. London: Verso.

Prewitt, Kenneth. 1965. "Political Socialization and Leadership Selection." *Annals of the American Academy of Political and Social Science* 361:96–111.

Prewitt, Kenneth. 1966. "Makerere: Intelligence vs Intellectuals." *Transition* 27:35–39.

Prewitt, Kenneth. 1968. "Political Perspectives of Opinion Leaders in Uganda." *Social Science Information* 7:53–78.

Prewitt, Kenneth. 1969. "From the Many Are Chosen the Few." *American Behavioral Scientist* 13:169–87.

Prewitt, Kenneth. 1970. *The Recruitment of Political Leaders: A Study of Citizen-Politicians*. Indianapolis: Bobbs-Merrill.

Prewitt, Kenneth. 1971a. "Introduction." In *Education and Political Values: An East African Case Study*, edited by Kenneth Prewitt, vii–xi. Nairobi: East African Publishing House.

Prewitt, Kenneth. 1971b. "Perplexities of the Political Identity Questions: The Case of Uganda." In *Education and Political Values: An East African Case Study*, edited by Kenneth Prewitt, 199–249. Nairobi: East African Publishing House.

Prewitt, Kenneth. 1971c. "University Students in East Africa: A Case of Political Quietude." In *Education and Political Values: An East African Case Study*, edited by Kenneth Prewitt, 141–70. Nairobi: East African Publishing House.

Prewitt, Kenneth. 1980a. "A Defense of NSF." *Society* 17:15–16.

Prewitt, Kenneth. 1980b. "Social Science Utilities." *Society* 17:6–8.

Prewitt, Kenneth. 1984. "Social Science and the Third World." *Society* 21:84–89.

Prewitt, Kenneth. 1985. "Security, Peace and Social Science." *Society* 23:12–15.

Prewitt, Kenneth. 1996a. "Annual Report of the President." In *Social Science Research Council: Annual Report 1995–1996*. New York: Social Science Research Council.

Prewitt, Kenneth. 1996b. "Presidential Items." ITEMS 50:31–40.

Prewitt, Kenneth. 1996c. "Presidential Items." ITEMS 50:15–18.

Prewitt, Kenneth. 2000. "Political Science for Design of a Sensible Census." *PS: Political Science and Politics* 33:139–42.

Prewitt, Kenneth. 2003. *Politics and Science in Census Taking*. New York: Russell Sage Foundation.

Prewitt, Kenneth. 2004. "Political Science and Its Audience." *PS: Political Science and Politics* 37:781–84.

Prewitt, Kenneth. 2013. *What Is Your Race? The Census and Our Flawed Efforts to Classify Americans*. Princeton, NJ: Princeton University Press.

Prewitt, Kenneth, Heinz Eulau, and Betty H. Zisk. 1966. "Political Socialization and Political Roles." *Public Opinion Quarterly* 30:569–82.

Prewitt, Kenneth, and William Nowlin. 1969. "Political Ambitions and the Behavior of Incumbent Politicians." *Western Political Quarterly* 22:298–306.

Prewitt, Kenneth, assisted by Okello Oculi. 1971. "Political Socialization and Political Education in the New Nations." In *Education and Political Values: An East African Case Study*, edited by Kenneth Prewitt, 1–22. Nairobi: East African Publishing House.

Prewitt, Kenneth, and Alan Stone. 1973. *The Ruling Elites: Elite Theory, Power, and American Democracy*. New York: Harper and Row.

Prewitt, Kenneth, George von der Muhll, and David Court. 1970. "Social Experiences and Political Socialization: A Study of Tanzanian Secondary School Students." *Comparative Political Studies* 3:203–25.

Pritchard, Rosalind M. O. 2011. *Neoliberal Development in Higher Education: The United Kingdom and Germany*. Oxford: Peter Lang.

"Professor Theodore Levitt, Legendary Marketing Scholar and Former *Harvard Business Review* Editor, Dead at 81." 2006. *Harvard University Gazette*, July 20. https://news.harvard.edu/gazette/story/2006/07/professor-theodore-levitt-legendary-marketing-scholar-and-former-harvard-business-review-editor-dead-at-81/.

Psacharopoulos, George. 1980a. *Higher Education in Developing Countries—a Cost-Benefit Analysis*. Washington, DC: World Bank. http://documents.worldbank.org/curated/en/home.

Psacharopoulos, George. 1980b. *Information: An Essential Factor in Educational Planning and Policy*. Paris: United Nations Educational, Scientific and Cultural Organization.

Psacharopoulos, George. 1981. "Returns to Education: An Updated International Comparison." *Comparative Education* 17:321–41.

Psacharopoulos, George. 1985. "Returns to Education: A Further International Update and Implications." *Journal of Human Resources* 20:584–604.

Psacharopoulos, George. 1991a. *The Economic Impact of Education: Lessons for Policy Makers*. San Francisco: International Center for Economic Growth.

Psacharopoulos, George. 1991b. "From Manpower Planning to Labour Market Analysis." *International Labour Review* 130:459–70.

Psacharopoulos, George. 1994. "Returns to Investment in Education: A Global Update." *World Development* 22:1325–43.

Psacharopoulos, George. 2004. "The Empirical Basis of Task Force Conclusions." *Comparative Education Review* 48:75–78.

Psacharopoulos, George, assisted by Keith Hinchliffe. 1973. *Returns to Education: An International Comparison*. San Francisco: Jossey-Bass.

Psacharopoulos, George, Jee-Peng Tan, and Emmanuel Jimenez. 1986. "Financing Education in Developing Countries: An Exploration of Policy Options." Washington, DC: World Bank.

Quelch, John A. 2003. "The Return of the Global Brand." *Harvard Business Review*, August, 22–23.

Quelch, John, and Rohit Deshpande, eds. 2004. *The Global Market: Developing a Strategy to Manage across Borders*. San Francisco: Jossey-Bass.

Quelch, John A., and Nathalie Laidler. 1993. "Harlequin Romances—Poland (A)." Harvard Business School Case 594-017. Cambridge, MA: Harvard Business Publishing.

Rafael, Vincente L. 1994. "The Cultures of Area Studies in the United States." *Social Text* 41:91–111.

Rancière, Jacques. 2011. *Althusser's Lesson*. Translated by Emiliano Battista. London: Continuum International.

Ravallion, Martin, and Adam Wagstaff. 2012. "The World Bank's Publication Record." *Review of International Organizations* 7:343–68.

Raza, S. Asad. 2006. "A Report from the NYU Strike." *Minnesota Review* 65–66:149–54.

Readings, Bill. 1996. *The University in Ruins*. Cambridge, MA: Harvard University Press.

Rhoads, Robert A., and Carlos Alberto Torres. 2006. *The University, State, and Market: The Political Economy of Globalization in the Americas.* Stanford, CA: Stanford University Press.

Rich, Andrew. 2004. *Think Tanks, Public Policy, and the Politics of Expertise.* Cambridge: Cambridge University Press.

Ritzer, George. 1993. *The McDonaldization of Society.* Newbury Park, CA: Pine Forge.

Robertson, Roland, and Habib Haque Khondker. 1998. "Discourses of Globalization: Preliminary Considerations." *International Sociology* 13:25–40.

Robinson, Pearl T. 2004. "Area Studies in Search of Africa." In *The Politics of Knowledge: Area Studies and the Disciplines,* edited by David Szanton, 119–83. Berkeley: University of California Press.

Rodney, Walter. 1990. *Walter Rodney Speaks: The Making of an African Intellectual.* Trenton, NJ: Africa World Press.

Rohde, Joy. 2013. *Armed with Expertise: The Militarization of American Social Research during the Cold War.* Ithaca, NY: Cornell University Press.

Rooks, Noliwe M. 2006. *White Money/Black Power: The Surprising History of African American Studies and the Crisis of Race in Higher Education.* Boston: Beacon.

Roosevelt, Kermit. 1976a. *The Overseas Targets: War Report of the OSS (Office of Strategic Services).* Vol. 2. New York: Walker.

Roosevelt, Kermit. 1976b. *War Report of the OSS (Office of Strategic Services).* Vol. 1. New York: Walker.

Rosenberg, Justin. 2000. *The Follies of Globalization Theory.* London: Verso.

Rosenberg, Justin. 2005. "Globalization Theory: A Post Mortem." *International Politics* 42:2–74.

Ross, Andrew. 2008. "Global U." In *The University against Itself: The NYU Strike and the Future of the Academic Workplace,* edited by Monika Krause, Mary Nolan, Michael Palm, and Andrew Ross, 211–23. Philadelphia: Temple University Press.

Ross, Andrew. 2009. *Nice Work If You Can Get It: Life and Labor in Precarious Times.* New York: New York University Press.

Ross, Andrew. 2011. "Human Rights, Academic Freedom, and Offshore Academics." *Academe* 97:11–17.

Ross, Andrew. 2017. "Repressive Tolerance Revamped? The Illiberal Embrace of Academic Freedom." *AAUP Journal of Academic Freedom* 8:1–16.

Rostow, W. W. 1938. "Investment and the Great Depression." *Economic History Review* 8:136–58.

Rostow, W. W. 1939. "Investment and Real Wages 1873–86." *Economic History Review* 9:144–59.

Rostow, W. W. 1941. "Business Cycles, Harvests, and Politics: 1790–1850." *Journal of Economic History* 1:206–21.

Rostow, W. W. 1942a. "Adjustments and Maladjustments after the Napoleonic Wars." *American Economic Review* 32:13–23.

Rostow, W. W. 1942b. "Price Controls and Rationing: Some Aspects of Price Control and Rationing." *American Economic Review* 32:486–500.

Rostow, W. W. 1946. *The American Diplomatic Revolution: An Inaugural Lecture Delivered before the University of Oxford on 12 November 1946.* Oxford: Clarendon.

Rostow, W. W. 1947. "The Inter-relation of Theory and Economic History." MC 188 (Box 10.f319). Institute Archives and Special Collections, MIT Libraries, Cambridge, Massachusetts.

Rostow, W. W. 1948. *British Economy of the Nineteenth Century.* Oxford: Clarendon.

Rostow, W. W. 1949. "The Economic Commission for Europe." *International Organization* 3:254–68.

Rostow, W. W. 1950a. "Government and Private Enterprise in European Recovery." *Journal of Economic History* 10:105–13.

Rostow, W. W. 1950b. "The Terms of Trade in Theory and Practice." *Economic History Review* 3:1–20.

Rostow, W. W. 1950c. "The United Nations' Report on Full Employment." *Economic Journal* 60:323–50.

Rostow, W. W. 1951a. "The Historical Analysis of the Terms of Trade." *Economic History Review* 4:53–76.

Rostow, W. W. 1951b. "Some Notes on Mr. Hicks and History." *American Economic Review* 41:316–24.

Rostow, W. W. 1952a. *The Dynamics of Soviet Society.* New York: Norton.

Rostow, W. W. 1952b. *The Process of Economic Growth.* New York: Norton.

Rostow, W. W. 1954a. "Factors in Economic Growth and Their Interrelations." MC 188 (Box 10.f306). Institute Archives and Special Collections, MIT Libraries, Cambridge, Massachusetts.

Rostow, W. W. 1954b. *The Prospects for Communist China.* New York: Technology Press of Massachusetts Institute of Technology and John Wiley and Sons.

Rostow, W. W. 1956. "The First Take-Off: The British Industrial Revolution, 1783–1892." MC 188 (Box 10.f309). Institute Archives and Special Collections, MIT Libraries, Cambridge, Massachusetts.

Rostow, W. W. 1957a. "The Agenda for 1957." MC 188 (Box 10.f279). Center for International Studies, MIT. Institute Archives and Special Collections, MIT Libraries, Cambridge, Massachusetts.

Rostow, W. W. 1957b. "The Interrelation of Theory and Economic History." *Journal of Economic History* 17:509–23.

Rostow, W. W. 1960. *The Stages of Economic Growth: A Non-Communist Manifesto.* Berkeley: University of California Press.

Rostow, W. W. 1992. "The London Operation: Recollections of an Economist." In *The Secret War: The Office of Strategic Services in World War II,* edited by George C. Chalou, 48–60. Washington, DC: National Archives and Records Administration.

Rostow, W. W. 2003. *Concept and Controversy: Sixty Years of Taking Ideas to Market.* Austin: University of Austin Press.

Rowan, Hobart. 1981. "The Washington Agenda." *Institutional Investor*, September, 337–38.

Rudenstine, Neil L. 1993. "The President's Report: 1991–1993." Harvard University Library. https://iiif.lib.harvard.edu/manifests/view/drs:427018329$1i.

Rudolph, Susanne Hoeber. 2005. "Perestroika and Its Others." In *Perestroika! The Raucous Rebellion in Political Science*, edited by Kristen Renwick Monroe, 12–20. New Haven, CT: Yale University Press.

Rupert, Mark. 2000. *Ideologies of Globalization*. London: Routledge.

Rusk, Dean. 1990. *As I Saw It*. Edited by Richard Rusk and Daniel S. Patt. New York: Norton.

Said, Edward. 1983. *The World, the Text and the Critic*. Cambridge, MA: Harvard University Press.

Said, Edward. 1993. *Culture and Imperialism*. New York: Vintage.

Salmi, Jamil. 2009. *The Challenges of Establishing World-Class Universities*. Washington, DC: World Bank.

Salmi, Jamil. 2016. "Peril and Promise: A Decade Later." *International Journal of African Higher Education* 3:43–50.

Salmi, Jamil, and Nian Cai Liu. 2011. "Paths to a World-Class University." In *Paths to a World-Class University: Lessons from Practices and Experiences*, edited by Nian Cai Liu, Qi Wang, and Ying Cheng, ix–xviii. Rotterdam: Sense.

Samoff, Joel, and Carol Bidemi. 2004. "The Promise of Partnership and Continuities of Dependence: External Support to Higher Education in Africa." *African Studies Review* 47:67–199.

Santos, Boaventura de Sousa. 2007a. *Another Knowledge Is Possible: Beyond Northern Epistemologies, Reinventing Social Emancipation: Toward New Manifestos*. New York: Verso.

Santos, Boaventura de Sousa. 2007b. *Democratizing Democracy: Beyond the Liberal Democratic Canon*. New York: Verso.

Santos, Boaventura de Sousa. 2007c. "Human Rights as an Emancipatory Script? Cultural and Political Conditions." In *Another Knowledge Is Possible: Beyond Northern Epistemologies*, edited by Boaventura de Sousa Santos, 3–40. New York: Verso.

Santos, Boaventura de Sousa. 2014. *Epistemologies of the South: Justice against Epistemicide*. New York: Routledge.

Santos, Boaventura de Sousa, João Arriscado Nunes, and Maria Paula Meneses. 2008. "Introduction: Opening Up the Canon of Knowledge and Recognition of Difference." In *Another Knowledge Is Possible: Beyond Northern Epistemologies*, edited by Boaventura de Sousa Santos, xix–lxii. New York: Verso.

Sartori, Giovanni. 1970. "Concept Misformation in Comparative Politics." *American Political Science Review* 64:1033–53.

Saul, Stephanie. 2015. "N.Y.U. Labor Guidelines Failed to Protect 10,000 Workers in Abu Dhabi, Report Says." *New York Times*, April 16. https://www.nytimes.com/2015/04/17/nyregion/nyu-labor-rules-failed-to-protect-10000-workers-in-abu-dhabi.html.

Saunders, Frances Stonor. 1999. *The Cultural Cold War: The CIA and the World of Arts and Letters*. New York: New Press.

Saunders, Frances Stonor. 2000. *Who Paid the Piper? The CIA and the Cultural Cold War*. New York: New Press.

Scheibla, Shirley Hobbs. 1981. "McNamara's Ban: The Treasury Means to Change the World Bank's Ways." *Barrons' National Business and Financial Weekly* 61 (August 17): 11, 18–19.

Schlesinger, Arthur, Jr. 1992. "The London Operation: The Recollections of a Historian." In *The Secret War: The Office of Strategic Services in World War II*, edited by George C. Chalou, 61–68. Washington, DC: National Archives and Records Administration.

Schmidt, Brian C. 1998. *The Political Discourse of Anarchy: A Disciplinary History of International Relations*. Albany: State University of New York Press.

Schmidt, Brian C. 2011. "The Rockefeller Foundation Conference and the Long Road to a Theory of International Politics." In *The Invention of International Relations Theory: Realism, the Rockefeller Foundation, and the 1954 Conference on Theory*, edited by Nicolas Guilhot, 79–96. New York: Columbia University Press.

Schmidt, Brian C. 2012. *International Relations and the First Great Debate: The New International Relations*. New York: Routledge.

Schoenbaum, Thomas J. 1988. *Waging Peace and War: Dean Rusk in the Truman, Kennedy, and Johnson Years*. New York: Simon and Schuster.

Schueller, Malini Johar. 2007. "Area Studies and Multicultural Imperialism: The Project of Decolonizing Knowledge." *Social Text* 25:42–62.

Schultz, Theodore W. 1961. "Investment in Human Capital." *American Economic Review* 51:1–17.

Schultz, Theodore W. 1971. *Investment in Human Capital: The Role of Education and of Research*. New York: Free Press.

Senghor, Léopold Sédar. 1981. "Foreword." In *The McNamara Years at the World Bank: Major Policy Addresses of Robert S. McNamara 1968–1981*, edited by the World Bank. Baltimore, MD: Johns Hopkins University Press.

Sexton, John. 1996. "The Global Law School Program at New York University." *Journal of Legal Education* 46:329–35.

Sexton, John. 2004a. *The Common Enterprise University and the Teaching Mission*. NYU. http://www.nyu.edu/about/leadership-university-administration/office-of-the -president-emeritus/communications/the-common-enterprise-university-and -the-teaching-mission.html.

Sexton, John. 2004b. *The Research University in a Global Context*. NYU. http://www.nyu .edu/about/leadership-university-administration/office-of-the-president-emeritus /communications/the-research-university-in-a-global-context.html.

Sexton, John. 2004c. *The University as Sanctuary*. NYU. http://www.nyu.edu/about /leadership-university-administration/office-of-the-president-emeritus /communications/the-university-as-sanctuary.html.

Sexton, John. 2005. *Dogmatism and Complexity: Civil Discourse and the Research University*. NYU. http://www.nyu.edu/about/leadership-university-administration /office-of-the-president-emeritus/communications/dogmatism-and-complexity -civil-discourse-and-the-research-university.html.

Sexton, John. 2007. "Fire and Ice: The Knowledge Century and the Urban University." NYU. https://http://www.nyu.edu/about/leadership-university-administration /office-of-the-president-emeritus/communications/fire-and-ice-the-knowledge -century-and-the-urban-university.html.

Sexton, John. 2010. "Global Network University Reflection." NYU. http://www.nyu.edu /about/leadership-university-administration/office-of-the-president-emeritus /communications/global-network-university-reflection.html.

Sexton, John. 2013. *Baseball as a Road to God: Seeing beyond the Game*. New York: Gotham.

Sexton, John, and Abraham M. Lackman. 2005. "City's Economic Future Linked to Brain Power." *New York Observer*, February 21. http://observer.com/2005/02 /citys-economic-future-linked-to-brain-power.

Shaw, Eric H., and D. G. Brian Jones. 2005. "A History of Schools of Marketing Thought." *Marketing Theory* 3:239–81.

Shaw, Timothy M. 1983. "Debates about Africa's Future: The Brandt, World Bank, and Lagos Plan Blueprints." *Third World Quarterly* 5:330–44.

Shaw, Timothy M. 1985. "Introduction: Are the 1980s Characterised by Crisis and/or Conjuncture?" In *Africa Projected: From Recession to Renaissance by the Year 2000?*, edited by T. M. Shaw and O. Aluko, 3–13. New York: St. Martin's.

Sherwood, Marika. 1996. *Kwame Nkrumah: The Years Abroad 1935–1947*. Legon, Ghana: Freedom.

Shivji, Issa G. 1993. "Rodney and Racialism on the Hill, 1966–1974." In *Intellectual at the Hill: Essays and Talks 1969–1993*, 32–44. Dar es Salaam: DPU.

Shukaitis, Stevphen, and David Graeber. 2007. *Constituent Imagination: Militant Investigations Collective Theorization*. Oakland, CA: AK Press.

Sibley, Elbridge. 1974. *Social Science Research Council: The First Fifty Years*. New York: Social Science Research Council.

Sigel, Roberta S. 1970. *Learning about Politics: A Reader in Political Socialization*. New York: Random House.

Slaughter, Sheila, and Larry L. Leslie. 1997. *Academic Capitalism: Politics, Policies, and the Entrepreneurial University*. Baltimore, MD: Johns Hopkins University Press.

Slaughter, Sheila, and Gary Rhoades. 2004. *Academic Capitalism and the New Economy: Markets, State, and Higher Education*. Baltimore, MD: Johns Hopkins University Press.

Smith, Adam. [1776] 1999. *The Wealth of Nations: Books I–III*. Edited by Andrew Skinner. New York: Penguin Books.

Smith, James Allen. 1993. *Strategic Calling: The Center for Strategic and International Studies, 1962–1992*. Washington, DC: Center for Strategic and International Studies.

Smith, R. Harris. 1972. *OSS: The Secret History of America's First Central Intelligence Agency*. Berkeley: University of California Press.

Smith, Steve. 1987. "Paradigm Dominance in International Relations: The Development of International Relations as a Social Science." *Millennium: Journal of International Studies* 16:189–206.

Soley, Lawrence C. 1995. *Leasing the Ivory Tower: The Corporate Takeover of Academia*. Boston: South End.

Solovey, Mark. 2013. *Shaky Foundations: The Politics-Patronage-Social Science Nexus in Cold War America*. New Brunswick, NJ: Rutgers University Press.

SSRC. 1965a. "Committee Briefs." *Items* 19 (June): 23–25. https://items.ssrc.org/print -archive/.

SSRC. 1965b. "Personnel." *Items* 19 (March): 11–14.

SSRC. 1966. "Personnel." *Items* 20 (September): 36–42.

SSRC. 1967a. "Personnel." *Items* 21 (March): 8–11.

SSRC. 1967b. "Personnel." *Items* 21 (September): 33–39.

SSRC. 1968. "Personnel." *Items* 22 (September): 32–39.

SSRC. 1969. "Personnel." *Items* 23 (September): 39–46.

SSRC. 1970. "Personnel." *Items* 24 (September): 31–39.

SSRC. 1971. "Personnel." *Items* 25 (September): 32–38.

SSRC. 1973. "Personnel." *Items* 27 (June): 20–24.

SSRC. 1976. "Fellowships and Grants." *Items* 30 (June): 24–32.

SSRC. 1977. "Fellowships and Grants." *Items* 31 (March/June): 16–23.

SSRC. 1979. "Kenneth Prewitt Elected President of the Social Science Research Council." *Items* 33 (March): 1–2.

SSRC. 1990–91. *Social Science Research Council: Annual Report 1990–1991*. New York: Social Science Research Council.

Staff. 1967. "SDS Sits-in on Dow Recruiter." *The Tech* 87 (November 7): 1. http://tech.mit .edu/V87/PDF/V87-N43.pdf.

Staff. 1969a. "Johnson Confronted on I-Lab." *The Tech* 89 (April 22): 1. http://tech.mit .edu/V89/PDF/V89-N18.pdf.

Staff. 1969b. "NAC Plans Court Protest; CIS Will Be Closed Today." *The Tech* 89 (November 4): 1. http://tech.mit.edu/V89/PDF/V89-N42.pdf.

Staniland, Martin. 1983. "Who Needs African Studies?" *African Studies Review* 26:77–97.

Starkey, Ken, and Nick Tiratsoo. 2007. *The Business School and the Bottom Line*. Cambridge: Cambridge University Press.

Steger, Manfred. 2002. *Globalism: The New Market Ideology*. Lanham, MD: Rowman and Littlefield.

Steger, Manfred. 2008. *The Rise of the Global Imaginary: Political Ideologies from the French Revolution to the Global War on Terror*. Oxford: Oxford University Press.

Steger, Manfred, and Paul James. 2015. *Globalization: The Career of a Concept*. New York: Routledge.

Steger, Manfred B., and Amentahru Wahlrab. 2017. *What Is Global Studies? Theory and Practice*. New York: Routledge.

Stein, Sharon, and Vanessa de Oliveira Andreotti. 2016. "Higher Education and the Modern/Colonial Global Imaginary." *Cultural Studies ↔ Critical Methodologies*, October 5, 1–9.

Stern, Nicholas, and Francisco Ferreira. 1997. "The World Bank as 'Intellectual Actor.'" In *The World Bank: Its First Half Century (Volume 2: Perspectives)*, edited by Devesh Kapur, John P. Lewis, and Richard Webb, 523–609. Washington, DC: Brookings Institution Press.

Steward, Julian H. 1950. *Area Research: Theory and Practice*. New York: Social Science Research Council.

Stripling, Jack. 2014. "A Trustee's Connections May Complicate NYU-Abu Dhabi Labor Probe." *Chronicle of Higher Education*, May 29. https://www.chronicle.com/article /A-Trustee-s-Connections-May/146843.

Suárez-Orozco, Marcel M., and Desirée Baolian Qin-Hilliard. 2004. *Globalization: Culture and Education in the New Millennium*. Berkeley: University of California Press.

Szanton, David L. 2004. "Introduction: The Origin, Nature, and Challenge of Area Studies in the United States." In *The Politics of Knowledge: Area Studies and the Disciplines*, edited by David Szanton, 1–33. Berkeley: University of California Press.

Takeuchi, Hirotaka. 2004. "'The Globalization of Markets' Revisited: Japan after Twenty Years." In *The Global Market: Developing a Strategy to Manage across Borders*, edited by J. Quelch and R. Deshpande, 37–77. San Francisco: Jossey-Bass.

Tedlow, Richard S., and Rawi Abdelal. 2004. "Theodore Levitt's 'The Globalization of Markets': An Evaluation after Two Decades." In *The Global Market: Developing a Strategy to Manage across Borders*, edited by J. Quelch and R. Deshpande, 11–30. San Francisco: Jossey-Bass.

Teilhard de Chardin, Pierre. 1999. *The Human Phenomenon*. Translated by Sarah Appleton-Weber. Brighton: Sussex Academic Press.

Teune, Henry. 1982. "The ISA." International Studies Association. http://www.isanet.org /Portals/0/Documents/Institutional/Henry_Teune_The_ISA_1982.pdf.

Thies, Cameron G. 2002. "Progress, History and Identity in International Relations Theory: The Case of the Idealist-Realist Debate." *European Journal of International Relations* 8:147–85.

Thompson, E. P. 1995. *The Poverty of Theory: Or an Orrery of Errors*. London: Merlin.

Thompson, John M. 1972. "Foreign Area Fellowship Program to Merge with Other Area Programs of the American Council of Learned Societies and Social Science Research Council." *Items* 26:41–44.

Thurow, Lester. 1970. *Investment in Human Capital*. Belmont, CA: Wadsworth.

Tomkins, Richard. 2003. "Happy Birthday, Globalisation." *Financial Times*, May 6, 14.

"Transcript of Morrill Act." 1862. Our Documents. Accessed February 2016. https:// www.ourdocuments.gov/doc.php?flash=true&doc=33&page=transcript.

Tsing, Anna Lowenhaupt. 2005. *Friction: An Ethnography of Global Connection*. Princeton, NJ: Princeton University Press.

Tsvetkova, Natalia. 2008. "International Education during the Cold War: Soviet Social Transformation and American Social Reproduction." *Comparative Education Review* 52:199–217.

Tuchman, Gaye. 2009. *Wannabe U: Inside the Corporate University*. Chicago: University of Chicago Press.

Twombly, Susan B., Mark H. Salisbury, and Shannon D. Tumanut. 2012. "Study Abroad in a New Global Century: Renewing the Promise, Refining the Purpose." In *ASHE Higher Education Report*. New York: Wiley.

UCS. 2018. "Founding Document: Beyond March 4." Union of Concerned Scientists. https://www.ucsusa.org/about/founding-document-beyond.html.

University of Minnesota. 2007. *Accountable to U: University Plan, Performance, and Accountability Report*. Office of the Senior Vice President for Academic Affairs and Provost. Minneapolis: University of Minnesota.

U.S. Congress. 1958. "National Defense Education Act of 1958" (Public Law 85-864). https://www.gpo.gov/fdsys/pkg/STATUTE-72/pdf/STATUTE-72-Pg1580.pdf.

Vansina, Jan. 1994. *Living with Africa*. Madison: University of Wisconsin Press.

Vawda, Ayesha Yaqub, Peter Moock, J. Price Gittinger, and Harry Anthony Patrinos. 2003. "Economic Analysis of World Bank Education Projects and Project Outcomes." *International Journal of Educational Development* 23:645–60.

Venn, Fiona. 2002. *Oil Crisis*. London: Routledge.

Vitalis, Robert. 2002. "International Studies in America." *Items and Issues* 3:1–2, 12–16. https://items.ssrc.org/print-archive/.

Vitalis, Robert. 2015. *White World Order, Black Power Politics: The Birth of American International Relations*. Ithaca, NY: Cornell University Press.

Vujakovic, Petra. 2009. "How to Measure Globalisation? A New Globalisation Index (NGI)." In *WIFO Working Papers*. Vienna: Österreichisches Institut Für Wirtschaftsforschung.

Wagley, Charles. 1948. *Area Research and Training: A Conference Report on the Study of World Areas*. New York: Social Science Research Council.

Wallerstein, Immanuel. 1997. "The Unintended Consequences of Cold War Area Studies." In *The Cold War and the University: Toward an Intellectual History of the Postwar Years*, edited by Noam Chomsky, Ira Katznelson, R. C. Lewontin, Laura Nader, David Montgomery, Richard Ohmann, Immanuel Wallerstein, Ray Siever, and Howard Zinn, 195–231. New York: New Press.

Wallerstein, Immanuel. 2004. *World-Systems Analysis: An Introduction*. Durham, NC: Duke University Press.

Walsh, Jack. 1982. "GM Truck Aim: Widen Share of Global Sales." *Automotive News*, September 6, 18.

Waltz, Kenneth N. (1954) 2001. *Man, the State, and War: A Theoretical Analysis*. New York: Columbia University Press.

Ward, Robert E., and Bryce Wood. 1974. "Foreign Area Studies and the Social Science Research Council." *Items* 28:53–58.

Washburn, Jennifer. 2005. *University Inc.: The Corporate Corruption of Higher Education*. New York: Basic Books.

Watts, Michael. 1997. "African Studies at the Fin de Siecle: Is It Really the Fin?" *Africa Today* 44:185–92.

Weber, Luc E., and James J. Duderstadt. 2008. *The Globalization of Higher Education*. London: Economica.

Weinberg, William, and Allan Weisenfeld. 1953. "Prosperity versus Strikes." *Industrial and Labor Relations Review* 7:123–26.

Weir, Robert M. 2007. *Peace, Justice, Care of Earth: The Vision of John McConnell, Founder of Earth Day*. Kalamazoo, MI: Press On.

West, Michael, and William G. Martin. 1995. "Guest Editors' Introduction." *Issue: A Journal of Opinion* 23:3–4.

West, Michael O., and William G. Martin. 1997. "A Future with a Past: Resurrecting the Study of Africa in the Post-Africanist Era." *Africa Today* 44:309–26.

"Why They're Slowing Growth." 1975. *Business Week*, February 24, 54–58.

Wildavsky, Ben. 2010. *The Great Brain Race: How Global Universities Are Reshaping the World*. Princeton, NJ: Princeton University Press.

Wilder, Craig Steven. 2013. *Ebony and Ivy: Race, Slavery, and the Troubled History of America's Universities*. New York: Bloomsbury.

Wiley, David. 2001. "Forty Years of the Title VI and Fulbright-Hays International Education Programs: Building the Nation's International Expertise for a Global Future." In *Changing Perspectives on International Education*, edited by Patrick O'Meara, Howard D. Mehlinger, and Roxana Ma Newman, 11–29. Bloomington: Indiana University Press.

Wilkie, William L., and Elizabeth S. Moore. 2003. "Scholarly Research in Marketing: Exploring the '4 Eras' of Thought Development." *Journal of Public Policy and Marketing* 22 (2): 116–46.

Williams, Jeffrey. 2006. "The Pedagogy of Debt." *College Literature* 33:155–69.

Wilson, Peter. 1998. "The Myth of the 'First Great Debate.'" *Review of International Studies* 24:1–16.

Winks, Robin W. 1987. *Cloak and Gown: Scholars in the Secret War, 1939–1961*. New Haven, CT: Yale University Press.

Wolfensohn, James D. 2005a. "Coalitions for Change: Address to the Board of Governors at the Annual Meetings of the World Bank and the International Monetary Fund." In *Voices for the World's Poor: Selected Speeches and Writings of World Bank President James D. Wolfensohn, 1995–2005*, 154–65. Washington, DC: World Bank.

Wolfensohn, James D. 2005b. "New Directions and New Partnerships: Address to the Board of Governors at the Annual Meetings of the World Bank and the International Monetary Fund." In *Voices for the World's Poor: Selected Speeches and Writ-*

ings of World Bank President James D. Wolfensohn, 1995–2005, 28–40. Washington, DC: World Bank.

Wolfensohn, James D. 2010. *A Global Life: My Journey among Rich and Poor, from Sydney to Wall Street to the World Bank*. New York: PublicAffairs.

Wooldridge, Adrian. 2011. *Masters of Management: How the Business Gurus and Their Ideas Have Changed the World—for Better and for Worse*. New York: HarperCollins.

Worcester, Kenton W. 1996. "Survey of International Field Research Fellowships, 1990–1995." *Items* 50:8–14.

Worcester, Kenton W. 2001. *Social Science Research Council: 1923–1998*. New York: Social Science Research Council.

World Bank. 1971. "Education Sector Working Paper." Washington, DC: World Bank.

World Bank. 1974. "Education Sector Working Paper." Washington, DC: World Bank.

World Bank. 1980. "World Development Report, 1980." Washington, DC: World Bank.

World Bank. 1981a. "Accelerated Development in Sub-Saharan Africa: An Agenda for Action." Washington, DC: World Bank.

World Bank. 1981b. "World Development Report 1981: National and International Adjustment." Washington, DC: World Bank.

World Bank. 1998–99. "Knowledge for Development: World Development Report." Washington, DC: World Bank.

World Bank. 2000. *Higher Education in Developing Countries: Peril and Promise*. Washington, DC: Task Force on Higher Education and Society, World Bank.

World Bank. 2003. *A Guide to the World Bank*. Washington DC: World Bank.

World Bank. 2011. "Education Strategy 2020." Washington, DC: World Bank.

World Bank. 2011. "Learning for All: Investing in People's Knowledge and Skills to Promote Development." Washington, DC: World Bank.

Wriston, Walter B. 1992. *The Twilight of Sovereignty: How the Information Revolution Is Transforming Our World*. New York: Scribner.

Zeleza, Paul Tiyambe. 1997a. *Manufacturing African Studies and Crises*. Dakar: Council for the Development of Social Science Research in Africa (CODESRIA).

Zeleza, Paul Tiyambe. 1997b. "The Perpetual Solitudes and Crises of African Studies in the United States." *Africa Today* 44:193–210.

Zeleza, Paul Tiyambe, and Adebayo Olukoshi. 2004. *African Universities in the Twenty-First Century*. Vol. 1. Dakar: Council for the Development of Social Science Research in Africa (CODESRIA).

Zemach-Bersin, Talya. 2009. "Selling the World: Study Abroad Marketing and the Privatization of Global Citizenship." In *The Handbook of Practice and Research in Study Abroad: Higher Education and the Quest for Global Citizenship*, edited by R. Lewin, 303–20. New York: Routledge.

Zimmerman, Robert. 1998. *Genesis: The Story of Apollo 8: The First Manned Flight to Another World*. New York: Dell.

Zisk, Betty H., Heinz Eulau, and Kenneth Prewitt. 1965. "City Councilmen and the Group Struggle: A Typology of Role Orientation." *Journal of Politics* 27:618–46.

Index

Abu Dhabi (NYU campus), 171–72, 176, 177, 183–88, 228–29nn23–25
academic networks, 41, 45–46, 147–48, 159–60
ACLS (American Council of Learned Societies), 145, 220n4
advertising campaigns, global, 99–100, 113–14
Africa: debt crisis in, 20, 75–80, 125; economic underdevelopment of, 77, 164; expansion of education in, 70–75; re-imagining of, 16–17; treatment of, in area studies, 38–39; and World Bank, 20, 69, 70–80, 125, 134–37
African-American studies, 206n46
African and African American scholars and students: in African studies crisis, 163, 164; in area studies, 58–60; effect of banker's imaginary on, 132; marginalization of, 37–38, 60; resource gap for, 147–48
African higher education: in alternative imaginaries, 193–94; in banker's global imaginary, 20, 119, 120, 126, 127–33, 136–37, 164, 218–19nn19–21; commercialization and commodification of, 132, 133, 136–37; effects of defunding on, 119, 120, 131–33, 218–19nn19–21; funding of, 20, 71–73; migrations of scholarship

in, 73–74, 164; national development imaginary in, 62–64, 70–75; NGO-ization of, 132; political socialization in, 153–54; radicalism in, 63–64, 74–75, 133; and rate-of-return calculation, 128–29; structural adjustment of, 126, 127–33, 164; student activism in, 74
Africanists/African studies scholars, 38, 146–47, 148, 163–64, 165, 220n6
African students, 37–38, 74, 193–94, 203n24
African Students Association, 38
African Studies, Joint Committee on, 146–47
African Studies Association (ASA), 41, 147–48
African studies programs: in black colleges and universities, 37–38, 43, 146, 147–48; Cold War popularity of, 42; funding of, 41, 163–64; modernization and decolonization in, 59–60, 148; racism in, 60; in rise of area studies, 37–38; SSRC in development of, 38, 146–50. See also area studies programs
Agricultural Trade Development and Assistance Act, 225n5
alternative imaginaries, 190–94
Althusser, Louis, 198nn16–17; "Ideology and Ideological State Apparatus," 22–26

American Council of Learned Societies (ACLS), 145, 220n4

American government. *See* federal government

American Political Science Association (APSA), 47, 165–66

Amnesty International, 228n25

Anders, Bill: *Earthrise*, 5–8, 6, 7

Anderson, Benedict, 197n11

Andrews, Kenneth R., 95

anticolonialism, 11–12, 19–20, 31–32, 42, 58–60, 64

Anti-politics Machine, The (Ferguson), 70, 208n8

antipoverty programs, 71–73, 124–25, 133–35

antiwar activists, 8, 58–59

Apollo 8 mission, 5–9

Appadurai, Arjun, 17, 25–26

Applbaum, Kalman, 86

Area Research Training Fellowships, Committee on, 144–45

Area Studies, Committee on (Columbia University), 39–40

area studies programs: area-based knowledge, 159–60; CENIS in, 50; criticisms of, 149–50; decolonization in, 19, 58–61, 149; definition of, 220n5; functions of, 156–57; funding of, 19, 21, 31, 38–43, 142–43, 146, 150–64; in marketization of universities, 137; military/academy collaboration in, 34–35; in modernization theory, 32, 58–61; and national imaginary, 36–43; national units in, 31–32; radicalism in, 59–61, 149, 206n46; and rise of global studies, 161–64; SSRC debates on, 21, 142–43, 144, 150–61, 166–67; SSRC in production of, 143–50. *See also* African studies programs; social sciences

Area Studies: With Special Reference to Their Implications for Research in Social Sciences (Hall), 39–40

Army Specialized Training Program, 34–35

Asian satellite campuses, 175–76

Asian studies, 59

Asquith Commission and colleges, 72–73

austerity measures, 131–32, 135–36, 163–64

Axial Ages, 178–79, 180–81

Ballantine, Duncan, 71

Ballon, Hilary, 182

banker's global imaginary: African higher education in, 20, 119, 120, 126, 127–33, 136–37, 164, 218–19nn19–21; defunding of higher education in, 20, 127–33, 135–36; geopolitical stability in, 118–19; rate-of-return accounting in, 20, 118, 119, 126–30; structural adjustment in, 20, 118–26, 133. *See also* Clausen, A. W.

Bank for Reconstruction and Development, International (IBRD), 65, 207n2. *See also* World Bank

Bank of America, 120–22

Baseball as a Road to God (Sexton), 227n17

base-superstructure model, 22–23

Becker, Gary: *Human Capital*, 128

behavioral models, military funding for, 42–43, 203n27

Berg, Elliot, 78–79

Berg Report, 76–77, 78–80, 210n17

Berlin, Isaiah, 96

Black, Eugene, 209n10

black colleges and universities, 37–38, 43, 146, 147–48

branch campuses, international, 21, 171–72, 175–76, 177, 183–88, 228–29nn23–25

Brand, Stewart, 197n10

branding/rebranding: of global education, 172–76; of Harvard Business School, 110; of institutions of higher education, 170; in marketing, 94; of NYU, 169, 171–72, 176–83

Brandt Commission Report, 64, 76–78, 209–10nn15–16

Brandt, Willy: *North-South: A Programme for Survival*, 76–78

Bretton Woods crisis, 3–4

British Economy of the Nineteenth Century (Rostow), 205n38

Brown, Clarence J., 101

Bunche, Ralph, 37

Bundy, McGeorge, 206n44

Bush, Vannevar, 33–34; *Science: The Endless Frontier*, 35

Business Research, Bureau of (Harvard), 107–8

business schools: curricula, 102, 103–4, 110, 111, 112; "globalization" in, 83–84; Harvard Business School, 101, 102, 106–11, 214n34; market imaginary reproduced by, 102–11; marketing in, 86; in reproducing the global imaginary, 102, 103–5, 106, 111

Canagarajah, A. Suresh, 15

Capitalism and Freedom (M. Friedman), 216n11

Carnegie Commission on Higher education, 221n9

Carnegie Corporation and Foundation, 40–41, 45–46, 47–48, 50, 103–4, 136

Carnegie Endowment for International Peace, 174

Carnegie Foundation for the Advancement of Teaching (CFAT), 151, 200n6

cartography of academic knowledge production, 21–22, 193

case studies (Harvard Business School), 107–9, 214n32, 214n34

CENIS (Center for International Studies, MIT): authorship policy of, 206n43; funding of, 29–30, 50, 199n2; interdisciplinary philosophy and research of, 29–30, 199nn1–2; and modernization theory, 48–50, 51–56; protests of, 60–61; radicalization of, 59

Central Intelligence Agency, 49–50. *See also* OSS

Cheche (Dar es Salaam), 74

Chenery, Hollis: *Redistribution with Growth*, 67–68

China, in modernization theory, 53–55

City in Modern Africa, The (SSRC), 146–47

Clausen, A. W.: Berg Report, 76–77; career of at Bank of America, 118, 120–22; reimagining of the World Bank by, 20, 118–24. *See also* banker's global imaginary

Clausen Bank: defunding of African higher education by, 20, 119, 127–33; economic policies of, 124–26; and global financial markets, 76–77, 79–80, 118–24; rate-of-return accounting on education, 126–30; vision of education of, 20. *See also* World Bank

Coatsworth, John, 178, 227n14

Cold War universities: federal funding of higher education in, 19, 30–32, 35–36, 38–43, 199n2; federal government in, 30–33, 190; national imaginary in, 9–10, 19, 36–49, 202n16; philanthropic organizations in, 29–30, 31, 59

Collaborative Research Networks (SSRC), 159

colonialism: and African debt crisis, 77; anticolonialism, 11–12, 19–20, 31–32, 42, 58–60, 64; post-war colonial imaginaries, 32–33; reimagined by John Sexton, 179–80; science as, 35

Comaroff, Jean and John, 15

Commerce Department, Commercial Services Program, 175

commercial banks, 65–66, 120–22, 125, 126, 216n10

commercialization of higher education, 10–12, 132, 174, 218n19

Committee on Engagement (SSRC), 159

Committee on International Relations (SSRC), 45

Committee on Problems and Policy (SSRC), 220n1

commodification of higher education, 111, 130, 133, 136–37, 190

Communist Communication project (CENIS), 207n50

communist insurgency, Western fear of, 66, 69–70

Comparative Politics, Committee on, 145, 220n3

Conable, Barber, 133, 216n9

Concerned Asian Scholars, Committee of, 59

Conference on Theory of International Politics, 45

Congress for Cultural Freedom (CIA), 202n16

Connell, Raewyn, 15

consumers, 84, 86, 87–91, 92–93, 110–11, 128

contested imaginaries, 19–20, 75–80

contrapuntal method, 18–19

corporations in the marketing imaginary, 95–97, 99–101, 102, 105–6

corporatization of higher education, 10, 168–69, 187, 194

cosmopolitanism, globalization as, 178–80

Cousins, Ewert, 178, 180–81

Crossing Borders program (Ford Foundation), 162

Cuban Revolution, 1959, 66

cultural identity, 36, 112–14

culture wars, 151

curricula: in African universities under structural adjustment, 132–33; business school, 102, 103–4, 110, 111, 112; at NYUAD, 177, 184; in political socialization, 153–54; in study abroad programs, 175

debt crisis, African, 75–80, 125

decolonization: of the academy, 15–16; in African studies, 59–60, 148; and area studies, 19, 58–61, 149; debates on in African universities, 74–75; higher education in, 72–74, 189–90; in modernization theory, 48–49, 63, 128; in national imaginary, 45–46, 48–49

defunding of higher education: of African higher education, 20, 131–33, 218–19nn19–21; of area studies, 142–43,

150–64; and banker's global imaginary, 20, 127–33, 135–36

democracy: and foreign student recruitment, 174–75; and globalization, 109; in modernization theory, 32, 51–52, 55, 63; in national imaginary, 19; in political socialization theory, 153; in social sciences funding, 29–30

democratic inclusion/expansion: of American higher education, 11–12; in area studies, 58–59

Department of Defense (DOD), 42–43

Department of Homeland Security (DHS), 2

development: in banker's global imaginary, 128, 133–37; education in, 70–75, 141, 209n10, 219n22; and global knowledge economy, 133–37; international aid for, 54–55, 66, 69–70; in modernization theory, 48, 49–58; in national development imaginary, 62–64, 65–75; in social sciences funding, 29–30; World Bank education funding in, 71–72

development economists, 124–25, 216n9

Development Research Center, World Bank: *Redistribution with Growth*, 67–68

diversity, 58–60

domestic policy emphasis: in banker's global imaginary, 118; in Berg Report, 78–80; in national development imaginary, 63. *See also* structural adjustment

Donham, Wallace B., 108

Drucker, Peter, 87–88

Dubai: Knowledge Village, 176

Du Bois, W. E. B., 148; *The World and Africa*, 37

Dulles, Allen, 49–50

Dunn, Frederick, 45

Dynamics of Soviet Society, The (Rostow), 53–54, 206n41

earth, images of, 5–10, 6, 7, 197n10

"earth," meaning of, 197n9

Earthrise (Anders), 5–9, 6, 7

East Africa Journal (Nairobi), 73
ecology of knowledges, 21–22, 193
Economic and Political Development Program (at CENIS), 29–30
economic convergence, 97–98
economic determinism (Marx), 50–51
economic growth: in African debt crisis, 75–76, 78–79; in federal funding of higher education, 35; in modernization theory, 51–53
economic knowledge production, 19–20, 65
economy, global, 79, 110, 118–24, 127–30, 168–70
education: in banker's global imaginary, 126–30; bilateral aid for, 209n9; crisis narrative of, 10–12, 197n12; as fixed capital, 216n11; global, as revenue stream, 21, 172–76; in global knowledge economy, 135–37; as global market, 130; as human capital, 1–2, 20, 71–73, 126–30, 131–32, 141, 200n6, 216n11; monetary value of, 127–30; as national development, 70–75, 209n9; in national development, 219n22; primary education, 128–30, 216n11, 217n17, 219n22; privatization of, in rate-of-return calculations, 130; rate of return on, 20, 126, 127–31, 217n12, 217n17; secondary, 129–30, 216n11, 219n22, 223n16; World Bank in, 13–14, 19–20, 70–75, 127–33, 134, 135–37, 209n10; World Bank research and publishing on, 136–37
"Education Sector Working Paper" (World Bank), 72
edu-theological global imaginary, 21, 171–72, 177–88, 225n3
Eisenhower, Dwight D., and administration, 53–55
embodied practices in knowledge claims, 15–16
epistemology/epistemic approach: to African studies, 148–49; in debates over area studies, 142, 144, 160, 165–66; in worlding the global, 15, 191–92

Ethnographic Board (SSRC), 144
exclusion, 14, 43, 171, 183
exploitation: in African debt crisis, 77; by NYU, 21, 169, 183–88, 228–29nn23–25

faculty: business school, in knowledge production, 103–5; in edu-theological imaginary, 180, 187; gender and racial hierarchies of, 14; migrations of, 73–74; postwar diversity and growth of, 58–59; in protests against the university, 60–61; in strike at NYU, 168–69; in war effort, 33–35
Featherman, David, 157–58
federal government: in Cold War universities, 30–33, 190; and modernization theory, 49–50, 51–52, 55–57; in national imaginary, 19, 36–37, 38–39, 41–42, 43–44, 48–49; in production of area studies, 144–45; study abroad supported by, 225n5; and war mobilization, 33–36. *See also individual agencies*
Federal Reserve, U.S., 76
Ferguson, James: *The Anti-politics Machine*, 70, 208n8; *Global Shadows*, 16–17
Field Development Working Group (SSRC), 159
field research: in area studies, 149–50; SSRC funding for, 38, 146–47, 149, 159, 161–62, 221n9
financial market, global, 20, 76–77, 79–80, 118–26, 133, 135
Financing Education in Developing Countries (World Bank), 129–30
fixed capital, education as, 127–28, 216n11
Ford Foundation, 29–30, 40–41, 50, 103–4, 136, 162, 206n46
foreign aid, 54–56, 66, 69–70, 132–33
Foreign Area Fellowship Program (FAFP), 146, 147–48, 220n6
foreign policy: in debates on area studies, 155; in modernization theory, 31–32, 48, 54–58; in national imaginary, 44, 46–48; in rise of global studies, 162–63

foreign scholars in area studies centers, 41–42

foreign students, 21, 172, 173, 174–76, 226n9

Fox, William T. R., 44–45

free trade, 54–55, 175–76

Friedman, Milton: *Capitalism and Freedom*, 216–17n11

Friedman, Thomas: *The World Is Flat*, 97, 212n14

Fulbright program, 173

Gates, Robert, 1, 196n2

generalizability of social scientific knowledge, 52–53, 143, 152–57

geopolitical stability, 54–55, 63, 75, 118–19, 162

Ghana, 132, 176

GI Bill (Servicemen's Readjustment Act), 36

global, the: reworlding of, 189–94; worlding of, within American higher education, 15–19

"global" and academic disciplines, 155

global imaginary: alternatives to, 190–94; contested, 19–20, 75–80; as knowledge production, 4–5; modernization theory in, 61; print culture in, 9, 197n11. *See also* banker's global imaginary; edu-theological global imaginary; marketing imagination; national development imaginary; national imaginary

globalization: "age of globalization studies," 3–4; conditions for imagining differently, 192; in debates over area studies, 152–56, 158–61; definition and usage of, 83–86, 111, 112, 164–65, 196n3; global education in, 172–76; impact model of, 10; as market imaginary, 20, 84–86, 95–101, 112–17; pluralization of, 165, 224n25; reimagining of, 25–26

global knowledge economy, 133–37, 166–67

global-local distinction, 149–50, 158

global networked university: limits of edu-theological imaginary in, 183–88; NYU

imagined as, 170–71, 176–83; resource scarcity in rise of, 170–72; as revenue stream, 21, 172–76

Global Shadows (Ferguson), 16–17

Global South. *See* Third World

global studies, 21, 142–43, 161–64, 165–66

"globe," meaning of, 197n9

Graduate Student Organizing Committee (GSOC)/United Auto Workers Local, 168–69, 224n1

graduate students: in edu-theological global imaginary, 188; funded by SSRC, 146; in migrations of scholarship, 73–74; protest by, 59–61, 193; strikes by (NYU), 168–69, 193, 224n1

Graves, Harold, 71

Grey Advertising: "Global Vision with Local Touch" campaign, 100

Guilhot, Nicolas, 1

Guyer, Jane, 163

Hall, Robert: *Area Studies*, 39–40

Hansberry, Leo, 37

Hansen, Harry, 88

Harlequin Enterprises case study, 113–14

Harvard Business Publishing, 214n32

Harvard Business Review, 85, 105–6, 110–11, 116

Harvard Business School, 101, 102, 106–11, 214n34, 214n32

Hauser Global Law Program, 177, 226n12

Heginbotham, Stanley, 157

Heidigger, Martin, 199n3

Herskovits, Melville J., 220n6

heterogeneity: in African debt crisis reports, 76–77; in American higher education, 12–14, 33, 161; and area studies, 166; in market imaginary, 115

hierarchies: in academic knowledge production, 14, 191, 197n13; in African Studies, 147–48, 164; in contrapuntal method, 18

higher education: American system and characteristics of, 10–14; as extraworldly spaces, 9; political economy of, 21, 23, 25–26, 142–43, 165–67; and rate-of-return accounting, 126–30; worlding the global in, 15–19

Higher Education in Developing Countries: A Cost-Benefit Analysis (Psacharopoulos), 129

Higher Education in Developing Countries: Peril and Promise (World Bank), 135–36, 141, 167, 219n23

human capital, 1–2, 20, 71–73, 126–30, 131–32, 141, 200n6, 216n11

Human Capital: A Theoretical and Empirical Analysis (Becker), 128

Human Capital Committee (SSRC), 159

humanities: and African studies, 148–49; in Cold War universities, 36, 202n16; de-funding of, 151–52; in SSRC area studies, 143, 145, 149–50

Human Rights Watch reports on NYUAD, 185–86, 228–29nn23–25

Human Terrain System, 1–2

IBRD (International Bank for Reconstruction and Development), 65, 207n2. *See also* World Bank

IDA (International Development Association), 66, 207n2

imperialism: African universities challenging, 73–74; American, African studies critiques of, 148–50; American higher education in, 11–12, 15–16, 19; and area studies, 38, 59, 60–61, 193

India, 29–30

individualized development, 134–35

Indonesia, 29–30

industrialization, 29–30, 32, 51–53, 205n38

inequities: of gender, 14; of race, 14, 60, 147–48, 217n12

infrastructure investment, 65–66, 67, 71–72, 132–33

In Search of Excellence (Peters and Water-man), 105–6

institutional worlds, 18–19

intellectual property in university funding, 151–52, 222n11

intelligence agencies. *See* security agencies/apparatus

interdisciplinary area studies centers, 41–42, 46–47, 142, 143. *See also* CENIS

International Center for Settlement of Investment Disputes (ICSID), 207n2

International Communism Project, 207n50

International Development Association, International (IDA), 66, 207n2

International Financial Corporation (IFC), 207n2

International Relations, 19, 31–32, 43–46, 197n13, 200n4. *See also* social sciences

international state systems, 44, 189–90

international students, 21, 111, 172, 173, 174–76, 226n9

international studies, 19, 31–32, 46–49, 50, 58–59. *See also* social sciences

International Studies Association (ISA), 47–48

international trade agreements, 175–76

Isaacman, Allen, 220n6

Isaacs, Harold, 59

Italy, 29–30

Items (SSRC), 156–57, 158–61

Jackson, C. D., 54–55

James, Paul, 17

Johnson, Lyndon, and administration, 56–57

Joint Committee on African Studies (SSRC), 147–48

joint committee structure of the SSRC, 148–49, 152, 158–62

kafala system at NYUAD, 185, 187

Keith, Robert, 88

Kennedy, John F., and administration, 8–9, 56–58

Kerr, Clark, 13

Keynesianism, crisis of, 3–4

Killian, James, 49–50

Kindleberger, Charles, 51

Kluckhohn, Clyde, 53

knowledge economy, World Bank and, 133–37

Knowledge for Development (World Bank), 135, 219nn22–23

knowledge production, material conditions of, 16, 21–22, 102, 107, 191–92

Krueger, Anne, 124–25

Kuklick, Bruce, 57

labor, exploitation of by NYU, 169, 183–88, 228–29nn23–25

labor economics, field of, 127–28

labor force/market. *See* human capital

Labor Workshop, Columbia University, 127–28

Lagos Plan, 64, 76–77, 79, 209n14

Lambert, Richard D., 220n5

language training (OSS), 34–35, 41, 159, 161

Learning about Politics: A Reader in Political Socialization (Sigel), 223n16

Lending in Education (World Bank), 71

Lesotho, 70, 208n8

lesser developed countries (LDCs). *See* Third World

Levitt, Theodore: and *Harvard Business Review*, 110–11, 215n38; on mandarinism by business school faculty, 104–5; "market imagination" of, 86–101, 212n13; as marketing guru, 106; in rise of "globalization," 83–86; self-promotion by, 100–101; on social responsibility, 212n11. *See also* marketing imagination

Levitt, Theodore, works of: "The Changing Character of Capitalism," 92; "Globalization of Markets," 91, 106, 112–17; "The Globalization of Markets," 20, 83–85, 95–101; "The Immiseration of Marketing in Academy," 104–5; *The Marketing Imagination*, 93–95, 100–101, 118; "Marketing Myopia," 88–91, 212n9

Lewis, David Levering, 179

Life magazine: "The Incredible Year '68," 6–8, 7

Liyong, Taban Lo, 74

locational endowment of NYU, 177, 179–80, 181–82, 182–83

MacArthur Foundation: Partnership for Higher Education in Africa, 136

Makerere University, 132, 218n19

Man, the State, and War (Waltz), 45

management gurus, 102, 105–6

manpower. *See* human capital

marginalization: of African studies, 163–64; of black scholars, 37–38, 60; in creating NYUAD, 183. *See also* inequities; racism

marketing: academic field of, 84–85, 86–88; branding/rebranding in, 94; consumer-centric, 92–93; global education in, 172–74; global strategies of, 109, 111; of higher education, 20–21, 137; of realist International Relations theory, 46; statistical modeling in, 104

marketing concept, 88–91, 212n9

marketing imagination: business schools in reproduction of, 102–11; and creativity, 86–90, 94; and globalization, 20, 84–86, 95–101, 112–17; Levitt's approach to, 91–95; markets reconceptualized in, 86–91; and reproduction, 212n13. *See also* Levitt, Theodore

Marketing Imagination, The (Levitt), 93–95, 100–101, 118

market research, 87–88, 89–90

markets: in banker's global imaginary, 119–24, 125–26; capital, 65–66, 121; global networked university in, 170; and knowledge bank, 134–36; in market imaginary, 84, 95–97, 113–15, 210n1; in national development imaginary, 79–80; reconceptualization of, 86–91, 95; standardization of, 95–96

Marshall Plan, 65

Martin, William G., 163

Mason, Edward, 71

Massachusetts Institute of Technology. *See* CENIS

material practices, 24

Mayer, Edward, 100

McClelland, Charles, 48

McNamara, Margaret Craig, 69

McNamara, Robert: and Brandt Report, 78; on commercial bank loans to developing countries, 216n10; education and career of, 66–67; and modernization theory, 19–20; national development imaginary of, 65–70; on the "Rostow Thesis," 57; in Third World education, 71–72; as World Bank president, 62–63. *See also* national development imaginary

McNamara Bank: collaborative research by, 68–69; criticism of, 120; in development, 62–64, 65–75; impact on higher education, 63–64; poverty reduction policies of, 124–25; prioritization of human capital by, 130; in scientific and economic knowledge production, 68–69; in Third World education, 71–73, 75, 76; use of "human capital" by, 127. *See also* national development imaginary

meaning, production of, 115

Merriam, Charles E., 144

methodology: in area studies, 39–40, 144, 149–50, 152–57, 165–67; in business school training, 104–5, 108

Middle East satellite campuses, 175–76

Mignolo, Walter, 15–16

migrant workers at NYUAD, 185–87, 188

militarized university, 11–12, 16, 33–36, 59, 60–61

military funding, 42–43, 203n27

military-industrial-academic complex, 2–3

Millikan, Max, 50, 51, 54–55; on *The Dynamics of Soviet Society*, 206n41; *A Proposal: Key to an Effective Foreign Policy*, 54–55

Mincer, Jacob, 128

Minerva Consortium, 1–2, 196n2

Mittelman, James, 146, 165

Modelski, George, 17

modernization theory: and CENIS, 19, 48–50, 51–56; in Cold War social sciences, 32–33, 48–49, 58–61; foreign policy in, 31–32, 48, 54–58; and human capital theory, 128; in national development imaginary, 63, 66, 67–68, 69; reimagined as globalization, 191–92; Rostow in development of, 49–58. *See also* national imaginary

mondialisation, 225n3

Mott MacDonald, 186

"Mr. Perestroika": "On Globalization of the APSA and APSR," 165–66

Mubadala Development Company, 185–86

Mubarak, Khaldoon Khalifa Al, 186–87

Multilateral Investment Guarantee Agency, 207n2

multinational corporations, 95–97, 99–101, 102

multiversity, 12–14

Murapa, Rukudzo, 60

Nancy, Jean-Luc, 224n3

National Academies, 2

National Defense Education Act (NDEA), 41–42, 145, 173, 196n2

national development imaginary: education in, 63–64, 70–75; and McNamara Bank, 65–70; modernization theory in, 63, 66, 67–68, 69; structural adjustment policies in, 125; World Bank policy in, 19–20. *See also* McNamara Bank

national economies: in banker's global imaginary, 118–19, 123–24, 128–29; in national development imaginary, 63, 69–70

national imaginary: area studies in, 58–61; in Cold War universities, 9–10, 19, 36–49; contradictions in, 58; modernization in, 32, 49–58, 61; war mobilization in, 33–36. *See also* modernization theory

National Labor Relations Board (NLRB), 168–69, 225n1

National Science Foundation (NSF), 35

national security: and area studies, 148–49, 155–56; in Cold War funding, 29–30, 31–32, 35, 44–45; economic and political growth in, 55–56, 63; and Minerva Consortium, 1; national development imaginary in, 63–64; in post-WWII knowledge production, 189–90; and study abroad programs, 172–73. See also security agencies/apparatus

National Security Council, 175

nation-states: in African studies, 148; in Cold War scholarship, 2–3, 9–10, 19, 31–32, 61, 189–90; in international studies, 48; in market imaginary, 84; in modernization theory, 52, 57–58; in national development imaginary, 63

Naval Research, Office of, 49

neo-classical economics, 115, 127–28

New York University (NYU): Abu Dhabi (NYUAD), 171–72, 176, 177, 183–88, 228–29nn23–25; branch campuses of, 176; graduate student strike at, 168–69; "Statement of Labor Values," 185–87

Ngũgĩ wa Thiong'o, 74

Nixon, Richard, and administration, 75–76

Nkrumah, Kwame, 37–38, 202n18

nonacademic institutions in American higher education, 12–14. See also federal government; philanthropy/philanthropic organizations

non-Western world: area studies in knowledge production on, 142–43, 144–45, 189–90; in Cold War funding of social sciences, 31; in creation of area studies, 32, 36–43; decolonization of, in radicalization, 58–59; information sources from, 15, 154–55; in modernization theory, 32, 48–49. See also Third World

North-South: A Programme for Survival (Brandt), 76–78

North-South dichotomy, 122–24

NYU Framework 2031, 181–82

Office of Public Information, 173

Omega Point, 180–81, 227n16

onto-theological perspective, 225n3

Organization for Economic Cooperation and Development, 209n9

Organization of African Unity (OAU), 77

Organization of Petroleum Exporting Countries (OPEC), 76

OSS (Office of Strategic Services), 34, 51. See also Central Intelligence Agency

Owuor-Anyumba, Henry, 74

pan-African intellectuals, 73–74

Parsons, Talcott, 53

Partnership for Higher Education in Africa, 136–37

patents in university funding, 151–52, 222n11

"Perspectives on Globalization" (Harvard case study), 109

petrodollars, 76, 121, 183–84

philanthropy/philanthropic organizations: in academic knowledge production, 61, 103–4; aid for education in developing countries by, 209n9; in area studies debates, 142, 143, 144, 146, 150–51, 165; in Cold War university funding, 29–30, 31, 39, 40–41, 44–46, 59, 200n6; in development of modernization theory, 48; Partnership for Higher Education in Africa, 136–37; in rationalizing of American higher education, 200n6; turn towards cross-regional programming by, 161–62. See also individual organizations

Political Behavior, Committee on, 201n12

political economics, 84, 210n1

political economy of higher education, 21, 23, 25–26, 142–43, 165–67

political socialization, 153–54, 155, 222n12, 222–23nn15–16

politics of worldliness, 192–93

postcolonial theory, 74

postsecondary education. *See* higher education

poverty, 58, 66, 67–68, 124–25

practitioner-focused academic journals, 102, 110–11

Preston, Lewis T., 133

Prewitt, Kenneth: in debates over area studies, 21, 142, 152–56; on political socialization, 153–54, 155, 222n12, 222–23nn15–16; on public utility of social sciences, 223n17; reform of the SSRC joint committee structure by, 158–61, 166–67

primary education, 128–30, 216n11, 218n17, 219n22

print culture, 9, 197n11

Project Camelot (U.S. Army), 42, 203–4n27

Project RAND, 201–2n12

Project Themis, 42–43

Project Troy (Office of Naval Research), 49

Proposal: Key to an Effective Foreign Policy, A (Rostow and Millikan), 54–55

Prospects for Communist China, The (Rostow), 53–54, 206n43

protests, 59–61, 193, 206n46

Psacharopoulos, George, 129–30, 217n11, 217nn14–15, 217–18nn17–18, 219n23; *Higher Education in Developing Countries*, 129; "Returns to Education," 129–30, 217n17

psychological warfare tactics, 42–43, 49, 203n27

Qatar Foundation: Education City, 176

R1 universities, 147, 221n9

racism: in African studies programs, 60; in International Relations programs, 44, 197–98n13; and political socialization, 222n12. *See also* inequities; marginalization

radicalism: in African universities, 63–64, 74–75, 133; in alternative imaginar-

ies, 193–94; in area studies, 59–61, 149, 206n46; in reimagining globalism, 25–26

rate of return: on American higher education, 217n12; in banker's global imaginary, 20, 118, 119, 126–30; empirical data in, 217–18nn17–18; in global knowledge economy, 136–37; primary education in, 128–30, 217n17

Reagan administration, 120

realist vision of International Relations, 44–46

rebranding. *See* branding/rebranding

redistribution, economic, 67–68, 77

Redistribution with Growth (Chenery and the Development Research Center), 67–68

Regional Advisory Panels (SSRC), 159

research, federal funding of, 151–52, 221–22nn10–11

Research and Analysis (R&A) branch of the OSS, 34

resource scarcity: in debates on area studies, 150–61, 163–64; in defunding of area studies, 142–43, 150–61; of NYU, 181–82; in reorganization of knowledge production, 166–67; in rise of the global networked university, 170–72; in social science research, 142–43

revenue streams, 21, 111, 171–76, 225n6

right-wing counterrevolution, 130

Rist, Leonard, 127

Rockefeller Foundation, 40–41, 44–46, 47, 50, 70–71, 136

Rodney, Walter, VI, 74–75

Rosenberg, Justin: "Globalization Theory: A Post Mortem," 3–4, 26

Ross, Andrew, 187

Rostow, W. W.: in development and application of modernization theory, 49–58; influence of, on the McNamara Bank, 67–68; and modernization theory, 48–49; and rise of modernism, 19

Rostow, W. W., works of: "The Agenda for 1957," 48–49; *British Economy of the Nineteenth Century*, 205n38; *The Dynamics of Soviet Society*, 53–54, 206n41; *The Process of Economic Growth*, 52–53; *A Proposal: Key to an Effective Foreign Policy*, 54–55; *The Prospects for Communist China*, 53–54, 206n43; *The Stages of Economic Growth*, 56–58, 67
Rudenstine, Neil, 110
Ruml, Beardsley, 144
Rusk, Dean, 45, 204n31
Russian Institute, 201n12

Saatchi & Saatchi, 99–100
Said, Edward, 18
Santos, Boaventura de Sousa, 15
Sassen, Saskia, 17–18
satellite campuses, 175–76
Schlesinger, Arthur, Jr., 34
Schultz, Theodore, 128
science: funding for, 35, 36; and policy in Project Camelot, 42–43, 203–4n27
Science: The Endless Frontier (Bush), 35
Scientific Research and Development, Office of, 34
secondary education, 129–30, 216n11, 219n22, 223n16
security agencies/apparatus: in academic knowledge production, 36, 61; African studies in, 148–49; and area studies, 39, 142; and CENIS, 51–52, 205n35; in funding higher education, 31, 36; and International Relations, 44, 200n4; in modernization theory, 49–50, 52, 57–58; on national development, 67; as post-graduate schools, 201n11; universities as strategic reserves for, 1–3, 189–90
Seitz, Earl W., 100
Senghor, Léopold Sédar, 69
Servicemen's Readjustment Act (GI Bill), 36
Sexton, John: *Baseball as a Road to God*, 227n17; edu-theological global imaginary of, 21, 176–88, 226n12, 227n14; "Global Network University Reflection," 178–79; institutional growth and transformation strategy, 169. *See also* New York University (NYU)
Shanghai, NYU campus, 171–72, 177
Smith, Adam: *Wealth of Nations*, 216n11
social movements in alternative imaginaries, 193–94
social relations, 9, 17–18, 198nn16–17, 225n3
social sciences: Cold War funding of, 29–33, 35; in Cold War universities, 9, 19, 36–49; and commercialization, 12; funding in shift back to core areas, 150–52; generalizability of, 143, 152–56; "globalization" in, 115, 117; International Relations, 19, 31–32, 43–46, 197n13, 200n4; international studies, 19, 31–32, 46–49, 50, 58–59; and language of globalization, 21; in military mobilization, 34; post–Cold War globalization studies, 2–3; public utility of, 223n17; reorganization of, 29–33, 142–43; in reproduction of modernization as national imaginary, 32, 43–44, 46–49. *See also* area studies programs
social whole, 22–25, 198n17
Sorrell, Sir Martin, 99–100
"southern theory," 15
Soviet Union, 3–4, 8–9, 42, 53–54
"Soviet Vulnerability" study (CENIS), 49–50
Special Operations Research Organization, 204n27
Spykman, Nicholas, 47–48
SSRC (Social Science Research Council): African field research funded by, 38, 146–50; Committee on World Regions, 39; debates over area studies, 21, 142–43, 150–61, 166–67; Exploratory Committee on World Area Research, 39; joint committee structure of, 158–61; and production of area studies, 143–50; and resource scarcity, 150–61

Stages of Economic Growth: A Non-Communist Manifesto (Rostow), 56–58
Staniland, Martin, 59–60
State Department, U.S., 172–73, 225n5
Statistical Control, Office of (Air Force), 66–67
Steger, Manfred, 17
strategic interests. *See* national security
strategic knowledge reserves, 19
structural adjustment: of African studies, 163–64; and African universities, 126, 127–33, 164; in banker's global imaginary, 20, 118–26, 133; in Berg Report, 78–80; in national development imaginary, 125; state services under, 127
Stuart McGuire shoe company, 100
study abroad programs, 3, 21, 172–74, 225–26nn4–6
Summer Case Writing Program (Harvard), 108
symptomatic reading, 198n16

Task Force on Higher Education and Society (World Bank): *Higher Education in Developing Countries*, 135–36
Teilhard de Chardin, Pierre, 180–81, 227n16
think tanks, 13–14
Third World: in alternative imaginaries, 193–94; American perspective in studies on, 155–56; in area studies, 145; in banker's global imaginary, 20, 122–23, 125, 129–30, 216n10; demands for non-western knowledge in, 15; education and national development in, 62–64, 70–75, 135–36; in global knowledge economy, 141; and Mc-Namara Bank, 62–64, 67–68, 69–70. *See also* non-Western world
Thompson, Kenneth W., 45
Title VI (NDEA) programs, 41, 145, 147–48, 162
Tomkins, Richard, 112
Tourism Development and Investment Company (TDIC), 184–85

transcendence: of the global imaginary, 24; of the global university, 171, 176–77, 180–81, 182; of the market imaginary, 84–85, 114; theological imagery of, 180–81, 227n17; through social sciences, 152, 155, 156–57, 160
Transition (Kampala), 73
Turner, James, 60

"undercommons," 193
underdevelopment, economic, 54–56, 77, 164
underfunding of developing world universities, 135–36, 223n16
UNESCO, 135–36, 225n5
Union of Concerned Scientists, 60–61
universalism, abstract, 192–93
universalizable theories, 40, 156–57
University of Amsterdam, 179–80
University of Chicago, 127–28
University of Dar es Salaam, 74–75
University Programs, Office of (DHS), 2
University Students African Revolutionary Front, 74
"U.S. Africanists' paradigm," 148

Vansina, Jan, 146–47
Veteran's Administration, 36
Vietnam Caucus, Asian Studies Association, 59
Vietnam War, 204n28
Vitalis, Robert, 44–48, 198n13, 202n19
vocationalization of African higher education, 132
Voices of the Poor (World Bank), 134–35
Volker, Paul/Volker Shock, 76

Wallace, Robert, 101
Waltz, Kenneth: *Man, the State, and War*, 45
war mobilization, 33–36
war on terrorism, 1–2
"Washington Formula," 59–60
Wealth of Nations (Smith), 216n11
Weissman, George, 101

West, Michael O., 163
white American scholars, 14, 147–48, 164
"whole-culture approach" to area studies,
  145
Wolfensohn, James, 108, 133–37
Wolfensohn Bank, 133–37
Wolfers, Arnold, 47–48
Wood, George, 66
working conditions at NYUAD, 185–88
"world," meaning of, 197n9
World and Africa, The (Du Bois), 37
World Area Research Committee (SSRC),
  144–45
World Bank: antipoverty agenda of, 71–72;
  Berg Report, 76–77, 78–80; Clausen's corporate strategy for, 118–24; and contested
  imaginaries, 75–80; in education, 13–14,
  19–20, 70–75, 127–33, 209n10; *Financing Education in Developing Countries*,
  129–30; founding mandate of, 65–66;
  globalization of, 124–26; *Higher Education in Developing Countries: Peril and
  Promise*, 167; human capital analysis by,
  127–30; institutions comprising, 207n2;

Knowledge for Development, 135; knowledge production by, 19–20, 65, 133–37; in
  national development imaginary, 62–64,
  65–75; reimagined as apolitical, 124;
  reputational rankings of universities by,
  219n24; *Voices of the Poor* study, 134–35.
  See also Clausen Bank; McNamara Bank;
  Wolfensohn Bank
World Bank Group, 207n2
World Banking Division, Bank of America,
  121
world economy. *See* economy, global
World is Flat, The (T. Friedman), 97, 212n14
World Regions, Committee on (SSRC), 144
World Trade Organization: General Agreement on Trade in Services, 175

Yale Institute of International Studies (YIIS),
  44–45
Young, Crawford, 146

Zayed bin Sultan Al Nahyan, 184
Zemach-Bersin, Talya, 174
zero point, xiv, 16

www.ingramcontent.com/pod-product-compliance
Lightning Source LLC
Chambersburg PA
CBHW050337270326
41926CB00016B/3495